"A superbly written, broadly researched biography of a fascinating, audacious, stubborn and deeply religious woman."
—*St. Anthony Messenger*

"Mother Angelica is one of the greatest entrepreneurs of all time, and is truly one of my heroes. With his 'insider' perspective, Raymond Arroyo has done a masterful job capturing not only Mother's immeasurable accomplishments but also her remarkable personality. Like Mother herself, this book has the unique combination of being both inspiring and entertaining."
—THOMAS S. MONAGHAN, founder of Domino's Pizza and Chancellor of Ave Maria University

"The book is a solidly researched, professionally told account of one of the most improbable successes of recent years."
—*National Review*

"*Mother Angelica* is a fascinating read about an amazing woman."
—*St. Cloud Visitor*

"Raymond Arroyo, one of America's leading journalists in reporting religion, has written a fascinating story of how faith transformed a cloistered nun into a media giant. This is an exciting rendition of a story that is more extraordinary and surely more heartwarming than fiction."
—ROBERT NOVAK, syndicated columnist

"Mother Angelica's personal words to me, her courageous example, and her constant prayers helped inspire my portrayal of Jesus in *The Passion of the Christ*. No one could have captured the essence of this modern-day saint better than Raymond Arroyo. His narrative gifts and understanding of Mother are clearly evident in this truthful and often candid depiction of one nun's struggle to bring God to the multitudes. Surely this book, and Mother's life will have an incredible enduring legacy."
—JAMES CAVIEZEL, actor

"It is a great read . . . Mother Anglica is an important part of the history of religion—and not only of Catholicism—in the last half century, and in *Mother Angelica* she receives a critical appreciation worthy of her person and achievements."
—*First Things*

"Raymond Arroyo captures the life of this complex woman dubbed the 'miracle woman' by members of Pope John Paul II's curia in his book . . . Mr. Arroyo's book is a must read for Catholics or anyone interested in the Church. With great reverence and wit he paints a masterful portrait of the woman who brought Rome to the masses."
—*The U.P. Catholic*

"If Rita Rizzo was an unlikely candidate for a Poor Clare's convent, Mother Angelica was an even more unlikely choice to establish, in Alabama, the business empire that is the Eternal Word Television Network. In this candid, captivating biography, Raymond Arroyo delivers not just a great story of a savvy and courageous woman, but multiple examples of the claim that all things are possible with God. I highly recommend it."
—RON HANSEN, author of *Mariette in Ecstasy*

"A page-turner about an elderly nun? It seems improbable, but when the nun is the formidable Mother Angelica and her biographer the eloquent Raymond Arroyo, the result is a book that few readers will be able to put down. Arroyo has produced a spellbinding tale of how Rita Rizzo emerged from a broken home, battling poverty, illness, and uncomprehending clerics to become the queen of Catholic media and a leader of the New Evangelization in America."
—MARY ANN GLENDON, Learned Hand Professor of Law, Harvard University and author of *A World Made New: Eleanor Roosevelt and the Universal Declaration of Human Rights*

"*Mother Angelica* is the beautifully told story of a beautiful woman of God whose toughness, tenacity, drive and determination built a network to bring the Catholic truth and culture to a nation that has never been more desperately in need of them."

—PAT BUCHANAN, columnist and author of
The Death of the West

MOTHER
ANGELICA

MOTHER ANGELICA

The Remarkable Story of
a Nun, Her Nerve, and a Network
of Miracles

RAYMOND ARROYO

Image Books

Doubleday

NEW YORK LONDON TORONTO SYDNEY AUCKLAND

AN IMAGE BOOK
PUBLISHED BY DOUBLEDAY
Copyright © 2005 by Raymond Arroyo

A hardcover edition of this book was originally published in 2005 by Doubleday.

Published in the United States by Doubleday, an imprint of The Doubleday Broadway
Publishing Group, a division of Random House, Inc., New York.
www.doubleday.com

IMAGE, DOUBLEDAY, and the portrayal of a deer drinking from a stream
are registered trademarks of Random House, Inc.

Book design by Fritz Metsch

A Spanish edition of this book, *Madre Angelica*, is being published simultaneously by
Image Doubleday (ISBN 978-0-385-52116-1)

Library of Congress Cataloging-in-Publication Data
Arroyo, Raymond.
Mother Angelica : the remarkable story of a nun, her nerve, and a network of miracles /
Raymond Arroyo.—1st ed.
p.   cm.
Includes bibliographical references.
1. M. Angelica (Mary Angelica), Mother, 1923–   2. Poor Clares—United States—
Biography.   3. Eternal Word Television Network.   I. Title.
BX4705.M124A77   2004
271'.97302—dc22   2004062117

ISBN 978-0-385-51093-6

PRINTED IN THE UNITED STATES OF AMERICA

5   7   9   10   8   6   4

For the mother of my children, Rebecca
my mother, Lynda
and
all mothers everywhere

But the foolish things of the world hath God chosen, that He may confound the wise; and the weak things of the world hath God chosen, that He may confound the strong.

I CORINTHIANS 1:27

CONTENTS

INTRODUCTION

THE FOLKS AROUND HANCEVILLE, Alabama, called it "that nun deal," "the palace," or "the Shrine," depending on whom you talked to. I would trek out there most Saturday mornings. Veering off Interstate 65, past cattle drowsing in the Alabama heat, I turned right at Pitts Grocery and raced by a row of newly built homes, concrete saints peering at me from their well-tended front gardens. Unlike the occupants of the RVs and air-conditioned tour buses on all sides, I was less interested in Our Lady of the Angels Monastery than in the woman who built it.

During the final approach to the mammoth stone-faced edifice Mother Angelica called home, I would silently review the questions I intended to put to her. This would be my last chance to prepare for the five-hour encounter that lay ahead: a sit-down interview with the world's most outspoken contemplative. Since cloistered nuns are forbidden direct contact with the outside world, our interactions were restricted to the community parlor: a plain room with a wall of metal latticework separating nun from visitor. On the surface, discussing the intimate details of one's life through bars would seem counterproductive. But in our case, the arrangement lent the proceedings a confessional air. It was as if the black laced metal grille between us liberated the seventy-nine-year-old abbess, allowing her to revisit the past with an honesty and candor she could not permit herself otherwise.

She would arrive ready to talk.

"Heyyyy, *paesan,*" Mother Angelica squawked as she entered the parlor on the other side of the grate. She paused in the doorway, her arms open, as if making a stage entrance. A quick warmth overtook the spare rose-tiled room.

Caught in the flow of a chocolaty Franciscan habit, all five feet five of her appeared amazingly young and lithe this day. Her rounded cheeks spilled over the sides of the wimple, like a pink pillow crammed into a shoe box. The down-turned smile, cherished by millions, pinched her eyes into slits of piercing gray.

Even though she was a good forty minutes late, no explanation was offered. Mother Angelica lived in the present moment.

"Well, let's get to it," she announced, as if I were the overdue party. Glimmers of affection and mischief danced behind her glasses as she sidled close to the bars, offering her hands through the grate. Once she took hold of me, she cut to the important stuff: "How 'bout some lunch? What we got, Sister?" Mother asked over her shoulder. The ever-attentive Sister Antoinette dashed off to the kitchen to check the cloister bill of fare.

Later, over half-eaten cookies and milky tea, a napkin tucked beneath her chin, Mother put aside her well-crafted personal anecdotes (perfected over a twenty-year career of unscripted television) and began revealing parts of her past no one, including her sisters, had ever heard before. Whether it was fate or just good timing, I caught Mother Angelica during a reflective moment in her life. She had just realized a long-sought goal: the completion of a new multimillion-dollar monastery. She seemed genuinely content, finally ready to look back on all she had survived and accomplished. Seated in an overstuffed leather chair, she struggled with memory and time to unearth the truth.

"Do you sense a split in yourself—in your personality?" I asked her this day. Whenever Mother emitted a long, almost bothered sigh, repositioning her body in the chair—as she did then—I knew a revelatory moment was upon us. Shooting a finger inside the starched white wimple that surrounded her face, she rubbed her temple as if she were physically trying to loosen the past from her memory. How often I would sit there waiting, staring past the metal florets dotting the grille, thinking how much they were like Mother herself: steely yet feminine; guarded yet open; forged by fire and lasting. Then the answers would come.

"Did I ever tell you about throwing the knife at my uncle? I want the real me to be known, because nothing I have or do is me. It's some street woman that got sick and was given many things." Then with slow precision, she added, "The real me is *not* what you see."

In the grated parlor of her cloister, for the better part of three years, I pursued "the real" Mother Angelica. From 1999 to the end of 2001, the woman *Time* magazine called "the superstar of religious broadcasting," and easily one of the most powerful and influential people in the Roman Catholic Church, met me for a weekly date of sorts to resurrect the past and appraise her life.

These visits were brave exercises for Mother Angelica. It is one thing to permit a neophyte to rifle through your history; he is disadvantaged from the outset, and knows only what the printed record affords. But I had known Mother personally and as an employee for five years when I began interviewing her. I had been near her in good times and bad, in public and in private. For two years, I occasionally cohosted her popular *Mother Angelica Live* TV program, and served as news director for the network she had founded. In some ways, she was like a grandmother to me—a grandmother with whom I shared an uncommon ease and kinship. Our mutual Italian heritage probably helped. We could converse about any issue and did not avoid the occasional ribbing.

"We had words once," Mother confided to a friend in my presence; "Raymond didn't get to use any of them." Despite differences and disagreements, we remained close. My peculiar vantage point allowed me to see Mother Angelica as she truly was: a simple, deeply spiritual woman struggling to do God's will and to overcome her personal failings.

I slowly began to recognize the other Mother Angelica, encased within the cherubic face beyond the metal bars. Rita Rizzo, the sickly girl who, with only a high school diploma, had fought her way out of poverty and single-handedly created the Eternal Word Television Network (EWTN), the largest religious broadcasting empire in the world—succeeding where all the bishops of the United States (and several millionaires) had failed. Here was a modern Teresa of Avila; an outspoken firebrand who, with a radical faith and determination, had surmounted obstacles that would have hobbled most men. She had beaten back sexism, bankruptcy, and corporate and ecclesial takeover attempts in order to provide moral leadership to "the people." Physically, this suffering servant had endured a mystical dance of pain and providence that would exact a terrific price and yield astounding rewards. The woman John Paul II declared "weak in body but strong in spirit" publicly challenged cardinals and bishops in the name of orthodoxy, broadcast a commonsense traditional vision of the Church in the post–Vatican II period, and became an ecumenical spiritual beacon to millions.

Still, she remains a mystery even to her legions of followers. How did this neglected, withdrawn child of divorce rise to become one of the most revered and feared women in Catholicism? How did a cloistered nun with no broadcast experience conquer the airwaves? How did stomach ailments, shattered vertebrae, an enlarged heart, chronic asthma, paralysis, and twisted limbs actually further her mission? What fueled her well-known public battles with Church hierarchy over practice and devotion? How has her television network and religious order managed to thrive while others have collapsed? And, most important, how is her message being received in the Catholic Church today, and what impact will it have on the future?

These nagging questions and my familiarity with bits of her hidden story convinced me that a full-scale biography of Mother Angelica was needed and timely. With trepidation, I approached the woman herself, fully realizing her participation would probably be minimal, due to the continuing demands of her network and the responsibilities of running a religious community. Angelica's reaction was typical and immediate: "Why not begin and see what happens?" As she had undertaken every major initiative of her life, trusting in God's providence, she embarked on this most invasive project with total commitment.

We decided it was not to be an authorized biography and that editorial control and interpretation would be mine alone. True to form, Mother allowed me complete journalistic freedom. She would make herself available for extended interviews on weekends or after her live show, usually for several hours, as time permitted. No question would be off-limits, no topic too sensitive. Fully cooperating with my research, Mother Angelica granted me unfettered access to her community archives, personal correspondence, friends, physicians, and the sisters of Our Lady of the Angels Monastery. The community historian, Sister Mary Antoinette, became my greatest ally, patiently answering questions, providing crucial information, and suffering calls morning, noon, and night.

And then just weeks after we had completed the final interview for this biography and our last live show together, Mother Angelica was felled by a debilitating stroke. It robbed her of speech and sealed her memory, rendering it unlikely that Mother Angelica will ever grant another interview—and certainly none with the depth, duration, or intimacy of those I conducted. Without my knowing it, I was recording the final testament of Mother Angelica, the last word on her remarkable life.

One evening, before shooting her live show, she gave me but one instruction, which has haunted me to this day: "Make sure you present the real me. There is nothing worse than a book that sugarcoats the truth and ducks the humanity of the person. I wish you forty years in purgatory if you do that!"

Hoping to steer clear of that ignoble end, I have written a book that does not avoid controversy or the seeming contradictions inherent in Mother Angelica's character: the cloistered, contemplative nun who speaks to the world; the independent rule breaker who is derided as a "rigid conservative"; the wisecracking comedian who suffers near constant pain; the Poor Clare nun who runs a multimillion-dollar corporation.

Herein are the remembrances of friend and foe alike, any and all I could find who had crossed her path. Criticisms of Mother Angelica are also unblinkingly considered here, as is her prodigious broadcast output and its development.

To properly appraise a life like Mother's, backward glances are necessary. Only by looking back can we see the twists of fate and grace that shaped this most unlikely life. Like the rest of us, nothing happened for Mother Angelica in a flash. Hers is a tale of mostly painful, confused, and, to the outsider, lunatic steps leading to a satisfying end. But the inspiration of her story resides in the struggle—a struggle that has for the most part been concealed or lost over time.

During the last five years, I have retraced her temporal and spiritual life from Canton, Ohio, to Hanceville, Alabama; unearthed people and stories Mother had long forgotten; weighed her gifts and failings; and discovered a faith rare in our day. I believe this mosaic constitutes the most complete picture of Mother Angelica—from inside and out.

In April 2001, after a particularly grueling interview session, Mother began to withdraw softly into the recesses of her cloister. Then on the threshold, she spun around like a coy young girl, slapping a hand on the rounded door frame. "You now know as much about me as God does," she said with a wry smile. "But there are *some things* even you will never know."

"You don't mind if I keep trying, do you?" I asked.

She cackled gaily, retreating into the hall.

What follows are her candid memories, the fruits of my research, and "some things" neither Mother Angelica nor I ever expected to uncover.

Raymond Arroyo
New Orleans, 2005

Prologue

ON CHRISTMAS EVE morning, 2001, the crumpled abbess lowered herself into the waiting wheelchair and tried to reassure her daughters. For weeks, the sisters had tensely monitored her every move, hoping their vigilance could somehow stave off the next illness or setback. From the nuns' shared looks of desperation to the reflexive aid they offered whenever she stumbled or even hesitated, she could feel their worry. "Jesus is coming today," she announced with calm determination on that morning. Pointing to the hallway, she directed the sister pushing her out of the cell. "I'm going to the chapel to wait for Him."

She wouldn't have to wait long.

Gliding past the closed doors of the great monastery hall, filled only with the sound of sisters rustling into their habits, the old nun looked as if she had just returned from the front lines of an extended war campaign. And perhaps she had. Public battles with a cardinal and her local bishop, a Vatican investigation, the death of a cloistered friend of forty-nine years, and constant health troubles had taken their toll on Mother Mary Angelica by late 2001. Even the millions who invited her into their homes each week might not have recognized her. A sling held Angelica's shattered right arm, the result of a fall a few days earlier. A patch covered her sagging left eye, which refused to close—a memento of the stroke she'd suffered in September. And the mouth that made bishops tremble and carried salvation to the lost on seven continents drooped pathetically, disrupting the once-jolly face. Angelica was now a living icon of "redemptive suffering," the embodiment of what she had long preached to her sisters.

One of the junior professed nuns carefully maneuvered Mother's wheelchair over the polished green marble and jasper floor of the monastery chapel. The familiar smell of honeyed incense embraced Angelica as she entered. Angels peered down from the stained-glass windows surrounding the chapel, offering their own salute as the sun broke in from the east. Washed in the shifting colors of their angelic light, the abbess rolled toward her Spouse. She was too infirm to don the habit for Him that morning, so in a cream-colored robe and matching ski cap, she dutifully came to pay Him homage, bearing the marks He alone had allowed.

Despite her condition, there was no bitterness as she approached the nearly eight-foot-high monstrance holding the consecrated Host. There was her Lord and Savior, enthroned high above the center of the multimillion-dollar chapel she had built for Him. Nothing was too much for her Lord. The scars of the present moment were merely new offerings to Him. They had long communed in pain, she and her Spouse. She recognized His touch and accepted it. She had learned that in pain—through pain—there were miracles, if she could but muster the faith to trust Him completely and submit to His providential designs.

Following Mass and the recitation of the rosary, her sisters began to scatter out of the chapel. In solitude, Mother Angelica weakly craned her head upward, training her good eye on Christ in the Blessed Sacrament, as she had for fifty-seven years of religious life. Then He drew near.

As if suddenly filled with concrete, her head flopped to the side. Weary and disoriented, Angelica's eyes rolled to the ceiling.

"Reverend Mother, are you all right?" Sister Faustina asked. "Reverend Mother?"

Mother Angelica did not respond. Why does she have this dazed look on her face, Sister Faustina wondered. Is her blood sugar plummeting? Is the diabetes acting up? Why can't she focus? The

sisters gathered around, calling her name, trying to get some response. To stabilize her blood sugar, a tall glass of orange juice was
brought in, which she downed. But it did no good. The nuns rushed
Angelica back to her cell, to check her vital signs.

Sister Margaret Mary, still wearing a nightgown, met them in the
hallway. Margaret Mary was Mother's sometime nurse, responsible
for dispensing medication and general health advice to the seventy-
nine-year-old. When she first saw the disoriented abbess, the nun
voiced her worst fear. "She's had a stroke," Margaret Mary said
numbly.

Back in her cell, Mother's blood pressure was normal, but an
oxygen mask failed to revive her. Sister Mary Catherine, the vicar
and Mother's second in the monastery, decided they should take
Angelica to the nearby Cullman Regional Medical Center. The
hour trip to Birmingham was deemed too far a journey. They loaded
the abbess into an ambulance and sped to the hospital.

Save for the constant yawning for air and the unfocused rolling
of her eyes, she was unresponsive.

At the hospital, Mother Angelica was ushered through a battery
of tests while the sisters prayed. Ending the suspense, Mother's
physician, Dr. L. James Hoover, sheepishly entered the waiting
area. He wore a festive bright red sweater that seemed to mock the
occasion, and his hands were thrust in his pockets. There was an
air of resignation in his gait.

"There is nothing we can do for her," Hoover apologetically
drawled. "She's had a stroke and she's bleeding from the brain."

"Well, what's going to happen?" Sister Margaret Mary demanded.

The doctor dodged the nun's eyes. "She's just going to drift off.
One in a hundred patients are candidates for surgery, but with her
age and health . . ."

The nuns instantly grasped the terrible decision facing them: do
nothing and watch their Reverend Mother slip away, or risk the
drive to Birmingham for a perilous brain surgery, which might kill
her. While the weighty choice was made, the woman who had created the largest religious broadcasting empire in the world lay com-

atose in the emergency room. Having been rescued by so many miracles in the past, she teetered on the brink of that eternity she had long pointed others toward.

Somewhere in the deep recesses of her traumatized mind, Mother Angelica, perhaps unconsciously, made a decision to fight. She would desperately cast herself into the hands of God, as she always had. For Angelica, there was no other way.

I

One Miserable Life

MOTHER ANGELICA came into the world overlooked and certainly unwanted, at least by her father. She was born Rita Antoinette Rizzo in the unassuming town of Canton, Ohio, on April 20, 1923.

Aside from being the home and burial place of President William McKinley, Canton was a forgotten industrial hamlet an hour or so outside of Cleveland. Great scattering streaks of brown smoke billowed from her chimney-dotted skyline, an emblem of the productivity issuing from the little town. Steel was the backbone of Canton: the building block of the new century and the lure for thousands of immigrants. From Canton's mills and production lines spilled the ball bearings, streetcars, bricks, telephones, and pipe fittings that would propel the nation into its greatest period.

Apart from the industry, Canton was, as it is today, a pleasant green pasture of rolling hills in the middle of the country, a place to raise a family and avoid the chaos and congestion of city life. That is, unless you lived in the southeast part of town, where Rita Rizzo was born.

In 1923, southeast Canton was known as the red-light district, or "the slums," according to some. For the blacks and hordes of Italian immigrants who worked in the Canton mills, the southeast was home. Italians were confined to the district by a combination of illiteracy and the constant tribute demanded by their wayward countrymen. It was a ghetto ruled by the Black Hand, a criminal organization with roots in Sicily. And though the mobsters carried black-handled revolvers as they conducted business in the neighborhood, the name Black Hand originated in the old country. Mob activity flourished during that era. A train of organized corruption ran from Cleveland to Canton to Steubenville. Cherry Street was the center of the Canton action, an avenue where racketeering joints and roving prostitutes vied for the same souls as St. Anthony's Catholic Church.

Mob slayings were a common occurrence in southeast Canton. Former members of the neighborhood still speak of people being blown up on porches, shot on street corners, or dropped in local rivers. Even today, well into their eighties, some of the locals talk of the Black Hand in muted terms and refuse permission to publish their names, for fear of reprisals.

This ethnic ghetto—where hookers tapped bordello windows to attract their johns; where shopkeepers lived across the street from female assassins; where parish priests tried to lead small-time hustlers to a better life; where the profane mingled with the sacred, and everyone struggled to make ends meet—this was the world that awaited Rita Rizzo's coming in 1923.

She was born in the sprawling home of Mary and Anthony Gianfrancesco, her maternal grandparents, who lived a block off the notorious Cherry Street. The house at 1029 Liberty was bordered on one side by an open field crawling with well-tended grapevines. Attached to the other side of the house, dominating the corner of Liberty and Eleventh streets, was Grandpa Gianfrancesco's saloon, a local watering hole and lunch spot for recently arrived immigrants and their American relations.

Rita's birth was a painful one for her mother, Mae. It took several hours and fifteen stitches to bring the nearly twelve-pound child into the world—facts Mae Gianfrancesco Rizzo never tired of repeating to her only daughter.

"My grandmother said I had rosy cheeks, a full head of hair, and was ready to go," Mother Angelica recalled with a cackle a lifetime later. "She said I looked like I was six months old."

John Rizzo, Rita's father, never wanted a child. When his wife of two years informed him she was pregnant, he "flew into a rage, violently ripping at her hair." Mae Rizzo believed this incident and the mental anguish that followed destroyed her milk supply.

When they first met, John seemed ideal to Mae. Tall, thin, dignified, he had a quiet demeanor and dressed impeccably. He wore spats and carried a cane. In a ghetto teeming with common laborers and hoodlums, John Rizzo was a dream come true. A tailor by trade, he was strolling down Eleventh Street when Mae's singing first drew him to the Gianfrancesco's kitchen door.

As Mae washed dishes, she would sing along to whatever Italian opera was spilling from her father's gramophone in the living room. Since her birth, music had always been there, as much a part of her life as Papa's saloon or the cast-iron stove in the kitchen. Mae wanted to be a singer, and she certainly had the looks for it. She was a striking woman, with dark eyes, sharp features, and an intense severity that attracted the glances of men in the neighborhood. Family photographs reveal a young woman who appreciated her good looks and knew which fashions would complement them. Oversized hats, billowing dresses, gloves, and parasols adorned Mae's comely frame. Her beauty captivated John.

Yet for all her charms, Mae, even as a young woman, was convinced she had been cheated by life. She traced her troubles back to the fifth grade, when, during a fire drill, a male classmate took her by the hand. Whether Mae was resisting his advances or just in a foul mood, she pulled a plank from a nearby picket fence and cracked the boy over the head with it. Presumably, the teachers complained. Her mother, never one for conflict, decided that Mae had had enough education. She was removed from school and did not return. Later in life, the feeling that she didn't know enough or wasn't smart enough would leave deep scars on Mae Gianfrancesco—scars that would eventually burden her daughter.

When John Rizzo sauntered up to the kitchen door and complimented her voice, Mae must have thought him an answer to prayer. Here was a chance to escape the crowded, tempestuous household of brothers. A chance to start anew and maybe get an education. At twenty-two, Mae seized her chance at happiness and married John

Rizzo on September 8, 1919, over the objections of her parents, who "never liked him."

Four years later, on September 12, 1923, the couple conveyed their five-month-old daughter, Rita Rizzo, to the font of St. Anthony's Church on Liberty Street. It was an established custom at the time to baptize infants within days of their birth, but a pair of tardy godparents had necessitated a delay. So when the Rizzos finally approached the font with the hefty child, who seemed much older than five months, the astonished priest turned to Mae. "Why didn't you wait till she could walk here?" he asked.

Freshly baptized, Rita was carried by her mother to a side altar dedicated to Our Lady of Sorrows. Surely Mae felt an affinity for this particular image of Mary. On the altar of the Madonna, whose exposed heart bore swords of anguish, Mae placed her only child. "She told me that she said, 'I give you my daughter,'" Mother Angelica remembered a bit sadly. "I'm sure she thought she would have other children, but she never did."

It is no wonder. The Rizzo marriage was already crumbling. John's inability to support the family financially seemed to be a contributing factor.

"My father could never make a decent living," Mother Angelica insisted. "Finally, my mother got him to rent a house. . . . One night I was in my crib. And I started crying, yelling, and screaming. So she got out of bed to check on me, and there were roaches everywhere, all over me, all over the wall. The wallpaper was moving. It was just full of roaches." After some choice words to John, no doubt deriding his failings as a provider, Mae bundled Rita up and went to her parents' home for the night. This would become a regular pattern throughout their marriage.

The relationship was further undermined by John Rizzo's overbearing mother, Catherine. Around 1926, Catherine Rizzo could find no domicile, despite the fact that she had eleven children, including John. So it was decided she would join the young Rizzo family in Canton—at Mae's urging.

"She didn't have enough foresight to figure out that if eleven children didn't want their mother there must be something wrong,"

Mother Angelica said sardonically. "So [my mother] took her in and that's when the trouble started."

In fact, the trouble probably started much earlier. John had been physically and verbally abusing Mae for years, according to court documents. So while it's unlikely that Catherine Rizzo destroyed the marriage, she certainly created flash points for the couple to war over.

The determined Mae met her equal in Grandma Rizzo. A big woman, with a mouth to match. She suffered no fools—especially in the kitchen. Grandma Rizzo's gastronomic standards were high, and Mae's cooking, as well as everything else the woman did, was just not up to par, and certainly not good enough for her son. The regular criticism became too much for an insecure person like Mae to bear.

One afternoon, Mae had just popped a chicken into the oven, bone and all—a pet peeve for Grandma Rizzo, who proudly deboned her fowl in minutes. Before the oven door had closed, the old lady began chastising Mae for her culinary shortcomings. Three-year-old Rita clung to her mother's side. After listening intently for several minutes, the child stepped between her mother and Grandma Rizzo.

"I said to my grandmother, 'Oh shut up. You all time talk, talk, talk.' Well, my mother grabbed me up and gave me a hundred kisses because I was defending her," Angelica recalled. "My father would never defend her!"

This would be the first, although not the last, time Rita would raise her voice in almost visceral defense of her mother. It is also the first glimpse of the outspoken quality that would come to define her character. But the intervention did little to quell the acrimony between Mae and her mother-in-law.

Sometime between 1927 and 1928, according to Mother Angelica, a possessed Mae climbed the stairs of their home in search of a gun to kill the old woman. "If my father's mother had been there, she would have done it. Luckily, she had left for Reading, Pennsylvania, to live with her daughter . . ."

By November of 1928, John Rizzo was also living elsewhere. For two years, he lost himself in California, providing no explanation and no forwarding address. Without money or a job, Mae had to support what was left of her family. Like refugees, she and five-year-old Rita returned to her parents' home, though they were not exactly welcome there. The Gianfrancesco home was already filled to capacity. Mae's four brothers (Tony, Pete, Frank, and Nick) and the elder Gianfrancescos occupied the two bedrooms, forcing Rita and Mae to sleep in a renovated attic. Over the years, Mother Angelica often told a story about that first winter in the house. As she and her mother slept in the upper room, a storm blew open the windows, depositing snow on top of them. Given the resources and generosity of the Gianfrancescos during this period, it seems odd that they would subject their own daughter and grandchild to such brutal conditions.

Anthony Gianfrancesco was far from poor, despite the poverty around him. He owned three homes in the neighborhood, which he rented to family and to Canton's newly arrived Italian immigrants at cut-rate prices. Anthony had emigrated from Naples, Italy, to Colorado, where he worked in a gold mine, before moving to Akron, Ohio. There he met and married Mary Votolato. Conflicts with his mother-in-law spurred a resettling in Canton and a new business venture.

The saloon bearing Anthony Gianfrancesco's name became a safe harbor for foreign families afloat in a strange new land. In southeast Canton, the saloon was the center of Italian public life, a place where countrymen could speak their native tongue, mingle with their own, and share the indignities endured that day at the hands of the Americans. Mother Angelica remembered her grandfather providing Italian newcomers with clothes and helping them find work. Grandma Gianfrancesco would often feed the immigrant families in a room above the saloon, where the Italian lodges would sometimes meet. It was a family place. Inebriation was forbidden, and if the tab got too high or the hour too late, the Gianfrancescos would send their customers home.

It is likely that hard liquor or beer was served in the Gianfrancesco establishment during Prohibition, which hit Canton on

January 16, 1920, and would not be repealed until February 1933. Mother Angelica vividly recalled one event that happened in either 1929 or 1930.

"I couldn't have been more than four or five, and my grandfather didn't want me in the saloon. He gave me a small mug of beer with a big collar on it. I had four or five pretzels, and he said, 'Go outside and sit on the curb and enjoy yourself.' So I'm out there on the curb drinking this beer and eating pretzels when the Salvation Army Band shows up. Well, they're praying all kinds of psalms in front of me and praying for my salvation. They must have been shocked to see this kid drinking beer. I remember yelling up to my grandfather, 'There's a big band down here.' "

The little girl with the Buster Brown haircut had a front-row seat on life unvarnished. At the corner of Liberty and Eleventh streets, she observed the people and the ways of the world, not all of them as benign as the passing Salvation Army Band. On her curbside outings, she would converse with prostitutes, members of the mob, men returning from the mills, Mamooch—an Italian woman who roamed the streets, praying—and the black people who shared her neighborhood. This moving carousel of humanity would instill within the child an empathy for strangers and teach her to relate easily with individuals from disparate backgrounds. In this laboratory of life, young Rita absorbed the misery of the world and the hidden humor few ever managed to find.

About this time, Mae Rizzo set up a dry-cleaning shop next to her father's saloon, after a brief apprenticeship with a tailor and cleaner. It would be the first of many entrepreneurial efforts she undertook to provide for Rita without family assistance. If she had to live beneath her parents' roof, Mae was determined to show them she could support her daughter—alone.

Mae demonstrated the same independent streak in matters of faith. Though the Gianfrancesco clan were not churchgoers, Mae began frequenting St. Anthony's. The church and its pastor, Father Joseph Riccardi, gave the abandoned wife a sense of comfort and peace. As a volunteer, she organized Italian festivals in the parish; one of these would provide the setting for Rita Rizzo's first public

performance. A couple of years after Al Jolson's *The Jazz Singer* took
the country by storm in 1927, Rita impersonated him onstage.
Wearing a little boy's suit, the six-year-old walked into the crowded
church hall to sing "Danny Boy."

"The stage looked gigantic to me. . . . My mother was petrified,
so she says, 'Look, I'm going to be right there in the audience so you
keep your eyes on me and you'll be okay. You just sing your song.
Okay?' I said, 'Okay,' and all of a sudden my uncle pushes me out,
the big curtains part, and there I am. So I start singing the song.
And just at the place where Al Jolson begins to cry because Danny
Boy dies, I couldn't find my mother. Someone must have stepped in
front of her. So I'm crying my eyes out. I keep singing, but I'm crying like a baby and I'm going 'Oh Danny boy.' Pretty soon, the whole
place is crying. Then suddenly, I see my mother and I'm all happy
again, singing away. It was perfect. My uncle Nick went bananas.
He picked me up and threw me in the air, and the people were
yelling and clapping."

Even at a tender age, Rita would draw acclaim not so much for
her performance as for her ability to display honest emotions in
public. The audience connected with the basic humanity they saw
coming from the child and responded with their love. This momen-
tary joy would not last long, however.

In the late 1920s, the Black Hand unleashed a renewed campaign of fear and violence in Canton. Their wicked spree went
largely unchallenged by the Canton police, who were complicit in
their crimes. In one of the most notorious murders of the era, Don
Mellett, the crusading publisher of the *Canton Daily News,* was
gunned down in his garage after writing a series of articles exposing
bootleg operations and prostitution rackets in town. Canton's police chief Saranus Lengel, a detective, and others were later con-
victed of the murder.

Lacking confidence in law enforcement, Rita, Mae, and many of
their neighbors turned to the only stable institution available to
them: the Catholic Church, which was relatively strong in Canton
and an active force in the lives of parishioners.

In a story related by Mother Angelica, her mother, and some locals, Father Joseph Riccardi discovered that the mob was burying bootleg liquor in a place beyond suspicion: St. Anthony's schoolyard. The locale served the double purpose of providing the mob with a great cover for their illegal hooch as well as a way to humiliate the straight-arrow priest. Standing his ground, in defiance of a death threat, Father Riccardi installed floodlights in the schoolyard and alerted local authorities. Someone should have told the thirty-two-year-old priest that the authorities were on the mobsters' payroll.

But it was Father Riccardi's announcement that St. Anthony's would be relocated from the heart of Mafia territory to the comparatively tranquil Eleventh Street, SE that really drew the ire of the Black Hand. The church provided their neighborhood and "businesses" with a cloak of respectability. It also may have been a useful meeting place to conduct affairs in relative secrecy. Whatever their motive, the mob was dead set against the relocation, preferring to have the new church built on Liberty Street, in place of the old one. Coerced parishioners petitioned the court for an injunction, which halted building at the Eleventh Street site for a time.

Eventually Riccardi prevailed, and a new St. Anthony's sprang up in a better part of southeast Canton. Bishop Schrembs, the ordinary of Cleveland, sang the young priest's praises: "Father Riccardi was fighting for the upbuilding of a decent, clean living Italian colony, free from the influence of gambling resorts, bootlegging joints, and infamous houses which infested the neighborhood of the old church site."

On Sunday, March 10, 1929, the Black Hand responded. Following the nine A.M. Mass, Father Riccardi walked to the rear of the church to perform a baptism. In the vestibule, he met Maime Guerrieri, a twenty-seven-year-old greasy-haired woman accompanied by her five-year-old daughter. "I'm glad you sent your little girl back to school," the priest said, trying to make conversation with the woman. Before he could say anything else, Guerrieri pulled out a revolver and fired five shots at point-blank range. Two bullets hit the priest. Father Riccardi died later that day.

At trial the accused, Guerrieri, was found "not guilty of murder . . .

on the sole ground of insanity." The faithful of the parish were shaken, and the six-year-old Rita had encountered her first martyr.

"You never saw a whole parish cry as they did. It was just a serious, terrible breach of justice—no one was ever punished." Mother Angelica knitted her brow and shook her head in disgust at the memory. "I think in our lives, that was a big loss, because Father Riccardi was somebody who understood us."

For Rita and Mae, the final pillar supporting their lives had crumbled. Then in October 1929, the Great Depression hit, devouring the scant savings of people in southeast Canton and elsewhere. For the rest of her life, Mae Rizzo refused to deposit her cash in a bank. Always prepared for a second crash, Mae hoarded her money in a bag for easy accessibility. The death of their pastor and the financial insecurity of the times ushered in a downward spiral of hard knocks, which would test mother and daughter.

In 1930, John Rizzo returned to Canton and visited his family at the Gianfrancescos' home. Though Mae still had feelings for John, her trust in him had died long ago. The awkward meeting went nowhere and Mae abruptly asked him to leave. On September 24, 1930, she filed a divorce petition at the Stark County Courthouse in Canton. The document mentioned John's "extreme cruelty"—the beatings, the verbal lashings, and his failure to provide for the family. It begged the court to grant Mae alimony and custody of Rita.

The seven-year-old child tried to make sense of it all: the abusive marriage, the long absence of her father, and the emotional decomposition of the only parent she really knew. Though it would have been natural for her to turn to her mother for comfort, Rita knew, even at seven, that this was impossible. Unable to cope with the finality of the divorce, Mae was increasingly hysterical and given to crying fits. Rita had only herself to rely upon.

"Sometimes I used to wonder if there was a God, and if there was such a person I couldn't figure out why He wouldn't let me have a family, like the other kids," Mother Angelica observed, a faraway look in her eyes.

"She was an adult all her life," Angelica's cousin Joanne Simia said. "She never had a childhood."

In later life, through her television network, Rita brought light to the dark places of the world, places where the forgotten congregated: bars, nursing homes, hospitals, and run-down motels. When she spoke, they felt she understood their pain, their busted marriages, their alcohol addiction, their dysfunctional families. She seemed like one of them. Behind the veil, the twinkling eyes, and the crinkled smile, they sensed that she, too, had been wounded. And indeed she had been.

The Beginning of Hell

ON MARCH 10, 1931, the court awarded Mae custody of Rita and five dollars a week in child support. "And that's when hell began," Mother Angelica observed. The stigma of divorce and the challenge of making a living at the height of the Depression would rack the lives of both Rita and Mae. It didn't help that John Rizzo rarely made his child-care payments. At times, Rita would go to the courthouse and find no funds waiting for her. On one such occasion, the spunky nine-year-old tracked her father down at the men's store where he worked.

"I asked him for alimony and he gave me fifty cents. So the next week, I went up to the courthouse. The desk looked like it was twenty feet high, so I said to the woman that I had come for the alimony payment. She said, 'Honey, your dad gave you five dollars last week.' I said, 'No, he didn't; he gave me fifty cents.' So she showed me the receipt I'd given him the week before. He had added a dot and an extra zero to make it look like five dollars. I never went back. I never went back looking for alimony again."

To make ends meet, Mae opened another dry-cleaning business. Following disagreements with her brothers, she moved out of her parents' house. Between 1933 and 1937, Mae and Rita would occupy a series of run-down, occasionally rat-infested one-bedroom apartments, usually partitioning the room for maximum usage. The front end was for the business, the back end for sleeping. When Rita and her mother were not getting along, the girl would stay with family friends, occasionally lodging with Victoria Addams, a woman who was dating John Rizzo. The serial instability had a negative impact on Rita.

At St. Anthony's School, her grades slipped. Some of this could be attributed to the cruel treatment she received from the nuns as a child of divorced parents. In the early 1930s, divorce was considered a shameful act and a grave sin in the minds of most Catholics, particularly Italian Catholics. At St. Anthony's, Rita Rizzo was the only child of a broken marriage.

In 1933, the sister in charge of Rita's class asked every student to sell a subscription to a Catholic magazine. Rita said she would take two, because her aunt Rose would likely buy one. The nun snapped back, "Oh, you just take one. You want to be so much and in the end you don't amount to anything." Tears trailed down Rita's cheeks. "I hated those nuns, I hated them," she said later. When Rita returned home, Mae knew something was wrong, but Rita refused to talk. Mae got a classmate's mother on the phone and was incensed to learn of the treatment her daughter had received. In retaliation, she pulled Rita out of St. Anthony's and sent her to a public school.

Later, a priest would persuade Mae to reenroll Rita at St. Anthony's. But the following year at Christmas, there would be another unpleasant parting. At the conclusion of a Christmas party, the nuns distributed toys to Rita and her peers. Each child tore at the wrapping paper, producing new trinkets, waving them about, to the delight of their cohorts. When Rita's name was called, she went forward to claim her present.

"I got this yo-yo. It was old and scratched, had some knots in it—you couldn't use the thing. So I went home, and my mother asked where I'd gotten it. When I told her Sister had given it to me, that was the final straw."

Mae and Rita sped to St. Anthony's rectory, where Mae gave the pastor a piece of her mind. She considered the used gift a put-down—and her child would be put down by no one. Before leaving, she withdrew Rita from St. Anthony's for the last time.

The stigma of divorce would also separate Mae from the church that had long been her support. Having avoided confession since the divorce, she was encouraged by her friends to seek the sacrament from a missionary visiting the parish. When Mae confessed to committing the sin of divorce, the priest "hit the ceiling." "You what?" the priest railed. "Do you realize that by getting a divorce you were excommunicating yourself?"

"Instead of being kind or loving to her, he blasted her!" Mother Angelica said. "She didn't even get a chance to say that she wasn't remarried and was obeying Church law."

Mae stormed out of the confessional and would not return to church for a decade.

At about the same time, Mae's business was failing. Customers picking up their clothes would promise to pay the following week, but the cash rarely materialized. Too proud to return to her family, Mae and Rita scraped by as best they could, at times sharing a piece of bologna and bread for supper. Committed to her ideal of self-sufficiency, Mae refused to approach the Gianfrancescos for a handout, no matter how dire the circumstances.

To the outside world, Mae Rizzo seemed the picture of confidence. She still wore her fashionable hats and maintained the slightly imperious facade that kept strangers at arm's length. All who knew her recalled a compelling raconteur, a woman who could hold an audience's attention no matter what story she was telling. Her daughter would inherit the gift. But emotionally, Mae Rizzo was falling apart. By 1934, poverty and chronic depression pushed her over the edge. At home, before her bewildered eleven-year-old daughter, Mae would burst into tears, lamenting the life she had inflicted on her child, the lack of education that restricted her options, and the husband who had wronged her. Three years after the divorce, Mae was incapable of tearing John Rizzo from her heart. Just the sight of him with another woman would enrage her.

John Rizzo's dating only compounded Mae's depression, producing dark, destructive thoughts. "She was always threatening suicide," Mother Angelica revealed. "And when I came home from school, I never knew if I would find her dead or alive. I couldn't study or concentrate."

The fixation with Mae's state of mind, and the unceasing battle to survive deprived Rita of all outside relationships. An underlying sense that she had somehow contributed to her mother's condition only intensified her attachment to Mae, who became her sole focus. "Much of the time I took care of her," Mother Angelica told me. "That's why I never had friends, never played with dolls. To me, life was very serious."

Reversing roles, Rita became the parent and Mae's emotional caretaker. At eleven years of age, barely able to see over the dashboard, Rita was already driving Mae's car, delivering starched clothes to her mother's customers and collecting payments on Saturdays. At times, she would bring home a profit, sparking a celebration at the public library, where Mae would pore over books and Rita would indulge in the comics and a box of caramels. But more often than not, the girl returned from her deliveries empty-handed, and Mae's tears would flow. Rita helplessly absorbed her mother's sadness.

"Had the Lord not pulled me up, I would have had one miserable life," Mother Angelica said during a moment of reflection. "I never saw any change occur. I felt I was born that way and I would die that way. I was not bitter, just resigned."

Then the miraculous intruded on Rita Rizzo's life for the first time. Returning from a downtown visit to the dentist, the lanky child looked both ways as she dashed across a large boulevard to catch a bus. Worn-out socks flopped about her ankles. She headed for the median in the center of the street, when a woman shrieked. Glancing over her right shoulder, Rita saw two headlights bearing down on her. She froze. The engine's gruff rumble grew louder. With only seconds till impact, Rita closed her eyes, paralyzed with fear.

"All of a sudden, it felt as if two hands under my arms picked me up—I can almost feel them when I talk about it—and put me on the island where the cars were parked," Mother told me in an awe-filled whisper. She claimed that the passersby were amazed by what they saw and stared at her in disbelief.

The next day on the bus, the driver told Mae he had witnessed "a miracle," and had never seen "somebody jump so high before." Both mother and daughter considered the "lifting" a touch of grace during an otherwise-dismal moment in their lives.

By the time fourteen-year-old Rita started high school, in 1937, she and her mother could no longer go it alone. Financial pressures forced them to return to the Gianfrancesco home, where Grandma, Grandpa, and Uncles Pete and Frank were still in residence. But the house was different now. Anthony Gianfrancesco had suffered a stroke after losing his temper with someone in the saloon. Paralyzed on one side, he hobbled around the house with the aid of a cane. The condition aggravated his hot Italian temper and added to the anxieties of the household. Regardless of the domestic challenges, and Mae's wounded pride at having to return, at least she and Rita could expect regular meals and a roof over their heads.

To spare her mother any additional anguish, Rita strove to keep her grades up at McKinley High School, with mixed results. During her sophomore year, Ms. Thompson, her economics teacher, spotted something in the lean, solitary underachiever. In class, the teacher announced that there was someone in the room who could be an A student and the most popular student in the school if she applied herself. Ms. Thompson cornered Rita after class.

"You know I was talking about you," the teacher said.

"Yes," Rita replied.

"Well, what are you going to do about it?"

"Nothing," Rita said defiantly. "I don't like people, and I don't like you."

On her way home, Rita regretted the nasty remark, but she found it difficult to restrain her choleric temperament. She couldn't have friends, anyway. They would make Mae uneasy, and anyone demanding Rita's attention would be perceived as a threat. For Mae's sake, Rita had become an avowed loner.

Days after her chat with the economics teacher, the McKinley High bandleader approached Rita, asking if she would like to be a drum majorette and lead the band. In restitution for her cocky answer to Ms. Thompson, and without knowing anything about music, she accepted the challenge. Looking back, Mother Angelica feels that Ms. Thompson and the other teachers may have been conspiring to help her. In the summer of 1939, Rita took up the baton.

"She could twirl very well," fellow majorette Blodwyn Nist recalled. "She had those big hands and did a beautiful job." Nist and
Rita were the first female majorettes in McKinley High's history,
performing together at games, parades, and other community func-
tions. According to Nist, Rita was an outgoing girl with a strong
sense of right and wrong.

But there appears to be a disparity between Angelica's recollection of herself during this period and the public memory. Either
Rita had taken a cue from her mother and adopted a cheery public
mask to hide the insecurities and fears that clouded her daily life or
the newfound socialization thrust upon her as a majorette exposed
the lighter side of her personality. Whichever the case might have
been, none of Rita's peers were close enough to know the truth. According to interviews with her classmates, Rita had no intimate
friendships at McKinley High and, aside from her majorette duties,
kept to herself. Like her mother, Rita could be doggedly self-
sufficient and distrustful of outsiders.

She never attended a school dance, and no one recalled her dating. "I never had a date, never wanted one," Mother confided to me.
"I just didn't have any desire. I suppose having experienced the
worst of married life, it was not at all attractive to me."

In 1939, the din of the football games grated on Rita's nerves.
Crowd noise and even school chatter irritated the sixteen-year-old.
It felt like the world was coming in on her. To escape the cacoph-
ony, she would literally flee from McKinley High in the afternoons.
Wearied by her jumpy state, she sought medical attention. The
doctor diagnosed Rita as having a calcium deficiency, which contributed to a nervous condition. He prescribed calcium shots and
nerve medication. But a mineral shortage was probably not the
source of her problems.

At home, Mae was going through her own meltdown: Crying fits
were becoming more frequent, as were her suicide threats. The tactics Rita normally used to extract Mae from her deep depression
proved unsuccessful. Worried that her mother was "not herself"
and suffering from "total fatigue," Rita decided Mae needed time
away from Canton. With her grandparents' blessing, Rita sent Mae,

who was in the depths of her first nervous breakdown, to Philadelphia to be with her sister, Rose.

Left behind with feelings of guilt and anxiety, Rita tried to maintain a normal routine. She went to classes, earned money teaching baton-twirling, and lived with the Gianfrancescos. But a despondency soon set in: a dread feeling that her fortunes would never improve and that her mother might not recuperate. From this apathetic cauldron of misery would arise a pain that would reshape Rita Rizzo and draw her to a life she could not have imagined at the time.

2

The Gift of Pain

SNOW BLANKETED the stoops of Eleventh Street that night in 1939. It fell in great dollops, burying the lower part of the weathered picket fence that fronted the Gianfrancesco home. Picking at congealed pasta in her grandmother's spacious wallpapered kitchen, the smell of oregano and garlic hovering in the air like incense, Rita Rizzo was about to birth a part of the persona that would overshadow the rest of her life.

Though her tired brown eyes registered no emotion, conflicted feelings of relief and longing welled up within Rita as she considered her mother's absence from the well-worn table. Seated across from her, the bachelor of the Gianfrancesco clan, Uncle Pete, hunched over his plate, mimicking the comedians he heard on the radio. Grandma Gianfrancesco waved a long, thin upturned hand, which didn't correspond with her plump frame, toward the girl's plate, encouraging her to eat. Rita rearranged the food but consumed very little. Whether it was the nerve medication or the stress, her stomach felt strange. A dull nausea would settle in sporadically, disrupting some meals. Rita ignored it.

The seventeen-year-old was far too busy to think of herself. To earn money, she divided her free time between giving baton lessons and working at a factory that made liturgical candleholders. Each week, Rita dutifully sent a dollar of her income to her mother, who, after a month, still remained in Philadelphia.

Rita's uncle could not resist commenting on the arrangement. "When's your mother coming home?" Uncle Pete asked, his mouth half-full. Rita shrugged from the other side of the table. "Why doesn't that lazy woman come home?" Pete continued stabbing the red mass before him, giggling. "Pretty good deal—you work and send her money, while she's on vacation in Philly."

Rita never looked up from the pasta. But her down-turned eyes were now alive with anger, hurt, and an instinctive hatred of injustice. She alone knew what her mother had endured. She had seen Mae ridiculed for her divorce, watched her iron other people's clothes late into the night, seen the statuesque woman confidently march off to job interviews, only to return home a defeated mess of screeches and tears.

"What a lazy woman! That's the life," Uncle Pete continued.

Without a word, Rita pinched the sharp point of the bread knife on the table and hurled it at her uncle's head. The knife pierced the wallpaper inches from the stunned target. Pale and shaken, Uncle Pete hardly breathed. Grandma Gianfrancesco gently lowered her fork, as if any sudden movement might provoke more flying silverware. The criticism of her mother quieted, Rita pushed away from the table and fled furiously into the snow. Here was an early glimmer of the indignation that would appear whenever she felt those close to her were under assault.

"I walked and I walked that night. And I realized then that there was something inside of me that was capable of evil—to kill somebody," she later recalled. "At that point, I determined that whatever it was—I guess you'd call it anger—I had to control it completely. You can see God's providence, because He let me see what I was capable of. And I knew I *had* to change, but I didn't know how."

Rita's grades reflected her inner turmoil. At the end of junior year, she had missed nearly two months of school and had failed three subjects. All this was withheld from her mother, whose tears Rita dreaded more than anything else. She clandestinely began summer school, creating fictions to justify her absences from the house.

The summer course work effectively ended Rita's career as a

drum majorette. Though she later said it was the "dumbest thing" she'd ever done, leading the band gave Rita an ease and confidence before crowds she might otherwise never have attained. The only known picture of Rita in her majorette uniform discloses a natural performer, cocksure and sassy, relishing a perfect pose: her head thrown back, one leg stylishly bent.

Upon her return from Philadelphia, Mae Rizzo was better, if not cured, and armed with a new sense of purpose. She committed herself to finding regular employment, though her job search went nowhere.

Rita internalized Mae's disappointment and, despite her own scholastic struggles, resolved to take action. In an audacious move, Rita marched down to city hall to see Canton's Republican mayor, James Seccombe. Spying an employment angle, the politically savvy Rita, without consulting her mother, submitted Mae's name for a city job.

"My mother has worked in the precincts for the Republican Party all her life," Rita explained to Mayor Seccombe. "At this point, she can't find a job. I think she deserves something for all her work."

"I think so, too," the mayor said, impressed by the girl's tenacity. "She'll have to pass a civil service examination."

"That's okay."

"Have your mother write a letter to the executive committee," the mayor instructed. Rita sprinted home to tell her mother the good news.

Mae was euphoric until she heard about the examination. Then panic set in. Beset by her old insecurities, Mae was ready to give up. "I can't pass anything," she said.

"Try, just try," Rita encouraged.

At McKinley High, Rita faced an onerous senior year loaded with extra courses to make up for those she had flunked the year before. Transcripts show that her course work included economics, bookkeeping, salesmanship, typewriting, and even blueprint reading. Each class would lend her a crucial skill in later life, but at the time they were just a disparate collection of courses chosen to secure a diploma.

No longer a majorette, Rita retreated into her shell, single-mind-edly intent on graduating with everyone else.

The Gift

RITA WAS ON HER WAY HOME from school one day in December 1940 when she received what she would later call "the greatest gift God ever gave me." Her stomach heaved and quivered as she reached the Gianfrancesco house. Doubling up in the doorway, she felt her knees and elbows go to jelly, and perspiration covered her brow. A few glasses of warm water provided by her grandmother did no good. The spasm continued for a full hour.

When it passed, diarrhea plagued Rita for the next twenty-four hours. Her once-full cheeks hung like saddle bags from the sides of her porcelain face. Each time she attempted to eat, it felt as if bits of glass were tearing through her intestine. In the days that followed, food refused to stay down, forcing her to adopt a restricted diet of crackers, tea, and anything soft that her system could tolerate.

By early 1941, the spasms were striking the eighteen-year-old about three times a week. Yet even in the midst of this physical strain, Rita remained fixated on her mother's welfare.

Weeks after taking the civil service exam, Mae had heard nothing from city hall. The suspenseful wait possibly contributed to her second nervous breakdown—and a repeat visit to Philadelphia for six weeks.

Plunged into a sobering adulthood on the eve of her graduation from McKinley High, Rita was again without her mother. While not resentful of Mae's absence, Angelica told me it brought her to the realization that no one could be expected to sustain her life—not her mother, not her father, not even her grandparents. The future would depend entirely on her own resourcefulness. With that un-derstanding, Rita began a solitary job search.

Emotionally spent and unemployed, Mae Rizzo was strapped for cash upon her return to Canton. On May 22, 1941, she petitioned the Stark County Court to collect $2,098.50 in back alimony from her ex-husband. Whether the court awarded her the money is unclear, but on July 1, 1941, having passed the civil service exam, Mae became a bookkeeper at the Canton Waterworks office. The job brought a sense of security and balance to Mae's life. In a show of financial abundance, the room she shared with Rita at the Gianfrancesco home was spruced up with satin bedspreads, dust ruffles, window treatments, and lamps she could never have afforded previously. The newfound amenities were little comfort to Rita, whose stomach disorder was getting worse.

In late July, Rita's worried grandparents asked their physician, Dr. James J. Pagano, to examine the girl's stomach. Pagano had been making regular house calls to Liberty Street since Anthony Gianfrancesco's stroke. Initially, the doctor thought Rita suffered from ulcers or gallbladder complications. He prescribed suitable medications, but they did nothing to alleviate the pain or stop the spasms—a fact that invalidated his diagnosis.

By the time Dr. Pagano sent Rita to Mercy Hospital for X-rays in November 1941, she had lost twenty pounds. The tests conclusively identified her ailment as ptosis of the stomach, commonly known as a "dropped stomach." The condition pinched the entryway of the organ, causing an obstruction that blocked the passage of food. A custom-designed medical belt to suspend Rita's stomach was the proposed remedy. The belt made Rita's life bearable, even as the world was falling apart.

In December 1941 the Japanese attacked Pearl Harbor, dragging the United States into worldwide conflict. For a steel town like Canton, the war brought jobs. Rita joined the ranks of the more than fifteen thousand Canton women on wartime payrolls. Her confident attitude and senior-year elective courses enabled her to land a post in the advertising department of the Timken Roller Bearing Company in early 1942. At the time, Timken was a powerhouse, producing 100,000 seamless gun barrels for 37-, 40-, and 75-mm guns over a two-year period.

As secretary to the Timken vice president of advertising, Peter Poss, Rita wore many hats. She wrote and edited copy, organized layouts for ad campaigns, and even learned to operate some machinery. "Mr. Poss thought she was tops," Elsie Machuga, a coworker at Timken, recalled. "She was sort of his girl Friday."

One day in April 1942, Rita retired to the ladies' lounge at Timken. She lay down, elevating her feet on the arms of the sofa, trying to impede the stomach spasm she could feel coming on. Within moments, a stabbing pain ran through her abdomen. Even the medical belt could no longer control her undulating stomach.

On May 13, Dr. Wiley Scott examined Rita for the first time. He determined that the medical belt had to be enlarged into a sort of corset, and he suggested that she sleep with her feet elevated eight inches to maintain the stomach suspension. The corset was not to be removed unless she was in bed with her feet up. She obeyed the doctor's orders, and her stomach pains subsided. Rita returned to work.

On July 10, 1942, Mae Rizzo was changing her father's bed linens when "two tall men in white" entered the room. The men called out to Anthony Gianfrancesco while Mae dumbly looked on, clenching a pillow in her teeth. As she struggled to shake the thing into a fresh pillowcase, her father sat up. Anthony focused on the strangers, muttered, "Yes," and fell back into the arms of death. Whether the men in white were angelic presences remains a mystery. But Mae was certain she had seen them, and she would relate this story for years to come.

If anybody could have used a pair of angels at the time, it was probably Rita. By November, her "nerves were worse than ever" and the spasms had returned. "I couldn't sleep or eat. My hands would shake and my left arm would get numb," Rita wrote of the illness. Her only relief, the surgical corset, began to cut into her hips, causing blisters—which would later rupture with the continual wearing of the garment. To allow the skin time to heal, she removed the corset and stayed at home in bed. During her confinement, Rita was eager to assess her condition. One day she elected to get out of bed without the corset to test her recovery. A nauseating pain swiftly rolled through her stomach. When she glanced down, Rita was terrified by what she saw. As if marked by a faded bruise, the skin of her belly held a bluish tint. And more alarming, protruding from the left side of her abdomen was a lump the size of a lemon.

3
The Healing and the Call

THE AGENTS of divine providence are often mundane and, for the most part, unspectacular. For Rita Rizzo, the call of God would issue not from a star in the East or a column of fire, but from the mouth of a housekeeper who worked on the outskirts of Canton.

Mae Rizzo's thoughts were fixed on her daughter's torturous stomach spasms as she bounced homeward in a bus on Friday afternoon, January 8, 1943. Her back rigid, her hair like a finely wrought sculpture, Mae gazed out the window, wondering where this illness would lead. Rita didn't look well. How much longer could she survive on crackers, tea, and stale bread? Rita was shriveling before her eyes and there was nothing she could do about it. The recent death of Mae's father stirred up morbid thoughts. She couldn't bear losing Rita. Rita was all Mae had.

This private angst became public when Catherine Barthel boarded the bus and sat next to Mae. The petite Barthel was a friend who cleaned houses for a living, including a ramshackle residence in northeast Canton. Mae exposed her fears to the woman, vividly explaining Rita's latest sufferings. The bus lurched and rolled. Two gold angels blowing trumpets atop the tower of the courthouse hurried past the window.

"Why don't you take Rita to Mrs. Wise?" Barthel suggested.

Mae had never heard of Rhoda Wise. A stigmatic and a purported miracle worker, Wise lived in a white clapboard shotgun house a block away from the city dump. It was one of the homes Catherine Barthel cleaned each week. Wise believed herself to be the recipient of a miraculous healing—a healing that would leave a trail of supernatural phenomena in its wake.

The stout woman's sweet blue eyes masked the physical hell she had endured for nearly a decade. In the early 1930s, Rhoda Wise's belly swelled with what she thought was a child. Doctors later discovered that she was carrying a thirty-nine-pound ovarian cyst. The hospital visit to remove the growth would not be her last. Depressed and suicidal, Wise was committed to a state hospital in 1933. Abdominal adhesions would repeatedly force her back into the operating room.

During a rare period of good health, Wise accidentally stepped into an open sewage drain on her way home from a Christmas party in December of 1936. Her shredded right leg became infected and within months it began to turn inward. A succession of casts designed to straighten the leg had no effect.

In 1938, during yet another round of abdominal surgeries at Mercy Hospital, Wise was visited by one of the Sisters of Charity of St. Augustine. Arrayed in white, Sister Clement prayed with the ailing woman and introduced her to the rosary and other Catholic devotions. Being a Protestant, Wise summarily dismissed the nun's suggestions, particularly the idea that she should offer nine days of prayer to Saint Thérèse of the Child Jesus for a healing. The pain convinced her otherwise.

During a subsequent visit to the hospital, Wise prayed the nine-day novena to Saint Thérèse and soon converted to Catholicism. She left Mercy Hospital with a new faith and an open wound, which exposed a section of her bowel. The ruptured bowel would frequently discharge, burning Wise's skin as it oozed.

On the night of May 27, 1939, Wise claimed, Jesus entered her room and sat on a chair adjacent to her bed. The Savior appeared iridescent to her, His light filling the room. Before leaving, Christ promised to return.

Rhoda Wise's suffering was so intense that she prayed for death, until the night of June 27, 1939, when the light returned to her room. According to Wise's diary, Jesus stood in the doorway as Saint

Thérèse approached the bed. The saint put her hand on the open wound, saying, "You doubted me before. You have been tried in the fire and not found wanting. Faith cures all things." When the mystical pair withdrew, Wise "was astonished to find the wound on my abdomen . . . entirely closed . . . the ruptured bowel, too, was entirely healed."

Wise claimed Saint Thérèse made a later visit, this time splitting her cast in two before healing her right leg. After prolonged evaluation and inquiry, Monsignor George Habig, Wise's reluctant spiritual director, told friends and church officials that he believed the healings to be authentic and supernatural. News of the miraculous healings drew between three hundred and five hundred people a week to Rhoda Wise's home. Curiosity seekers, skeptics, and pilgrims stood in line to enter the front room of the small shanty for a chance to touch the visionary. Wise became a cult figure.

On Good Friday in 1942, what appeared to be blood spilled from gashes on Wise's forehead. Over the next few years, she would intermittently suffer Jesus Christ's Passion: profusely bleeding from her head, hands, and feet between noon and three o'clock on Fridays. Unknown to her devotees at the time, Wise had offered herself as a "victim soul" (like Saint Thérèse) for the good of priests and religious two years earlier. Her idea, rooted in Catholic tradition, was that suffering offered to God could compensate for the spiritual failings of others.

From 1940 until her death, Rhoda Wise would be the instrument of countless miracles. News reports of the time contain testimonies of people suffering from cancer, ear infections, mental disturbances, and goiters—all healed after visiting the portly mystic. Catherine Barthel relayed bits of this to Mae Rizzo during their bus trip.

In Barthel's wondrous tale, Mae found hope. After all, Catherine knew this Wise woman and worked for her. It had to be true. During the walk home, Mae delighted in the possibility that Rhoda Wise could free Rita from her stomach affliction. Even if the chances were remote, it was worth a try.

Rita wasn't so sure, and Wise's reputed signs and wonders were less than convincing: "I was so engrossed in survival that religion did not affect me. . . . My faith was not at a high level, if it was at any level at all. But I was so happy that my mother wanted to go that I figured, What can I lose?"

On that same night in January, Rita and Mae climbed into a taxi and braved a blizzard to see Rhoda Wise. When they got to the shotgun house, the squat, jovial owner, whose pink skin was like a carnation petal, met them at the door.

Wise invited Rita and her mother into her bedroom. A long altar arrayed with statues of Saint Thérèse, the Blessed Mother, and the Sacred Heart of Jesus dominated the room. In front of the altar, on the right, was the wooden kitchen chair where Jesus purportedly sat during His visits with Wise. She recommended that Rita sit in "our Lord's chair" while she chatted with Mae. Before the half-hour visit ended, Wise gave Rita "prayers to the Little Flower and told [her] to make some sort of a sacrifice—and to promise to spread devotion [to Saint Thérèse] if [she] was cured." That was it. Wise did not touch Rita or pray over her. She just offered the novena prayer card and showed her guests to the door.

Rita went home and did as she was told. Her mother and grandmother joined her each day to recite the nine-day novena. Rita's spasms continued, and so did the pain.

Nothing happened until the early morning hours of January 17, 1943, once the ninth day of the novena had passed. In the dark of those early hours, Rita felt "the sharpest pains" she had ever encountered. "It seemed that something was pulling my stomach out," she claimed. To avert the pain that she knew awaited her, Rita considered attaching the corset before rising. Then a voice commanded her to get up and walk without it.

"I knew I didn't need that brace and I knew I was healed," Mother Angelica said, even though her stomach still hurt. "I did have a pain, but it was different from the other pain."

She tentatively ambled into the kitchen, where Grandma Gianfranceso was cooking. "Grandma, I want a pork chop," she said.

The saggy woman spun around. "*Testadura!* You can't eat pork chops."

"Yeah, I can, Grandma." Rita lifted her pajama top, exposing her midsection. The blue coloration was gone. So was the lump. "I've been healed."

The old lady turned to her frying pan and started grilling a pork chop. When Mae entered the kitchen and heard the news, she was hysterical. Caught somewhere between elation and fear, Mae got so worked up, Grandma Gianfrancesco had to slap her across the face to steady her emotions. Mae threw the kitchen door open and yelled over the grapevines to her brother Nick's house: "Rita's cured. Rita's cured. It's a miracle."

Rita beamed as she stood in the empty lot next to the house, surrounded by the Gianfrancescos. To prove the authenticity of the miracle, she encouraged her ten-year-old cousin Joanne to repeatedly hit her stomach. The child complied. Today, Joanne is still convinced: "It was like a rock, completely healed."

Presumably to confirm the healing, Rita's stomach was X-rayed on February 6, 1943. In a letter to Monsignor Habig, dated March 19, 1943, Rita's physician, Dr. Wiley Scott, wrote the girl off as a "neurotic female with a mentality which is very open to any suggestive influence." By her own admission, Mother Angelica suffered from a certain neurosis during this period, but her choleric temperament and strong will hardly seemed susceptible to outside influences.

Dr. Scott contended that his alterations to Rita's corset in May 1942 produced a "mental suggestion" that made her feel as if her condition had improved. The suggestion couldn't have been too persuasive. Otherwise, she would not have complained of worsening pain eight months later, nor sought the services of a healer. It is also hard to imagine that a mere "mental suggestion" had the power to remove a discolored abdominal lump.

Near the end of his letter, Dr. Scott decried the healing, definitively ruling that "there was no anatomical change shown by the x-ray of February 6, 1943." But this diagnosis is questionable. Since earlier in the same letter, Dr. Scott contradicted himself when he wrote, "I had looked at the x-rays she first had taken at Mercy Hospital. *I have not seen those of February 6, 1943* [italics added]." If he hadn't seen these X-rays, taken after the supposed healing, how could the doctor credibly evaluate Rita's present condition or offer an honest medical opinion based on a comparative study? Either this was a flagrant typo or it is evidence that Dr. Scott never saw the posthealing X-rays and rendered a judgment based largely on Rita's emotional state and previous office visits. As Rita's medical records have since been destroyed, there is no way to solicit an independent analysis.

"All I know is I was gaining weight, which I was losing before. I wasn't interested in the doctor's report. I could have cared less," Mother Angelica said. For Rita the healing was a transforming experience, a milestone that would entirely reorient her life.

The Love Affair

"WHEN THE LORD came in and healed me through the Little Flower, I had a whole different attitude. I knew there was a God; I knew that God knew me and loved me and was interested in me. I didn't know that before. All I wanted to do after my healing was give myself to Jesus."

Unsure of how to do that, Rita turned to the holiest person she knew. Rhoda Wise would become her model of sanctity and a seminal spiritual influence. Every Sunday, the Rizzos joined the crowds packing Wise's house. There, Rita literally learned holiness at the feet of Rhoda Wise. She recalled sitting next to the mystic on a "little stool, and I would hold her feet up, because some people would squeeze the stigmata."

From Wise, she would learn how to deal patiently with overanxious crowds who at times mistook the object of God's grace for God Himself.

Fulfilling her promise to spread devotion to the Little Flower and the Sacred Heart, Rita sent personal letters, prayers, and Sacred Heart badges to anyone who wrote to the Wise house. One letter from September of 1943 revealed the depth of Rita's conversion: ". . . before I was cured I was a lukewarm Catholic . . . now I love [our Lord] so that there are times when I think I will die. When I think of all that He has done for me and how little I have done for Him, I could cry."

Privately, Rita adopted a series of devotional practices that, in retrospect, seem like a dress rehearsal for religious life. As a thanksgiving and reminder of her healing, she restricted herself to crackers and tea on Saturdays. She began reading spiritual literature, such as Mary of Agreda's *The Mystical City of God.* On her way home from work, Rita would often stay on the bus, bypassing her grandmother's house to go to St. Anthony's, where she would recite the Way of the Cross. The exposure to Rhoda Wise and her stigmata somehow made Christ's Passion real for Rita. No longer a theory or a distant tale, the Passion became a present reality. Each weekday, she meditated on the sufferings of Christ, using the light she gathered to view her wounds in a new way.

At Timken, a picture of Jesus impaled by a crown of thorns sat on the edge of Rita's desk. When accused by a coworker of "pushing her religion," Rita responded, "If you have a picture of a movie star or someone you love, you put it out there. Well, this is my love, and it's going to stay there."

By all indications, Jesus was her love. The only possible challenger was a man named "Adolph" Gordon Schulte. A boarder at Rhoda Wise's home, Schulte frequently took Rita to a Canton eatery called the Purple House. The occasional outings would lead some, such as Rhoda Wise's daughter, Anna Mae, to think that the two were "going together." Schulte contested the notion. "She was attractive, interesting, and nice to talk to," Schulte told me. "But there was nothing serious about it. It was very casual."

Rita's best friend at the time, Elsie Machuga, concurred: "I think that he liked to be around her, and he would bring her religious things all the time. But she was nice to everybody."

Questioned about the relationship, Mother Angelica spoke frankly: "I was never a sexpot, and I never wanted a date. Sexually, I'm a eunuch. I could care less. It's just not my bag."

On one occasion, Rita did engage in a public display of affection. Steven Zaleski, a Canton native and acquaintance of Rita's at the time, recalled a mission at Sacred Heart Church on Clark Avenue. When the congregants came forward to venerate a carving of the crucified Christ, Rita "kissed Him on the heart with great fervor. Very personal. Like He was her lover."

In her bedroom, mimicking the example of Rhoda Wise, Rita erected an altar at the foot of her bed. Covered in light fabric, it held two large statues of the Sacred Heart and the Blessed Mother surrounded by tiny images of the Infant of Prague, Saint Anthony of Padua, and, dead center, Saint Thérèse of Lisieux. An unadorned wooden kneeler stood before the altar, where Rita would pray in the wee hours—a practice discouraged by her mother. One morning, Mae was horrified to find a penitential chain dangling from beneath Rita's pajamas.

"She got the hint that something was going on, and she wasn't happy about it," Mother Angelica recalled with a laugh more than fifty years later. Rita's love of Christ began to take precedence in her life, gently replacing all other attachments, including her attachment to Mae Rizzo.

Perhaps threatened, Mae warned Rita about being "overly pious" and voiced her concerns to Grandma Gianfrancesco. "She doesn't belong to us anymore," the wizened old woman told Mae ominously. This is not what Mae wanted to hear. At roughly the same time, she received more bad news.

During the summer of 1943, John Rizzo married a second time. At fifty years of age, he wed a twenty-four-year-old woman who had gone to school with Rita. There is no record of Mae's reaction, but Rita's healing, coupled with steady employment, probably softened the blow. Mae had shed the Rizzo name by this time and was calling herself Mae Francis. She insisted that Rita adopt the new name, as well.

On a fall afternoon in 1943, twenty-one-year-old Rita Francis had completed her customary Way of the Cross at St. Anthony's. She knelt at the side altar, facing the statue of Our Lady of Sorrows—the same statue that had gazed upon her on the day of her baptism. When Rita intoned the closing prayer of thanksgiving, she was overcome by a "deep awareness" that she "had a vocation." There was suddenly a sense that she had to "go wherever the Lord would send" her. No doubt, troubled by thoughts of the bitter nuns she hated from grade school, Rita hesitated for a moment before returning to her inspiration. Mother Angelica told me, "I've always felt if the Lord says do something, you do it." And she did.

For guidance, she sought out Monsignor Habig, Rhoda Wise's spiritual director. He affirmed the religious vocation and agreed it should be kept secret so as not to agitate Mae Francis unduly. To nurture her calling, Rita spent more time at Rhoda Wise's house.

The Wise home was an oddity by any measure. Visitors to the house described a bright light that appeared in the front bedroom whenever Rhoda spoke to Jesus. They also claimed to have heard an occasional clicking sound resonating throughout the shanty, which Mrs. Wise attributed to the presence of Saint Thérèse. In the 1940s, these inexplicable occurrences and the mystic herself attracted a constant stream of visitors to the home, nuns among them. A friend to many religious, Rhoda Wise would become Rita's vocational resource. Learning of Rita's intention to enter religious life, the mystic furnished the young woman with a list of communities and superiors to contact.

But Rita's grades had been so poor that none of the teaching orders would accept her. Later at the Wise house, she met a group of Josephite nuns who worked with the deaf in Buffalo. This piqued Rita's interest, and she resolved to visit the Josephites in upstate New York.

The Buffalo Bluff

TO MAKE THE TRIP to Buffalo without detection, Rita would have to escape town clandestinely. Rita's friend Elsie Machuga and her mother, Anna, were very supportive of Rita's religious vocation. They encouraged her to follow God's promptings, even if it meant leaving Mae behind. So in late 1943, the Machugas became her accomplices.

The story, created for Mae's benefit, was that Rita and Elsie were headed to Cleveland for the weekend. Mae was distrustful of the story, since Rita hardly ever spent a night away from home. But she eventually accepted the idea. The Cleveland ruse would afford Rita the time to visit the Buffalo community and return home Sunday evening without Mae being the wiser. At least that was the plan.

On Sunday evening at 10:00 P.M., the phone rang at the Machuga house. Elsie picked up the receiver, thinking it was Rita, back from her Buffalo adventure. Instead, the enraged voice of Mae Francis filled her ear.

"Where is Rita? How come you're home already?" Mae barked.

"She'll be there pretty soon," Elsie replied.

"You're an instigator and you're going to be responsible for anything that happens to her," Mae screamed. "I'm going to come down there and *cut you up* if anything happens to her." There was a sudden pause. Elsie could hear Rita's voice in the background.

"Here she is," Mae announced sharply, and the phone went dead.

The next day at work, Rita apologized to Elsie for her mother's behavior.

Though still ignorant of Rita's vocation, Mae must have sensed her daughter pulling away. Mae's desperate emotional attachment suffocated the young woman. "I think what clouded her life was beginning to cloud my life," Mother Angelica explained to me later.

Mae's fixation on past hurts and a paranoid suspicion of anyone in her daughter's life inhibited Rita's growth as a person. Even though Mae experienced her own conversion and a genuine deepening of faith after Rita's healing, she could not bring herself to assert complete independence. The twenty-one-year-old crutch was still required, as illustrated by an oft-repeated story. Mae claimed that Rita, as a child, once told her, "Someday I'll build a castle and take you with me to live in it." Less than twenty years later, these cherished words would take on prophetic dimensions, but at the time they suggested a woman parasitically dependent on her daughter for survival and sustenance.

Meanwhile, Rita secretly pursued the religious vocation she felt God calling her to. A letter from the Josephite Sisters was excitedly shared with Monsignor Habig. It indicated that some of the Josephites felt Rita had a contemplative vocation, but they voted to accept her into the active order anyway. With a thin-lipped grin, the old monsignor placed the letter aside. "No, you can't go there," he told Rita. "But I know where you *should* go." Certain that a contemplative vocation would better suit her, and possibly fearing interference from Mae Francis, he gave Rita the address of the St. Paul Shrine in Cleveland. "This is where God wants you," Monsignor Habig told her. It was a cloistered Franciscan contemplative monastery.

"I didn't have the foggiest idea what a contemplative monastery even meant," Mother Angelica said later, but she accepted the monsignor's word on faith and made arrangements to visit the Cleveland monastery.

The Visitation

PETER POSS, Rita's supervisor at Timken, gave her the day off, dropped her at the bus station, and underwrote her journey. Poss also agreed to pick Rita up at five P.M. and deliver her home by suppertime, so as not to arouse Mae's suspicions.

The visit to the St. Paul's Shrine was overwhelming. Located at the corner of Euclid Avenue and East Fortieth Street in Cleveland, the Victorian Gothic church was a citadel of the ancient faith in the modern world. Constructed in 1875, the massive sandstone church seemed propelled heavenward by a spired bell tower encircled by four minaretlike turrets. Attached to the side of the church stood a five-story brick monastery built in 1931. Rita entered the intimidating structure with some reticence.

Sister Magdalene, a genial nun, ushered her into a parlor draped in shadows. The pronounced silence and the thick metal grille probably disturbed Rita. When she attempted to initiate conversation, hoping someone on the other side would respond, a door on the grille began to move. Silently, like ghosts, two nuns stood on the other side of the open grate, wearing deep brown habits, black veils drawn over their faces. Rita stared at the shadowy figures. She had never been inside a monastery before, nor had she ever encountered nuns like these. The sisters slightly raised their veils, introducing themselves in subdued German-accented voices. One was Reverend Mother Mary Agnes, the abbess of the monastery; the other, Mother Mary Clare, was the vicar. For some time, the nuns discussed their way of life and their expectations for a postulant.

Rita considered the surroundings and the strange ways of the nuns, and then, perhaps without fully understanding why, she arrived at a decision: "I thought, Well, Lord, this is where you want me, this is where I'm going."

Before leaving, Mother Agnes asked Rita if she wished to be a first choir sister or a second choir sister. First choir sisters sang the Divine Office each day and took solemn vows; second choir sisters were lay sisters and attended to the day-to-day cleaning of the monastery. Not understanding the distinction, Rita replied, "I'll try singing."

"Oh, can you sing alto?" Mother Agnes beamed. "We need one so badly."

Even though Mae had said she was "tone-deaf," Rita agreed to sing alto and became a first choir sister.

"This was another providential thing," Mother Angelica told me. "If I hadn't been a first choir sister, I could have never been an abbess. Lay sisters were not allowed to be superiors—and once you made your decision, you could not transfer to the other state."

Rita promised to enter the monastery on August 15, 1944, at the age of twenty-one.

Upon returning to Canton, Rita described the wonders of the Cleveland monastery to her friend Elsie, and shared her plans for departure. "I just thought, Well, you go, girl," Machuga recalled later.

On a Friday afternoon in 1944, Rhoda Wise lay in her bed, under the influence of a painful ecstasy. While her wounds bled, she began to speak. It was the only time Catherine Barthel could recall Wise saying anything during one of her supernatural agonies. "Rita? My Rita?" was all Wise said. Later, when Barthel questioned the statement, Wise claimed to have been responding to something Jesus had told her about Rita Francis. Interviewed in the 1980s, Barthel offered no further clue as to what that "something" was. Visitors to the Wise home later remembered the mystic prophesy-

ing that Rita "would do great things for the Church." Mother Angelica herself received word of this pronouncement. While impossible
to verify, the statements are ultimately not as important as the mark
Rhoda Wise would leave on Rita Rizzo.

From Mrs. Wise, Rita personally learned that suffering could be
a gift from God. This lesson would powerfully shape her religious
life and the lives of countless others. Where direct communication
with the divine would be skeptically dismissed by most, Rita, after
her association with Wise, considered it something natural, even
commonplace. To young Rita, mystical experiences with the saints
or Christ Himself were not to be dismissed or questioned, but
heeded and acted upon.

In August 1944, Rita visited the Wise house for what she expected to be the last time. Decades later, Rita would inherit the
home and establish a shrine there. Though it is infrequently visited
today, the house and the woman who owned it remain close to the
heart of Rita Rizzo.

At the Gianfrancesco home, Rita relished her final moments, secretly recording images of her family that would have to last a lifetime. Although she could share her decision to enter religious life
with friends and strangers, Rita could not bring herself to inform
Mae. Unable to gauge her mother's reaction, Rita said nothing, and
on August 15, 1944, she left the house for work, as usual. Peter Poss
drove her to the bus station, once again paid her passage to Cleveland, and promised to send, by special delivery, a letter she had
written to Mae Francis. This was the only way Rita could go
through with her decision.

As the bus doors closed on her difficult childhood, the shattered
family, and the burden of Mae, Rita looked to a serene future with
her love, Jesus. Thoughts of prayer and silence contended with the
guilt of abandoning her closest friend on earth. Still, she had to proceed with the elopement. It was what God wanted. Soon locked
away from the world, Rita expected to be free of its concerns. As
she completed the sixty-mile journey to her new home, Canton receded into memory. She imagined she would never see it again, and
that she would gently slip into a new life of submissive anonymity.

4
Bride of Christ

THE LETTER marked "Special Delivery" awaited Mae Francis when she entered the front room of the Gianfrancesco house on August 15, 1944. She ripped at the right-hand side of the envelope and pried out its contents. Recognizing the familiar handwriting, Mae froze. Her eyes flew to the underlined phrases slashed across the bottom of the page. The script had a tense, hurried bent.

August 14, 1944

My own dearest Mother,

When you receive this letter I will be in Cleveland. I have entered the Adoration Monastery at 40th and Euclid. You know it better as St. Paul's Shrine. This my dearest mother I realize is a shock to you. But if I were to ask your permission you would never have granted it. To have to enter in this way has hurt me tremendously. I wanted you to give me to Our Lord as His Spouse. It may be difficult for you to understand but this is His Most Holy Will. You have done <u>many wonderful things</u> for Our Lord since my cure. <u>He has a work for you to do. There are many souls that you can lead back into the true fold. Your work is on the outside winning souls for Him. Heed His plea and give all generously, without reserve, to His Most Sacred Heart.</u> Because I will be His Spouse, <u>His love for you will</u>

increase greatly. He loves you very much to ask this sacrifice of
you. He wants to be first in your heart. You have put me before
Him in the past. Our Lord has tried to make you understand
this all during your life. Do not, my dearest mother, attach
yourself to anyone or thing on earth, but attach yourself to
God alone who is patiently waiting for all your love. A cloister,
my mother is a heaven on earth. It is the greatest privilege
given to man on earth. This Our Blessed Mother said to
Blessed Mary of Agreda. There will I tell Him with every
breath that I take that I love Him. There will I make reparation for all the cold hearts in the world. Something happened
to me after my cure. What it was I don't know. I fell completely in love with Our Lord. To live in the world for the past
19 months has been very difficult. I love you very much and I
have not forgotten what you have done for me. My love for you
has increased since my cure, but if I were to stay in the world
another month I would leave it completely and enter into Our
Eternal Home. I am not of the world. Please Trust Him. You
can always write and you can see me once every two months.
You will see me with the grate open. I will write once a month.
We belong first to God then to our parents. We are His children. I ask your blessing that I may reach the heights I desire.
I love you very much. I want to thank Grandma for everything
she has done for me. My Beloved will reward her greatly. She
will also be able to see me with the grate open. Love you.

Always Yours,
Rita xxxxxx

Tears streamed down Mae's face. First the man she loved had
abandoned her, now her child, her rock, had followed suit. Hurt
gave way to anger. A rant of self-pity began that would go on for
hours. "My only child is gone," she screamed hysterically. When
she showed the letter to Grandma Gianfrancesco and Uncle Pete,
they joined Mae's wild display.

"It was like I died," Mother Angelica explained. "They said you
could hear my mother screaming all over the block. She ran down to

see the priest because she suspected that I had to get some baptismal and birth certificates. The priest said yes, he had given me one, but he didn't feel it was his place to tell [my] mother I was leaving."

In the ensuing months, Mae would feel a deep sense of betrayal and a fresh anger whenever she thought about Rita. She told friends that Rita was "ungrateful" and had left her "totally alone."

A Very Regimented Kind of Life

ON THE EVENING of August 15, 1944, Rita stepped off Cleveland's Euclid Avenue into the darkness of the St. Paul Shrine of Perpetual Adoration. Inside, she was instructed to kneel before the enormous wooden enclosure door. The portal to her new life opened, and there in the dim hallway, illuminated by a few exposed bulbs, were Mother Mary Agnes, Mother Mary Clare, and the sisters of the order in two single-file rows, facing one another. Veils concealed the identity of the nuns. When Rita stood, the sisters turned toward the interior of the cloister and led her in song to the chapel. The otherworldly ritual and its formality filled Rita with a wonder that awakened her excitement. Soon she would be a prisoner of divine love, a Franciscan nun of the Most Blessed Sacrament.

The French order of Poor Clares was founded in 1854 by Father Bonaventure Heurlaut and Josephine Bouillevaux (later Mother Marie de St. Claire). Father Bonaventure, a zealous overachiever, envisioned a religious order dedicated to worshiping Jesus Christ in the Blessed Sacrament (according to Catholic doctrine, the consecrated Host, or Blessed Sacrament, is no symbol, but the actual body, blood, soul, and divinity of Christ). What Father Bonaventure lacked was a female superior. When he met the eldest daughter of the mayor of Maizieres, Josephine Bouillevaux, he discovered his foundress.

Known for her strong will, Bouillevaux, like Father Bonaventure, heard voices and received messages from God. Together, they established the Sisters of the Immaculate Conception in a Paris apartment on December 8, 1854. The order owed its name to the dogma of the Immaculate Conception, proclaimed on the very same day by Pope Pius IX. The dogma insists that the Virgin Mary was protected from the stain of original sin, her soul having been immaculate from her conception. To honor the Virgin, Bouillevaux, now Sister Marie de St. Claire, consecrated herself and all her future daughters to the Mother of God. She declared that every nun of the order would henceforth take the name Mary.

Eventually, the sisters would relocate to Troyes, France. Under the patronage of the local bishop, they established a permanent monastery and took the name the Franciscan Nuns of the Most Blessed Sacrament. Continuing the tradition of Saint Francis and Saint Clare of Assisi, the order maintained an impetuous spirit and a childlike reliance on God in all things.

With Mother Marie de St. Claire as superior, the order's mission was to adore the Blessed Sacrament in a spirit of perpetual thanksgiving, making reparation for mankind's ingratitude toward God. In a move that would take on great significance for Mother Angelica, the order was declared a pontifical institute by Pope Pius IX on September 15, 1868. From that time on, the religious order would answer only to the Holy See in Rome.

From the motherhouse in France, a new foundation of sisters was established by Mother Mary of the Cross in Poland and later in Vienna, Austria. Mother Mary of the Cross died in 1906, shortly after receiving the solemn vows of a Viennese nun named Sister Mary Agnes. In 1921, that nun crossed the ocean and founded the first American branch of the order in Cleveland, Ohio.

This was the same nun, now Mother Mary Agnes, who, beneath the intricate network of exposed mahogany beams in the Gothic chapel in Cleveland, accepted Rita's promise to join the Franciscan nuns in the summer of 1944.

Following the ceremony, Sister Veronica, the novice mistress who whispered as if the angels were eavesdropping on her conversations, led Rita to the novitiate on the second floor. Here as a postulant, separated from the larger community, Rita would discern whether the cloistered life was truly for her.

Traditionally, a woman remained a postulant in the order for six months. After that time, she would become a novice, receiving the habit and a new name. Still later, if it was determined that she could withstand the life, the sister was allowed to take temporary vows. With the permission of the solemnly professed nuns, these vows were renewed annually for three years. After six years the sister could proceed to her solemn vows. The process was an arduous one. Rita would have problems from the start.

The average day at the St. Paul Shrine permitted little flexibility. The nuns maintained a rigorous schedule to accommodate the praying of the Divine Office. They were expected to pray in unison four times a day, adore the Eucharist for two hours, attend Mass, and recite the rosary. Time for spiritual reading, recreation, household duties, and meals rounded out their routine. Activities were intensely regulated, including the mandatory 4:50 A.M. rising time. Once the wooden clapper sounded in the hall each morning, the rule obligated the nun to announce *"Ecce adsum"* ("Here I am, O Lord, to fulfill Thy holy will in all things"), bless herself, and kiss the floor three times in honor of the Trinity. Washing was to be done kneeling on the floor. These and other rules were militantly observed and deviations were not tolerated. Those who could not measure up to the high standards were asked to leave.

Wearing a simple black dress and a cap, Rita attempted to conform to monastic life. She cleaned floors and baked altar breads as part of her initial assignments. During her first weeks in the cloister, she arrived late for prayer and made a habit of disturbing the elder sisters by barging through the enclosure doors.

None of this escaped the watchful gaze of Mother Agnes. In her Germanic way, the abbess began to prune Sister Rita, imposing a series of humiliations on the young postulant to teach her obedience. Each time Rita happened upon the abbess, she was to cease all activity, kneel down, and kiss the scapular of the Reverend Mother. But Mother Agnes did not stop there. In the presence of the entire community, the abbess would point out Sister Rita's faults, especially her volatile style of entering a room. As a penance, the plucky nun was made to kneel in the middle of the refectory, where the sisters ate, and recite a prayer that began "I am nothing. I can do nothing. I am worth nothing. I have nothing but my sins."

"Applesauce," Sister Rita would sometimes mutter under her

breath after finishing the litany. The penance would be repeated "Monday after Monday after Monday," until the nun accepted it as truth. While these tests moved her contemporaries to tears, Sister Rita was neither broken nor particularly disturbed by them.

"My whole life was a matter of survival, and I think that attitude of survival just changed places," Mother Angelica told me. "In the monastery, I had a lot of security; I didn't have to worry about anything."

But after only a month in the cloister, Rita came down with pneumonia. Monastery records indicate that she was given "permission to go to the hospital." Sometime later, following a bout with a sore throat, she left the cloister a second time to have her tonsils removed. The postulant's poor health became a source of concern for her superiors.

In late September 1944, Sister Rita was called to the parlor. Required to have a chaperon present when meeting guests, Rita was joined by Sister Veronica. On the other side of the open grille sat Uncle Nick Gianfrancesco. His deep recessed eyes held a misty sorrow. He had come to inform Rita of Grandma Gianfrancesco's passing and, as Mae's emissary, tried to convince her to return home. Somehow, he couldn't find the words. For the better part of an hour, while Rita talked of the new abbreviated black veil she had just received and the beauties of the monastery, Uncle Nick wept as if he were attending a wake. To Nick Gianfrancesco, the alien environment must have seemed like a prison.

"Are you happy here?" he asked in a voice broken with emotion.

"Oh yeah, Uncle Nick, I am."

Satisfied, he dabbed his eyes and left for Canton.

Back home, Mae Francis could still not accept what Rita had done. The canny abbess, correctly assessing the family situation, wrote to Mae, asking her to visit the monastery for another sister's investment ceremony. The idea was to slowly introduce the hostile parent to the ways of the cloister.

When Mae finally broke down and visited Cleveland in November 1944, she was allowed to see Mother Agnes, but not Rita. To offset Mae's disappointment, the abbess made "a big fuss over her," building bonds of trust through kindness. Repeated visits would wear down Mae's resistance to Rita's vocation. Occupying the extern apartment during her monastery sojourns, she now felt like part of the family. Mae began to understand.

Throughout her postulancy, Sister Rita immersed herself in spiritual writings. She studied everything from *Lives of the Saints* to the rule of her order. These works, coupled with "a very regimented kind of life," slowly shaped Rita in her newfound Franciscan spirituality. As she adjusted to life behind the cloister walls, she strove to suppress the forceful personality that had endeared her to coworkers and friends in Canton. But cracks surfaced.

On December 28, the feast of the Holy Innocents, the elder sisters went up to the novitiate to mix with the postulants and novices. "My, you're quiet," one of the nuns said to Sister Rita. "Yeah, and I have nothing to be sorry for," Rita shot back, referring to the habit of admitting faults in the cloister.

Keeping the brash side of her personality under wraps was challenging. Coping with a physical woe that had been afflicting her since early December only added to Sister Rita's crankiness. From the constant kneeling during prayers, penances, and work assignments, Rita's knees were swollen with fluid. Mother Angelica later described them as "two puffy water-filled grapefruit." She could manage to walk, but kneeling became impossible—and kneeling was a major part of contemplative life at the time.

A meeting of the professed nuns to vote on Sister Rita's admission to the novitiate was scheduled for February 1945. But her bad knees and other health problems forced a postponement of the vote.

"In those days, health meant everything," Mother Angelica remarked. "If you had health, you had a vocation."

For the moment, Sister Rita's vocation was in serious jeopardy.

More Stars

EACH FRIDAY, the messages Rhoda Wise received during her painful ecstasies were hungrily devoured by her followers. Like a human telegraph, her devotees spread the weekly messages far beyond the confines of Canton. For believers, these were news flashes from the Almighty. Mother Agnes, the abbess of St. Paul's Shrine, considered herself a believer.

One afternoon, while Sister Rita was still a postulant, she was invited to the office of the abbess.

"Is anyone here insulting you?" a concerned Mother Agnes asked, peering through her wire-frame glasses.

"No, Reverend Mother."

"Now think," the abbess announced in her clipped German accent. "Is anybody here insulting you?"

"No," Sister Rita replied, as if accused of a crime she had not committed.

"Are you sure?"

"Yes, Reverend Mother."

"Well, I don't know, then." Mother Agnes wore a troubled expression.

"Sister Agnes was with Mrs. Wise during her agony and the Lord said, 'Tell Rita every little worry will be erased from her heart. For each insult, each heartache, more stars.'" Neither Sister Rita nor Mother Agnes could decipher the message at the time, but the stars were coming.

In the spring of 1945, on Rita's twenty-second birthday, Mae Francis finally saw her daughter through the parlor grille. They talked of home, the struggles they had endured, and the life Rita had chosen. Mae missed her daughter, but she realized the futility of fighting Rita's call. In a diary entry written that same evening, she gave her daughter away:

April 20, 1945

To the King of Kings in the Most Blessed Sacrament
Your Majesty,

Today I offer Thee my beloved daughter on her 22nd birthday. I give Thee gladly what you wanted and placed in my care. I have tried my best to raise her as I thought best. Forgive me dear Lord today all the offenses I have committed against Thee. I thank Thee also for the deep wound Thou has placed in my heart. I beg Thee to shower many Graces and blessings upon her all the days of her life and bless those you have chosen to have charge over her. ~~I bless her also, for~~ I humbly beg to receive only the crumbs for I know that Thou lovest me. I humbly ask ~~today~~ for the Grace of loving you more and more and the grace of winning many souls for Thee.

Your New Mother

Having received Mae's blessing, Rita yearned for her wedding day. Months passed, but permission did not come. Mother Angelica believes she was nearly thrown out of the monastery on at least two occasions. Each month, the sisters questioned her commitment to cloistered life. And each month, Sister Rita was resolute, declaring her intention to stay.

With the first year anniversary of Sister Rita's entrance to the convent approaching, and her knees swollen like melons, Mother Agnes decided the local bishop should determine her fate. Normally, the professed nuns would have judged Rita's fitness for the novitiate by a chapter vote. But in this instance, Mother Agnes probably knew that Rita lacked the three-fourths majority needed to become a novice, so she personally intervened, putting off the chapter vote and calling in an outside party.

Father Floyd Begin, an emissary of the bishop and later an auxiliary bishop of Cleveland, met Sister Rita in the parlor. He asked why she wished to remain in the monastery. Rita argued that it was necessary to fulfill her vocation and that, if given time, her watery knees would improve. Apparently, Father Begin was moved by her earnestness. The bishop permitted Sister Rita to remain in the cloister for another six months. During this interval, she would be closely scrutinized by the nuns.

To spare her knees, Rita stayed off of them as much as possible and went about her duties. Some of the professed sisters noticed her lack of improvement, however.

During the six-month trial period, Mother Luka, a small woman with an apologetic face, who had been a pharmacist before religious life and was now in charge of the infirmary, beckoned Rita there. She was more refined than the other professed sisters, but she spoke the same Teutonic-laced English.

"Sister Rita, you have got to kneel, or they are going to send you home," Mother Luka warned.

"But look at my knees," Rita implored.

"They are terrible, but there is nothing I can do about it." The old nun was sympathetic but firm. "Please kneel."

Sister Rita followed orders. By shifting her weight to her shins, she was able to kneel during the Divine Office and throughout the day. Regardless of the physical cost, she was determined to claim her spot in the community.

The strategy worked. In October 1945, more than three-fourths of the solemnly professed nuns voted for Sister Rita to take the veil and enter the novitiate.

"I think in my heart Mother Agnes did it because she had a lot of faith and love for Mrs. Wise," Angelica speculated later. "She had heard about 'the more insults, the more stars,' and I think that was the only reason the chapter voted for me to get the habit."

The wedding commenced on November 8, 1945. Mae Francis arrived early, carrying a cake and flowers. Her sister-in-law, Rose, had fashioned a handmade wedding dress for the occasion. As a special tribute, Mother Agnes forfeited her right to select Rita's religious name, allowing Mae that honor. Mae chose the name Angelica, because Rita had been, in her words, an "angelic and obedient daughter."

Bishop Joseph Schrembs presided over the vesting ceremony, lending it the appropriate grandeur. At the penultimate moment, the abbess rose, scissors in hand, to snip Rita's last connection to the world. Her curly brown locks fell to the chapel floor. The nuns peeled away Rita's wedding dress and replaced it with a brown tunic, a scapular, and a white veil. The holy habit enveloped every part of Rita Rizzo, as did the love she felt for her Spouse. For Rita, this was no mere intellectual union, but the beginning of a lifelong bond—an intimate personal experience of communion with Jesus

Christ. Her mother, uncles, and friends sat on the public side of the chapel, sobbing in approval. As she stood behind the grille, she looked like the rest of them, save for the glow of fulfillment on her face.

Rita Rizzo was no more. Sister Mary Angelica of the Annunciation stood in her place.

To commemorate the occasion, Sister Angelica spent the afternoon in the parlor with her mother. The meeting inspired a letter, written that night:

To the mother in law of Jesus and my own sweet mother,

Today the greatest possible honor has been bestowed upon you and I. To have me marry an earthly king would be an honor, but to be espoused to the King of Kings is an honor that even the angels cannot understand. We shall have to wait until the day eternity dawns for both of us to realize what it means. So many souls in the world much better than I am, He might have chosen, but His eyes rested on you and me. It is as if He were walking through a field of beautiful flowers looking, looking passing many beautiful ones by, and then suddenly He stops and picks a small flower weak and hardly able to hold up its little head, and He walks away having made His choice. It must be, because there is no one on earth that needs Him more than we do, needs Him every moment of the day. Let us then spend the rest of our lives in thanking, praising, and loving Him. Shall any sacrifice be too hard for us, whom He ever holds in His arms?

Shall we not be filled with spiritual joy knowing the loving eyes of God rests upon us?

May my sweet Spouse keep you very close to His Sacred Heart. There is no loneliness for one who realized His sweet presence and the presence of your angel.

I want to thank you once more for bringing me into the world, for taking such good care of me, for your many sacrifices, for all your love and devotion, thanks for everything.

May I become worthy of such a mother. I ask for your blessing on this our day of days that I may become what Jesus
wants me to be.

> Your loving child, and spouse of Jesus,
> Sister Mary Angelica

The confined life of the cloister brought to the surface the failings of those locked within its walls. Temperament, family background, education, and talent were so diverse from sister to sister
that disagreements invariably arose. Feelings were wounded and
grudges nursed. In this microcosm of life, the nuns strove to conquer their personal imperfections for the good of the community.
Sister Angelica was no exception. To control her anger and quick
tongue, penitential practices were undertaken. But stricter discipline was needed to shake off her impatience, especially when en-
countering certain sisters.

"One time I said to the Lord, 'Today come hell or high water I'm
not going to be impatient,' " Angelica recalled. "And by nine came
hell and high water! I blew it."

In the fall of 1945, when plans were under way to establish a
monastery in New Orleans, Bishop James McFadden of the
Youngstown Diocese called Mother Agnes with an alternative
proposition.

John O'Dea, the retired owner of Eller Manufacturing, a steel
plant in Canton, wanted to donate his home and estate to a contemplative order. John and Ida O'Dea's only stipulation was that
perpetual adoration of the Blessed Sacrament be maintained in the
home. After due consideration, Mother Agnes accepted the O'Dea
offer, abandoned the New Orleans plans, and set about picking six
nuns to establish the new foundation in Canton. Mother Mary
Clare, the vicar in Cleveland, would be abbess of the Canton
monastery. Mother Luka would become her vicar.

The abbess called Sister Angelica of the Swollen Knees to her
office. Mother Agnes addressed the nun sternly. "Mother Clare and
I have made a decision," she said. Sister Angelica imagined all the
horrible things to follow: You must return home. You have no voca-

tion. Physical health is a consideration. . . . "Mother Clare feels the five stories of steps here are causing your knee problems, so we have decided to send you to the new foundation in Canton."

Under normal circumstances, only professed nuns were eligible for membership in a new foundation, and transferring a sister to her hometown was verboten. But this was no ordinary circumstance. Either Angelica's condition would improve or she would be evicted from religious life.

Canton was to be a last chance: the arena where her vocation would be tried, and a final judgment rendered. With apprehensive obedience, Sister Angelica accepted the transfer.

5
Sancta Clara

SISTER ANGELICA'S knees stung as she piled into John O'Dea's limousine with the other five sisters and departed the St. Paul Shrine on October 1, 1946. Joining Angelica for the trip to Canton were Mother Clare; Mother Luca; Sister Veronica, the novice mistress; Sister Mary of the Cross, a transfer from another order; and Sister Joanne, a postulant.

It had been a hard good-bye, especially for Mother Clare. The seventy-three-year-old abbess left behind Mother Agnes, her dearest friend, whom she had met in the Vienna convent in 1921. During the drive, the abbess betrayed no emotion, holding her head high, like a marble bust, for the benefit of the other sisters.

Sister Angelica's new home bore no resemblance to her digs in southeast Canton. The twenty-four-room O'Dea estate sat at 4200 Market Avenue North, situated on fifteen lush acres in a tony section of town. Surrounded by a small forest interrupted by manicured lawns, the Tudor-style O'Dea house, with its multiple fireplaces and rich paneling, seemed too swank for Poor Clare nuns. Adjustments would be required.

The premier objective was to build a temporary chapel in the large living room. The remainder of the mansion would be partitioned to create a refectory, infirmary, workrooms, and bedrooms. That first night, several beds were situated dormitory-style, with sheets hung between them for privacy. To slip her bloated knees beneath the covers without irritation, Sister Angelica billowed the blankets and shimmied into a comfortable spot.

Waking on the morning of October 2, Angelica threw back the sheets, hardly believing what she saw. "Both knees were normal"; the swelling had subsided and the water was gone. "And that convinced them that I had a vocation," Mother Angelica told me with astonishment. "That convinced Mother Clare. And so I only waited two more months to make my profession." The rapid improvement of her knees was viewed by Angelica as a signal grace from God, an affirmation that she belonged in the order and in the Canton monastery.

In the meantime, she was still in the midst of her canonical year: a period set aside to conform to the patterns of contemplative life. During the canonical year, a sister was allowed no communication whatsoever with family or friends.

As the in-house chapel was not yet completed, Sister Angelica and the other nuns were driven to St. Peters, where they attended Monsignor Habig's morning Mass. Near the end of the service, a familiar cough seized Angelica's attention. "I heard my mother, and knowing my mother, as she was very emotional, I didn't know what to do." Once again, Rita Rizzo's concern for Mae's emotional state forced all other thoughts aside.

Released by the final blessing, the nuns processed single file out of the church, with Sister Angelica holding up the rear. In her peripheral vision she could see an addled Mae standing near the confessionals. There was no guessing what Mae might do. Dying inside but obedient to the rule, Angelica avoided her mother's eyes, staring forward instead. Except for the open-palm wave and a shifting expression of sorrow on her face, Mae made no move as Rita passed.

Later that afternoon, Mother Clare confessed that she and the other sisters were "edified" by Angelica's restraint at Mass. The incident confirmed the nun's readiness for first vows. It did not, however, merit the nun any special treatment.

During her first weeks at the O'Dea house, Sister Angelica ran her bathwater into one of the massive claw-foot tubs. As she went to turn off the spigot, the porcelain knob crumbled in her hand, slicing a gash between her middle and ring fingers. Mother Luka applied a bandage to stanch the bleeding, but the right hand swelled. With her first profession only months away, all Angelica could think about was her ring finger. Following the European tradition, wedding bands were worn on the right hand in the order.

The next day, Mother Clare "was furious" at *culpas*. Taken from the Latin word meaning "faults," *culpas* was the time set aside before meals on Mondays, when each sister confessed a fault before the entire community. The abbess would then prescribe a just penance.

"Mother, I accuse myself of breaking a porcelain knob on the bathtub," Sister Angelica declared, kneeling on the floor of the refectory.

"I know! We're only here a few weeks and you're already breaking the place apart," Mother Clare shouted in a staccato German accent.

When Sister Angelica returned to table, she matter-of-factly ate her food. A weepy, badly shaken postulant asked, "How can you eat a meal after that?"

"I'm hungry," Angelica replied, shrugging.

The tough knocks of childhood had given Sister Angelica advantages over her peers: a thick skin and the ability to hold firm in times of adversity.

At the dedication ceremony in the O'Dea mansion on October 4, Bishop James McFadden enthroned the Blessed Sacrament within the monstrance for adoration in the temporary chapel. The monastery would henceforth be known as Sancta Clara, in remembrance of Saint Clare.

For all its grandiosity, the house was actually quite small. Once partitioned in half—the externs living on one side and the cloistered nuns on the other—it provided little refuge for a nun hoping to avoid sisters who were considered unpleasant.

Sister Mary of the Cross, appropriately enough, was a tall, big-boned nun with wide cheekbones and beautiful blue eyes. As community librarian, she brandished an absolutism that vexed Sister Angelica.

An avid reader at the time, Angelica consumed several volumes of John of the Cross as well as the writings of Saint Teresa of Ávila, Brother Lawrence of the Resurrection, Paul of the Cross, and others. She would repeatedly read these works at Sancta Clara, capturing them in her nearly photographic memory. Since books were due back in the library by week's end, the nun also learned to accelerate her reading time.

Sister Mary of the Cross kept the library under lock and key. Her system allowed the nuns to select books from a listing of titles posted each week, but no one was permitted to browse the secured stacks.

"That's what made me mad," Angelica recounted, as if it had happened the previous Wednesday. "I didn't know why you couldn't just pick out a book! There's a big difference between a title and a book. If you got stuck with a cookbook when you wanted a spiritual book, you had to wait a week to get another one. So I'd order three and I figured I'd get one good one. My Italian temper was always up."

This would not be Angelica's last entanglement with Sister Mary of the Cross.

By its very nature, the cloistered life exaggerates flaws and magnifies insignificant conflicts. The close proximity of brash personalities at Sancta Clara turned the place into an incubator of quiet resentments and unspoken rivalries.

"It was a cross of learning to live with one another . . . a cross of learning to love," Mother Angelica reflected. "The cross of: How do you live with people who are so opposite from you, whose thoughts are so different?" She told another biographer, "A lot of times I was on edge, I have to admit."

Civil Wars and Civil Rights

COMMUNITY ECCENTRICITIES erupted into full civil strife the day of Sister Angelica's first profession ceremony. A blizzard spit snow and ice all over Canton on January 2, 1947, delaying the guests and stalling the arrival of Bishop James McFadden.

Through the makeshift wooden grille in the O'Dea living room chapel, Mae Francis, Rhoda Wise, and other guests watched the nuns gather on the cloister side. Sister Angelica knelt on a prie-dieu, her head piously bent.

Intruding on the peace, the choir director, Mary of the Cross, began heatedly arguing music technique with her sister organist. Voices slowly escalated. Suddenly the two nuns were at each other: the organist refusing to play, Mary of the Cross threatening to toss her into the snow if she didn't.

"And I'm sitting there trying to re-collect myself for my vows," Mother Angelica told me. "The people must have thought we were nuts."

The nuns returned to their corners, the organist resuming her somber melody and Mary of the Cross taking her place at a prie-dieu. Moments later, a bug scampered across the wooden floor. Mary of the Cross rose up, lifted the kneeler with both hands, and pounded it on the ground, attempting to annihilate the insect. Like a madwoman with a jackhammer, she repeatedly wielded the prie-dieu, hurling it and herself at the crawler. The organist, thinking the display an underhanded critique of her playing, pounded the keys all the harder. Sister Angelica could not believe what she termed "the shenanigans." Then the bishop walked in.

Sopping wet and complaining about his car, which was stalled several blocks away, the bishop requested a change of socks. Mother Clare sent Sister Angelica to fetch him a new pair. When she returned to her place at the opening of the grille, the bishop laid a fitting crown of thorns atop Angelica's head.

At the point in the ceremony where the bishop was to slip the profession ring onto Sister Angelica's finger, he couldn't get the band past her swollen knuckle. Pantomiming the placement of the ring, Bishop McFadden said, "I espouse you to Jesus Christ, son of the most high God."

"With everything going on there, I'm thinking, Oh Jesus doesn't love me. You know? . . . I mean, it was a real spiritual experience!" Mother Angelica recalled sarcastically. "But that's the way God works with me. As I look back, before anything big that was com-ing, something happened to me."

In spite of the farcical atmosphere, Sister Angelica took her first vows seriously. In a typewritten letter to her mother after taking the vows, she referred to herself and Jesus as "the espoused" and "the Royal Couple." The pair, she wrote, "wish[ed] to express their gratitude to their friend and member of their personal court." Farther down she wrote, "The spouse has asked the Bridegroom to fill you with his peace and consolation." She signed the letter "Jesus and Angelica."

There is a freeness and unity of voice when Angelica writes of her feelings and those of the Messiah. Inherent in the letter is her strong belief that she was wed not to a concept or an idea, but to a person. This core conviction and love of her Spouse would govern all her actions from that time forward. During their honeymoon, Sister Angelica grew closer to her "Bridegroom" than she would have thought possible.

Angelica experienced a series of minor maladies—headaches, ingrown toenails, and the like. Although trivial, these ailments were enough to make Angelica cranky when Mother Clare scheduled her for adoration at three A.M. Angelica grudgingly arrived at the appointed time but "wasn't happy to be there." She addressed her resentment to Jesus: "I got all these painful things, and adoration on top of it. What do you think I am, a horse?"

"No, you're my bride," she felt Him respond in the quiet.

"God, I never said that to Him again, I tell you."

Though Mae Francis visited Rita regularly, she deeply felt her daughter's absence at home. Rita was sympathetic. Some undated letters from this period demonstrate Angelica's continuing concern for her mother. In one letter, she urged Mae, "Don't be lonesome sweet heart. I love you very much. Only people that have no one to love them can be lonely. You have Jesus and me and the sisters."

In another letter, Sister Angelica assumed the role of teacher, imparting spiritual advice to Mae:

Dearest Mother,

There is never a day passes [sic], I do not thank Jesus for such a loving self-sacrificing mother. Darkness may overshadow you at times, but it is only that you may enjoy the everlasting light more fully. . . . Keep loving, it is what makes us pleasing to Jesus, it is the one thing necessary. . . .

Lovingly,
Sister Angelica

With the arrival of new postulants, there were now thirteen sisters in the cramped monastery. To alleviate the crowding, new buildings and an elaborate chapel would be added to the house.

The construction was fraught with setbacks. During excavation in March 1950, the crew broke a sewer main running to the house. They also miscalculated the size of the new buildings and unnecessarily removed a group of trees in the yard. Had they listened to the mouthy twenty-six-year-old nun spot-checking blueprints, they might have avoided the errors. Sister Angelica frequently dropped in on the workmen and was known to engage in technical squabbles with them. By May, there was no one left to spar with. A union strike kept the crew home and brought construction to a standstill. Though the community calendar notes the nuns' frustration with the delay, another project revived their spirits.

Sancta Clara hosted its first Interracial Day in August. On the front lawn of the monastery, Bishop McFadden celebrated Mass for three busloads of black pilgrims from Cleveland and their white counterparts. Organized by Mae Francis's black friend, Dr. Norma Marcere, the event probably did not enjoy widespread support in the community. Nevertheless, the sisters considered it a success.

Hosting this event at a time when integration was still taboo illustrates the countercultural mind-set of the monastery and its inhabitants. Notwithstanding the fact that there were few black Catholics in town and no black sisters in the community, the nuns of Sancta Clara followed the racial situation with great interest. Having shared a neighborhood with black people and having experienced the prejudice lobbed at Italians, Sister Angelica was particularly attentive.

Between 1950 and 1953, a string of young aspirants would enter

Sancta Clara in hopes of joining the community. Three in particular would forge lifelong bonds with Sister Angelica.

Elizabeth Olson, or Sister Mary Joseph in religious life, had a serenity and an easy smile that endeared her to the nuns when she crossed the threshold in 1950. Of Swiss/German extraction, the accomplished seamstress devoted herself to making habits when not at prayer. Whether at work or recreation, in the chapel or out, Sister Joseph seemed branded by a perpetual wide-eyed look of awe, as if the angels in their glory had just shown themselves.

In January 1951, Kathleen Myers of Louisville, Ohio, arrived at Sancta Clara. There was a nervous quality about the attractive girl with the weak chin and the wide, toothy smile. Kathleen had graduated from college and worked as a secretary at an art house before entering the monastery. Had she not become a nun, she might have pursued the arts. After taking the veil, she became the community sketch artist, scribe, poet, and lead soprano. In religious life, she would be known as Sister Mary Raphael.

Raphael heard Sister Angelica long before she ever saw her. Working as an extern, a sister who runs outside errands for the cloistered community, she was delivering food at the turn. Akin to a drop box at a bank, the turn permitted food and goods to enter the enclosure without human contact. Raphael had just placed some groceries in the turn door when a chirpy voice rang out. "Isn't God good?" it said, the words reverberating in the metal drum from behind the grille. "You're the new postulant, aren't you? Isn't God good?" She would soon discover the answer to that question with some assistance from the owner of that detached voice.

Evelyn Shinosky, later known as Sister Mary Michael, reverted to Catholicism after her parents left the Catholic Church to join a national Polish breakaway community. Short, plucky, and without artifice, Evelyn was a dedicated worker. Her cooking talents and willingness to serve distinguished her in the community. Even today, Sister Michael's hooded eyes hold a steely sweetness. She described the Angelica she met in the early 1950s as unique and industrious: "She was out of the ordinary, and into everything."

The Crucible

THERE WAS plenty for Sister Angelica to get into in the new monastery. Dedicated in October of 1951, the eucharistic shrine and sprawling living quarters were standing, but the effects of the hurried work were evident. Every time rain fell, the basement walls darkened with moisture; water finally beaded up on the plaster and trickled to the ground. The architect had neglected to leave an inch of space between the outer bricks and the inner wall, thus trapping moisture within. Sister Angelica had detected the flaw in the plans early on, but her warnings were ignored. With physical evidence at hand, Angelica re-presented her criticisms to Mother Clare.

"Mother, we've got to fix this place up; it's falling apart."

"We don't have the money for it, Sister Angelica," Mother Clare replied.

Angelica had a ready-made solution: "I'll get some of the boys over here," the nun announced.

The "boys" from the old neighborhood in southeast Canton were persuaded to join the nun's crew; for the most part, they donated their labor.

"I got as many honest ones as I could, and a few mixed in between," Mother Angelica said with a knowing smile. Thus began the first of Angelica's many building projects.

Common laborers and syndicate sidemen traipsed through the halls of Sancta Clara when their day jobs ended. Uncle Nick Francis was tapped to be the late-night contractor. Around the monastery the men became collectively known as Angelica's "Tonys."

"Let's get it right this time, boys," the bespectacled nun called out to her troops in the basement.

Armed with a high school course in blueprint reading and a regular diet of *Popular Mechanics,* along with architectural and carpentry magazines, Sister Angelica was the perfect monastic foreman. The handy nun knew her way around tools, could repair leaky faucets, and build cabinets if necessary.

"She was sort of the Miss Fix It," Sister Mary Anthony, an extern at the time, remembered. "Anything broke, you called Sister Angelica."

Her duties were not limited to the mechanical. The young sister juggled an unusual array of positions within the convent, simultaneously holding the positions of community bursar (bookkeeper), portress, and economist (buyer of supplies).

At the same time, she would stay up with her "Tonys" until two o'clock in the morning, plying them with instructions and stale doughnuts. Three hours later, she would rise with the rest of the community and begin her day of prayer anew.

Amid the great activity, Sister Mary of the Cross and her "almost violent" outbursts remained a distraction. In what appears to have been more than a personality conflict, Sister Angelica was greatly troubled by the disobedience she saw in the bold sister. Several nuns confirmed that Mary of the Cross would contradict Mother Clare and could resort to shouting to get her way. In a calendar entry from May 22, 1950, Mary of the Cross wrote of being reprimanded, most likely at the hands of Mother Clare: "Received the worst public—I don't know what to call it—today. I am 'digging my own grave'—will have to be 'chastised' in public . . . and this was for me! . . . Mary I cling to you with all my love. Call me home soon Mother!"

This entry provides some understanding of the situation in the monastery and offers a rationale for Angelica's frustration with the nun.

In the spring of 1952, Mother Clare summoned Sister Angelica to the parlor, where visitors were waiting. She expected to find her mother or maybe her uncles there. But seated on the other side of the double grille was the lean figure of her father, John Rizzo. A study in guilt, he slumped pathetically in the tiny room, his sister Mary from Pennsylvania next to him. At fifty-six he was still handsome, and gentler than Angelica had remembered.

"Your aunt is here," John Rizzo began hesitantly, indicating the unknown woman beside him. "She came to visit me, so I thought I would bring her over."

Moments later his voice was drowned in sobs. To keep Angelica from seeing the tears, he pressed the heels of his hands to his eye sockets. Perhaps he wept over the discarded family he might have had, or to mourn the years spent away from the veiled stranger with his dark eyes—a stranger John would never know now. Composing himself, his eyes falling everywhere but on Angelica, John asked, "Are you happy here?"

"Yes, I am," the nun replied.

"I felt sorry for him," Mother Angelica admitted. "For some strange reason, I don't remember having any resentment toward him. I didn't hate him or love him."

Noticing some grease spots on Angelica's habit, John asked if he could bring her some dry-cleaning fluid. She mentioned her favorite brand, and John vowed to return.

A few weeks later, he reappeared in the parlor with a gallon of fabric cleaner.

"Is there anything else you need?" Rizzo asked.

"No, I don't think so, Dad." It was the first and last time she would call him "Dad."

A lifetime of questions hung in the silence between them, and so many regrets.

"Can I come back?" John asked sheepishly.

Unsure of the rules governing visitations, Angelica agreed to ask permission. John started to leave, then sat down again. "I want you to know I'm sorry, and I want your mother to know I'm sorry."

Sister Angelica was stunned by his words: "That was like a million dollars to me, because I didn't know him well enough to think he could be sorry . . . and I really wanted to see him again."

But the cloister rules allowed parents to visit only once every two months, forcing Angelica to choose between her mother and father. When Mae discovered that John Rizzo was visiting the cloister, she issued an ultimatum: If he visited their daughter again, she would not. Uncertain what to do, Sister Angelica left the decision to her abbess.

In a letter to John Rizzo, Mother Clare explained the limitations on visits to the cloister and rendered a judgment: Since Mae had raised Rita, Mother Clare decided she should be the only parent allowed to see Angelica.

The letter devastated John Rizzo, according to his sister. He died of a heart attack six months later, on October 29, 1952. Sister Angelica's only comfort was the fact that he had received last rites at the hospital.

In the cloister, Sister Mary of the Cross continued to grate on Angelica's nerves. "I thought she was God's worst," Mother Angelica recalled years later. "Every day I was mad about something new she'd do. I wasn't at all spiritual at the time, because I had *her* on my mind."

During an eight-day retreat in 1952, Angelica admitted her disgust with Mary of the Cross in the confessional of a Father Paulinus. In Mother Angelica's recollection, the confession ended like this:

"What is your name?" the priest asked.

"Sister Angelica."

"Angelica, you're an ass."

"What?" the incredulous nun asked.

"You heard me. I said you're an ass." Then the priest changed tactics. "Why did you come here?"

"I came here to be a saint."

"Then why don't you love her?"

"God Almighty is having a hard time loving her."

"I asked why aren't *you* loving her?" The priest bore in. "If you want to be a saint, you should expect somebody hard to live with. You should expect that kind of suffering—and make every effort to love her."

Sister Angelica began to realize that observing the constitutions was not enough to attain holiness. In the face of blistering tirades and what she termed "schizophrenic" behavior, Angelica made an earnest attempt to befriend Sister Mary of the Cross.

"Suddenly, when I made an effort to love her, I found myself able to be more patient and loving toward everybody," Mother Angelica said. "When you're concentrating on anything that's disruptive in your life, you really don't love anybody."

In the lead-up to her final vows, Angelica embraced the self-forgetfulness and self-denial demanded by religious life. Even Mother Clare's humiliations became easier to bear.

Believing that "those who are going to lead need to be humbled,"

the seventy-nine-year-old abbess must have seen leadership possibilities in Sister Angelica. She told her on one occasion, "Sister, if
you don't change your manner, I'm going to change your name."

"If Mother Clare had to make a point to the community, Angelica became the fall guy," Joan Frank, a former nun at Sancta Clara
remembered. "If everyone was doing something, Angelica was singled out."

But despite the severe treatment, the abbess had a great respect
for the twenty-nine-year-old nun. As a sign of Mother Clare's confidence in Angelica's leadership abilities, she entrusted her to organ-
ize work assignments and keep the sisters busy. On her own
initiative, Angelica led a cleaning party of nuns to the basement.
One of the sisters, a transfer from another order, objected to the
work and complained to Mother Clare.

The abbess promptly revoked Sister Angelica's assignment. The
nun shed angry tears of rejection in her cell. "I thought I did what
Mother Clare told me to do, and here I was out of work," Mother
Angelica told me.

The vicar, Mother Luka, brushed softly into Sister Angelica's
room, wearing her usual sympathetic, hangdog expression. Sitting
on the edge of the bed, the old nun counseled her. "Angelica, one
day you will be a good superior, but not now."

Angelica would have been content achieving the rank of
solemnly professed sister. "I didn't give a damn if I was ever superior. That was the attitude I had then."

After nearly nine years in the cloister, Sister Angelica reached
her goal and took her final solemn vows on Friday, January 2, 1953.
Her old spiritual director, Monsignor George Habig, officiated in
the new chapel. Angelica promised to "live during the whole term
of (her) life . . . in obedience, without property, and in chastity." At
the high point of the ceremony Angelica laid prostrate as the sisters
draped a black shroud over her. The symbolism of dying to the
world and rising again into a new life deeply affected the new
solemn professed—even if her stomach was levitating at the time.

"Somebody decided to put one of those money belts around my
tummy with all these prayer petitions in it. My mother had peti-

tions in there, my aunt and uncle, the sisters, all the people I went to school with," Angelica said. "I bent over, but my stomach never touched the floor."

On August 12, 1953, Sister Angelica's friend Mother Veronica departed Canton to found a new monastery in Washington, D.C. Like orphans, the crop of novices was left in the hands of Mother Mary Immaculate. Deprived of Veronica's motherly warmth, the sisters were subjected to a nun they describe, respectively, as "rigid," "melancholic," "sarcastic," and "a tough perfectionist."

A teacher from Ireland, Mother Mary Immaculate had the perfect name. In dress and behavior, she was flawless, expecting nothing short of perfection from her charges. Though she would one day become abbess in Canton to great acclaim, at the time she could be unusually harsh with the novices.

"Mother Immaculate made me feel like I was going to hell one day," Sister Michael ruefully recalled.

The Fall

INSPIRED BY Mother Veronica's departure to build a community in Washington, Sister Angelica began formulating her own ideas about a new monastery, with a special focus, as early as 1953. Joan Frank remembered working in the garden with Angelica when she first mentioned the possibility of establishing "a monastery for little Negroes down south." As conceived, the foundation would recruit black sisters to the contemplative life. "She definitely wasn't racist; she spoke about the black people very affectionately," Frank recounted.

"Her mother loved the Negroes," Sister Michael told me. "I think some of that probably rubbed off on Sister Angelica." Seeing Mae Francis freely interact and befriend blacks before integration certainly laid the groundwork for Angelica's brainchild. The community's established interest in racial issues, evinced by the Interracial Days hosted by Sancta Clara, only fortified the vision. Sister Angelica quietly mentioned the possibility of establishing a Southern foundation to friendly nuns, but for the moment the idea failed to develop beyond talk.

Then one afternoon in 1953, providence would again painfully intrude upon Sister Mary Angelica, with lasting results. Assigned to clean the hallway and bedrooms of the second-floor novitiate, the nun chose a modern approach. To expedite the work, she poured a soapy solution onto the floor and piloted a commercial electric scrubber across the surface. Angelica had the height, if not the girth, to master the unruly machinery. As she slid the polisher side to side in neat rows through the foam, the cord caught beneath the brushes. The heavy contraption bucked and shuddered, throwing Angelica off balance.

"The whole machine just popped up and the handle hit me in the stomach and threw me on that slippery floor," Angelica explained, wincing in anticipation of what was to follow. "I fell down and had such a pain." The left side of her back stung. The ache radiated from the small of her back to the middle of her left leg. Angelica used the wall to regain her balance, eventually finding her feet. Once up, she shuffled to the capsized scrubber, repositioned it, and finished the job. She imagined the back pain would dissipate over time. Three years later, she was still waiting.

In late 1953, Mother Clare had her own health problems. The abbess suffered two heart attacks, returning to the community greatly diminished. In this weakened state, she quietly turned to Sister Angelica, her oft-humbled daughter, to fill the leadership gap.

Freeing the Captives

ELEVEN NOVICES had abandoned Sancta Clara by the fall of 1953 in order to escape the harsh regimen of Mother Mary Immaculate, the novice mistress. The nuns who remained in the "extremely strict" environment suffered from nervous colitis, crying jags, and feelings of unworthiness. The gratuitous attention paid to faults drove one sister to a nervous breakdown and paved the way for another. "It was like a kind of bondage," according to Sister Raphael.

When Mother Mary Immaculate went on an eight-day retreat, the abbess asked Sister Angelica to stand in for her.

In November 1953, Angelica bounded into the novitiate with a cheerful optimism, an antidote to the gloom and doom normally spread on the second floor of Sancta Clara. For eight days Sister Angelica took charge of the novices' religious education, formation, and daily routine. She stressed God's love for the sisters and urged each of them to become His alone.

Sister Raphael, a novice at the time, "was very bitter" about Angelica filling in for the novice mistress. After trying to conform to the stiff pattern of religious life established by Mother Mary Immaculate, here was the community maverick introducing something entirely different. Sister Raphael wanted none of it, and she was "rude to say the least."

During that first week, Angelica tried everything to win the novice's confidence, with little success. "Leave me alone," Sister Raphael would say. "I don't want your help." When the demands of the cloistered life got too intense, Raphael would retreat to an emotional cocoon and hide in her cell. Sister Angelica had seen it all before. To draw the young woman out, she slipped a note beneath Raphael's door one day. When no response came, she took matters into her own hands and entered the novice's room. Raphael was balled up under the covers, crying in self-pity. "You get out of there," Angelica said, ripping the sheets off the novice and pulling the mattress from under her. Sprawled out on the floor, Raphael began to laugh—and a lifelong friendship was sparked.

Angelica introduced Raphael and the other novices to the spiritual classics she had absorbed throughout her religious life. Heavy emphasis was placed upon Saint John of the Cross and his "dark night of the soul"—a period of spiritual deprivation on the road to deeper mystical union with God. In the spirit of Brother Lawrence of the Resurrection, the sisters were told to practice "complete abandonment to God and [to find] happiness in doing as He wills whether He leads . . . by suffering or by consolation." She used examples from the lives of the saints as models for religious life. Sister Angelica taught that the saints "didn't break the rules; they simply rose above them." Joan Frank mused: "And it seems that's how she saw herself: rising above the rule."

In eight short days, change swept through the novitiate. A freeing, intoxicating light suddenly invaded the clenched lives of the young nuns. During her animated talks about submitting to divine providence and conversing with God throughout the day, Sister Angelica forged a lasting bond with Sister Joseph, Sister Raphael, and others.

At the conclusion of Mother Mary Immaculate's retreat, several of the novices claimed to be in the midst of the "purgative way" of prayer, while others were suffering "the dark night of the soul." Angelica had made her mark. Mother Mary Immaculate was not impressed.

Upon Mary Immaculate's return and the reinstitution of her hard ways, Sister Raphael suffered "a minor breakdown," ending up in the infirmary. At the time, Angelica was in charge of the sick bay. As a rule community sisters were forbidden any interaction with the novices. But in the infirmary, who was looking? There, Angelica continued mentoring Sister Raphael in the spiritual life. By the novice's own admission, Angelica helped her to escape the "pitfalls that had trapped" her.

Sensitive to the problems in the novitiate, Sister Angelica began quietly mothering the other novices as well. When a young sister appeared depressed, she would whisper, "Jesus loves you" as they passed in the hall. If a novice was corrected by Mother Mary Immaculate, Sister Angelica would "chime in, saying, 'I did that all the time when I was a novice,' " Joan Frank recalled.

To mitigate the novices' miseries, Mother Clare secretly authorized Angelica to provide spiritual direction to some of the young sisters. Knowing the older nuns would challenge this suspension of the rule, Mother Clare insisted the spiritual guidance be handled discreetly.

Sister Michael remembered Mother Clare personally asking her in 1953 if she desired spiritual direction from Sister Angelica. The young nun refused the offer and returned to her normal routine.

It was the kindly seamstress, Sister Joseph, who would be Angelica's first spiritual daughter. They met clandestinely beyond a garden gazebo at the end of the sprawling lawn. The O'Dea woodshed would also serve as a rendezvous location, "because not many sisters went down there," according to Sister Michael.

Even with her injured back, which now affected her posture, Sister Angelica raced about the monastery, keeping appointments with her spiritual charges. Sisters Raphael and Assumpta would drop by Angelica's cell off the upstairs sewing room for consultations. Quietly running her needle through a garment, Sister Joseph sat in the sewing room, providing a lookout. "I would be the watchdog as she gave spiritual direction," Sister Joseph revealed.

Despite the precautions, Mother Mary Immaculate, acting on a tip, soon became aware of the covert sessions. She confronted the abbess about Angelica's stealthy spiritual direction of the novices— a violation of the community rule. Concealing the truth, Mother Clare denied deputizing Angelica to guide the nuns and called the accused to her office.

During an overheard conversation, Sister Angelica tearfully told Mother Clare that the older sisters "had turned on her," inflicting hurtful wounds. The abbess consoled Angelica, instructed her to dry her tears, and admitted in confidence that "for some reason God wasn't blessing the community." Perhaps to remedy the situation and to protect the novices, the abbess permitted Angelica to continue her spiritual directing activities.

Quietly, and in the face of complaints, Mother Clare set Sister Angelica on a leadership path within the community. Her advancement was threatened only by her deteriorating back condition and rivalries within the cloister. But through faith, these apparent obstacles would propel the nun toward a life's work and a destination as inscrutable as God Himself.

6
Providence in Pain

ANGELICA LIMPED through the halls of Sancta Clara inspecting the handiwork of her crew the way a detective appraises a murder scene. Dark-rimmed glasses reduced her pupils to glistening black pinpoints that scanned each wall, hunting for any slipup. At her urging, Uncle Nick Francis and the Tonys had spent days slathering the interior of the monastery with a fresh coat of donated paint. Completing her rounds, she confronted the workmen. They held their breath awaiting her verdict. As she drew closer, a mischievous smile of satisfaction broke beneath the nun's generous nose, and her eyes turned to half moons. This was what they had come for—not money or adulation—but to win her approval. This curious motive would mark Angelica's relationship with workmen throughout her life.

For a nun, she had an uncommon ease with men. There was no distance between Angelica and her Tonys; they shared a mutual respect. And though she would morally challenge the boys on occasion, there was none of the condescending pretension they normally received from nuns or clergymen. Sister Angelica wasn't pretending to be better than anybody—and she offered the men what no one else cared to: a shot at redemption by virtue of their labor. Angelica relished the interaction with the Liberty Street crew. She caught up on the latest neighborhood news, offered advice, and could always be relied on for a laugh.

But this outward cheer camouflaged a back pain that had retarded her brisk pace. For the better part of three years, since her fall, Sister Angelica had experienced a constant stinging sensation on the left side of her back. Her spine now seemed to be shifting and each day it was harder to straighten up. Instead of improving with time, her back condition had worsened. Angelica realized that she was suffering from something far more serious than a sprain. Medical attention was now warranted.

Aside from her physical state, Angelica's prospects were looking up in 1955. At thirty-two, she was the community economist, responsible for purchasing goods for the monastery and overseeing any work on the cloister grounds. She enjoyed a following among the young sisters and was viewed within the community as an emerging leader.

In early June 1955, her friend Mother Veronica returned to Canton from the Washington monastery. It is likely that she came at the behest of the abbess to salvage the troubled novitiate. The only way to end Mother Mary Immaculate's reign of terror was to replace her. Mother Veronica reclaimed her old job as novice mistress and Sister Angelica regained an important ally.

That same summer, Angelica sought a medical appraisal of her back pain. An entry in one of two surviving calendars from Sancta Clara written by Mother Mary Immaculate reads:

June 13, 1955

Dear Sr. M. Angelica returned home from the hospital today. The doctor ordered a brace for sister to relieve the pain in her back caused by a fall. She is to wear it for one year.

Doctors claim it is nerve pressure by bone out of place from birth.

The physicians believed that Angelica's fall in 1953 had aggravated a preexisting spinal defect. To relieve her compressed spine, Angelica was fitted for a body cast and made to use oversized crutches. The idea was to create space between the vertebrae, thereby easing her pain. When that remedy failed, leg and neck traction were attempted. According to Sister Raphael, Angelica hung suspended from a hospital-bed contraption for six weeks. Her allergy to pain medication only added to her misery. Without a buffer, Angelica endured needles to the spine and other oppressive treatments. All told, she spent four months in the hospital, but with no positive result. Immobilized by a back brace, a dejected Sister Angelica retreated to the monastery.

To eliminate Angelica's pain and restore her posture, her physicians suggested a spinal fusion. So on July 31, 1956, she returned to Mercy Hospital to face the scalpel, which she hoped would end her torment.

The Outrageous Bargain

THE NIGHT BEFORE the surgery, Dr. Charles Houck, a thirty-six-year-old orthopedic surgeon, coolly stepped into Angelica's room for a courtesy call. Already anxious, she found little comfort in the surgeon's bedside greeting.

"Sister Angelica, there's a fifty-fifty chance you'll never walk again," the doctor said flatly. His approach was clinical, and she thought him "kind of a sour guy." "So in the morning, if you can't move your leg, don't be surprised." Having performed his duty, he bade her good night, turned on his heel, and stepped back into the corridor.

In the darkened room, with only her fears, Sister Angelica panicked. Will I be in a chair for the rest of my life? On crutches? Crippled? the nun thought to herself. She tried praying her beads, hoping that the repeated pleas to the Virgin would calm her. But thoughts of a future confined to a wheelchair interrupted. The Lord had healed her stomach pains; why couldn't He heal her now? Caught between prayer and frenzy, clawing at her sheets, Angelica struck an outrageous bargain with God. "Lord, if you let me walk again, I'll build you a monastery in the South," she pledged.

For at least three years, Sister Angelica had discussed her vision for a southern monastery dedicated to blacks. Now in a moment of crisis, the repressed inspiration became a spiritual bargaining chip.

The fear of being paralyzed aroused her commitment to the project, lending it a divine urgency.

Recent national events seemed to cry out for such a monastery. The year of Angelica's surgery, the U.S. Supreme Court affirmed its ban on segregation in public schools; thousands of blacks, following the lead of Rosa Parks, began occupying seats normally reserved for whites on public buses; and Dr. Martin Luther King, Jr., made national headlines by organizing protests and boycotts throughout the South. Sister Angelica had an innate feel for the times.

Mother Angelica told me, "I remember we had heard about the racial tension in the South, and I don't know if that's what was on my mind, or if I just felt sympathy. I'm not too sure what happened."

But in a letter she wrote on March 25, 1957, what had happened became abundantly clear:

> Having worked with the Negros [sic] before entering the Holy Order, I came in order to pray and sacrifice for them. A year ago when the doctors were doubtful that I would walk again, I turned to our Lord and promised if he would grant me the grace to walk, I would do all in my power to promote a cloistered community among the Negros [sic]. It would be dedicated to the Negro Apostolate by prayer, adoration, sacrifice, and union with God. It would ceaselessly make reparation for all the insults and persecution the Negro race suffers and implore God's blessings and graces upon a people dear to the Heart of God.

Beyond the contemplative mission to pray for humanity in general terms, Angelica was promoting a type of intercessory activism: the establishment of a house of prayer in the midst of a specific people who were suffering a unique social oppression.

As they wheeled Sister Angelica into surgery, everything was riding on her walking again. Practicing what she had taught the novices, the thirty-three-year-old abandoned her health and her monastery to the will of God.

After the initial incision to Angelica's back, Dr. Houck ruled out a spinal fusion. In the blood-soaked wreckage, he discovered an extra vertebra crowding its neighbors. The resulting "kissing vertebra" was the principal source of Angelica's pain. A malformed spine and a nerve attached to a bone on the left side of her back presented even greater challenges to the surgeon, as he attempted to remove the extra vertebra.

"During the surgery, something went wrong," Sister Bernadette confided to me, her thick eyebrows rising. "Sister Anita, an elderly sister at the hospital, told Sister Juliana, an extern at Sancta Clara, that during the surgery the doctor made an incision—and he knew that she would never walk again. When he made that cut, he threw his instrument on the floor and walked out."

Mother Angelica confirmed the story. According to her, a Muslim doctor finished the operation and sewed her up. To compensate for the bleeding, three bags of donated blood mingled with her own. The names on the transfusion bottles were Luntz, Goldberg, and Cohen—a fact that furnished Angelica with a story she would repeat to Jewish groups for decades. "I've never been the same since," she would say with great chutzpah.

The spinal surgery was considered a failure. Though Angelica could move both legs when she woke from the anesthesia, walking was another matter. She remained in the hospital, recuperating, for at least two months.

Returning to Sancta Clara, Sister Angelica was confined to the infirmary, where a procession of nuns collected around her bedside.

"She never appeared sick," Sister Joseph, a regular visitor, remembered. "She always had that gift of leadership. She had a magnetic personality, and when she counseled you spiritually, you felt she could guide you, and lead a community."

Suffering altered the teachings and person of Sister Angelica. In the infirmary, she began to use her personal experience to concretize and explain lofty spiritual concepts to the other sisters. Pain had become a tool of understanding, increasing her empathy for others and deepening her own spiritual sense. Through necessity she learned to rely on God in all things, and found strength in weakness.

With her intimates, Angelica shared her vow to establish a community in the South, giving them additional incentive to rally her to health. Sisters Joseph and Raphael practically tripped over each other attempting to assist the ailing nun. In her first weeks home, they vied for the honor of shuttling Sister Angelica through the monastery in a rickety wooden wheelchair. Eventually, Angelica herself ended the competition, graduating to a back brace, leg brace, and crutch. With their assistance, she took her first wobbly steps of independence, to the delight of her supporters. God had fulfilled His part of the bargain.

In late 1956, on her feet and out of the infirmary, Sister Angelica shifted her focus to the establishment of the new foundation. Armed with what she considered a spiritual mandate, she enlisted the support of Mother Clare's successor, the new abbess of Sancta Clara, Mother Veronica.

"No" was Mother Veronica's first response, but under the pressure of Angelica's insistent pleas, the abbess slowly relented. Once convinced, Mother Veronica became a quiet advocate of the new foundation. Her letters and private conversations testify to her belief in Sister Angelica, a nun she considered "a genius."

With the support of the abbess, Angelica and her small band of nuns turned into a prayer militia, storming heaven for their Southern monastery. Still a practical question remained: Where to establish it?

When a couple came forward offering free land in Florida, Angelica interpreted their charity as a sign from God. She dashed off a letter to a Florida bishop, asking permission to found the monastery in his diocese. The bishop declined the offer.

One nun's family suggested that the bishop of Mobile, Alabama, might welcome such a foundation. In prayer, Sister Joseph received strong confirmation that Angelica should write the bishop of Mobile. As she prepared to do so, her old nemesis, Sister Mary of the Cross, threw an obstacle in her path.

By 1957, the relationship between Mary of the Cross and Angelica was much improved. Through Sister Angelica's tireless efforts to show love to the domineering nun, Mary of the Cross had taken a liking to her. But whatever fondness existed quickly dissipated when Sister Mary of the Cross announced her intention to found her own new monastery in St. Cloud, Minnesota.

Lacking the sisters necessary to establish two monasteries, Mother Veronica found herself in a quandary. On the one hand, a very vocal senior sister was demanding her own foundation; on the other, a younger nun with the markings of a leader felt God had called her to the South. Never one for confrontation, the abbess devised a solution to the stalemate—one worthy of Solomon. On behalf of each sister, Mother Veronica would write letters of introduction to the bishop of St. Cloud and the archbishop of Mobile-Birmingham. The first nun to receive a positive response from a bishop could proceed with her foundation; the other would have to abandon her plans.

On January 8, 1957, Mother Veronica mailed the two letters at the same time. In her message to Archbishop Thomas Toolen of Mobile, Mother Veronica wrote:

> Our great desire is to be in the midst of the colored people to intercede for them; we understand this mission would have to be more or less secret in order to prevent race difficulties; but we would like to be there for the colored, and in time, in the course of years, would hope even to have colored applicants for our community . . . the principal idea is to pray for them.

The official record of monastery business, the Sancta Clara Protocol, mentions only the possibility of a St. Cloud foundation on January 9, 1957. Mention of the Birmingham foundation would not surface in the protocol until years later. This is not surprising, since Sister Mary of the Cross was the community secretary and thus responsible for the official record.

The rivalry inside Sancta Clara grew intense.

Competing prayers and constant checks of the daily mailbag exacerbated tensions in the cloister. Sister Angelica and her followers prayed incessantly for a successful outcome, mindful that their fate would be determined by the archbishop's promptness.

"Mine wrote first; hers didn't write for a couple of months," Mother Angelica told me with a satisfied smirk.

Archbishop Toolen's letter of January 12, 1957, warmly invited the Franciscan nuns into the diocese and encouraged them to establish the community in Birmingham, home to a quarter of a million black people. Nowhere in the letter, nor in his later correspondence, does the archbishop write "Ya'll come," as reported in numerous published accounts. Nevertheless, Sister Angelica and her supporters were euphoric over what he did write.

With Bishop Toolen's permission secured, the sisters asked their local bishop to bless the new foundation. On February 28, 1957, Bishop Emmet Walsh of Youngstown dropped a bombshell. He felt the community in Canton was not strong enough to sustain the departure of the six nuns required by Church law to establish a new foundation. The loss of a council sister (Sister Angelica) was particularly worrisome to the bishop. He bluntly instructed the nuns to drop the idea of a new monastery.

No doubt prompted by Sister Angelica, the abbess wrote a second letter to Bishop Walsh on March 7, 1957. While accepting the bishop's decision, she revealingly pleaded Angelica's cause:

> To her it is a mission God has inspired her to fulfill; she has no rest, nor does she give me any in her effort to do what she thinks God is asking of her. . . .
>
> She is young—thirty-four, but she has been our bursar for several years and has business ability beyond the average. She has been figuring and planning for years and in her mind she has a complete plan for both building and maintaining the monastery. . . . If you could have a talk with this sister, Your Excellency, I believe you would understand how our resistance was broken down.

In a follow-up letter of March 25, 1957, Sister Angelica argued her own case to the bishop. Her powerful will and mission were apparent, as was the determination to do whatever was necessary to accomplish her goal.

Your Excellency,

> . . . Will your Excellency permit me to follow the example of
> our holy Father Francis who, having been refused at the front
> door, counseled his followers to return at the back door. I
> know your decision has been a prudent and fatherly one, so
> this letter is not intended to change Your Excellency's mind.

She then explained her commitment to establish a "Negro apostolate" and added:

> Since our Lord seemed to show His Will by permitting me to
> walk again and to enjoy perfect health, against all the doctors'
> expectations, I took this as an indication that as He had ful-
> filled His part, I must fulfill mine. . . . As always your deci-
> sion was accepted as God's Will and Reverend Mother has
> made it very clear to me that for the present, nothing will be
> done, nevertheless, it leaves so many things in mid-air; the
> help that has been offered by friends involving work to be
> done as well as donations and offers of financial assistance,
> also there are the three young ladies who are waiting to join
> me in this particular field of work. . . . Would Your Excellency
> approve of this project and give your consent to it when the
> beginning of a new foundation will in no way weaken our
> community? This assurance from you would leave me free to
> continue building up, hoping and planning for something that
> will eventually be a reality—even if now I will have to move
> my horizon to a further distance.

For a letter "not intended to change" the bishop's mind, Sister
Angelica made a strong case for a reversal.

Bishop Walsh's response was sympathetic, allowing preparations
to continue. But he stopped short of granting definite approval to
the foundation. The letter was viewed as a victory in the
monastery—a delay, but not a deathblow to the Southern foundation. For the next three years, Mother Veronica and Sister Angelica

maintained constant contact with the archbishop of Mobile, stoking his interest in the foundation while continuing plans at home.

Though they were separated by cloister walls, the bond between Mae Francis and Sister Angelica remained strong. Mae must have been informed about the Birmingham foundation by this point. An undated letter to Mae shows that Angelica had fully assumed the role of mother in their relationship. Along with the spiritual instruction, the letter contained a foretaste of the future:

> . . . your soul is beautiful and close to God because of suffering. . . . Loneliness is one of the best tools God uses to bring us closer to Him. . . . Why . . . Because it empties our heart of all created things and images, and we find no consolation either in creatures or ourselves . . . there is no one but God . . . you are close to me yet it's so natural to want to give out once in a while . . . please do . . . your cross is my cross . . . we are one . . . so you can't be selfish and keep it, so there. . . .

Then there is a handwritten addition at the bottom:

> Someday you'll be working [for] and adoring Him— He has plans for us— Don't worry—
>
> S. Angelica

The cryptic close seems to indicate that Sister Angelica and Mae had already agreed on some future course of action. The margin contains a brief handwritten note from Mother Veronica, who probably knew Angelica's intentions for her mother. It reads: "All for love of Him. M.M. Veronica. I love you. What Sr. says is true."

The Master Builder

IN MARCH 1958, Sister Angelica's left leg would occasionally go numb below the knee, but that did not stop her from taking on another building project.

Some of the nuns longed to have a grotto in the backyard dedicated to the Virgin Mary. The job of building it fell to Angelica. She called "every good, pious Catholic" she knew, seeking help with the project, but no one offered their time.

"I'm having a hard time getting people," she told Mother Veronica. "I do know some people who are a little different. I could call them."

"I don't care, as long as we get it built," the abbess said.

Sister Angelica called a pool hall in southeast Canton and roused the Tonys. Recognizing the voice on the other end of the line, Angelica screamed out, "When did you get out of jail?" After chitchatting, she got down to business. "I need some of the boys; I'm having a hard time down here."

Sixty-two bricklayers, masons, and ditchdiggers from the neighborhood showed up to build the grotto. Uncle Nick, who sold insurance, made time to oversee the job. Though the community newsletter reported that the work was donated, the Sancta Clara Protocol claimed it was a "contract job."

Whatever the financial arrangement, Sister Angelica paced the job site like a general contractor, giving orders and making snap decisions as needed.

Near the end of the project, in the fall of 1958, Uncle Nick noticed Sister Angelica's left leg swiveling awkwardly as she walked. To compensate for the spinal pain, she would throw her body to one side, disturbing her alignment.

"It was getting harder to walk and harder to straighten out," Mother Angelica said. "I walked kind of bent over—I couldn't stand the pain."

Still, there was work to do. Having produced a marble niche for the Virgin, the nun with the "bizarre gait" turned her attention to landscaping. She visualized a row of shrubs framing the stone pathway and a backdrop of hemlock trees behind the grotto.

"I'll get 'em for you," a workman named Pitzigill assured Angelica. "How many you think we need?"

"Where you gonna get these?" she asked.

"Eh, don't worry about it. Me and the boys'll go out some night and pick 'em up." Pitzigill dropped his voice. "There's a guy in North Canton got hundreds of 'em."

"You gonna go and take them?"

"Yeah, what's wrong with that?"

"You can't go steal those trees," Angelica said, sounding every inch the mother superior.

"You can't steal trees," Pitzigill protested. "Trees belong to God. You gonna use 'em for God, so how can you steal them?"

Rejecting his offer and his reasoning, Sister Angelica set out to raise the money for the trees honestly. She called the head of the local syndicate. In addition to the money, she had a spiritual goal in mind.

"I need six hundred dollars' worth of hemlock trees," she told the mob boss.

"All right, I'll write you a check."

"No, I don't want you to do that. I want you to get checks from all the boys and give them to me. I'm going to put their names on a piece of parchment, roll it up, and put it inside the statue of Our Lady."

"Are you nuts? I can't do that," the made man said.

"Nobody's going to see it; it'll be buried in concrete, like you're going to be one of these days if you don't straighten up."

The mob boss said nothing.

"See what you can do," Sister Angelica said, placing the phone on its cradle.

A few days later, a stretch limo appeared in front of the monastery. Angelica linked arms with the syndicate head and led him to the Marian grotto.

"You really want people like me to buy those trees?" the mobster asked.

"Yes, I do. I need people like you to buy these trees so that one day, if you're ever in a lot of trouble, you'll remember the Lord and His Mother," Angelica said.

She slipped the man a Sacred Heart badge and showed him out of the monastery. Within days the mail brought a pile of checks bearing the names of well-known businessmen from the Canton community. In calligraphy, Sister Raphael committed their names to a parchment scroll and placed it inside the statue of Mary, where it rests today, surrounded by hemlock trees.

In the fall of 1958, winds of change swept through the Roman Catholic Church. The stout, jolly Cardinal Roncalli became Pope John XXIII, successor to Pope Pius XII. It was assumed that the seventy-seven-year-old Italian would be a "caretaker Pope," cleaving to tradition and offering no surprises. Roncalli proved conventional wisdom wrong.

In Canton the sharp winter chill of 1958 sent spasms through Sister Angelica's back and left leg. Retreating to bed, she unfastened her leg brace and tried to find some comfort by reclining. As she lay on the mattress, images coalesced on the wall of her room. At first, she dismissed the vision, but it refused to leave her mind's eye. Pressing taped pieces of graph paper to the wall, her back pinching, Sister Angelica attempted to capture what she saw there. The result was a crude pencil-drawn architectural plan; a blueprint for the new monastery.

During recreation periods, Angelica and her fellow nuns painstakingly created a scale model of the plan, using bits of cardboard and wrapping paper. Without the proper permissions, the monastery began taking shape, even as Sister Angelica's physical condition degenerated. Walking had become a trial for the nun. Finding stationary activities more agreeable, she would write out budgets and income flow charts for the new monastery in order to limit her physical exertion. But privately she wondered how a crippled nun could possibly lead a new community.

Stumped by the continuing numbness and flailing left leg, her doctors sent Angelica to the Cleveland Clinic for observation on April 27, 1959. She underwent intensive physical therapy, working out daily on the parallel bars and practicing exercises to strengthen her spine. Days of testing revealed little. The doctors found no loss of movement in Sister Angelica's back, and only stiffness in her left hip, knee, and ankle. They found no explanation for the continuing leg pain.

Back at Sancta Clara, snail-like progress was being made on the new monastery. Though Archbishop Toolen was still eager to have the monastery in Birmingham, the Youngstown ordinary, Bishop Walsh, had yet to give his final okay. To end the stasis, the business-minded Angelica wrote Bishop Walsh on August 7, 1959. Utilizing novel arguments, she pressed him for an answer:

About three years ago Your Excellency gave Our Reverend Mother permission to have my friends prepare for the future foundation in Alabama. To date the property given to us has increased in value and we have several bricklayers and trades-men, all friends, ready to donate their labor. They would like to start in the winter because they do not work up here at that time and would be able to build the monastery during the winter months. . . .

I am enclosing a crude sketch and plan which I made. . . . I know the plans must seem a little ambitious at first sight but as we have nothing in the way of a building to start with in Birmingham, if we did not build, it would mean the remodel-ing of an old home which would entail much expense both in purchase and in remodeling costs. . . . The plan and building as it is drawn up would cost around $130,000.00. But with the donated labor and the proper selection of building materials we have figured it around $75,000.00. . . .

I have also enclosed a proposed income and expense sheet for the foundation. The figures are based on what we have done here. . . . The sisters there will be expected to practice poverty to a great degree which is as it should be and we hope to work enough to support ourselves. . . . The Rosaries we hope to sell mostly in the North and also the Publication will be sent to people in the North. As we intend to do most of the printing, half-tones, etc. ourselves this will decrease the ex-penses of the publication. . . .

During my recent trip to the Cleveland Clinic the Doctors told me that the only way to prevent the left limb from com-plete disability is to go to a hot climate. The nerve in the spine is exposed and cold winter months are very hard. I am willing to accept whatever Jesus wants from me but thought if your

Excellency thought we might go to Alabama we would be able to start soon and it would only mean one more winter to endure. Even though the use of my left limb is at stake, I am willing to give it to Our Lord if Your Excellency thinks we are not ready yet.

The emotional plea for the preservation of her extremity and Angelica's single-minded tenacity apparently touched the bishop.

By November of that year, Bishop Walsh approved the general concept and began studying what waivers from Church law would be needed to make the monastery a reality. Sister Angelica's age was a concern for the Church. In April 1960 she would be only thirty-seven years old, while the order's constitutions demanded that an abbess be at least forty. Sister Raphael had similar problems, as she was a few years shy of thirty-five, the age required to be a vicar. Then there was the matter of the two lay sisters who wished to be upgraded to choir sisters in the community. Only Rome could grant these special dispensations. Throughout 1960, papers ricocheted from the chancery of Birmingham to Youngstown to Sancta Clara to Rome, then back again.

As a member of the community's governing council and a potential abbess, Sister Angelica became officially known as Mother Angelica in 1960. But titles were not her goal. Inspired by the positive response of Bishop Walsh, she moved on to the next challenge: raising capital for the Birmingham foundation.

The Angler

HER FIRST IDEA was to raise earthworms in Sancta Clara's basement and sell the slimy live bait to fishermen at two cents a head. "Oh God, no," Mother Veronica said in response to Angelica's proposal.

While flipping through a copy of *Popular Mechanics* in November 1959, Sister Angelica spied an ad for fishing lure parts. The innate marketer sensed opportunity on the glossy page. She needed a product with appeal in Canton as well as in the predominantly Protestant South. Rosaries and altar cloths were out of the question. But fishing lures had secular appeal and could possibly turn a profit.

Mother Veronica tentatively signed off on the idea and committed five dollars for the purchase of a starter kit.

When the box arrived, Angelica surreptitiously carried it upstairs to the laundry room, where Sisters Raphael and Joseph were working. Prying open the box, they strung the sharp and confusing contents together, literally spilling their blood for the foundation. Punctured fingers were a small price to pay for the glittering creations scattered across the tabletop. Now it was time for a test.

Bent over one of the monastery tubs, the three nuns laughingly dragged their lures through the brine. Tiny propellers twirled, metallic tails wiggled, and Sister Angelica thought she might be onto something.

A visiting electrician provided confirmation. When he finished repairing the monastery's refrigerator, talk turned to the electrician's weekend fishing trip to Miami.

"Wait a minute—I got something for you," Angelica told him. She returned to the kitchen with a handful of lures.

"Where'd you get them?" the repairman asked.

"I made 'em."

"I paid a dollar and a half apiece for lures like this this morning."

Sister Angelica's eyes lighted up. At a buck and a half apiece, the profit potential was incredible.

The electrician's fishing trip turned out to be a smash, and he raved about the lures. Using his endorsement, Angelica convinced the abbess to invest six hundred dollars in the fishing-lure business, certain she could find a market for the things.

Her background in advertising at Timken Roller Bearing came in handy. Understanding the importance of a brand name, she dubbed the enterprise St. Peter's Fishing Lures. "It seemed the only name for cloistered nuns to call a project like this," Angelica said at the time.

Her layout experience enabled her to create a professional-looking piece of direct mail for the lures. Sister Raphael's cartoon angel, "Little Michael," with his cocked halo and fishing rod, appeared on all materials. Beneath shots of the lures were tantalizing names, such as St. Raphael's Dry Fly, Little Jonas, St. Michael's Wet-Fly, and Double Trouble. A Jewish friend printed up color brochures with an explanatory note: "The purpose of the course is to raise funds to aid the Great Fisherman in His quest for souls. With every lure goes a prayer that He will bless your fishing."

The pitch and the product were winners, and Mother Angelica knew it. With a mailing list of two thousand fishermen, the nuns aggressively stuffed envelopes for a marketing blitz in January 1960. Before mailing the flyers Mother Angelica, Sister Raphael, and Sister Joseph dragged the mailbag into the chapel to ask God's blessing upon their efforts. "Well, here they are Lord," Mother prayed. "If You bless us, we'll have money to buy land." With hopes high, the nuns mailed their ads.

"I was learning I can't do anything; divine providence has to do everything," Angelica recounted. "After you send out mail, there is nothing you can do but wait." She expected an immediate deluge of orders.

Two fishermen responded.

"Mother Angelica and Jesus were not on speaking terms that week," Sister Raphael later wrote.

"Lord, I can't believe this," Angelica fumed in the chapel, avoiding eye contact with Her Spouse in the Blessed Sacrament. "Now You know we have to have a means of making a living! We don't have anything now."

In addition to sending flyers all over the country, Angelica, the marketer, dropped a few notes to members of the media. If the fishermen did not respond, the press soon did. On April 10, 1960, *Our Sunday Visitor* and the *Canton Repository* simultaneously ran stories on the "Convent of Double Trouble." Hundreds of lure orders flooded into the Canton monastery, and the story became a national sensation.

Swept along by Mother Angelica's personal notes and Sacred Heart badges sent to select media, the story was picked up by the *Miami Herald,* the *Denver Register,* the *Cleveland Plain Dealer,* the *Chicago Sun-Times,* and other major papers throughout the United

States and Europe. In 1961, *Sports Illustrated* ran a feature on St. Peter's Fishing Lures and presented Mother Angelica (who had never cast a line in her life) with a plaque commending her "special contribution to a sport."

To meet the national demand for the lures, Angelica created an assembly line in the monastery. During work periods, the nuns would drop into her workshop, spending up to three hours a day constructing the lures.

Looking up from the dexterous fingers stringing and twisting the lures into being, Mother Angelica marveled at the dedicated sisters surrounding her. For the first time, she felt part of a family: "Now I had someone else in my life," she commented later. These loyal sisters were her daughters and she was their mother; one in prayer and purpose. Rita Rizzo had finally arrived home.

Her sense of family would include her lay helpers as well. The St. Peter's Fishing Lures mailings never referred to customers as "clients" or "friends." The 1961 Christmas message set the tone for her interaction with the public for years to come:

Dear Family,

We just wanted you to know that *your* cloister is almost complete and that you have given Jesus the most wonderful gift in the world for a birthday present—a new and beautiful throne.

Mother Angelica allowed her extended family to feel a sense of personal ownership over her projects. Everybody was in it together. This concept would continue and thrive as she took on new and larger apostolates.

With Sisters Joseph and Raphael committed to the Birmingham foundation, Mother Angelica lacked two sisters. Like any practical Italian, she sought her first prospect in the kitchen. Sister Michael loved the Canton monastery and had no desire to go south. But when Mother Angelica personally invited the nun with hooded eyes to join the new foundation, she had a change of heart. "I don't know why, but I said yes," Sister Michael recalled. "Later I wished I hadn't said yes, but I've never regretted coming." Angelica next approached Sister Assumpta. Though several months away from her final vows, the young nun also consented to join the Birmingham foundation. Mother Angelica's family was now complete.

On October 29, 1960, Mother Veronica wrote Bishop Walsh, subtly prodding him to make haste with permissions for the Birmingham community. She insisted that the financing for the foundation was secure: Sancta Clara promised to donate one thousand shares of bank stock to the new community, a Canton couple had committed to buying a small house for the sisters, and the fishing lures had turned a $4,500 profit. The abbess promised that the departure of five sisters to Birmingham would not cause the Canton community to suffer. But the suffering had already commenced.

Sister Mary of the Cross, still smarting over her unborn St. Cloud community, openly challenged the authority of the mild Mother Veronica. Other sisters were troubled by severe mental and emotional disorders. One nun, later expelled from the community, chased Mother Angelica up a flight of stairs with a butcher knife.

All was not well in Sancta Clara, and Angelica eagerly anticipated moving on.

Writing the Sancta Clara Protocol entry for February 3, 1961, must have been a torture for Sister Mary of the Cross. It reads: "Rome granted the Alabama Foundation all permissions to proceed."

It was now official. Mother Mary Angelica would soon be an abbess—initially to four sisters, and later to millions. She finalized plans for her maiden voyage to the city she would soon call home: a place known for its racial strife and its anti-Catholic attitudes.

7
The Foundation

UNCLE NICK FRANCIS's chromed sedan fractured the ice of Sancta Clara's circular drive on the morning of February 26, 1961. He arrived early to ferry the sisters to Cleveland to catch their flight bound for Dixie. Mother Angelica was about to step into a world filled with unknowns—a place sketched in her mind by the impressions of monastery visitors, and the occasional dispatches found in the *Canton Repository.* She had read of black men sitting in at lunch counters, organized marches in nearby Montgomery, and racial violence that sometimes ended in death; but apart from that, she knew little about Alabama and still less about Birmingham.

Alabamy-Bound

BY 1961, the iron-ore industry that sustained the city of Birmingham had faltered. A plunging steel market collapsed the town's prospects and fueled hatred. Ku Klux Klan members and others used the economic woes to demonize blacks, Jews, and Catholics. Hell brewed in the tranquil green hills of Birmingham, earning it a reputation as one of the most segregated cities in the South.

At the same time, this buckle of the Bible Belt glittered with a flourishing faith. Baptist churches dotted the steep hills while Methodist, Presbyterian, and AME sanctuaries clustered near town. The Catholic community, made up largely of Italian, German, and Irish immigrants, accounted for less than 2 percent of the population. With their statues and annually smudged foreheads, they were an anomaly in a region not particularly receptive to strangers.

Heeding Pope Pius XII's call to offer aid to the black race, a handful of Catholic religious orders migrated to the area. Their numbers were minuscule and they languished in the "missionary territory"—but at least they fared better than their forefathers.

In the first part of the twentieth century, Birmingham Catholics were the targets of religiously motivated violence. In a case eerily reminiscent of Father Riccardi's Canton slaying, the rector of St. Paul's Cathedral was gunned down on the church's steps in the 1920s. Subsequently, locals remember a convent being burned to the ground. These expressions of displeasure with the Catholic in- filtration would take varying forms over the coming years.

In the early 1960s a spree of unsolved black and Jewish house bombings would earn the town the nickname "Bombingham." In a few short years seething racial tensions would turn "Magic City" into a national flash point of hatred and violence. But Mother An- gelica knew none of this as she left for Alabama.

She happily sped to Cleveland in Uncle Nick's car, her dream monastery, like a cardboard dollhouse, teetering on her knees. She held it close for safekeeping. Sitting next to her, Mother Veronica gazed at the blizzard of thick flakes skittering past the car window. Angelica's attention was elsewhere. She thought only of her mis- sion: to find land and build a prayer "community among the Ne- groes" in Alabama.

The snowstorm knocked out power at St. Paul's Shrine, but the sisters lighted up at the sight of Mother Angelica. Even the rheumy-eyed abbess, approaching her seventy-fifth year in the or- der, remembered her much-disciplined charge. Mother Agnes blessed the new foundation, spiritually linking Angelica to the women who had raised five foundations of the Franciscan Sisters of the Most Blessed Sacrament in the United States, and eleven other monasteries in Poland, India, Germany, France, and Italy.

The incessantly falling Cleveland snow hampered the Trailblazer, delaying the first air flight of her life. Arriving late in Atlanta, the nuns missed their Birmingham connection and were forced to spend the night in a motel.

For two nuns unaccustomed to the world beyond the cloister, much had changed. Their motel visit became a comedy of errors. Unfamiliar with recessed showerheads, Mother Angelica was mysteriously spritzed each time she went to fill the bathtub. And when Mother Veronica ordered her to douse the lamplight, each rotation of the switch only made the bulb brighter. "I think the devil's in that light," a wide-eyed Angelica told her superior.

The 1961 motel stay is significant, as it marks the first time Mother Angelica actually saw a television set. She watched no programming, because "you had to put a quarter in it or something." But in that Atlanta motel room, she made the acquaintance of the instrument that would transform her life.

In Birmingham the next day, Mothers Angelica and Veronica settled in with the Sisters of the Holy Trinity. The Trinitarians would host the nuns throughout their search for land, doing so at the behest of the archbishop, whom the nuns were scheduled to meet that first afternoon in town.

With open arms, Archbishop Thomas Toolen greeted Mother Angelica from atop the winding staircase of his residence. The rotund, merry man, who wore a black cassock with an enormous magenta cummerbund cinched just under his armpits, barreled down the staircase, sprigs of white hair escaping his skullcap. With his oversized head and large ears, he could have passed for Charles Laughton. Mother Angelica remembered him as "very fatherly" and "so human."

In his parlor, the archbishop told the sisters he had the perfect mansion picked out for their new foundation. The nuns exchanged looks. As Mother Veronica glanced down in prayer, Angelica began her pitch. She pulled out cash-flow projections, budgets, and finally, to seal the deal, her ambitious monastery model. As the dazzled archbishop took this in, Mother Angelica reminded him that the fishing-lure business had already netted eleven thousand dollars in profits, and more was expected. Sufficiently convinced of the need for a customized monastery, the archbishop gave the go-ahead to purchase land in Birmingham. Nowhere in either the history of the order or in the press of the time was there any mention of the monastery being built so that the nuns could pray for the maligned black community or to welcome black vocations to the contemplative life. For the safety of the sisters, their mission would be kept secret.

After Mass each morning, Angelica and Veronica would scout land in the area; they visited mansions and mountain plateaus, but nothing seemed right for the foundation.

In the meantime, Mother Angelica began to acquaint herself with the local Italian community. Like her Tonys back home, Italian Catholic businessmen were enthralled by the entrepreneurial Calabrese nun. Her vision and earthy humor were magnets for these *paesans,* who outdid one another offering services and materials. One of the first was a builder named Tony Oddo. Introduced to Angelica by a priest, he agreed to build her monastery at a reduced price.

Protestants were no less generous. When Wilmont Douglass signed on as architect, he was so stunned by the model, the plans, and the fishing lures, he called a local PR man to scare up some publicity for the nuns. The *Birmingham Post Herald* and the *Birmingham News* each ran stories on the fishing-lure nun and her dream to build a monastery.

But for all the acclaim and acceptance in Birmingham, Mother Angelica's land hunt was stalled. By March she had no prospects. Everything the nun saw was either too far out of the city, too expensive, or not zoned for a monastery. Angelica displayed resilience and faith during the delay. She wrote to the sisters in Canton, "It's pretty obvious that *He* is guiding this foundation and we have only to love and wait for His sweet providence to show us the way." But after nearly two months in Birmingham, all Mother Angelica had secured was a builder, an architect, a forty-dollar checking account, and a determined belief that God would not abandon her.

The Hand of Providence

ON MARCH 16 the high-pitched voice, which sounded like a whistling teakettle, fell over a public audience for the first time. At a formal tea hosted by some society ladies on the lower level of the Trinitarian sisters' convent, Mother Angelica was making her way around the room, glad-handing and introducing herself, when the call came. A Trinitarian sister struck a gavel to draw the attention of the assembled. She then beckoned the thirty-eight-year-old Mother Angelica forward to offer a few words.

"I could have crowned her! But she sweetly smiled and stepped aside," Angelica wrote of the sister that day. "Jesus helped me—and they started asking questions and looking at [the] lures and saying, 'Isn't this wonderful.'" The initial public speech was uneventful, but the fact that this cloistered nun had broken her silence in public was revolutionary.

When Angelica returned upstairs, Mother Veronica had already booked her next speaking engagement. As a favor to a Birmingham monsignor, she was to give a talk on Vocation Day at a local Catholic high school the following Thursday. Angelica grudgingly accepted the task, but at the time, she considered such talks an ordeal.

For a glimpse into her speaking technique, an entry she made in the community history on March 22, 1961—the day before the speech—is illuminating: "I think the best preparation is to have no preparation. Jesus will tell me what to say when the time comes."

Four real estate agents were contacted to find land for the foundation while Mother Angelica renewed an independent search. Ridiculing her handicap, she repeatedly climbed overgrown mountainsides in full habit, using her crutch to clear the way as she sought the hallowed spot. On certain properties she would plant religious medals every few feet or press a relic of Mother Cabrini to the soil, in an effort to win God's favor. This would go on for months.

Back home in Canton, a new play, entitled *Sister Was a Sport,* opened at the Players Guild on April 18, 1961. Inspired by Mother Angelica's fund-raising exploits, it told the tale of Sister Mary

Helen, a once-expert angler who is inspired to sell custom-designed fishing lures when the monastery falls on hard financial times. Though none of the Sancta Clara sisters saw the show, Mae Francis did not miss it.

Some in the theater remember Mae offering her own running commentary during the performance. "Oh, they got that wrong," she muttered aloud in the dark whenever the fictional narrative strayed from reality.

Without Angelica knowing it, hundreds were witnessing the stage version of at least a part of her life. Back in Birmingham, she watched, with only casual interest, the medium that would transmit her image and ideas far beyond the confines of any theater. To keep up with the world, Mothers Angelica and Veronica would join the Trinitarian sisters after supper on most evenings to watch NBC's nightly newscast, *The Huntley-Brinkley Report*. This was the first television program Mother Angelica ever viewed.

On Mother's Day, Cooper Green, the former mayor of Birmingham, took Angelica to see a stretch of land in Irondale. Long before the suburb was immortalized in Fannie Flagg's *Fried Green Tomatoes at The Whistle Stop Cafe*, the village was little more than a collection of hillside shanties perched on the far side of Mountain Brook's splendid mansions.

A long, lonely road led to ten acres of gently sloping mountainside, an ideal setting for a monastery. Adjoining the property, situated on its own acre and a half, sat a small two-bedroom house. When Mother Angelica discovered that the house was in foreclosure, she had a practical notion: The nuns would need a base of operations and facilities during construction of the monastery, so why not buy the little house? Sensing God's providence, Angelica quickly placed a contract on the fifteen acres, the house next door, and another three and a half acres "for protection so no one [could] build too close to us."

"God is good. He made us look a little while, but He gave us more than we ever expected and that's just like Him," Mother Angelica said at the time. "It pays to trust the Good God."

Meanwhile, the zoning board refused to grant a building permit for the land, which jeopardized the project. Mother Angelica started working the phones while Cooper Green placed a call to the mayor. "Feeling kinda sick" and not knowing if she would get her permit or not, Angelica was presented with closing papers for the Irondale properties.

"We were so deep in it all anyway, we signed it. Might as well gamble all and trust the Lord," she wrote to the sisters at Sancta Clara.

God rewarded her blind trust. By the summer of 1961, Mother Angelica had building permits and deeds to fifteen acres of Birmingham real estate. The purchase cost was thirteen thousand dollars, the precise amount earned by the fishing-lure business.

The Boss

ARCHBISHOP TOOLEN applied his considerable heft to the back of a shovel, driving it into the rocky ground on July 24, 1961. Having intoned prayers in Latin and English before a hundred onlookers, the cleric broke the soil and initiated the building of Our Lady of the Angels Monastery. "I feel sorry for these workmen with two nuns telling them what to do," the archbishop joked.

In the shadow of churning bulldozers and uprooted pine trees, surrounded by the laughter of their supporters, Sister Joseph and Mother Angelica could barely contain their joy. Pictures from that day show an ebullient Angelica, glowing with determination and confidence. There is triumph in her eyes.

As building began, the Birmingham team changed. Mother Veronica stayed behind to attend to the Canton community, and in her place Sister Joseph became Angelica's construction partner. But it was Mother Angelica who ran the show. When a concrete-block vendor stopped by the site to present an estimate, one of the workmen yelled out, "You better see Mother, she's the boss on this job." Technically, Tony Oddo was the monastery contractor, but at every turn it was Mother Angelica who approved orders, caught mistakes, made the tough calls, and kept an eye on the budget.

As the rocky land was being cleared, the architect warned

Mother Angelica against building on the sloped property. The excavation costs would be enormous, he told her, and even if the monastery could be erected there, he foresaw a gaping fifty-by-sixty-by-twenty-foot cavern where the courtyard was to be.

"We'll find a hill around here somewhere and just put it in there," Angelica replied. When Sam Saiia of Birmingham Excavating Company donated a crew to do thousands of dollars' worth of digging, Mother Angelica pressed forward confidently. Dynamite loosened the rock, dirt was moved, but as the walls went up, the cavern the architect had predicted sat in the middle of the construction site.

Mother Angelica paced the perimeter of the hole one afternoon, aware that she had a major problem on her hands. A slack, saliva-drenched southern voice interrupted her thoughts. "Got a big hole there," a lined old man yelled from across the pit. Hocking his moistened tobacco into the abyss, he sauntered closer to Angelica. "You need some dirt? I got a hill in back a' my house, and every time it rains, damn thing's in my basement. You want it?" She did. Within days, his hill became fill, and the problem was solved. It was to be one of Mother Angelica's lesser donations.

Cossette Stevenson of Stevenson Brick and Tile Company donated the bricks for the monastery. Joe DeMarco donated the concrete blocks for the interior. A Jewish-owned company supplied all the tile for the building and gave the nuns a thousand-dollar discount on appliances. The monastery had become an ecumenical touchstone in Birmingham, an inspired project that Protestants, Jews, and Catholics could support. The personality of Mother Angelica made it so.

By any standard, Angelica maintained a wearying daily schedule throughout the building of her monastery. On most days, she was up at five A.M. After Mass, the praying of the Divine Office, breakfast, and a bath, Mother arrived at the work site by nine o'clock. For the next eight hours, she would shadow the crew. Hovering with her ever-present crutch, she braved the Birmingham sun, offering the workers challenge and encouragement.

Of her daily sun exposure at the work site, she wrote, "When I take off my gimp I look like a clown: a perfect round circle of sunburn and a very red nose that makes others suspect that I either belong, or should belong to AA."

Retiring to the Trinitarian convent after 5:00 P.M., she prepared prints for bids, wrote checks, and made phone calls while Sister Joseph attended to the laundry. Mother's engagement in every phase of the building was total.

She briefly attempted to withdraw from the hands-on approach, but it didn't last long. On September 17, 1961, she wrote:

> For a couple of days we let the men go on their own and then went over to see what they did—and it was exactly nothing. So, from now on we keep after them. We are working on uncompleted plans and it is very hard to do. What isn't written they ask me about and we just pray we make the right decisions. The other day I got slightly perturbed at Mr. Douglas [the architect] and told him so . . . in no uncertain terms . . . and it really worked! They have 10 men working on [the plans] and they will be all completed by Tuesday or else. You know, if they think you're easy to get along with they'll try to put you off and put you off and think they can get away with it. So I guess now they know!!!

Slowly, the crew began to realize this was not your average cloistered nun. More often than not, she knew what she was talking about, could easily read plans, and had no reservations about expressing her displeasure with shoddy work. "I had to tell the bricklayers off when they got a little careless on the joints," Mother wrote in October 1961. "I think they got the idea when I told them they'd have to tear down any wall that didn't suit us."

More complicated than repairing a leaky basement or building a grotto in the backyard, this project required all she had learned. Day by day, Mother Angelica began to reconcile the requirements of her religious life with the demands of business. Balancing the bottom line with the desire to provide a good example proved a real challenge. She touched on the difficulty in a November letter:

When I read the life of St. Teresa of Avila and it said she went
to confession every day I could never figure out just why. You
know of course that she built 15 of these foundations, but
even then it never dawned on me why she had to go to confession every day . . . well . . . now I know!!! There are some
days I could go twice.

The day she arrived on the site and found the bricklayers missing in action must have been one such occasion. When Mother
questioned their whereabouts, one of the workmen said they were
finishing a house in another part of town and would be gone for
three days.

"And what are we supposed to do here for three days—play
checkers and let the building stand until they finish a house?"
Mother Angelica said. "Do you know where this house is?"

The workman said he did. Mother summoned Tony Oddo. "Mr.
Oddo, please get in your truck and go over to the house they are
working on and tell them when they are finished, to keep going and
just come over to pick up their tools—they're fired." Within an
hour, Angelica found a new team of bricklayers and work continued. In the aftermath of the incident, no man was ever late on her
site again.

Advances and Setbacks

ON SEPTEMBER 18, 1961, a train carried Mae Francis and her belong-
ings to Birmingham for what would be more than a casual visit. With
Rita gone, the loneliness of Canton had closed in on Mae. Now retired from the Canton Waterworks, she did what was expected and
permanently relocated to the South. The small house at the edge of
the monastery property would become her temporary home.

By 1961, Mae was a changed woman. She redecorated the two-
bedroom house, cooked lunch for the sisters in the afternoon, answered the phone, and offered comfort to her daughter. She had
developed a spiritual life and grown more mellow, but her attachment to Rita had not abated.

Shortly after Mae's arrival, Mother Angelica addressed three hundred people at a Birmingham diocesan function. A monsignor introduced her as "the biggest beggar this city has ever known . . . she gets her hands on you, you're finished!" Mother took to the podium, explaining the "nocturnal adoration" the sisters maintained before the Blessed Sacrament, and the constant prayer they offered for the people of Birmingham, "regardless of race or creed." A comic retelling of her efforts to extinguish the lamplight in an Atlanta motel, and similar challenges of coping with modernity, rounded out the talk. She hoped it would be the "last of the speeches."

But she was soon back at the rostrum, before a group of Jewish businessmen. Opening with talk of her transfusion and the Jewish blood they shared, Mother Angelica established an instant rapport with the audience. The comedic timing, picked up from the streets of Canton, paid off in spades. Soon men's groups, women's groups, the Kiwanis Club, Jewish temples, sewing circles, and students, not all of them Catholic, were clamoring for Mother Angelica to address their organizations. To familiarize the locals with religious life and whip up financial support for her increasingly expensive monastery, she accepted all invitations.

Money had become an issue for Mother Angelica by late 1961. Not only had the monastery gone over budget but the nuns' personal finances had also evaporated. At one point, she and Sister Joseph were down to forty cents. "Don't worry, the Lord will provide," Mother assured Sister Joseph.

Where Mother Angelica found rest in that belief, Archbishop Toolen found only anxiety. Her plan was to borrow $68,000 from the bank to offset the building cost overruns. But she needed the archbishop's approval to do so. Concerned about saddling a new community with such a heavy debt, the archbishop paid Angelica a personal visit on November 22.

The sheer size of the monastery set the archbishop back on his heels. Following a quick tour, he joined the sisters in the little home next door to the monastery. Plopping himself into a captain's chair, he told Mother she could not borrow any money and that building had to stop until she could raise the necessary funds to move forward.

"But Your Excellency, the bedrooms are just iron framing now; they'll begin to rust. It will be terrible," Mother pleaded, trying to convince him of the need to continue. The chapel was not even completed.

"I don't care," the archbishop said, starting to shift his bulk upward. "You just stop right now." As he rose, the captain's chair was still attached to his plentiful backside.

"Well, I didn't know what to do," Mother Angelica told me, holding for the laugh. "I didn't want to pull it off of him." A few wiggles later, the chair was free and the somewhat embarrassed archbishop left.

Not knowing what her next step would be, a disappointed Angelica grabbed her crutch and went out to the work site, where she called the crew together. "Well, we've run out of money and the archbishop said we have to stop building," she announced.

"He can't tell me to stop," the owner of Canterbury Electric shouted back.

"But I can't pay you."

"Sister, for you to owe me money is like having money in the bank," the electrician said. "I'm going to finish the job."

The plumber, the bricklayers, and Tony Oddo followed suit.

Now Mother needed a way to pay them. She wrote home to Sancta Clara, asking for a $25,000 loan, which the council approved. To contain costs, Mother Angelica and Sister Joseph personally laid wall tile in the bathrooms and cells of the monastery. They sanded cabinets and worked on the windows. The labor would cost Angelica more than time. "Sister spine gets to yelling once in a while, but Jesus gives the strength to keep going," she said during the construction.

Wanting for financial resources, Mother Angelica made the hard decision to build only half of the monastery originally planned. In hindsight, she saw the decision as providence in action: "Jesus prevented us from having enough money; He just gave us enough for half." Years later, His reasoning would become apparent to Mother.

For all of the support she garnered in Birmingham, there were those hostile to the idea of the monastery, to say nothing of the Yankee Catholic nun building it. At first, Angelica received anonymous letters accusing her of "taking all the money away from the Italians." Then things got more serious.

Starting on successive Saturdays in September 1961, generators were stolen and equipment at the work site was vandalized. Mother saw this as an effort to frighten her away from completing her mission. "That I want to see," she defiantly told the Canton sisters. For protection, a night watchman was retained and a system established where the nuns would flash the porch light of their small house in the event of danger. But Mother Angelica had underestimated just how lethal that danger could be. Several months later, frantically flipping the light switch, she would experience down-home terror personally.

8
A *Family Monastery*

RIVULETS WOUND ROUND the broken rock and earth surrounding the half-built monastery. Rain punished the pine trees as it fell on Old Leeds Road that evening. In the little white house, a quick walk from the work site, on the night of February 21, 1962, Mother Angelica, Sister Joseph, and Mae Francis were praying the glorious mysteries of the rosary when they heard a pounding near the back of the house. They dismissed the sound at first, thinking it a dog rattling trash cans in the carport. Then the pounding grew more intense, as if someone were trying to break through the back door. Glass could be heard smashing on the tiles in the kitchen. Petrified, Mae Francis ran to her bedroom. Sister Joseph scurried toward the kitchen, and Mother Angelica made for the front door, flicking the lights for help. But no one came. A gunshot rang out at the rear of the house.

Desperate for help, Angelica threw open the front door. In the amber light of the porch, curtains of rain obscuring her view, she waved and yelled to the watchman. The incessant drum of falling water was the only response. A flash of light and five shots broke the darkness; a bullet landed so close to Mother Angelica, she "could smell the gunpowder." "You never saw a crippled nun run so fast in all your life," Mother later said.

She tried to force the door shut behind her, but it wouldn't latch. Are they trying to get in? How many are there? Mother wondered. Throwing her weight against the door, she offered a panicked prayer. It was only when she glanced down that she realized the rug was sandwiched in the doorjamb. Sliding it back, she flipped the lock and reached for the phone. "It was as close to hell as we ever want to get," Mother Angelica said afterward.

Within days, the story was all over the newspapers and on radio. "I told Jesus that I could have thought of a better way of getting the monastery known than this incident," Mother wrote to the Canton sisters, "but He didn't ask my opinion."

Angelica recounted the harrowing story for the media, careful to add that the action was "not typical of Birmingham" and praising the people of all faiths who had shown such "kindness" since her arrival.

Authorities had no leads. Nearly two weeks later, the harassment resumed.

At 4:30 A.M., the high bark of their new puppy woke the sisters from a sound sleep. The familiar pounding had startled the animal. Over his clamorous bark, five shots snapped outside. This time, the nuns stayed indoors. When it was over, they found a bullet lodged in a window frame of the house, but nothing more.

Momentarily frightened, Mother resolved to go forward. In a dispatch to Canton, reporting the second attack, she wrote: "If it happens a third time I'll begin to enjoy it!" This nun had no intention of leaving—except to import sisters to the new foundation.

In the Family Way

ON MAY 8, 1962, in a nine-seat Pontiac station wagon loaned to her by a Birmingham car dealer, Mother Angelica, Mae Francis, Sister Raphael, Sister Joseph, Sister Michael, Sister Assumpta, and a lay couple pulled out of Sancta Clara's horseshoe drive and headed south.

"It was very hard when they left," Sister Anthony, a Sancta Clara nun, remembered. "Part of the community bond was gone. Raphael had that voice, Michael was the cook, Mother Angelica had all her talents, and Sister Joseph was the seamstress."

Mother Veronica would say Angelica "brought the cream of the crop along with her." Veronica had allowed her to do so. Her motherly devotion to Mother Angelica was so complete, she permitted choice sisters to depart the Sancta Clara community, causing an instability that would plague the monastery for years to come. For the good of the new foundation, Mother Veronica essentially sacrificed the old.

A euphoric cry sounded two days later when the station wagon pulled onto Old Leeds Road, affording the sisters their first glimpse of the building they had seen only in drawings, models, and photos. The modern chapel with its great sloped roof, designed to resemble an ark, pointed to heaven. From this focal point, the two pinkish wings of the monastery spread in separate directions, turning back on themselves to create a perfect square. The monastery conceived and birthed in pain had become a reality.

For ten days, Mother Angelica and the sisters hosted a well-publicized open house—a chance for the public to view the mysterious inner sanctum of monastic living before the nuns were locked away forever.

Seven thousand visitors eyed the eighteen Spartan cells—tiny rooms of painted concrete block with metal beds and matching side tables. A bare cross hung in each cell, a reminder that the sister who lived there represented Christ in her sufferings and penances. There was a simple workroom, a refectory for group meals, and a courtyard at the center of the complex. The only elaborate feature of the monastery was the chapel—by design.

"The entire project was planned so that complete concentration would be just on the Blessed Sacrament," Mother Angelica told visitors before the dedication. "Anyone, regardless of faith, is welcome to come and spend a few minutes or a few hours with God."

The chapel could seat about eighty people on the public side, but it seemed larger due to the space overhead. A sloped A-frame ceiling of varnished beams rose to meet a skylight, permitting natural illumination. In the middle of the chapel, perched atop the half wall separating the public from the cloister, two carved genuflecting angels held the monstrance containing Christ in the Blessed Sacrament. Directly above the monstrance, ostensibly suspended in air, a handmade crown of gold testified to the king enshrined in the chapel. Angelica had spared no expense on this house of God.

"Sisters, you can never go overboard when it comes to Our Lord and the things that belong to His worship," Mother Angelica told the nuns during the first days of the new foundation. "We must never feel that anything is too lavish or expensive when it comes to vestments or altar cloths or chalices. God has never been stingy with us, Sisters. He never said, 'Now you just stay in Canton and suffer these things.' He never said, 'Here, this little shack is good enough for a beginning—live in it for a while.' No, He inspired all these people to be generous and make this beautiful monastery possible."

On May 20, the day of the monastery's dedication, the tours ended, and so did the sisters' contact with the public. Nearly a thousand people came to bid them farewell. Mother Angelica collected her daughters from the assembled throng and headed into the monastery.

Before lumbering into the structure to bless each room, Archbishop Toolen told the well-wishers that the "powerhouse of grace and prayer" was a "monument" to Mother Angelica, to "her love of God and her love of people." Then he added, "This is a great day in the history of Birmingham and a great day in the history of the Catholic Church."

Wending through the halls, Mother watched the archbishop and his attendants pronounce prayers and baptize the rooms. After months of toil and twenty-five speeches to civic and church groups throughout Birmingham, and with ninety thousand dollars of debt, Mother Angelica retreated to her cloistered vocation once more. Following the blessings, Angelica fell on one knee, kissing Archbishop Toolen's ring. She closed the door behind him, turned the key, and established cloister, locking herself and her sisters away with God.

"After all the ceremonies were finished, I remember seeing Mother kneeling on her prie-dieu in the chapel, and she was crying. It was so emotional," Sister Michael recalled. "We were finally all here and we were enclosed."

Everyone except the community's first postulant: Mae Francis.

"She was an extern sister for some years—a difficult one," Mother Angelica told me. "It's very bad to have parents down when you have a new monastery and five sisters."

It seemed like a fine idea at the time. Sister Mae lived in the monastery but interacted with the public, spinning stories for the amusement of visitors while selling items near the chapel. Mae's desire to pass her later days with God, a wish expressed more than twenty years earlier, had become a reality. Angelica joked that she had become her own grandmother, since Mae now called her "Mother."

The presence of Mae Francis underscored Mother Angelica's intention to establish a family monastery. "I felt that a monastery should combine family life and monastic life. . . . Pius XII said a girl should go from one family to another. And boy that struck me hard," Angelica explained. "Me, of all people, talking about family—the girl who never had one. I think that's why the Lord never gave me a family, because I recognize family, I know the need for family. I know without family, you can't survive."

On the surface, the religious life at Our Lady of the Angels Monastery was as rigorous as that at Sancta Clara. Much of the day was reserved for prayer, and the imposed silence remained intact. What had changed was the approach to monastic living.

Sister Assumpta believed Mother was "more concerned with the contemplative" dimension in Birmingham. "We got rid of penances; we played Monopoly for recreation. She was trying to make a more relaxed foundation."

Eliminating public talk of faults and humiliating penances, Mother Angelica pioneered a monastery where there was "no longer an isolated individual, seeking self alone, but a togetherness . . . one in will, in purpose, in love."

To encourage total participation in the life of the monastery, Mother freely shared blessings and setbacks with her entire family. There were no secrets. Community decisions were arrived at in a similar fashion. Angelica would first consult with her sisters, collecting their views on a given matter. She then would consider her options alone before the Blessed Sacrament. Once she selected a course of action, the sisters would unify behind it and pray for a positive outcome.

Financial shortages would often challenge their family spirit and communal faith. "I can remember being down to three dollars in the checkbook," Sister Michael, who kept the financial books for the community, told me. "Mother had to worry, yet she had the faith that it was going to come."

Due to the generosity of Joe Bruno, a local grocer, the sisters never had to worry about food. Bruno purchased whatever the monastery needed each week, and he would continue to do so until his death in 1996.

The pressing problem, known to all the sisters in mid-1962, was the debt. Using the St. Peter's Fishing Lure mailing list, Mother Angelica began writing monthly letters to the family outside the cloister in hopes of inspiring donations. The responses, bearing the names of individuals needing prayer, contained slight offerings, but not enough to pay the banknote each month.

To supplement the income, Sister Mae peddled lures, rosaries, and charcoal sketches by Sister Raphael to monastery visitors. Prices fluctuated depending on Mae's perception of the visitor's financial condition. A person Mae perceived as poor was treated to a discount. The wealthy suffered price hikes. "That's justice," she crowed to Angelica when questioned.

During recreation in the summer of 1962, one of the sisters had a brainstorm. The nun suggested that Mother Angelica record a "little heart to heart talk" that could be sold to supporters. A group of enthusiastic laypeople agreed to cover the cost of recording and duplication. In August 1962, Angelica recorded her first talk, entitled "God's Love for You." Backed by piano accompaniment, the 45-rpm meditation explained God's personal love for each individual. By Christmas of that year, fifteen hundred copies had been sold.

As the Universal Church ached for a new way to engage the modern world, Mother Angelica stumbled upon one.

On October 11, 1962, Pope John XXIII floated down the main aisle of St. Peter's Basilica on the *sedia gestatoria,* past a canyon of white miters, to inaugurate the Second Vatican Council. Two thousand-plus bishops covered the ten-tiered platforms on either side of the aisle, filled with anticipation, and armed with their own notions of the future. Seated five hundred yards from St. Peter's main altar, Bishop Karol Wojtyla of Krakow knew he was entering a historic moment in Catholicism.

Pope John called the pastoral council to renew the message of the Roman Catholic Church in the modern age. But the council would have far wider effects than even the Pope could have envisioned at its inception.

About the same time, the family at Our Lady of the Angels Monastery welcomed a new member. Upon completing her term as abbess of Sancta Clara, Mother Veronica permanently transferred to the southern foundation. Her affection for Mother Angelica and the deteriorating personal conditions in Canton made the relocation inevitable. In a supreme act of humility, she submitted herself to her spiritual daughter, Angelica, offering quiet guidance and support whenever it was required.

"Do whatever the Lord tells you to do" was Veronica's constant refrain to the young superior. "Do what He inspires you to do."

Since her call to religious life, Mother Angelica had carefully heeded God's inspirations. These subtle and at times fleeting impulses would guide her community in large matters and small. Angelica craved inspirations and sought them out with a childlike simplicity, which caused some to scoff—until they witnessed the results. Her approach was straightforward: "If He wants it, we do it. And we do it no matter what it takes. That's what pushes me."

In September 1963, while Mother "felt pushed" to cut her second recorded talk, "The Presence of God," His absence could be felt in Birmingham. Downtown, in the basement of the Sixteenth Street Baptist Church, ten sticks of dynamite exploded, blowing out the stained-glass windows and killing four black girls. The heinous attack sparked outrage throughout the country and dealt the deathblow to segregation. For Mother Angelica, it was a distressing reminder of the early inspiration for her monastery that had failed to bear fruit. Somehow, the goal of establishing a foundation for black contemplatives got lost along the way. After being in Birmingham for more than a year, Our Lady of the Angels had not attracted one black vocation. In interviews, none of the founding sisters, including the abbess, had any recollection of dedicating their community to "the Negro apostolate."

It would be nearly a year before the monastery welcomed its first local postulant, and she was not black. In August 1964, a dark-eyed, olive-skinned graduate of John Carroll High School, Jo Ann Magro, became the first Birmingham native to enter the community. As Sister Mary Regina, she tended the monastery gardens and drew unintended laughs from the sisters for her chronic malapropisms.

Mae Francis was already arrayed in the habit by this time, and known as Sister Mary David of the Infant Jesus. Mother Angelica chose the name as a tribute to Mae's favorite biblical character: King David. Seven nuns now occupied the cloister. But Angelica keenly wanted to attract young vocations. And for that, changes were needed.

She first sought permission to alter the order's name from the Franciscan Nuns of the Most Blessed Sacrament to the Poor Clares of the Holy Eucharist. Mother thought the former name sounded like an active community and confused potential vocations. At the same time, she wrote to Rome, requesting special permission to pray the office in English and to modify the traditional habit slightly. Step by step, piece by piece, without even knowing it, Mother Angelica was at the forefront of John XXIII's renewal.

The Vanguard of Renewal

CONSISTENT WITH all that had gone before, pain preceded Mother Angelica's work of renewal. A diseased gallbladder "packed with some 50 stones" sidelined the abbess from October 1964 to early 1965. The surgery and recovery period furnished Angelica with a natural penance and time to reflect before spearheading an era of change in her community and elsewhere.

The Second Vatican Council decree on the renewal of religious life would not be finalized until October 1965. But before then, many outside the walls of St. Peter's assumed they knew what the document contained. While the council fathers were still deliberating the specifics of the decree, their *periti* (theological experts) offered magisterial speeches in public and wrote articles to prepare the Church for what was to come. Time would prove many of these exaggerated previews untrue. But somewhere betwixt the fantasy of the early prognostications and the reality of the Vatican II documents, something new was born: the spirit of Vatican II. This heady movement of renewal and possibility captivated the imagination of many in the Church. Mother Angelica was not immune to its charms.

In March 1965, at the suggestion of the Canon Law Society of America, Angelica and her sisters sat around their family table crafting a wish list of modifications to Church law they believed could hasten the renewal of religious life. The Canon Law Society was so impressed with the final result, they urged Mother Angelica to rework the letter into an article to be published in *Review for Religious* magazine. She did so. Two essays in the periodical from 1965 and 1966 reveal Angelica's surprisingly progressive vision for the future of contemplative life.

In "One Heart and One Soul," she scolded cloistered communities for their unwillingness to embrace the "directives and changes promoted by the Holy See." She foresaw monasteries where "formalism and regimentation [were] washed away," replaced by a "family spirit" and a deep communal "union with God." In a series of bold and personal proposals, Angelica called for:

- The reevaluation of religious constitutions every ten to fifteen years, suggesting that "many of the customs which we hold dear have become outdated and create among young aspirants a feeling of tension and restraint."
- The abolishment of rank (choir as opposed to lay sister), and all class structure in the enclosure.
- An end of the "public accusation of fault," or *culpas.*
- Dropping the "age requirements for the election of officers" in the cloister.
- And, finally, lifting the penalty of excommunication for

breaking the enclosure or failing to read a small part of the Divine Office. She wrote, "It is understandable why a priest is bound under pain of mortal sin in the recitation of the Divine Office (although the helpfulness of this has been questioned); but why nuns?"

In the article "Contemplatives and Change," Mother Angelica's critique of religious life was even more progressive and mildly feminist:

Why are so many of our monasteries becoming cold and regimented houses instead of homes of holiness? Through the centuries many cloistered religious have become enveloped in a cloud of small rules, customs, and traditions which are contrary both to the Gospel and to the spirit of their founders. . . . Rules that control standing, sitting, and walking tend to create an appearance of affectation. What we need is religious who are truly human, fully women, and imbued with the realization that unless the love of God shines forth from them and enhances their human personality they have failed in their duty of bringing Christ to the world.

Elsewhere in the article, Angelica criticized "the promotion of ascetical practices that tend to dehumanize the individual under the guise of virtue." She even called for the modification or elimination of the parlor grille. Quoting other superiors who believed "the grate [to be] a holdover from old antifeminist laws," she argued that "none of the men's contemplative orders have the grille."

Her writings drew the attention of not a few contemplative leaders, as Mother discovered when she attended an August 1965 meeting of major religious superiors in Denver. At the meeting, it occurred to Angelica that the superiors of the various orders should form an association to "exchange ideas" and share the needs and difficulties of renewal. Responding to the inspiration, she invited several superiors to Birmingham in early November to begin work on the forward-thinking association.

At Our Lady of the Angels, Mother implemented her own modernization plan. She relaxed some rules of abstinence, allowing the consumption of meat on feast days, and for the first time in the community's history permitted the sisters to watch the priest celebrate Mass. Prior to this, they could hear the celebrant on the other side of the reredos but saw nothing.

Intrigued by her articles, some religious communities began calling on Mother Angelica to "help them update." On October 19, 1965, Angelica and Sister Mary David drove to South Carolina to consult with a community of Poor Clares. It would be a long drive to South Carolina.

Sister David freely expressed her opinions and questioned Reverend Mother's every move. And though Angelica exercised more patience with Sister David than with any other sister in the cloister, being superior to one's birth mother had its disadvantages. Several hours of confined contact in the vehicle took its toll. Masking her agitation, Mother Angelica turned to the elderly nun, offering a restrained correction. "Oh, you're just like your father," Sister David snapped, turning to the window.

Perfectae Caritatis, the Second Vatican Council Decree on the Adaptation and Renewal of Religious Life, was promulgated by Pope Paul VI on October 28, 1965. It called for a period of "adequate and prudent experimentation" in religious life. It advised religious to modify the way they lived, worked, and prayed. All "obsolete practices" were to be suppressed, and habits were to be "simple and modest . . . suited to the circumstances." Like butane on a campfire, the council's decree inflamed Mother Angelica's determination to institute even more changes in her community.

In January 1966, half a dozen carpenters tore out the grille and turntable from the parlors of Our Lady of the Angels Monastery. A hinged wooden gate that could be opened for parental visits and other occasions served as the new partition.

Over a two-year period the nuns' habits were "renewed" as well. They wore veils and long beige dresses in the spring of 1966. But by 1967, mod beige jackets, abbreviated veils, and matching skirts became the standard. The jacket and veil ensemble would stay in vogue at Our Lady of the Angels Monastery for nearly eight years.

Mother Angelica resumed her speaking activities in 1967, though they were now restricted to her parlor. It was not uncommon for Mother to address a group of student nurses in the morning and converse with a busload of black women in the afternoon. Methodists, Baptists, Episcopalians, young and old, passed through the parlor to attend her extempore spiritual conferences.

The needs of fellow religious also concerned Mother Angelica. Learning at her association meetings of the few recreational options available to active-order nuns, she commissioned the building of a swimming pool and tennis court in the monastery's backyard. Sam Saiia again donated the crew for the excavation. Pete Cox threw in the five-thousand-dollar pool. Mother hoped the projects would create "good public relations" with the active sisters in Birmingham and members of the association.

But even as the sisters frolicked in the pool, and the winds of the Second Vatican Council blew through Our Lady of the Angels, Angelica could sense trouble on the horizon. Certain sisters visiting the monastery had discarded their religious habit in the name of renewal. The community history describes one group of nuns as wearing "an old habit cut short with pumps." Disturbed by the excesses but committed to her ideal of renewing the Church, Angelica took to the airwaves in one of her first television interviews with a local affiliate in September 1967. With an infectious exuberance, she explained the changes under way at the monastery, trying to put them in context. Along with the obvious evangelical benefits, Mother probably thought the exposure would engender donations, which had fallen off considerably.

Inspired Nuts

ST. PETER'S FISHING LURES was no longer reeling in the customers it once had. "We found out these Southern fish don't bite Yankee lures," Mother quipped to a reporter after dissolving the business.

Searching for alternative means of self-sustenance, the nuns stuffed envelopes for minimum wage, started a clipping service, and raised strawberries. But none of these efforts panned out. Mother Angelica was in a fix.

Ruth Sloan, a rail-thin woman who lived across the street from the monastery, sold dry-roasted peanuts out of her kitchen for extra income. On December 5, 1967, she casually mentioned her sideline to Mother Angelica. A wave of inspiration washed over Mother: the nuns could roast, bag, and sell their own peanuts. Within days, she sold the concept to her network of lay helpers. Having no money to sink into the project, she financed a peanut roaster.

Donning her marketing veil, Mother gathered the nuns around the family table to pick a name for the venture. The Li'l Ole Peanut Company, the name suggested by Sister Michael, was the choice by consensus. In just over a week the business was up and running.

Falling into a familiar production line, the sisters labored over the scalding nuts with the same intensity they'd once brought to lure assembly. The peanuts would "come out of the roaster and go into a conveyor belt and then up into a big bin that cooled them off," Sister Michael remembered. The nuns then packaged the nuts in specially made yellow-and-red cellophane bags emblazoned with the Li'l Michael mascot of fishing-lure fame.

Grocery stores, football stadiums, bars, drugstores, racetracks, and schools lapped up the holy home-roasted peanuts.

Mother Angelica added several supermarket chains to her clientele by personally meeting with store owners. She wangled free radio advertising for the company, and snapped up packing equipment at a greatly reduced price. By the end of 1968, Angelica had paid off the entire monastery debt, and the Li'l Ole Peanut Company posted a five-hundred-dollar profit.

On Ash Wednesday in 1969, Mother Angelica and her tight-knit family received an unexpected cross. On that day, Sister Mary David, oblivious to the presence of others, came tearing out of Angelica's office. She didn't notice Sister Veronica padding like a tortoise down the cinder-block corridor at the same moment. The two nuns collided in the hallway. Veronica was fine, but Sister David fell sideways against a doorjamb, cracking her right arm. As she hit the floor, her brittle hip gave way and shattered. Like a wounded animal, she moaned in anguish.

At the hospital, she was fitted with an artificial hip. But somewhere between the time of the operation and her return to the monastery on March 16, the hip popped out of its socket. Sister David blamed the doctors for her suffering and adamantly refused to return to the hospital for care. She would manage the pain with a cocktail of aspirin and angry outbursts hurled at any unfortunate party within reach. Condemned to a wheelchair, David plunged into self-pity and a profound bitterness.

Anxiety over her mother's condition—a thorn tended since childhood—stung Mother Angelica anew. Sister David demanded constant attention, and more often than not she wanted it from her daughter. Shouldering the responsibility of the community, and unable to improve her mother's condition, Angelica relied on her sisters for help.

To lighten Mother's load, they made Sister David the center of family life. Sacrificing her nights, Sister Raphael slept on a couch in the elderly nun's room in case of an emergency. Sister Michael concocted specialty dishes to lift Sister David's spirits.

"I figured, I'm a good cook, so I'll fix her a meal," Sister Michael said. "I took it into her room and she threw me out. I was so hurt; I was really hurt."

Nevertheless, Sister David's room became the new family meeting place. After supper, Mother Angelica and Sister Raphael would hoist David from her wheelchair and ready her for bed. The sisters sat on the floor in their nightgowns, sharing the day's events and playing with their dog, Prince—anything to make Sister David feel included and happy.

Outside the monastery, a trial of a different sort played out in the Church. The teachings of Vatican II trickled down to the parish level by 1969 and were implemented with varying degrees of success. Though the documents themselves held a truth and power, the imprecision of the language invited interpretations perhaps not envisioned by the council fathers. Innovators breathed their own

ideas into the documents, discarding long-cherished Catholic devotion and practice in the name of the council.

Ignorant of the actual documents of Vatican II, most Catholics
accepted the abrupt changes at face value, considering them valid
and compulsory. Almost overnight, the universal language of the
Mass, Latin, was jettisoned; the priest faced the congregation; devotions bequeathed by Catholic ancestors were summarily cast off;
and what had been sin in the past was now considered merely the
exercise of a free conscience. The Church seemed in flux, changeable, and without moorings. The laity reeled in confusion, while
Church architecture, vocations, and Mass attendance fell victim to
the chaos.

Mother Angelica appreciated the depth of the crisis when her
own chaplain suggested rearranging the chapel. The priest offered
to move the orblike tabernacle carrying the Blessed Sacrament
from the main altar to a less prominent spot. Instinctively thinking
of her Spouse, Angelica refused. If the chapel was for Jesus, He
should remain front and center, she thought. An unexpected visitor
from Rome would help Mother circulate this thought, and others
like it, outside her cloister.

On March 22, 1969, the Pope's diplomatic delegate to the United
States, Archbishop Luigi Raimondi, visited the monastery while on
other business in Birmingham. Struck by the engaging abbess and
her peanut operation, the archbishop promised to secure formal
permission for Mother Angelica to continue her parlor talks as a
"missionary activity"—an exceptional waiver for a cloistered nun.
Before leaving the monastery, the archbishop paused before the
wheelchair-bound Sister Mary David to offer his blessing. "You will
have a long Lent," he said. The prescient blessing could have been
imparted to the rest of the community and, for that matter, to the
entire Church in America. For all concerned, Lent had just begun.

9

The Spirit Moves

SWINGING A PICKAX in the withering Alabama heat, the abbess and her sisters cleared stones and debris from a graduated rock formation in front of the chapel. They planned to turn the rocky incline into an Eden of flowerbeds and dancing fountains, capped by a donated statue of Our Lady of the Angels. On this day, looking up from her work, Mother Angelica observed a familiar car entering the property. Hidden in the shadow of her broad-brimmed hat, a grimace overtook her face as the young priest drove up. No matter how many times she told him, he just wouldn't take no for an answer.

When the cleric lowered his car window, Angelica jammed her ax into the ground, hoping the appearance of busyness would discourage him from conversation. Her stratagem failed.

Father Robert DeGrandis was a young Italian Josephite priest pastoring a black parish in Birmingham. Known locally for his weekly radio show *Ask the Priest a Question*, DeGrandis regularly visited the monastery. His routine included two tasks: praying for several hours in the air-conditioned chapel (a tantalizing lure in the blazing summer of 1970) and badgering Mother Angelica to accept the Holy Spirit.

Father DeGrandis had recently become acquainted with the burgeoning Catholic charismatic renewal. Seeking the "gifts of the Holy Spirit" granted to the apostles at Pentecost, the charismatics

worshiped with an emotional passion. Like their Protestant counterparts, they spoke in tongues, received divine "words of knowledge," and occasionally displayed gifts of healing. Thousands were
part of the effusive movement in the early 1970s. But to enter this
spirit-enhanced life, one had to receive "baptism in the Holy
Spirit": an infusion that could only be called down by a brother or
sister already living "in the spirit." Father DeGrandis was determined Mother Angelica should have this gift.

"That priest is out there again," Mother Angelica muttered, tilt-
ing her straw brim to shadow her mouth. The sisters took note and
scattered across the rocky incline.

"Every time we saw Father De Grandis, we'd go in another direction," Sister Regina remembered.

The priest leaned out of the car window, yelling up to the sweaty
abbess, thereby initiating a conversation that had become so predictable, it could have been scripted. With nowhere to run, Angelica laid down her garden tool and faced him.

"This Holy Spirit is really wonderful," Father De Grandis crowed
like a vacuum salesman hawking the latest model.

"We have the Holy Spirit," Mother yelled back.

The priest insisted. "I could pray over you for the *baptism* of the
Holy Spirit."

"No, that's all right." There was an edge of finality in Angelica's
voice. "I *got* the Holy Spirit at confirmation."

Then on February 11, 1971, Barbara Schlemon, a charismatic reputed to have the gift of healing, passed through Birmingham and
asked Father DeGrandis to take her to meet Mother Angelica.

At Schlemon's suggestion, she and Father DeGrandis prayed
over Sister David, imploring God to heal the nun's incessant hip
pain and the compressed fracture of the vertebrae she had suffered
while using a walker. Softened by the prayer over her birth mother,
Angelica consented to Father DeGrandis's longtime request. "Okay,
if I let you pray for me, will you let me alone?" she asked the priest.

"Yeah, I just want to pray for you," DeGrandis reassured her.

In the chapel, Schlemon and the priest laid hands on Mother,
invoking the baptism of the Holy Spirit. "Is that it?" Mother Angel-

ica asked when it was over. She felt nothing and clung to her suspicions.

More than a week later, Angelica came down with a cold. To
make use of the downtime in her cell, she quietly began reading the
Gospel of John. "In the beginning was the Word and the Word was
with God and the Word was God." As she read, a foreign tongue
spilled from her mouth inexplicably. When Sister Regina came to
deliver a glass of orange juice, Mother tried to say thank you, but
"something else came out." To cover for the strange speech, Angelica pointed to her throat.

"What's the matter—you got laryngitis? You can't talk?" Sister
Regina asked.

Mother nodded.

Alone again, she attempted to pronounce familiar words. "I
couldn't . . . I couldn't speak English," Angelica said later.

At least her cold symptoms had dissipated. Venturing outside,
she paced between the chapel and the fountains, testing her voice.
"Words came out, but I didn't know what they were," Mother recalled. "It scared me."

Returning to the cloister, Mother Angelica found her native
tongue once more. Days later, she telephoned Father DeGrandis.
He snickered when she described her symptoms. "It's nothing. God
gave you the gift of tongues," the priest said.

Unsure of what to make of the "gift," Mother Angelica kept it
private.

Before this charismatic experience, Angelica had never meditated on the Scriptures with any seriousness. She had devoured
spiritual writings and the works of the saints, but not the Scriptures
per se. "I got initiated into the New Testament through this little
experience," she told me. An enthusiasm for the Word overwhelmed Mother Angelica during 1971. It would have serious repercussions in her personal life and forever change her message.

At the urging of Bishop Joseph Vath of Birmingham, Mother accepted invitations to speak outside the cloister to select Catholic
groups. A new crackle and vibrancy filled her speeches. She vividly
animated stories from the Bible, glazing them with a streetwise hu-

mor. For many in the audience, it was the first time they could relate to Abraham, Moses, Lot, and the apostles as people: flesh and
blood human beings like themselves, who hurt, laughed, struggled,
and made mistakes.

Evey Cox was one of those riveted by the slender nun's magnet-
ism. Her Catholic husband, Pete, had given the sisters their pool.
Though a member of St. Luke's Episcopal Church, Evey reasoned
that if Angelica could speak to Catholics, she could speak to Episcopalians, too.

Mother Angelica's appearance at St. Luke's Women in the
Church meeting was electric. Jean Morris, a parishioner at St.
Luke's, remembered feeling "the Holy Spirit flow" from Angelica
during the talk. In the rapturous clamor that followed, the women
begged Mother to lead them in a Lenten Bible study.

"I'm just learning Scripture myself, you know," Mother demurely
protested, trying to beg off.

Though not sure "how to teach a class," Mother eventually consented to the ladies' appeals. As would happen time and time again,
she threw herself into the project, unconcerned with the requisite
demands or the outcome.

Every Monday afternoon at one P.M., the women would congre-
gate at the monastery for the weekly Scripture study. In a small addition between the cloister and the peanut-roasting room, Mother
would address her guests for nearly two hours. Though it started out
as a largely Episcopalian gathering, Methodists, Catholics, and others
trickled in as the weeks went by. While the women hungrily gobbled
up each lesson, Mother Angelica received her own education.

"Giving this class, I realized how little people knew. I learned
from those women that they didn't understand the spiritual life:
how to live with Jesus, like the saints did. Then the Catholics came
along, and they didn't know Scriptures, but they knew the sacraments—which should have been enough. But they could never
grasp it and bring it into their hearts and live it." She felt called to
help the laity "live the Gospel" and develop an interior life. But for
the moment, how to proceed was unclear.

On the first Monday of Holy Week, Mother Angelica thanked

the ladies' Bible group for coming and wished them a Happy Easter. Lent was nearly over, and so was the Bible study, at least in Mother's mind. As they exited, the women promised to return the following week. "But Lent is over," Mother pleaded.

The monastery Scripture study would continue for four more years, with as many as fifty people in attendance per session.

"I never thought of what was next," Mother said. "To me, it was 'the present moment.' The Lord wanted me to help these women, and that's what I was doing."

With Easter approaching, Angelica felt guilty about keeping her gift of tongues from the sisters. Upon learning the truth, the whole community desired the charismatic gifts. On Holy Saturday in 1971, Father DeGrandis and Mother prayed over each member of the community. All but one nun experienced the baptism of the Holy Spirit, and everyone received something. Following this experience, Sister Joseph and other nuns believed the Lord began speaking to them. By Easter Sunday, the whole community was "speaking in tongues."

"It was all very strange," Mother Angelica remembered. "The gift of tongues didn't really last that long. I think the Lord used it to re-orient my soul, and the sisters toward the Scriptures, so that we talked about them, we read them, and we discussed them. It was really the beginning."

By mid-1971, Angelica was regularly addressing groups on Mondays, Wednesday nights, and Thursdays at the monastery. Inevitably, there were instances where people missed a session. "So somebody came up with the idea of taping the talks, and if we missed one, we could play the tapes later," Jean Morris recalled. They purchased a simple recorder and the cassette tapes were sold for a dollar apiece. Mother Angelica had stumbled upon a new vehicle to reach the laity.

Sensing the potential of the taped teachings, Angelica approached the only person she knew in the media, Father De Grandis, about getting on radio. His efforts must have been successful, because in November 1971, she began recording a ten-minute program for WBRC; it aired on Sunday mornings at 9:50 A.M.

Listening to tapes of the *Journey into Scripture* broadcasts is a revelation. Mother's voice is a high-pitched chirp—an almost musical thing that flutters in the upper range and rarely descends. The deliberate formality of her approach recalls visions of a nun teaching catechism class to inattentive students in a church basement. She is largely lecturing in these early attempts, speaking at, but not yet to, her audience. Then suddenly, she happens upon a personal anecdote that is so real, so accessible, laughter erupts in the background. Her comedic timing is perfect. These broadcasts would be a dress rehearsal for all her future efforts.

The nuns soon waded deeper into the media by purchasing secondhand tape-recording equipment and a dubbing machine to mass-produce Mother's talks. Sister Michael lost her tiny sewing room, which was converted into a makeshift studio. In this closet of a room, Mother Angelica spoke to the world outside the cloister, communicating a spirituality she felt the laity lacked. The present moment had offered her a challenge, and by early 1972, she responded with a tape ministry.

Within weeks the peanut roasters stopped churning. Mother attributed the demise of the Li'l Ole Peanut Company to a shifty supplier who tried to squeeze her for a few extra dollars.

"You mean a kickback?" Mother asked him directly.

"We call it advertising money."

When Mother refused the shakedown, the supplier got tough, threatening to withhold the peanuts.

"If I'm going to hell, it's not going to be over peanuts," Mother told the supplier. That was it. Standing on principle, she closed down the peanut business and watched with some sadness as the hard-earned equipment left the monastery. But by then, God had given her a new mission, and it was already attracting attention from high places.

One Dummy to Another

TO CULTIVATE a strategy for addressing the spiritual needs of the Birmingham diocese, Bishop Joseph Vath invited Mother Angelica to a committee meeting in June 1972. If anyone understood the spiritual state of the diocese in 1972, the forty-nine-year-old abbess certainly did. Angelica was speaking all over Birmingham at the time, bringing her distinctive Catholic spirituality to people of all faiths. Prayer is what the people needed, she believed. They didn't know how to pray. For years she had given lessons on the subject to the nuns and the laity. Some even thought the teachings would make a good book. Mindful of her lackluster English grades, Mother dodged the literary temptation until the diocese called.

She resolved to pen a practical prayer manifesto—a guidebook containing "prayer formats" with litanies, Scripture readings, and meditations organized to lead Birmingham parishioners to "a closer relationship with God and neighbor."

At the monastery, she enlisted her family's assistance on the project. The nuns tracked down Old and New Testament passages for meditation while Mother drafted teachings to guide the laity in prayer.

Sitting under the conical metal choir light in the chapel and scrawling on a yellow legal pad, Mother Angelica began her literary adventure. "Lord, I don't know how to write a book," she said to the Blessed Sacrament. "But if you want me to do it, I'll do it." Sitting in the hard choir stall, "a light popped on" in her mind, she recalled, and "the words would come in paragraph form."

On July 18, 1972, Mother Angelica distributed folders containing her booklet, *Journey into Prayer,* to the members of the diocesan committee. After listening to hours of first-phase plans to revive the diocese, Mother asked if she could read part of her book. Bishop Vath vetoed the offer, tossing the unread booklet to the middle of the table. "This will be the second phase," the bishop announced.

The cold dismissal hit hard, reviving childhood feelings of rejection in Angelica. Smothering her anger in the embrace of Sister Raphael and the other nuns, she tried to make sense of the situation. Her work—indeed her entire mission—had been ignored. The sisters calmed their abbess, assuring her that the work was inspired. They encouraged her to find some way to publish the booklet and get it into the hands of the laity.

Using the phone book, Mother Angelica located a publisher "on the other side of the railroad tracks." Jean Morris drove Mother and her manuscript to the Birmingham badlands. Morris, a willowy Episcopalian, had short black hair and perfect teeth. Like steel wrapped in velvet, her laugh and lilting accent concealed an inner strength. Having been drafted from the ranks of the monastery Bible study in 1971 to chauffeur Mother to speaking engagements, she soon became Angelica's regular traveling companion, confidante, and spiritual daughter. The nun's unhesitating approach to life and faith captivated Jean.

By mid-August 1972, *Journey into Prayer* rolled off the presses with the permission of the bishop and an imprimatur declaring it free of doctrinal error. The sisters left the free booklets in the vestibules of churches, in malls, and in bus stations—anywhere they could reach the common man. Almost immediately, Mother began writing her next book.

"Sometimes I would get up early; I couldn't sleep and I'd write," Mother Angelica said. She would usually work in the chapel, but occasionally inspiration struck while walking down the hall or taking a bath.

Sister Regina recalled watching Mother write in the chapel: "She would look up at our Lord. And there'd be a certain look in her eyes, like a droop, where you'd see mostly the white part—like the depth of her soul had been exposed. And you could see: It was like a tape recorder had gone on in her mind; she could hear the words, and she'd keep writing and writing."

"It's like a mystery story, I don't know what's coming next," Angelica told a reporter at the time. "When the thoughts stop, the book is finished."

Mother read the final scrawlings to the sisters. The nuns discussed the content, suggested changes, and then democratically decided the title for each booklet. From Sister Raphael's submitted sketches, the community would choose the cover art, and then it was sent off to the printer. Comparisons of the original handwritten manuscripts with the published works reveal very little editing, though a few paragraphs and sections were deleted in their entirety.

By the end of 1972, Mother had authored three more books: *In the Shadow of His Light, In His Sandals,* and *The Father's Splendor.*

Mother Angelica terminated her writing for a couple of months after a woman accused her of committing the grammatical sin of splitting infinitives. Mother wasn't even sure what a split infinitive was. When Sister Raphael learned the reason for Angelica's writing strike, a smile exposed her long teeth. "The people you're writing for don't understand what a split infinitive is, either," Raphael offered.

"That gave me courage," Mother told me. "I thought, It's from one dummy to another!"

Mother's writing resumed, and so did the publishing. Not even limited resources could deter her.

Our Lady of the Angels Monastery still had no money to speak of. Surviving on cassette sales and the stipends from Mother's speaking engagements, the nuns lived a life of true poverty. Even lawn-care expenses had to be contained. In the spirit of Saint Francis, Mother Angelica imported sheep and goats to graze on the monastery property in the summer of 1972. Chickens and a pig later frolicked in the sloped yard. Testament to the sisters' practicality, the pig would make his final appearance on their dining room table, proving there is more than one way for a Franciscan to enjoy an animal—and to maximize an investment.

In 1973, surrounded by a veritable zoo, Mother wrote the largest and most challenging of her books. The 116-page *Three Keys to the Kingdom* sought to purify the reader's memory, understanding, and will in order to make the person more receptive to the desires of God. One enlightening entry in the book explains Angelica's fearless approach to new initiatives: "We use the talents we possess to the best of our ability and leave the results to God. We are at peace in the knowledge that He is pleased with our efforts and that His providence will take care of the fruit of those efforts."

The sheer diversity of her own efforts was staggering. In addition to speaking engagements, the Bible study, running the monastery, taping the radio show, and writing, Angelica also became something of an activist. "Mother has always been a leader, a fighter, and one of the most imaginative people I have ever known," Jean Morris said.

In June 1973, the nun convinced Jean to donate five hundred dollars to produce FIGHT MIND POLLUTION bumper stickers, which would be distributed free of charge at the monastery. "The Christian should be alive and aware of the consequences of mind pollution, the most important form of pollution," Mother Angelica told a reporter from the *Birmingham Post-Herald* as part of her public-awareness campaign. Mind pollution included everything from pornography to indecent dress—anything that reduced "man to the level of an animal."

Never hesitating to use her public profile, Mother spoke out against the Equal Rights Amendment at a public hearing. She was also an early opponent of female ordination, unafraid to involve herself in public controversies. But in October 1975, Angelica had enough trouble at home to keep her occupied. The book ministry was in danger.

Mother had just submitted her latest book to the printer, a reflection on the Eucharist entitled *To Leave and Yet to Stay*. The printer refused to publish the spiritual booklet, claiming a change in ownership. But the community history suggests it was the content of Mother's latest book and not ownership issues that scuttled the deal.

No matter the reason, Mother Angelica was without a printer. The sisters assembled at the family table and considered their options. They could either abandon the book ministry or do the printing themselves. The nuns opposed establishing a print shop, arguing that a lack of space, training, and money forbade the endeavor. But Angelica spied the hand of providence in the crisis.

With two hundred dollars in the bank, Mother and Sister Regina priced printing equipment at a commercial showroom downtown. Like an Upper East Side heiress with an open line of credit at Bloomingdale's, Angelica impulsively picked out a printing press, a cutter, and a stapler, which collectively cost fourteen thousand dollars. Witnessing the spree, Sister Regina collapsed into a heap.

"Where will you get the money?" Regina asked the determined abbess as she rushed from the showroom.

"The bank," Angelica answered.

But after she visited banks all over town, no one would grant her a loan. The monastery was Mother's only collateral and no regular income existed. When one banker refused to issue the loan on faith, Angelica denounced him as a "pagan." Private fund-raising produced only four thousand dollars. Still, Mother remained optimistic.

"Money is His problem. Working for His kingdom is mine," Angelica said in 1975, referring to her Spouse. "He takes care of His problem, and I take care of mine."

On the morning of October 16, Albert Moore, a regular volunteer at the monastery, was talking to Sister David in the reception room when Mother strode up. She slapped him on the shoulder and cracked a joke: "Want to lend us $10,000?"

"Yeah, I'll sign for it," a solemn Moore told her.

"Are you joking?" Mother asked.

"No, are you?"

"I was, but I'm not now!"

By four o'clock, she had a check for ten thousand dollars, well in advance of the scheduled equipment delivery.

Every aspect of book production would be done in-house. To increase their self-sufficiency, in early 1976, Mother Angelica purchased a collator, a typesetting machine, camera equipment, and a heat seal–packing device. But for all her attention to technology, Mother never lost her simple reliance on God, even at the most mundane moments.

The day a nine-foot sink arrived for the print shop proves the point.

"Did you think to measure the size of the door before ordering the sink?" an angry deliveryman asked Angelica. "This sink will not fit through that door."

"Well, let's pray over it," Mother said calmly. She laid her slender hands on the sink and told the men to proceed with the delivery.

"You expect four men to lift that sink off that truck just to prove to you that it won't fit?" the deliveryman hollered. "God Almighty can't make that sink fit through that door!"

"Try it," Angelica said. Tipped on its side, the sink slipped past the door with half an inch to spare.

As they had once mastered peanut roasters and packing equipment, the sisters quickly learned the ways of paper and ink. In the brief four hours reserved for work, the nuns could produce as many as three thousand books a day. As the slim volumes poured from the machines, only one member of the community voiced her doubts.

A Rolling Trial

"TEN THOUSAND books! You gonna have all the closets full of books," Sister Mary David complained, referring to Angelica's first batch of self-published tomes. "How you gonna get rid of ten thousand books?"

Sister David was "a daily challenge" for Mother, a wild card loose in the community, as unpredictable as a Birmingham twister and sometimes just as lethal. Wearing an abbreviated mantilla atop her pile of thick white hair, she tore through the monastery in an electric wheelchair, removing all obstacles in her path, including furniture and fellow sisters, if necessary. And if David disagreed with Mother Angelica's daily lesson, even in the slightest, it was not uncommon for the elderly nun to roll to the front of the room, look her daughter straight in the eye, and announce, "That's the BUNK," and then leave in a huff. Angelica would continue talking.

Sister David was no less opinionated in her primary work assignment: reading the mail. Slitting the letters open, she offered a running critique of each correspondent. If the donation was too slight or the request too large, she would scrawl "Cheapskate," "Some nerve," or "Don't send books" on the envelope. But it was Mother Angelica and the projects she birthed that would elicit Sister David's harshest criticisms.

"She never approved of anything I did. Never. She'd always say, 'It's all useless; you're wasting your time and you're wasting money,'"

Angelica recalled. "I'd pass her room later and she'd be bragging on me. But she would never do that in front of me."

Even a gift could trigger Sister David's ire. "What do you want me to do with that?" she said one day, casting a hard eye on the carefully selected purse sitting on her lap.

"It's your birthday present," Mother Angelica replied.

"Aw, well, you never did have any taste," her mother said dismissively, regarding the bag as something foul.

Sister David stashed the purse for weeks, until one day Angelica saw it in her wheelchair. "Oh, you've got your new purse," she said.

"That's the one you gave me," Sister David responded. "There's nothing else around."

Despite the barbed comments and the slights, Sister David loved Mother Angelica. But it was a tortured love, one sifted through a lifetime of hurts and fears. The past never left her. When David looked upon her abbess, she still saw Rita, her rock: the little girl she had shivered beside on cold nights and had shared meals with to stay alive. Rita had been true to her word: She had built a castle and brought Mae to live in it with her. She belonged to Sister David, first and always. Sharing Rita with others was unimaginable. The attachment put the abbess in an uncomfortable position.

"As superior, if I made a decision favoring the sisters, she'd be mad," Mother Angelica said. "She had many beautiful qualities, which I don't want to put down, but she had clouds from her past that constantly tormented her."

These clouds drifted over the entire community. The nuns tolerated the continuing outbursts and nasty behavior because of their abiding affection for Mother Angelica. But patience with the old nun's antics was wearing thin. Sister David's primary caretaker, Sister Raphael, who warred with her own nervous personality, was especially frustrated. She wrote in an unpublished memoir: "[Sister David] never felt that the sisters loved her for herself. . . . As a result she often rejected our efforts to get close to her. She demanded so much of Mother's time that it was humanly impossible to satisfy her." Nevertheless, Sister Raphael tried, remaining at David's bedside as Mother's surrogate.

By the mid-1970s, Our Lady of the Angels Monastery was changing. Modifications made during the experimental period following
the Second Vatican Council were revised by Mother Angelica. Between 1974 and 1975, the nun's jacketed habit (which could have
easily been produced by the wardrobe department of *Star Trek*) was
replaced by a shin-length brown tunic topped by a beige collar and
veil. It was much closer to the traditional habit, allowing functionality without losing a sense of the past. In what may have been a defensive measure against the creeping modernity she saw
threatening the Church at the time, Mother reinstalled the parlor
grille. Contrasting with the easy interaction the sisters and the public shared on monastery grounds, the physical bars of the parlor underscored the separate life of the cloister. This fairly minor
architectural change hinted at Mother Angelica's evolving thoughts
on contemplative life—thoughts that would take decades to fully
develop.

Making Apostles

JESUS CHRIST entered human history with a redemptive message
and "a few stinky apostles" (to borrow Mother Angelica's words).
From this small crew, a faith spread like wildfire, continuing to
burn more than two thousand years after His coming. By the end of
1975, with more than twenty short books on the spiritual life to her
credit, Mother Angelica had the redemptive message down. What
she lacked were the apostles to help spread that message.

In January 1976, an Atlanta couple visiting the monastery asked
Mother to consider issuing condensed editions of her work. These
abridged versions of her spiritual booklets could be carried in the
pocket or purse of a lay missionary and distributed as needed.
"Minibooks," Mother called them that day. The couple loved the
idea, and Mother ran with it.

To accommodate the minibooks and maintain her current output, Mother planned a new print shop. Materials were donated and
new presses purchased. In July 1976, at a cost of more than
$100,000, the print shop was finally completed. A handwritten sign

hanging over the new room read: THE MASTER'S PRINT SHOP. WE DON'T KNOW WHAT WE'RE DOING, BUT WE'RE GETTING GOOD AT IT. Eventually, 25,000 books rolled off the presses each day.

A small army of charismatic minibook missionaries spread Mother Angelica's writings all over New Orleans and Atlanta. Soon orders were teeming in from Ohio, Pennsylvania, New York, and New Jersey as people requested thousands of copies of the books. Mother was about to leave for New Orleans to speak to a group of missionaries, when suffering, her longtime silent partner, appeared without warning.

Angelica experienced a tightening in her chest on July 15, 1976. It felt like a heart attack. The nuns rushed their fifty-three-year-old superior to South Highland Hospital, where an arteriogram revealed a heart abnormality. The organ was thicker on one side, limiting blood flow.

"I have trouble in the evenings," Mother confided to me. "That's why I'm on oxygen all night; it helps the blood travel more easily to that other side."

Medication was prescribed, but surgically there was nothing to be done. It would be one of the many physical crosses shouldered by Angelica for herself and others—a thing to be accepted, like an old friend.

"That has always been the preparation that God seems to give me," Mother said of pain in an interview. "It always seems to precede something that the Lord wants me to do."

Throughout the fall Mother gave speeches, mostly to charismatic prayer groups in New Orleans, Atlanta, and Clearwater, Florida. The slight nun with a wave of gray hair swept under her veil was on a mission to recruit apostles. From the stage Angelica tried to rouse "deadhead" Catholics from their lethargy.

"Give me ten Jehovah Witness type Catholics and I can change the world," she told the crowds, her intense eyes ablaze behind black cat glasses. "Every person should be a missionary. We need to get so excited about our faith that we want to share it with our neighbors." She added, "The books and minibooks are mustard seeds. Every housewife, every businessman can be a mission-

ary. . . . Drop a book, drop a leaflet wherever you go. You plant the
seed and then the Spirit will take over." Following her talk in Clearwater, eight hundred people came forward to distribute the thirteen
thousand books she had brought along.

Though she considered herself "a conservative liberal who happens to be charismatic," Mother Angelica had reservations about
some of what she saw happening at the charismatic gatherings. The
emphasis on healing and the gifts of the spirit seemed to be obscuring the importance of the sacraments in Mother's mind. "The
charismatic movement in general was going in the wrong direction.
With the books and the talks, I tried to bend them more to the
sacraments, the Eucharist, Our Lady, and a deep interior life—not
all the running around in tongues and all that kind of stuff. I could
see from the beginning it was not going to last," she told me.

A Catholic paper in Florida reported that she warned charismatics about "a disease called 'healingitus.' " Angelica argued that sick
people could be in better spiritual shape than those considered
healthy. Being a woman racked by illness of one kind or another,
Mother's personal bias was understandable.

Ron Lee, a retired air force officer, and his wife also saw the
problems in the charismatic movement. They were looking for
something deeper. When they heard Mother Angelica, they believed they'd found it. In June 1977, Lee approached Mother with
the idea of organizing her confederation of missionaries into a
worldwide movement. With her blessing, Lee became the "director
guardian" and the Catholic Family Missionary Alliance was born.

As envisioned by Lee, local branch managers known as "regional
guardians" would "teach and recruit" new missionaries, keeping
them supplied with Angelica's books and tapes. The missionaries
would distribute the books and equip every interested parish in the
country with a five-step plan of renewal designed by Mother Angelica. Eight thousand missionaries in the United States and abroad
were drawn to the CFMA. The vehicle had changed, but Mother's
mission remained the same: to call people to holiness.

Twenty-eight guardians from Indiana, Illinois, Florida, Georgia,
New York, New Jersey, Wyoming, Michigan, and Kansas attended a

retreat led by Mother Angelica in Birmingham on December 2, 1977. Standing in the chapel, they joined hands with the nuns, "forming a human seal, strong and protected by the angels," according to Sister Raphael. Mother laid her hands on each guardian, praying in tongues for their fidelity. Some sang out in holy gibberish, others were "slain in the Spirit." As the guardians departed the monastery grounds, the nuns trilled Mother's original musical composition "We Go Out into the World." Jean Morris was the only non-Catholic guardian in attendance.

"It was charismania at its height," Morris said of the CFMA. "Mother began to realize that people were taking the gifts rather than the Lord . . . and so she gradually pulled out of it."

But that would not occur until 1980. In the interim, she flew across the country, sounding the call to holiness before charismatic groups and dispensing her free tapes and books to any and all takers.

A seven-day trip to Chicago in March 1978 would decisively change Mother Angelica's life forever. Tom Kennedy, a retired marketing manager from the Chicago suburbs and the Midwest guardian, organized her visit. According to the itinerary, Angelica would offer workshops for her guardians, speak at parishes throughout Chicago, and talk with a few reporters. But it was the first appointment on the itinerary that would inspire Mother Angelica to reach unimagined heights: a visit to Channel 38, a Baptist-run television station atop a Chicago skyscraper.

10
Doing the Ridiculous

MOTHER ANGELICA ogled the compact studio with something bordering on covetousness. Nestled in the upper reaches of the Chicago skyscraper were a few cameras, a grid of lights, and a small set.

"Lord, I gotta have one of these," Angelica whispered in a private prayer. Then almost as soon as it was out, she hesitated. "What would twelve nuns do with this? I'm a cloistered nun, and I don't know anything about television." But she had already been bitten.

Tom Kennedy, the intense guardian with outer eye wrinkles like sunbursts, proudly ushered Mother and Sister Joseph into the high-rise studio. Like a miner approaching the mother lode, Angelica turned to her guide. "Tom, how much does something like this cost?"

Kennedy quizzed one of the technicians and reported back to Mother. "Nine hundred and fifty thousand dollars," he told her.

"Is that all?" Mother said, her doubts fading. "I want one of these."

Glancing out the window, she saw Channel 38's satellite equipment on the rooftop. Mother stared at it for a long moment. Without breaking her glance, she spoke to Sister Joseph: "Boy, it don't take much to reach the masses, you know."

Here was a vehicle that could effectively reach millions without the expense of printing and the exhaustion of travel. Angelica's fifty-seven spiritual books had touched a large audience, but one TV appearance could communicate to all of those people and more.

"My attitude is, if the Lord inspires me to do something, I attempt to do it. I start and it goes like a snowball downhill," Mother said. "I have to start; if it's not His will, it will either fall apart or something will happen to really hinder it."

At breakfast the following morning, March 9, 1978, Sister Joseph made a startling announcement. After praying about Mother's wish to establish a studio, she felt "the Lord spoke" to her. He said, "The media is Mine and I will give it to [Angelica]."

At first, Mother thought it a joke, but Sister Joseph was not laughing. "We took it with a grain of salt, but we hoped it would happen," Tom Kennedy recalled.

That evening, Mother spoke to hundreds of Catholics at St. Margaret Mary Church in the Chicago suburbs. The standing room–only crowd had weathered a blizzard and treacherous roadways to attend the talk. Mother made it worth their while. Standing before her SOUNDING THE CALL TO HOLINESS banner, she regaled the crowd with miraculous tales of the peanut business, the printing operation that had allowed her to reach the man in the pew, and even broke out castanets for an impromptu rhythmic demonstration.

In the middle of the talk, a lanky, slightly disoriented Nashville lawyer with fine white hair and square-framed glasses pushed through the crowd in the back of the church. He stood there, mesmerized by what he was hearing; a smile on loan from the Cheshire cat split his face.

Bill Steltemeier was attending a legal convention in Chicago that day, when he chanced upon a flyer for Mother Angelica's talk in the vestibule of the downtown cathedral. A married, ordained Catholic deacon of three years, Steltemeier was a senior partner in the Nashville law firm of Steltemeier & Westbrook, a real estate and commercial practice. On weekends, the spindly Vanderbilt Law School graduate served as a prison chaplain. Seeing Mother's flyer, he asked directions and headed toward St. Margaret Mary's Church.

Hopelessly lost in the blizzard, Steltemeier skidded past accidents and hazy interstate signs until he ran out of gas. He puttered to the next exit and rolled into the nearest gas station. Angry and tired, he asked the gas attendant the whereabouts of St. Margaret Mary's Church. He was a block away.

"I never heard anything like it," Steltemeier said of Angelica's talk. Like a man possessed, he walked past the standing throng and forced his way into a pew near the front. Mother Angelica looked in Steltemeier's direction only once. That's when he says he heard a voice. "'Until the day you die,' it said. It scared me to death," Steltemeier recalled. "I knew my life belonged to her from that first instance, no question about it."

At a reception following the talk, Angelica nodded and smiled at the lawyer from across the room, but they did not speak. A frightened Steltemeier got back into his car and returned to town. "I kept thinking, I'm not going to get involved," he told me.

On the return flight to Birmingham, Mother Angelica was consumed with the idea of television production. She quickly turned from the window to Jean Morris, who was in the adjoining seat, as if a fresh inspiration had just landed. "Do you know where we can make a tape?" she asked. Jean did not. "Well, find out and we'll make one," Mother ordered. The final product could be distributed to the Catholic Family Missionary Alliance, and then, if it was good enough, shopped to broadcasters. Emboldened by the charge, Jean located a fellow Episcopalian, who had a sound studio in town, and a Presbyterian minister with limited camera expertise.

A little more than a month after their first encounter, Bill Steltemeier drove down from Nashville to confront the nun who had haunted him since Chicago. "Every mornin', interiorly, I heard, 'Until the day you die,'" Steltemeier said with a rollicking Nashville twang. "I didn't know what to make of it."

Moving past the goats and the sheep in the front yard, he knocked on the monastery door and asked for the abbess.

Mother Angelica appeared in the doorway with a knowing grin. "I wondered when you were coming," she said. For Angelica, here was a Catholic lawyer with the practical business acumen she lacked. For Steltemeier, Mother represented a spiritual ideal to emulate and follow. Their connection was immediate. The faithful Sancho had found his Quixote. After talking the day away, he offered Mother a large donation and a promise to be a missionary guardian. Steltemeier would earn the title in the coming years.

Baptism in the Hermitage

MOTHER ANGELICA's first half-hour foray into television, *Our Hermitage,* was envisioned as a miniretreat with the abbess in a purported monastery. Sitting in a rocking chair, surrounded by a candle, a few books, and other furnishings (distressed by Sister Raphael to give them an "old look"), Mother would do what she had done for years: mine the Scriptures for practical life lessons for the audience.

On April 28, 1978, Angelica and Sister Raphael climbed into Jean Morris's Imperial, the trunk loaded with props, and headed to the studio. Once the set was dressed, Mother fearlessly strode before the cameras and began the taping.

The harsh lights and low-angle shots made her look like "Grandma Moses with an Andy Gump profile." Her voice sounded tinny, like Mickey Mouse. As she bent down to extinguish an unlighted candle, her head fell out of the frame.

"It was a disaster," Jean Morris recalled, laughing. "It really and truly was."

"I wasn't too good," Angelica conceded.

Without an audience, Mother's reliable fire never surfaced. The bland set only compounded a bad situation. On the ride home, Angelica was ready to throw in the towel. "I can't do this. I don't have it," she told Jean and Raphael.

"Yes, you do," Jean said sternly. "We'll start over again tomorrow."

It would take several tomorrows until they got it right.

As Mother attempted to perfect the first program, the guardians of the Catholic Family Missionary Alliance assembled for a retreat in late May. According to the community history, the third night of the meeting devolved into a "Katherine Kuhlman style event. It was a fiasco, like a three ring circus, [with] the leaders demanding cures and proclaiming miracles." Mother was livid and "reprimanded the guardians" for the display.

"It got to be too charismatic," Tom Kennedy said of the CFMA. "When she got more involved in the TV stuff, Mother just dropped the charismatic thing completely." It would be the start of a slow withdrawal from the Missionary Alliance, fueled in part by a shifting focus and disagreements with the lay leadership.

In early June, Mother returned to the studio to reshoot the first episode of *Our Hermitage*.

"I've never forgotten it. It was incredible," Jean Morris enthused. "The power was there; you could feel it."

The program opens with a wandering shot through Alabama underbrush as Sister Mary Raphael sings, "All I ask of you is forever to remember me as loving you." A still shot of a cottage appears and then dissolves to Mother Angelica seated in a faux-leather chair before a papier-mâché fireplace. Her nose looks huge in the light, her eyes lost in shadow behind her glasses. She seems tired and disconnected, probably owing to a bad asthma attack that had sent her to the hospital just days before the shoot. Angelica riffs on the Scripture, finding meaning in seemingly inconsequential details. The episode is dedicated to the multiplication of the loaves and the fishes. After Jesus performed the miracle, she explains, he told the apostles to collect the scraps from the crowd. Mother pounces on the tiny morsel, her passion suddenly exploding.

"Have you ever wondered what happened to those scraps after Jesus took them and filled those twelve baskets? I'll bet those apostles ate those scraps for months. You ever think of Thanksgiving dinner? I look forward to Thanksgiving dinner, except sometimes I'm still eating it at Christmas . . . that Thanksgiving turkey never disappears it just gets bigger and bigger."

While the audience is still laughing ("It's like putting them under an anesthetic"), Mother slips in her lesson.

"Most of you take the scraps of your life and you permit them to pour guilt on your poor souls, or resentment or regret. And you live in those regrets, and you live in that guilt. . . . I wish I had never felt angry or distressed, but I have. But I know that Jesus is going to take all the scraps of my life and your life and He will make something out of them that is so nourishing for our soul and so beautiful. . . . If you have anything in your past that you are sorry for and it seems they keep coming back and making you more miserable and more unhappy . . . let the Lord pick up those scraps. . . ."

For all its professional defects, the show captured Mother's practical teaching and her way with the Scriptures. The humor—the authenticity—was there.

It was decided that the one-thousand-dollar tape, principally financed by Jean Morris, should be submitted to broadcast outlets. Familiar with *The 700 Club,* Mother contacted the Christian Broadcast Network, hoping to interest them in the program.

Founded by the evangelical Pat Robertson, this fledgling nondenominational satellite network reached more than 3.5 million families with a combination of Bible teachings and inspirational programming aimed at a general Christian audience. In need of programming at the time, they agreed to look at Mother's tape.

Too precious to trust to the mails, Angelica asked Jean Morris to hand-deliver her only copy of *Our Hermitage* to CBN. Jean headed for Virginia Beach, Virginia.

Tom Rogeberg, CBN's manager of program scheduling, told me he had been praying for a "Roman Catholic program" to supplement the otherwise Protestant lineup when Jean Morris arrived on his doorstep. In a house adjacent to *The 700 Club*'s TV studio, where he worked, Rogeberg slipped *Our Hermitage* into the three-quarter-inch tape player.

"There was a glow about her and an absolute positive recognition that here was a woman who wanted to share the Lord with people," Tom Rogeberg said of that first viewing. "She had personality and zeal. I was immediately drawn to her and said, 'We need to have more of this.' "

Rogeberg wanted to run the show daily. But to do so, he needed sixty episodes in two months.

"Sixty episodes?" Angelica shouted into the phone. As she spoke to him, images of falling props, hasty exits, and inadvertently removed microphones flickered in her memory. "If that's what you need, that's what we'll do," she promised Rogeberg, defying her doubts.

Several days a week, Mother, Sister Raphael, and Jean Morris traipsed out to Channel 42, a local CBS affiliate, to tape three or four installments at a time. In what would become her pattern, Mother crammed for her shoots on the way to the studio. Flipping through the Bible in the backseat, she identified jumping-off points for her half-hour monologues.

To cover the sixty-thousand-dollar tape and production cost, the Catholic Family Missionary Alliance wrote letters to the editors of Catholic publications, requesting funds from readers. For her part, Mother Angelica returned to the speaking circuit, raising interest and donations among her faithful.

"For too long the TV tube has been in the hands of the enemy," Mother Angelica announced to a crowd of four thousand in Clearwater, Florida, on July 13, 1978. Her solution: a satellite to beam the teachings of the Church to the masses. The audience rose to its feet in rapturous support. This was the first public hint of Mother's intention to secure a television satellite, and the first time it was mentioned in her community history. While still new to electronic communications, she was already envisioning her next bold stride.

The frail, tortured Pope Paul VI, a man wounded by the volatility and disagreement of the post–Vatican II Church, found peace on August 6, 1978. In his summer residence at Castel Gandolfo, he was struck by a massive heart attack, intoned a prayer, and then hastened to his judgment. As cardinals prayed over the body of the deceased Pope, Mother Angelica laid hands on Matt Scalici, Jr., in her chapel.

Scalici had requested Mother's blessing before heading to Los Angeles to seek his fortune as a singer. The twenty-year-old with a bush of curly hair and a Burt Reynolds–style mustache had known the abbess since he was three. His parents, Matt and Phyllis Scalici, friends of Angelica, had practically raised him at the monastery. But in the summer of 1978, in the middle of completing a film and television degree at the University of Alabama, Hollywood beckoned. It seemed only natural to get Mother's blessing before the journey. Kneeling beside his Protestant traveling mate, Matt asked Mother to pray for him.

"I'm going to pray. I'm going to pray that you fail quickly, so you can come back home, because I need you here to help me with my TV apostolate," Mother told him. A spooked Scalici headed west as a new nun entered the monastery.

The ruddy, green-eyed Gayle Breaux had a voice like molasses dipped in the bayou. A native of Labadieville, Louisiana, Breaux held a graduate degree in music therapy and had been a teacher before entering religious life. In her first weeks, the future Sister Mary Catherine mastered operation of the printing presses. Her timing could not have been better. Just weeks after Sister Catherine's arrival, the construction of a second print shop concluded.

The sand and concrete blocks remaining from the project were quickly earmarked for another building. By October, two builders, Nelson Campbell and Jim Gardner, were hard at work on the sisters' new garage.

In Rome, a more difficult job had begun. Sequestered in the Sistine Chapel, the cardinals searched their ranks for a new Pope. The throne of Peter lay vacant for the second time in a year, as the new Pope, John Paul I, had succumbed to a heart attack only a month after taking office. The second history-making conclave of 1978 ended on the afternoon of October 16. For the first time in 455 years, the Catholic Church would be led by a non-Italian, and the only Polish Pope in history. With a glint in his eye and visible strength, Karol Wojtyla strode onto the loggia above St. Peter's Square, launching one of the most ambitious and far-reaching pontificates of all time.

Watching the first televised images of John Paul II with the other nuns in Sister David's room, Mother Angelica had no idea how closely the message and mission of this Pope would entwine with her own. Both the Pope and the abbess fell into the great works of their lives at nearly the same moment. In unison, they would initiate a powerful new evangelization felt around the globe.

In the Beginning Was The Word

THE WORD first drew her attention in a Catholic newspaper article sometime near the end of October. Based on the Irving Wallace novel of the same name, *The Word* was a four-part CBS miniseries scheduled to air in mid-November. In it, a newly discovered ancient scroll casts doubt on the divinity of Jesus Christ, threatening to undermine the very foundation of Christianity. In the end the scroll is proven to be a fraud.

Based on the plot summary, Mother Angelica considered the film "blasphemy"; a misuse of the airwaves that could only sow seeds of doubt in the minds of believers. She saw the film as an attack on her Spouse, the Word made flesh—which is what she told Jean Morris and Sister Raphael from the backseat of the Imperial en route to shoot episode seventeen of her new series, *In His Sandals,* a "sock-it-to-'em" exposition on the letters of Saint Paul.

Passing a bulletin board on her way into the Channel 42 studios, Angelica noticed for the first time that the station was a CBS affiliate. She asked to see Hugh Smith, the vice president and general manager of WBMG, to discuss the upcoming miniseries.

"Your network is going to show a movie called *The Word,*" Mother Angelica informed Smith with some annoyance, "and it is blasphemous to Our Lord."

"I haven't heard anything about this," a surprised Smith said. "But let me call the network." He retreated to the hall.

After a call to the coast, Smith returned to the studio. The movie was indeed scheduled to air, but the network had received no complaints. "I see no way we can cancel this program because of one person," he gently told Mother Angelica.

The airing of the miniseries could have a terrible effect on viewers, she protested. Sister Raphael and Jean Morris glanced worriedly at each other as Mother's expression began to change.

"Are you trying to tell me how to run my station?" Smith demanded.

"No. I think you have crummy programs, but I've never told you how to run your station. But this is blasphemy!" Angelica crossed her arms, her eyes narrowing. "Are you a Christian?"

"Yes," Smith said. "But do you think God cares what we do down here?"

"Yes, He cares, and I care." Angelica's voice was rising. "I will not put my programs on this station, nor make any other programs here, if you run that movie."

The vice president tried to reason his way out of the conflict, reminding Mother of the few TV studios in town. "You leave here, and you're off television. You need us."

"No, I don't. I only need God!" Mother was on her feet now, yelling. "I'll buy my own cameras and build my own studio."

"You can't do that."

"You just watch me," she said, staring Smith down.

In an interview, Hugh Smith did not recall the content of their conversation, but he described it as "very calm" and "not an acrimonious thing." Jean Morris, who was also present, disagreed.

"He didn't blow his top, but Mother blew hers," Morris claimed. "This was a very tense situation. We gathered up our set and materials and Mother, Sister Raphael, and I drove silently . . . without saying a word all the way to the monastery."

Back home, Mother Angelica fell into a rocker and described her exchange with Smith to the sisters. "I blew it," she told them. "I told the man we would build our own studio, and I wouldn't even know where to begin."

The sisters mulled over the problem. Sister Catherine recalled some of nuns shouting out, "The garage. Mother, let's make the garage a studio!"

Intrigued by the suggestion, Mother and the sisters traipsed down to the garage site behind the monastery. Angelica surveyed the leveled earth and considered each wooden spike marking off the perimeter of the construction. She instructed the builder to expand the slab to accommodate a "television studio." The man looked bewildered, as if the nun had just spoken to him in Aramaic. "I don't know anything about a TV studio," he said.

"I don't know anything about it, either, that's not the point. We're going to build one," Mother declared. With no dedicated funds, no business plan, and no hesitation, Angelica faithfully leapt into independent television production.

"Unless you are willing to do the ridiculous, God will not do the miraculous," Mother said of her sudden decision. "When you have God, you don't have to know everything about it; you just do it."

She contacted benefactors, seeking funds for the new venture. At the same time, her CFMA in Michigan began collecting donations for a traveling control room: a trailer capable of recording Mother's live talks on the road and her studio productions at the monastery.

In April a New York salesman came to Birmingham to submit an estimate for the studio lights. Forty-eight thousand dollars would be the cost. Knowing she couldn't afford anything near that, Angelica told the salesman, "Go back and sharpen your pencil."

"The best I can do is fourteen thousand eight hundred dollars," the salesman told her.

"Sold," Mother announced, though she didn't understand that the cheaper estimate was for lesser-quality instruments.

Providentially, the bargain-variety units were out of stock at the time of delivery, so the distributor sent what he had—an expensive Italian light package worth $48,000. Mother Angelica paid only $14,800.

In May 1979, her first Hitachi camera arrived, at a cost of $24,000. Including the building and the equipment, Mother now owed creditors more than $400,000. Collections taken after her speaking engagements partially paid the bills. On her visits to at least nine cities between 1979 and early 1980, she preached about the promise of television and the need to support her efforts. "And what if you fail?" one doubter asked. "Then I'm going to have the most lit-up garage in Birmingham," Angelica fired back from the stage.

In the early part of 1979, she spoke to a standing room–only audience in Philadelphia. A ragtag camera crew of equipment salesmen and friends went along to record the proceedings. On the stump, Angelica was electric; hilarious personal tales and Scripture fused with her Italian directness, creating a frenzy.

"The crowd was so whipped up by her that the floor of the church began to shudder," Matt Scalici recalled. "We couldn't hold the camera shots."

Corresponding with Mother Angelica's prayers, Scalici's run at Hollywood had quickly failed. Back in Birmingham, he assisted the abbess with her television plans and occasionally joined her on the road.

Not every outing was successful. A June trip to Houston, Texas, ended with Mother receiving "food poisoning and no love gift." When she returned home, Sister Mary David reached for the pillowcase that was normally loaded with donations. Finding none in the bag, she unleashed her displeasure on the nuns and her daughter.

Sister David detested Angelica's travels and worked to discourage future trips. "I go through hell worrying that the plane will crash and you'll get hurt," she would tell her daughter, laying on the guilt.

"Sister David never let anybody forget that Mother was *her* daughter," Jean Morris said. "She was the dowager queen. She was demanding, and when we went on trips, we didn't go anywhere that Mother didn't call home a couple of times a day, principally, I think, because she wanted David to know she was okay."

But the more Angelica traveled and the more people knew of her, the less Mary David felt connected. Sharing Rita was still impossible.

One Foot in the Air

BY LATE 1979, Mother's prerecorded programs were airing in some local markets on commercial television and nationally on CBN. She had recently completed fifty episodes of a new series shot in Atlanta. Unsure of what to do with the ever-increasing stockpile of tapes, Angelica wrote to all the bishops in the United States, offering free copies of her programs for education or rebroadcasting purposes. Not one bishop responded, according to Mother.

What she needed was a distribution organ, a way to reach the man and woman in the pew. Commercial television was dismissed as too costly. So Mother pursued the idea of delivering her programs via satellite. Conferring one day with an engineer, one of the five part-time employees working at the monastery, she asked, "How do you get from here in Birmingham to [the satellite up] there?"

"You need [a satellite dish], you need a license, you need an air search, and you need a lawyer," he told the intent nun.

"Which comes first?"

"A lawyer."

Angelica got a cable magazine and scanned the names of lawyers specializing in federal communications law until she came across the firm of Pepper and Corazzini. "I thought it would take an Italian to understand one, so I called them up," she said.

After a series of attempts, Robert Corazzini took her call. Corazzini was a lawyer who knew his way around the Federal Communications Commission. He secured licenses for several television entities and represented those on the forefront of the emerging cable world, including CNN founder, Ted Turner.

"Mr. Corazzini, I'm Mother Angelica from Our Lady of the Angels Monastery and I want to build a satellite network."

There was a marked silence on the line.

"I beg your pardon?" Corazzini asked. Angelica explained herself again. Despite his reticence, the lawyer agreed to visit Birmingham to discuss Mother's legal options.

"I remember sitting in a little kitchenette in the monastery over a cup of coffee with Mother Angelica and Sister Raphael, planning what we were going to do with the FCC," Corazzini recounted. Once the lawyer had gauged Angelica's seriousness, he offered her but one warning: "Once you begin, there is no turning back. Do you understand that?" Mother said she did, and Corazzini agreed to help her.

Of their collaboration, Corazzini said, "The great thing about Mother was that she had absolute faith that it was going to work. As long as we kept plugging, God would take care of it."

As Corazzini pursued her broadcasting license in Washington, D.C., Mother Angelica flew to North Carolina in January 1980. Her destination was PTL, a Protestant network founded by Assembly of God minister Jim Bakker and his wife, Tammy Faye. Mother

Angelica had appeared on *PTL* several times throughout 1979, to great acclaim, and was ranked in polls as an audience favorite. During one broadcast, she told Bakker, "I am convinced God is looking for dodoes. He found one: me! There are a lot of smart people out there who know it can't be done, so they don't do it. But a dodo doesn't know it can't be done. God uses dodoes: people who are willing to look ridiculous so God can do the miraculous."

Bakker was so taken with the nun, he dispatched a team of scenic designers to Birmingham to build her first studio set. The result was a powder blue living room with framed paintings of Jesus and the Pope decorating the walls. Programs recorded in the studio were fed to the control room—a white Winnebago parked outside. Emblazoned on the body of the so-called TV van was Mother's philosophy of the moment, the misspelled adage "Dodos for Jesus."

Angelica had collected a small team of dodoes by this time, regular employees like Matt Scalici; Virginia Dominick, whose family was close to Mother; and Mike and Martha Mooney, a Protestant couple devoted to Angelica's vision. Additional production staff was borrowed from the construction crew as needed.

With her attention now fixed on television, the Catholic Family Missionary Alliance had fallen off Angelica's radar by March 1980. Headquartered in Florida, the CFMA leadership took the organization in new directions. Angelica contended that "it fizzled out," and eventually Our Lady of the Angels Monastery would formally separate from the CFMA.

At about the same time, Bill Steltemeier drafted bylaws and created a board for a new nonprofit civil corporation to be called the Eternal Word Television Network (EWTN). The name reflected an enterprise born in controversy and founded on principle. It immortalized Mother Angelica's protest against the film *The Word* as well as her unstinting devotion to Jesus Christ, the Eternal Word made flesh.

Mother's target audience remained consistent. Dictated by her personal history, she wanted to reach the people she knew best, the people she was still a part of: "We're after the man in the pew, the woman who is suffering from heartache, the child who is lonely,"

Mother told the *New York Times.* "I'm hoping we can teach without teaching, enlighten the heart and relax the body." But financial hurdles stood in the way.

By mid-May, Angelica owed $380,000 on the studio equipment, and the vendor, Gray Communications, was demanding payment. While Bill Steltemeier hunted for money among business leaders, Mother went to the people, giving talks in New Orleans, Miami, Orlando, Houston, Grand Rapids, Kalamazoo, and Kenosha, taking up a collection in each town. But she hoped a visit to a Wisconsin-based foundation would end her days of passing the hat and relieve her financial burdens.

The De Rance Foundation was the brainchild of Harry John, grandson of Miller Brewing Company founder Fredrick Miller. The gangling, eccentric Harry John looked more like a homeless man than a millionaire. Several interviewees describe him as one who "didn't appear clean," a man who would attend business meetings wearing "a beret, suspenders, and clown pants." In the 1950s, this wild visionary, compelled by faith, plowed his entire 47 percent stake in Miller Brewing Company stock into the De Rance Foundation, a Catholic philanthropic venture that took its name from Armand-Jean De Rance, the seventeenth-century ascetic abbot who led the religious reform that produced the Trappists.

In 1970, John's sister Lorraine sold her 53 percent interest in Miller stock to New York industrialist Peter Grace. Grace quickly turned it over to Phillip Morris, increasing the value of the De Rance–held Miller stock several times over. Harry John later sold out to Phillip Morris for $97 million. With the cash, he underwrote deep-sea treasure expeditions, collected reams of religious art, fed his personal obsession with the Sacred Heart, and built a plum-colored headquarters for the foundation on the outskirts of Milwaukee. Mother Angelica entered the building in June 1980.

Dick DeGraff, a fund-raiser for a Wisconsin-based Catholic nonprofit organization, took Angelica to De Rance after learning that she needed money for a satellite dish. Racks of religious art, pickaxes, and bowls of exotic nuts littered Harry John's office. Though fascinated by the nun, he was not convinced she could start a TV network. He asked her to elaborate on her long-range plans and explain the function of a satellite dish. Angelica complied, and as a sign of her seriousness, she requested $480,000 to cover her debt and the expected cost of the dish.

"Let me think about it," John said.

"What do you need to think about?" Mother smiled. "I need it."

According to DeGraff, Mother Angelica was not happy nor assured of success on the drive back. "Pray," DeGraff told her.

"We always pray," Angelica responded ruefully.

In August the De Rance Foundation sent Mother Angelica a check for $220,000—hardly enough to bring down EWTN's mounting debt load or to offset the imminent financial bleed.

On September 18, 1980, already hundreds of thousands of dollars in arrears, Mother Angelica was about to order a thirty-three-foot satellite dish from Scientific Atlanta at a cost of $350,000 when she hesitated. Where would she get the money? And what if it never came? Most would have cut their losses and run. But Angelica proceeded with the order, exercising what she would later call her "theology of risk."

"You want to do something for the Lord . . . do it. Whatever you feel needs to be done, even though you're shaking in your boots, you're scared to death—take the first step forward. The grace comes with that one step and you get the grace as you step. Being afraid is not a problem; it's doing nothing when you're afraid."

Hers was a high-stakes faith. On the heels of the satellite order, Angelica instructed Bill Steltemeier to draft a purchase agreement with RCA for satellite-transmission equipment. The acquisition of the satellite dish, coupled with the transmission hardware, would bring Mother's debt burden to more than $1 million.

Steltemeier had to revise his first draft of the RCA contract, removing a clause that mortgaged the monastery property as security. "I got a lecture on how you can't mortgage holy ground," Steltemeier recalled. The revised contract was turned down by a string of RCA executives, until an Italian vice president called to speak to Mother Angelica.

"You really expect me to approve this contract?" he asked.

"Yes, I do, and so does God," Mother replied.

"I'm going to approve the contract, but you need a six-hundred-thousand-dollar down payment. Where are you going to get it?"

"God will provide," Angelica responded.

In Washington, her lawyer, Robert Corazzini, was ready to file the broadcast-license application with the FCC. He lacked but one thing: a $280,000 letter of credit guaranteeing the funds for the satellite purchase. Mother Angelica scrambled for the promissory note, writing to foundations and big benefactors.

She was sitting on the cloister side of her chapel, praying before Mass on October 29, when a "chubby guy," Lloyd Skinner, walked up with Joe Bruno. Skinner had recently sold a pasta company to Bruno and was visiting Birmingham.

"The Lord said to me, 'There's your letter of credit,' " Mother told me.

After Mass, Skinner and Bruno were shown the studio and the print shop. As they toured the facility, Mother mentioned her travels and the letter of credit she needed to "put the Church all over the country."

"Go get her a letter of credit," Skinner said, turning to Joe Bruno. "I have some stock that's not doing me any good. I'll send it to you."

By November 7, the letter of credit and the license application arrived at the FCC. But Corazzini cautioned that the competition could be fierce and that it might take months, possibly more than a year, to secure the license.

The nuns of Our Lady of the Angels prayed that God's will would be done in Washington. Their abbess headed for Milwaukee to meet with Harry John. This time, she asked him for $700,000 to pay off a portion of the satellite dish. So long as he could control the dish, John was willing to donate the money. It was a deal Angelica refused to accept, even as her options dwindled. Convinced that she needed independence, she accepted a bank loan for the money at a prime interest rate that could have been as high as 23 percent.

From a purely financial point of view, the prospects for the Eternal Word Television Network at the end of 1980 were bleak. The enterprise was strapped for cash, more than a million dollars in debt, and facing operating expenses of $1.5 million a year. Defying reason, Mother Angelica clung to her inspiration and to her God.

"He expects me to operate on a faith level, not a knowledge level," Mother said. "He expects me to operate—if I don't have the money, if I don't have the brains, if I don't have the talent—in faith. You know what faith is? Faith is one foot on the ground, one foot in the air, and a queasy feeling in the stomach."

Angelica's queasy feeling was about to intensify.

11

Cathedral in the Sky:
The Eternal Word Television Network

ON JANUARY 27, 1981, Mother Angelica triumphantly hobbled into the refectory bearing the FCC envelope in her slender hand. In the waning days of the lame-duck Carter administration, the Republican nun from Canton, Ohio, got federal permission to operate the first Catholic satellite television station in the United States. The speed with which the FCC granted the broadcast license exceeded all expectations: In only two months' time, the application had blazed through the bureaucratic process. For Mother, this rapidity was yet another sign of God's providence.

A charismatic in charge of sorting the applications at the FCC recognized Angelica's name, the story goes, and advanced her request to the top of the pile. An FCC policy of expediting cases with a compelling public interest may also have played a role; the nation's first Catholic network would certainly have qualified.

The twelve nuns of Our Lady of the Angels Monastery were to be the first religious ever granted an FCC license. Sister Raphael wept, other sisters laughed, and hugs were exchanged as they celebrated the miracle of the moment.

"A spiritual growth network must be rooted in the contemplative life," Mother said at the time. "I think this is why we were chosen. This is the most unlikely thing for a religious order, but God likes to do big things with little things."

Though they could now legally operate, the "big thing" had yet to be built.

Debt threatened to dash the network before it drew its first breath. To stabilize the situation, Angelica flew to Palm Beach with Jean Morris and Dick DeGraff on February 15 for a meeting with Peter and Margie Grace of the Grace Foundation. Mother requested a $635,000 loan, even though she hated asking for money. The few humiliating acts of begging in her life had been confined to John Rizzo's tailor shop, where she suffered the glare of strangers as he rifled through his pockets, withholding what should have been given freely. That same powerlessness ambushed her now as she sat smiling in Palm Beach.

Mother impressed Peter Grace, but he needed more time before agreeing to a loan. And Mother didn't have time. At that moment, her speaking engagements provided the only reliable income to the sisters and the network, income that barely covered employee salaries.

After she returned home, Angelica and her sisters went to God in frantic prayer. They joined hands in Mother's bedroom, imploring Him for the resources and guidance they so desperately needed. While supplicating, Sister Regina's eyes tightened. In her mind's eye she saw a white satellite dish before a darkened sky, a red flame shooting from its center.

"No one will be able to extinguish this flame," she announced to the sisters, claiming it was a message from God: "This is my network and it will glorify my Son." Regina wasn't certain if the vision was authentic or the product of her imagination. Welcoming any word of comfort, Mother and Sister Raphael elaborated on the message, praying that "the Word would envelop the entire world."

By early 1981, the board of the Eternal Word Television Network had taken shape. To shield the monastery from any financial fallout, the network was to be a civil corporation run by the laity. Bill Steltemeier would serve as president, with Matt Scalici, Sr., Dick DeGraff, and others serving on the board. The vicar and abbess of Our Lady of the Angels Monastery (Raphael and Angelica, respectively) were to have permanent board positions. As chairman,

Mother Angelica was vested with an absolute veto power over any board action. A New York theologian, Father John Hardon, was tapped to review the orthodoxy of religious programming submitted for broadcast. Hardon would unwittingly instigate one of the great crises of Mother Angelica's religious life.

Up in the Air

IN WHAT COULD charitably be described as an innocent lapse of judgment, Father Hardon privately shared with a Vatican official his apprehensions about a cloistered abbess traversing the country with regularity. Apprised of the situation, Rome shared his concerns. On February 16, 1981, the Sacred Congregation for Religious, with authority over Angelica and her cloister, notified Bishop Joseph Vath of Birmingham that Mother Angelica could break cloister to visit her studio but that all further travel was strictly forbidden. With the blessing and encouragement of her bishop, Mother had given spiritual talks outside the cloister for more than a decade. But on February 27, Vath revoked his long-standing permission.

The last financial support for Angelica's nascent network was withdrawn. Twelve talks booked for 1981 had been earmarked to cover operating expenses until the network began broadcasting. In a March 7 letter, Mother begged the bishop to allow her to keep the engagements and also made known her intention to ask the Congregation for Religious permission to egress from the monastery "to see to the work of the Eternal Word Television Network outside the studio itself when necessary." She also promised to notify the papal representative in the United States of her situation.

Bishop Vath phoned Angelica on March 10.

"Your Excellency, I have all these talks now that I'm obliged to give this year," Mother pleaded.

"Well, just cancel them," the bishop replied.

"Next week, I'm supposed to go to your hometown, New Orleans."

"Well, you can fulfill that one. And that's the end of this year."

"Bishop," Angelica said, desperate for some foothold. "Our

salaries are three thousand dollars a month, and the only way we can pay these salaries is from the talks I give."

"Well . . ." The bishop's voice trailed off. "I just spoke to the nuncio. He said you have to make up your mind if you want to continue this or seek exclaustration."

Mother's breath left her as if she'd been punched in the abdomen. "Exclaustration? I can't do that. My life is very important to me—my vocation!"

Exclaustration would have meant a withdrawal from the community and a suspension of Angelica's vows of poverty and obedience for a period of up to three years. In laymen's terms, it was an extended leave of absence from religious life.

"A no-return situation was thrown in my face: If you want this, take your habit off," Mother explained, still offended as she sat behind the monastery grille. "I was shocked at that."

At table, she read the bishop's letter to the community, setting off a firestorm in the cloister. Certain it was part of an effort to "destroy the network," the nuns shouted down the suggestion that their abbess should sacrifice her vows and community for the network.

"He can't do that; we have our rights," Sister Regina piped up. Mary David pounded the table. "I dare him to touch one hair on my daughter's head," the wheelchair-bound sister threatened. Mother Angelica was strangely silent and depressed, according to the sisters. She withdrew to the chapel, fell to her knees, and stared at the Blessed Sacrament. Before her Lord and Master, tears stained Angelica's cheeks.

"You could feel that Jesus was carrying her," Sister Regina observed later.

One by one, the sisters filed into the chapel, offering embraces of consolation. Throwing their arms around their embattled Mother, they huddled together, sharing her tears and pledging their fidelity no matter what happened.

"I've seen her cry bitter tears over what the Church was doing to her, and that was one of the times," Jean Morris recalled. "But the next day, she pulled herself together and found a way out. She was fighting battles outside and inside the Church."

Forced to choose between her vocation and the mission she felt God calling her to, Mother wrote the nuncio for assistance. Her fate and that of the network were in the hands of the papal representative, Archbishop Pio Laghi.

Two trucks carrying the unassembled thirty-three-foot satellite dish and associated machinery rolled onto the monastery grounds during the early part of Lent. Deep in the throes of the penitential season, Mother went out to greet the sacred load. Her mood lightened the moment she saw the equipment. Like a parent welcoming a child from an extended journey, she clasped her hands in satisfaction and pleasure.

A burly deliveryman with tattoos littering his biceps lowered himself from the cab of one of the trucks. Before he could unload the equipment, he told the abbess, he needed to collect the $600,000 down payment required by the contract. Mother went numb. She stalled for time, retreating to the chapel. She simply didn't have the money.

"I blew it, Lord," Angelica told her Spouse. There was nothing in her hand, no cards left to play. After a moment of prayer, she struggled to her feet, resolved to turn the deliveryman and the equipment away. As she pushed into the sunlight, one of the sisters called her to the phone. Bill Steltemeier was there. "It was a guy from the Bahamas—in a yacht—who was reading one of her minibooks and having trouble with his kids," Steltemeier told me in a giddy wheeze. "He said he was going to send her a donation: six hundred thousand dollars."

"Can you send it right now?" Mother asked the caller.

By lunchtime the money had been wired to her account and the equipment was unloaded.

On Sunday, March 8, the satellite dish dangled from a borrowed crane in the sisters' sloping backyard. Trees had been cleared on the periphery to allow the transmitter unimpeded passage to the cloudless blue skies above. The nuns stood on the sidelines, praying as each piece of the uplink was lowered into place.

"It was like our little firstborn back there," Sister Regina recalled. "We felt like spiritual mothers. There was something very special about that dish."

Like a spider inspecting a newly spun web, John Scalici, Matt's brother, hung from the end of the crane, appraising the great white bowl pointed to the heavens. Matt snapped a picture to capture the moment. When developed, the photo revealed a transparent red streak, like a laser beam, emitting from the center of the satellite dish. Skeptics would write off the red band in the photograph as overexposure or sun flares, but to Mother and her compatriots, it was divine confirmation of Sister Regina's vision—a supernatural manifestation of the never-to-be-extinguished flame of the Word. The photograph became an immediate inspirational icon, and it hangs in the network offices to this day.

Bad news traveled the phone lines to Mother Angelica on March 19. It was the secretary of the Papal representative in Washington calling. Having received her plea to speak outside the cloister, the nuncio forwarded his official response: "Obey the bishop and help the U.S. bishops." In a letter received subsequently, Archbishop Pio Laghi again suggested that Mother seek exclaustration, and he formally denied her travel request. Confined to the cloister, with no money to cover employees' salaries, Angelica turned to Bill Steltemeier.

To convey the urgency of the moment and the very real possibility of bankruptcy, Steltemeier hopped a plane from Nashville to Birmingham and begged Bishop Vath to reconsider his decision. But there was nothing the bishop could do, since the prime mover in this case was Rome, not Vath. To retain the staff for the rest of 1981, Steltemeier paid network salaries out of his own pocket.

In the meantime, Peter Grace offered some relief by granting Mother Angelica a $635,000 loan for two years at a rate of 7 percent. According to Dick DeGraff, who later worked for Grace, the billionaire adored Angelica and her dream network, but the people in his foundation were concerned about EWTN's fiscal solvency.

"I told Mother we needed a budget," DeGraff recalled. "She said, 'No, a budget is the devil's handiwork. We live on faith.' She had some crazy idea that you didn't need a budget. It was absolute presumption, in my opinion." But Angelica viewed budgets as limiting God's generosity and she adamantly refused to ever implement one.

In May, Mother realized that she would need assistance from someone in the Vatican to free herself from the travel prohibition. The nuns were at a loss, until they read of a catechetical conference in New York to be given by a high-ranking Vatican official, Cardinal Silvio Oddi, head of the Sacred Congregation for the Clergy. Though it was a long shot, perhaps he could intervene on Mother's behalf and secure the permissions she needed to finish building the network. It was imperative that she meet the cardinal face-to-face, and show him the facility if possible. Since Angelica could not go to him, Bill Steltemeier flew to New York to bring the mountain to Muhammad.

Steltemeier staked out Cardinal Oddi, planting himself in the first row of the conference for three days. As instructed by Mother Angelica, he ran rosary beads through his fingers, staring holes in the short, bald cardinal with a neck like a fire hydrant. At the conclusion of one of the talks, Steltemeier seized his moment with Oddi. No doubt distracted by the lawyer's bizarre attentions, the cardinal was curious.

"Your Eminence, Mother Angelica is building the first Catholic satellite network in the United States, and I need you to come down to see it in Birmingham." Steltemeier fleetly rattled away, turning on his persuasive Southern charm. "We're having a little trouble with the bishop. Could you please come down and give us your blessing?"

"I cannot. I have to leave tomorrow night for Rome," the cardinal replied in broken English.

Not missing a beat, Steltemeier leapt in. "I can get a Learjet, fly you down, and get you back in time for your flight." A fixed smile punctuated the offer.

The worn-down cardinal consented to the trip. Steltemeier reserved a plane through his law firm, and he and Oddi flew to Birmingham on May 21. Assured of Oddi's coming, Mother Angelica sent Dick DeGraff to Rome to follow up personally on what she hoped would be a positive visit for the cardinal. Angelica would leave no base uncovered.

The nuns and the staff, in their Sunday best, formed a receiving line when Cardinal Oddi drove up. As if they had known each other forever, Mother linked arms with the cardinal and led him through the print shop and studio, pointing out all that God had allowed. They then dodged the grazing sheep in the backyard to view the pièce de résistance: the satellite dish. Bill Steltemeier swung a censer, wafting trails of fragrant smoke as the cardinal blessed the earth station. Oddi later wrote in the monastery guest book:

I am happy to bless this initiative which will undoubtedly produce abundant fruits in the field of evangelization. . . . The Church should be the first to utilize the modern methods of transmission. May the Lord reward most generously this small group of consecrated nuns who have dedicated themselves with such strong faith to the accomplishment of this work.

"What do you want? What do you need?" Oddi asked at the conclusion of his visit.

Angelica and Steltemeier told him of the dire financial situation, Mother's need to travel, and the difficulties with Bishop Vath.

"I take care. Me fix it," the cardinal promised.

At the Vatican, Oddi assured the waiting Dick DeGraff that he would take care of everything. Within days, EWTN's new cardinal protector visited the Congregation for Religious, securing the exemptions from Church law that Mother desired. On June 10, formal permission to leave the monastery on network business, without jeopardizing her consecrated status, was granted for a three-year period.

The tenacious fifty-eight-year-old abbess, fortified by her steely faith, had demolished another obstacle. Her mission had been hampered but not stopped.

"The need we have for assurance and the absolute lack of willingness to take a risk for God is appalling to me. I'm sure our Lord asked a lot of people to build a network. There has to be a reason that He chose a few nuns who didn't know anything, in the wrong state of life, with no money, because it goes against reason," Mother Angelica explained to me. "The Bible says that God chooses the weak to confound the strong. Some people say I am a woman of great faith. I'm really a coward who keeps moving forward."

EWTN

EWTN WAS ENVISIONED as a "spiritual growth network," "a supplement to, not a substitute for, the Church." The mission statement of the Eternal Word Television Network clearly stated its dedication "to the advancement of truth as defined by the Magisterium of the Roman Catholic Church . . . to serve the orthodox belief and teaching of the Church as proclaimed by the Supreme Pontiff and his predecessors." It would be a "means by which the various organizations within the Church [would] have a nation-wide vehicle of expression . . . as long as their spirituality remain[ed] within the theological context of Mother Church." EWTN would be "media for orthodox endeavors," even as Mother's approach was profoundly unorthodox by almost any accepted business standard.

The network was to exist solely on the contributions of viewers. There would be no advertising, no shilling for funds, and no toll-free donation lines. "I feel in my heart that if I am more concerned with their souls and their happiness, and their family life . . . I think they will be inspired by God to give without me asking," Angelica told a cable magazine in 1981.

In the lead-up to the launch, Mother Angelica appeared on *Good Morning America,* the *Today* show, and on the front page of the *Wall Street Journal,* hawking her network and faith in divine providence. On August 15, the feast of the Assumption, Bishop Vath, the board of governors, Mother Angelica, and her sisters gathered in the chapel to prepare for EWTN's maiden broadcast. The bishop intoned a prayer, then joined a procession, led by a team of flag-bearers, to the control room.

Walking beside Sister Mary David's wheelchair, Angelica

clutched the hand of her doubting mother. Trailing behind them was the spent crew, who had worked late into the night, editing, scheduling, and shooting programs to fulfill EWTN's four-hour daily (seven days a week) programming commitment. Tom Kennedy and some of the Catholic missionaries carried banners while Harry John, Joe Bruno, and other benefactors joined the line of witnesses. Believers like Jean Morris stood shoulder-to-shoulder with some who never thought they would see the day, and who doubted Angelica's ability to sustain the network.

Mother squeezed through the crowd blocking the door to the control room. Fighting back tears, she offered her own prayerful composition:

O God, Lord of heaven and earth, You alone have accomplished all we have done. May this first Catholic Satellite Television Network be a tribute to the beauty of Your Church. May Your Son, the Eternal Word, be glorified through this great work of Your hands. Bless all the programs that will issue forth from its facilities. Just as Your Word issues forth from You, Lord Father, may that same Word touch each heart that listens to this network. Let Thy Spirit work with freedom through every teacher who proclaims Thy truth and Thy Church. Bestow upon this network the power to inspire men to seek holiness of heart, zeal for the extension of Thy Church, courage to seek after justice and human rights, and the patience to endure persecution. May Thy Paternal Blessing always rest upon it. Amen

Mother Angelica slashed the ribbon, entered the cramped control room, and sat before the operations console. At 6:00 P.M., she threw the switch, bouncing the signal up to Westar III, a secondary satellite accessed by few cable operators. The handful of viewers watching that first night saw a documentary on the Shroud of Turin; an introduction to the network by Mother Angelica; an old Bishop Sheen program; *Mother Angelica Presents,* featuring the nun speaking before a live crowd; an interview with Mother Teresa; and a Russian dance festival hosted by that great master of the dance, Orson Welles.

"Even though we were small and some people didn't like what we were doing, and most people thought it wouldn't work, I felt sure at that point that somehow it would be a great instrument in the Lord's hands. I was starting a new way to evangelize," Mother Angelica said of the first broadcast. "In that little studio, pulling that switch, I knew that the Lord could reach the world and every part of it. That was the day I was sure He was going to make it work."

Two months after the launch, only six cable systems, reaching about 300,000 homes, were airing EWTN's programming. Professionally, the network was not exactly up to industry standards. Early programming guides reveal a schedule stacked with studio lecture series, old movies, and syndicated programs from the 1950s and 1960s. *I Married Joan, Lassie, Robin Hood, Wok with Yan,* Bob Hope movies, and World War II musicals were shuffled with Catholic spiritual programming to fill out the grid. When she could, Mother personally finagled limited runs of films like *Joan of Arc* or *A Man for All Seasons,* but most of the time EWTN aired whatever was cheap and available.

Mother and Ginny Dominick essentially ran the network in 1981. The pair conferred on all aspects of operations and production, and shared a close professional and spiritual bond.

"Ginny was the daughter Mother never had," Marynell Ford, a future VP of marketing, observed. "There was a close relationship there, and I think in her heart of hearts Mother had a hope that Ginny would become a nun."

The tall, sandy blonde is remembered by early employees as a strong-willed, sensitive individual, unafraid to speak her mind and occasionally challenge Mother. For instance, Dominick opposed the idea of a satellite network before and after the launch. She felt Mother should continue producing her own show, but avoid producing less worthy programs featuring others in order to fill a broadcast schedule. Apparently, Angelica disagreed.

By the fall of 1981 the EWTN crew had swelled to twenty. Among the new family members was Chris Harrington, a Mississippi Catholic with a degree in broadcasting, who came to intern at the network and stayed for more than twenty years. A caring, stout, freckled soul with Coke-bottle glasses, Harrington quickly absorbed EWTN's mission, making it her own. For many of these early employees, as for the Tonys back in Canton, part of the mission was to please and win the personal approval of Mother Angelica.

"What I demand of the crew here is total commitment," Mother told a reporter in the 1980s.

Most of the original employees were Baptists who disagreed with key tenets of the Catholic faith. But they loved Mother Angelica. Their affection for her overcame any divisions and allowed them to work wholeheartedly for a Catholic corporation. They followed Mother's every order and never missed her Friday spiritual lesson. This ecumenical holdover from Angelica's days of leading the Bible study in her monastery parlor forged a kind of religious unity among the staff, a unity much needed, given the constantly shifting roles and responsibilities.

"No one ever had one job," Matt Scalici confessed, laughing. "We did whatever Mother wanted us to do at the time. Early on, I remember shearing the sheep."

Like everything else at EWTN, job duties evolved, as did the CEO.

To balance the demands of the cloister with those of the network, Mother Angelica set limits from the beginning. Time reserved for work in the cloister was spent at the network; all other times, including meals, recreation, and community prayer, would find her back in the cloister with her nuns.

"I always knew the sisters had to keep their cloistered life, because to me that was the backbone of anything we tried to do at the network," Mother insisted. "Without that, it would have just disintegrated."

Mother Angelica still oversaw the formation of the nuns, offered a daily lesson, and personally created a schedule for each sister. The nuns uniformly agree that the work of their abbess did not intrude upon their life in the cloister.

"I think the Lord gave me the grace to concentrate on the network, with all its multitudinous details, and then go back to the monastery and drop everything," Mother said. "Once there, I was not CEO; I was abbess. I had to be what the Lord wanted me to be in that moment."

With the network up and running, Mother's next task was to sell the EWTN concept to cable operators and secure a place on their individual systems. In 1981, cable television was in its infancy. The watershed Home Box Office live broadcast of the Ali-Frazier "Thrilla in Manila" heavyweight bout in 1975 set off the premium programming craze and started the race to cable television. If enough cable operators made room on their systems for a given signal, a satellite start-up could become a national network overnight. C-Span, Nickelodeon, CBN, ESPN, and Showtime had already been on the air for a couple of years by the time Mother Angelica got into the game. CNN had launched the year before and was still looking for subscribers.

Unlike most of her peers, Mother offered her network to operators free of charge. And though this was a big plus, there were drawbacks: Her network lacked the flash and instant appeal of other niche broadcasters, and EWTN was only available on a secondary cable satellite.

The first cable networks delivered programming by regional microwave transmission or "bicycled" tapes to local cable companies. That all changed in the early 1980s, when Home Box Office, Ted Turner, Mother Angelica, and others tried to convince cable operators to do something novel: invest $75,000 to $250,000 in a receiver satellite dish to pull programming from the skies. It was a whole new means of delivery, and the industry needed convincing.

To make the case, Mother Angelica became an annual fixture at cable conventions throughout the 1980s. Prowling the convention halls, she extolled the miracle of EWTN and the benefits of satellite delivery.

"Mother and Ted Turner were quite parallel in what they were doing at the time," observed Robert Corazzini, the lawyer they shared. "The two of them kind of played off of each other at the cable conventions, without having a formal relationship. Ted Turner was the likable bad boy, and right behind him, in her habit, came Mother Angelica, his total opposite."

The pair drew eyes. While big players like Turner convinced the cable operators to purchase their downlink satellites for purely financial reasons, Mother Angelica made them feel good about doing it. She rode the coattails of the big networks by proximity, while providing the cable industry with a benign religious presence that cable operators with small-town sensibilities could relate to. The one advantage Angelica always had over her competition was Angelica.

"She was more interesting for who she was, rather than for what she was selling," Bob Corazzini said of Angelica's convention visits. "And she understood that."

Squeezed into the corner of the Southern Satellite Systems booth she shared, sitting at a card table covered with her mini-books, Mother enchanted cable operators with personalized versions of the network's founding. Her humble beginning with two hundred dollars and no experience, the battle over *The Word,* and the decision to turn the garage into a studio were recounted until they crystallized into something approaching myth.

Angelica knew how to hold a crowd, or break one up. Finding herself before the *Playboy* booth one year, Mother, another nun, and Bill Steltemeier convened an impromptu rosary rally. As they prayed aloud, embarrassed patrons scattered and a few bunnies scampered for cover. "The girls with rabbit tails would see me coming and they'd turn around because they were half-dressed. Of course, I didn't think the back was any better than the front," Mother recalled. "I'd go up and give them a Sacred Heart badge, and they didn't know what to do with me." For her, the conversation was perfectly natural, like being a kid back on the venal streets of Canton. The iconic clash of a fully habited nun conversing with the scantily clad embodiment of sexual liberty no doubt attracted attention.

Along with the passersby on the convention floor, the Catholic bishops were also taking note of Mother Angelica. And some did not like what they saw.

A Threat from Within

WORD HAD REACHED EWTN that Mother was being derided as a schismatic, "a proud and disobedient nun" acting in defiance of the bishops. Bill Steltemeier and others believed that the statements originated not with the bishops themselves but with officials at the United States Catholic Conference, the bishops' bureaucratic entity in Washington, D.C., piloted by clerics and laymen.

Tension between Mother Angelica and the bishops conference was inevitable. The same year she founded EWTN, the U.S. bishops launched their own foray into cable television: the Catholic Telecommunications Network of America.

CTNA was a for-profit satellite-distribution network chartered to provide Catholic programming to dioceses around the country. At the time, it was the most expensive project ever undertaken by the bishops, carrying a price tag of $4.5 million in start-up costs alone. Through the sale of specialized services like teleconferencing, and by levying an annual five-thousand-dollar fee on network affiliates, CTNA intended to be self-sustaining in three years' time. Where EWTN went directly to viewers via cable, CTNA could be seen only by local bishops—or at least those bishops willing to expend capital on a receiving dish.

Getting 370 bishops to agree on magisterial teaching was difficult enough, but getting them to agree on what constituted Catholic programming was nearly impossible. To resolve the impasse, the bishops created a gatekeeper system, whereby they could individually control programming decisions. Diocesan affiliates received the daily CTNA feed; then the local bishop would determine which if any programming merited broadcast on his station.

"It was a flawed design from the start," Father Robert Bonnot, who later became president and CEO of CTNA, told me. "The irony of it was they were very concerned about gatekeeping their own network, and here was this nun in Alabama who could care less what the bishops wanted to have happen. Clearly, she was going out and doing what she needed to do to get on cable systems. CTNA was not free to do that."

Those running the bishops' network quickly realized that cable was the place to be, but Mother Angelica was already there. She was "the Catholic personality on the scene, much more than the bishops" in the opinion of Father Bonnot. This prominence diverted potential CTNA resources to EWTN and established a Catholic center of power and influence independent of the bishops' conference, fueling animosity. Privately, Mother and those in her camp feared CTNA's entry into the cable arena. After all, how many Catholic networks would the marketplace support or tolerate?

Publicly, Angelica dismissed what she called the "grossly exaggerated" rivalry between the two networks. "[CTNA] is a diocesan network [beaming] directly to dioceses—programs are scrambled for an exclusive audience," she told the *Los Angeles Times*. "Our programs are free and go directly to the people in their homes. It's like comparing the *Los Angeles Times* to the candy shop."

Acknowledged or not, the rivalry existed and battle lines formed. In the summer of 1981, a full year before CTNA actually began broadcasting, Richard Hirsh, the secretary of communications for the bishops conference, suggested in an interview that EWTN represented a "needless duplication" of Catholic media efforts. He went on to lament the fact that there was "no official contact with [Mother Angelica] whatsoever."

"I have absolutely no problem with the bishops," Angelica explained to a reporter. "I do not feel obligated to render an account to the USCC which is a lay entity." Announcing her network plans, she wrote a letter directly to every bishop in the United States, asking them to "suggest activities in your diocese that you would like to see broadcast nationwide on EWTN." Flouting the bishops' bureaucratic apparatus in Washington did not exactly endear the nun to the USCC staff. One anonymous USCC critic opined in the Catholic press, "Cloistered nuns should stay in their monasteries and not get involved in stuff like this."

The condescending tone of this criticism and others like it over the years revealed a discomfort, not only with Angelica's approach but, perhaps on a deeper level, with a woman providing leadership in a male-dominated Church. Calls for the admittance of women to the clergy and the ecclesiastic power structure had been sounding in Catholicism for more than a decade. But confronted with the reality of a traditional, orthodox woman wielding influence over the masses was too much for even feminist advocates to take. The added insult of Angelica's having accomplished this feat without earning the academic degrees so cherished by the Church structure at the time only widened the chasm between the nun and her detractors.

In the fall of 1981, Richard Hirsh and Father John Geaney, president of the Catholic communicators association, UNDA, undertook a peacekeeping reconnaissance mission to EWTN.

Father Geaney hoped the visit would answer some questions. "At the time, it was: Why do we need this—particularly her type of theology? Is this a good representation of the Church in terms of what the bishops and UNDA were trying to do? We were trying to present the Church in its fullness." The apparent supposition was that Angelica broadcast a narrow version of the faith and that only expert consultation could help.

By all indications, the meeting was amicable, albeit tense. Mother told "charming stories" about the origins of the place and asserted her view that EWTN could never be "run by a committee." The visitors admitted their frustration with the CTNA model and proffered the hope of future collaboration.

In February, Mother was invited to meet in Washington with a group of bishops overseeing Church media efforts. The president of the bishops conference, Bishop Louis Gelineau of Providence, Rhode Island, led the discussions. He assured Mother that there was no competition between EWTN and CTNA, listened to her well-honed stories, and asked the size of the network's budget.

"Well, Bishop, I don't have a budget," the nun said, to the delight of the handful of cuff-linked businessmen and bishops around the table.

"You have to have a budget in the television business. You can't operate without a budget, Mother," Bishop Gelineau said.

"Bishop, let me ask you what you mean by a budget." Mother Angelica eyed the others at the table. "I started off this year with three hundred thousand dollars in the bank. Now what do you think I had to take in last year to have three hundred thousand dollars in the bank?"

There was mumbling on all sides. "Six hundred thousand dollars?" the bishop offered, playing along.

"You see, Bishop, that's the point. The Lord gave me two million. If I had had your budget, I would've lost one point four million dollars."

"You should have heard them laugh," Bill Steltemeier told me. "They wished us well—I don't think they meant it, but they wished us well—and we left."

At the beginning of 1982, EWTN signed a contract with Wold Communications in Los Angeles to access the Westar IV satellite. The agreement stipulated that no pornographic content could follow or precede EWTN's nightly feed. Angelica's concern was that viewers watching EWTN's four-hour broadcast on a given channel not be subjected to salacious material either before or after her broadcasts. Whatever the satellite provider scheduled to bookend EWTN's programming would appear to be part of the Catholic channel's feed. Both parties agreed to the morality clause, and Mother signed the deal, even though the Wold monthly fees were more expensive than her previous satellite lease.

The sisters became aware of EWTN's financial bleed in March 1982. The stress of the ballooning debt compounded by tens of thousands spent each month caused Angelica to weep openly during supper. She told the nuns in the refectory that they were bankrupt. Unless $350,000 could be located quickly, the bank would take control of the network. Telegrams were sent out to big donors and prayers were fervently renewed.

Sister Mary David's health plummeted along with the finances. Returning from a Las Vegas cable convention and an appearance on *The Mike Douglas Show*, Mother found Mary David "stunned and starry eyed," according to Sister Raphael. The elderly nun had been struck by "several small strokes" and her hip pain had worsened.

To alleviate Sister David's suffering, Dr. Rex Harris, a bone specialist and visitor to the monastery, convinced the nun to have her dislocated hip prosthesis removed. After thirteen years of refusing to speak to a doctor, taking only aspirin to dull her pain, she agreed to the surgery.

At the hospital, Mary David's high blood pressure, and a seizure, caused the surgery to be delayed. By May 20, her condition had rapidly deteriorated and death seemed imminent. Holy oils were administered and the sisters prayed for their departing member. Then quite suddenly, the fiery nun rallied, cheating death and surprising the community. About a week later, doctors proceeded with Sister David's hip surgery.

Providence and Mother Angelica's donors had saved the network at the end of March. Less than a month after the urgent appeals for cash had gone out, the needed $350,000 trickled in from all over the country. Mother's "miracle a day" rolled on. But before she could recover from the latest financial crisis, Angelica embraced another, this one triggered by a deal that would make EWTN available to every cable system in the country.

During Sister David's health woes, a transmissions broker offered Mother eighty-eight hours on the most esteemed satellite in cable television: RCA's Satcom IIIR. "Now that's providence," Mother told a reporter in 1982. "Nobody gets on Satcom anymore; it's filled. And if there was the tiniest bit of space, believe me, you wouldn't get it—so we never even looked."

Relocating EWTN to the Satcom satellite meant access to nearly six times the number of cable systems (4,600) and a possible audience of 20 million households (up from 1.5 million on Westar). Even with the intimidating monthly transponder fee of $132,000, Mother Angelica was certain that this was where God wanted the network. She signed the contract on June 14, 1982, breaching the Wold contract, which had been signed earlier that year. Unable to afford two satellite leases, she unloaded one. Executives at EWTN contended the breach was justified due to a contract violation by Wold. Regardless of the consequences—and they were to be severe—EWTN was now part of the cable industry's number one satellite.

Sister Mary David's frequent outbursts in the cloister offended no one more than Sister Raphael. So as a sort of penance, the nun willingly slept on a cot at St. Vincent's night after night, attending to Mary David after her surgery.

In her fear and frustration, Sister David would spit her food across the hospital room or chastise Sister Raphael for lacking brains. It took everything for the vicar to maintain her toothy smile.

But as the weeks unfolded, Sister Raphael actually found herself growing attached to David. "As she grew to depend on me, my love and compassion grew until I found the thought of losing her almost unbearable," Raphael wrote of the old sister. The feeling was mutual. In the summer of 1982, Sister David began to call Raphael "Mama."

Once back at the monastery, David's old fears returned. So did her panic. In mid-August, she told her "mama" in a quivering voice, "Oh, Raphael, you're going to lose your David!"

"No, I'm not going to lose you. You'll always belong to me." Raphael's words had a sedating effect. But Sister David knew the end was near, and that knowledge plunged her into a painful introspection. Mae Gianfrancesco's wounds, tended for decades like mementos in a cedar chest, were suddenly unpacked by Sister Mary David. Lying in what she knew would be her deathbed, it all came back: the abuse inflicted by her husband, the missed education, the struggle to survive, the abandonment by her "ungrateful" daughter thirty-eight years ago.

Mother Angelica's arrival in her room interrupted the cascade of memories. But caught up in the past, Mary David could muster no greeting, only a grave question: "Why did you leave me?"

The wound of rejection bled, fresh as the day it had been inflicted. Even after sharing twenty years of religious life beneath the same roof, Mae could not accept Rita's sudden departure from her life. Soon, Mother Angelica would know exactly how she felt.

12
Death and the Dark Night

PERSPIRATION DOTTED Mother Angelica's forehead, testifying to the physical and spiritual exertion of the moment. Kneeling beside her mother's sickbed, she begged God for more time and thanked Him for the extension He had already granted.

Just minutes earlier on that Friday, August 20, Sister Raphael had clopped into the monastery apartment to check on Sister Mary David. From the door, she saw the sleeping nun's colorless pallor and taut expression. Leaning close to the bed, she was certain her "little David" had stopped breathing.

The gangly vicar scurried into the hall and paged Mother Angelica on the house phone. Spotting the abbess, she sputtered, "[David's] dead of heart failure," and ran for the doctor and a priest. Tears of loss welled up in Angelica's eyes, then a look of determination. She darted to Mary David's bed, grasping her mother's shoulders.

"Sister don't go—oh David! David!" Angelica shouted, shaking her mother hard. "Lord, You can't take her now. Please don't take her now. She's not ready yet. Please don't take her now." Mother Angelica continued joggling the old woman, fearful that she would die with "hatred in her heart" and face her Maker carrying unresolved "bitterness and anger" toward her former husband, John Rizzo.

Sister Mary David's eyes fluttered. She slowly regained consciousness and returned to the living. By the time Sister Raphael appeared in the doorway with Dr. Rex Harris, Mother Angelica was on her knees in prayerful Thanksgiving. "The air was just heavy, and I knew we were in the presence of God," Dr. Harris remembered. "It was just this absolutely incredible experience."

Rising to her feet like a woozy prizefighter in the twelfth round, Angelica told Dr. Harris and Sister Raphael, "I have asked the Lord to leave her with me for twenty-four hours." She would take it upon herself to prepare Sister David's soul for eternity, mothering Mae to the very threshold of death.

Once during Sister Mary David's final days, perhaps in response to her daughter's prayers, she bolted up in bed and focused on the door, as if a stranger had entered unannounced. Her nurse, Dorothy, saw no one. "You look so beautiful," David said dreamily, staring at the door. To Angelica, it was a sign that her mother had finally reconciled with John Rizzo. The last obstacle to Mae's passage had been removed.

On Sunday, following an examination, Dr. Harris told the nuns that Sister Mary David was moments from death. Fluid had filled her lungs and her heart was starting to collapse. Mother Angelica and Sister Raphael, sitting on the edge of the bed, helped Mary David renew her vows. As the formula was hastily repeated, the other nuns streamed in to pray for their fading sister. To fulfill David's wish to die before her Lord, Sister Michael carried the Blessed Sacrament to her room in a small metal case.

Tears spotting her polyester habit, Angelica clutched Mary David's hands and elevated the Host before her mother's tired eyes. "Oh David. Jesus loves you. I love you," she said again and again, kissing Mae's cheek. "Oh Mother, Mother." Her voice pinched with sorrow, Angelica watched Mae's eyes shift from the Host to her own moist face and back again. The pain, the sorrow, the regret that Mother Angelica had worked her whole life to dispel slipped away with Sister Mary David at nine P.M. on August 22.

"Mother yelled out 'Mama' and started to cry one of the heaviest cries," Sister Regina recalled. "It was the cry of a daughter losing her mother, and you could really see she was losing a part of herself."

"I cried for three days, because in spite of her harshness and her lack of encouragement, I loved her because she stayed with me," Mother Angelica said, looking past me, a hint of melancholy in her voice. "She loved me in her way."

Angelica's grief exploded at the funeral. She lamented the life her mother might have had, and perhaps her own inability to deliver Mae from the inner demons that tormented her. The abbess had given it her best, but in the end, Mae had been incapable of change. Beneath a canopy of solemn hymns sung by her employees, Mother Angelica reluctantly released the last link to her childhood, the final member of her immediate family.

Kneeling in the crypt before her mother's marble marker inscribed with words from Isaiah—"One thing I ask of the Lord, this I seek, to live in the House of the Lord all the days of my life"—Angelica was disconsolate. She privately grieved for hours on end, buckling under the weight of her loss.

When she surfaced at the network, another burden awaited her: the $132,000 monthly bill for transmission on the Satcom satellite. The arrangement put EWTN in a catch-22. They needed the more expensive satellite to build an audience, but the donor base was not expanding sufficiently to support the exorbitant overhead.

In August 1982, donations were so scant that Bill Steltemeier took out a personal loan of $66,000 to pay part of the monthly transponder bill. And though offerings eventually covered the loan, Steltemeier would repeat the desperate act before year's end.

Weeks later, in the midst of EWTN's cash crunch, the Catholic Telecommunications Network of America (CTNA), the bishops' fledgling satellite start-up, hit the airwaves. Though visible to only a few diocesan stations and a handful of homes, it posed an ominous threat from EWTN's perspective. According to records, Mother Angelica was told at the time that CTNA's intention could be to "absorb" her network and "take it over" at the first opportunity. If the bishops shifted strategy, taking their signal directly to cable systems, EWTN could be evicted from the airwaves. Lacking CTNA's imprimatur, Angelica's network would be seen as an interloper. With a little political pressure from the bishops conference, EWTN might be edged off cable systems and replaced with the bishops' feed. At least that was the fear within the EWTN camp. Interviews suggest that there were voices within CTNA urging direct distribution to cable operators, but how close this was to becoming a reality is hard to establish.

Mother Angelica viewed the competition between the networks as a struggle for the future of the Catholic Church in America. "Whoever has the media will have the Church," she told a consultant in October 1982. Mother believed EWTN represented the "voice of the Pope" in a Church confused about its future and forgetful of its past. Theologians, priests, laity, and even a few bishops openly agitated for optional celibacy for priests, changes in the Church's sexual teaching, and greater lay control of Church governance.

Concerned that these dissenting voices would find airtime on CTNA's feed, Angelica locked her sights on the new network. Some of the programs focused heavily on the social Gospel, downplaying the Church's moral teaching. Nuns and priests appeared on documentaries and talk shows in secular garb—an image that Angelica believed would confuse the laity and normalize progressive innovations. To keep CTNA in a holding pattern, isolated from cable operators, and to exercise some control over their programming, Angelica and her team devised a plan: She would cooperate with the bishops' TV venture by offering them an hour of free airtime each day. The access to EWTN's viewers would satisfy CTNA's craving to be seen on cable while granting Mother the prerogative to screen the content of their feed. To the public and the Vatican, Mother Angelica would be seen as establishing a working relationship with the bishops conference. She made the offer and awaited the bishops' response.

On November 12, dingy clouds dropped rain on St. Peter's Square, obscuring the morning sunlight. Mother Angelica and Sister Joseph, carrying a replica of their satellite dish, found cover beneath Bernini's colonnade as the runoff cleansed the cobblestones of the piazza. After a long wait outside the bronze doors, they climbed the smooth, shallow marble steps of the Apostolic Palace. It was to be Angelica's first personal encounter with Pope John Paul II. More than a personal pilgrimage, this was her chance to "present the Eternal Word Television Network to [the Pope] to use in any way he sees fit."

Following Mass in the Pope's private chapel, Mother Angelica extended the satellite miniature to the Pontiff. John Paul's eyes narrowed mischievously when he spotted the nun and her dish. "I have heard about you," the Pope said with a knowing smile. "You do good work."

Angelica sensed an instant bond. "I've always felt that the Holy Father understood what we were trying to do and why," she said of their first meeting. The photograph of that visit and the Pope's words would become important endorsements during a period of uncertainty for EWTN.

For the remainder of her Roman sojourn, Angelica met with Vatican officials. Her cardinal protector, Silvio Oddi, during one meeting advised her to reject any programming not in conformity with papal teaching. "Don't air it," the cardinal is quoted as saying. Mother and her network had been drafted into the cold war between the Vatican and an unruly American bishops conference.

Back in the United States, the bishops had yet to respond to Mother's offer of free airtime, but they had suggested a liaison meeting in December to further dialogue between EWTN and CTNA.

At the December 15 meeting in Washington, CTNA officials and bishops on the board raised an objection to EWTN touting itself as "the Catholic network," since it carried no imprimatur from the bishops. They were similarly perturbed that Mother Angelica had initiated a cable service without first consulting them. But as a member of a pontifical order, she did not need their sanction, so long as she had the approval of Rome. Steltemeier returned fire, producing letters illustrating how CTNA officials had actively dissuaded bishops from appearing on EWTN programs. Charges as well as financial reports were exchanged. In the end, the meeting only increased suspicion between the two organizations and confirmed the financial instability of Mother's prime competitor.

"CTNA was undercapitalized, so it was kind of dead from the beginning," Bishop Robert Lynch of St. Petersburg said of the network he would later oversee as general secretary of the bishops conference. To complicate matters, dioceses were still not signing up for the broadcast service, throwing off revenue projections. Sources reveal CTNA was hundreds of thousands of dollars in debt and had already burned through more than a million dollars by 1982. Poor finances were by no means restricted to CTNA. While Mother pushed the bishops to accept her offer of free airtime, EWTN struggled for solvency, as well.

In early December, Bill Steltemeier took out a $132,000 loan against his savings to pay a delinquent transponder bill; at the time, EWTN was operating under an outstanding debt of $2 million. By the end of the month, a new bill was due. Mother called Harry John of the De Rance Foundation and asked him to sign for a $130,000 loan. He consented, but the local bank refused to release the funds, certain that Mother would be unable to pay them back. Again she called Harry John. "I'll lose the network Monday without the money," she told him.

"We don't want that to happen, Mother. The network is important. We don't want you to lose it." Harry John loaned her the $130,000 dollars from his personal reserve, interest-free. The tortuous drama would play out every thirty days for years to come. "Every month we agonize over the payment of this huge sum in order to stay on the air," Sister Raphael wrote in 1983. "It is a heavy burden."

The spring brought a round of honors for Mother Angelica. She was named Italian American Woman of the Year in New Orleans, received an honorary doctorate in theology from the Franciscan University of Steubenville on May 7, and later that month received the John Paul II Religious Freedom Award from the Catholic League. Another unexpected surprise arrived at the monastery on May 11, complete with a police escort: a summons from Wold Communications demanding $1,440,000 for breach of contract.

According to Matt Scalici, EWTN's engineer, Mother Angelica had pulled the plug on the Wold deal when she discovered that EROS, a soft-core-porn channel, appeared in close proximity to EWTN's four-hour programming block, in violation of their agreement. She had conveniently found carriage on a better satellite in June 1982. A month later, pleased with the new arrangement,

Mother had instructed Bill Steltemeier to terminate the Wold contract, contending that the transponder was "bleeding pornography"
near her signal. Whatever the explanation for the withdrawal,
EWTN now faced a massive lawsuit and financial ruin.

Months of negotiations culminated in a June 1 meeting in Los
Angeles between Wold lawyers and EWTN. Bill Steltemeier,
Mother Angelica, and Sister Joseph were speeding to the meeting
in a cab when Mother spotted a church. She asked the driver to
pull over. In the darkened nave, the trio knelt in prayer.

After several minutes, Mother, her eyes closed in contempla-
tion, whispered to Steltemeier, "You go; I'm going to pray."

"Don't leave me," Steltemeier hissed in protest. "They're expecting you. They don't want to see me; they want to see you."

"We'll stay and talk to Jesus. You go. It'll be okay." Mother Angelica and Sister Joseph remained in place, untroubled and immovable. Defeated, Steltemeier snatched his briefcase and hoofed it up
the aisle.

Wold lawyers and executives met Steltemeier for a three-hour
negotiation. Steltemeier was clear that EWTN did not have the requested funds and simply could not comply with the conditions of
the settlement. Wold initially demanded that EWTN pay the $1.4
million penalty for breaking the contract, then unexpectedly softened its position.

"A miracle took place before my eyes," Steltemeier said. "They
agreed to settle for two hundred and fifty thousand dollars." What's
more, Steltemeier convinced Wold to stagger the payments over a
two-and-a-half-year period.

A beaming Steltemeier ran back to the church to report the final
settlement to Mother and Sister Joseph. When Angelica heard the
news, she turned toward the tabernacle. "Oh, thank you, Jesus. I
knew you'd do it," she said. The principals agree that Angelica's
faith contributed to the outcome, but on a natural level, Steltemeier's legal savvy and unflagging determination certainly had
some influence. The network president had perfected a cornpone
gullibility that led adversaries to underestimate his prowess. Be-

neath Steltemeier's laid-back Nashville exterior was a mind as sharp as his crooked canines.

"Without Bill's legal mind and his common sense, we would not have survived," Dick DeGraff affirmed. "Steltemeier was the layman that made that network go."

Mother Angelica Live

IN AUGUST 1983, on the second anniversary of the network's founding, Mother Angelica decided to try something new: a live program. Standing before oversized pictures of her meeting with the Pope, a monstrance, and a satellite dish, and surrounded by a row of fake ferns, Angelica bounced like a giddy girl. Clasping her hands in excitement, she told her audience, "This is our first live, live, I mean really live television program. You know we didn't know whether we were going to do this or not, but we just decided to put both feet in cold water and step forward."

Mother exuded a buoyant euphoria that night, a sense of excited innocence as she plunged into the universe of live talk. To fully explore the interactive possibilities, she agreed to do a series of live show pilots on Tuesday, Wednesday, and Thursday nights in October—just to test the waters.

There were good reasons to present Mother Angelica in a live format. She had a natural rapport with the audience—particularly with callers—and from a marketing perspective, it was crucial that new viewers see Mother Angelica and equate her with the network. By late 1983, ninety-five cable systems in thirty-one states were carrying EWTN, and many viewers were seeing it for the first time.

Fortuitously, the live show evolved just as Mother's national profile was rising. In Hollywood, a film biography was in the works, and screen legend Loretta Young was interested in playing the lead. Beverlee Dean, a former producer at ABC, was shopping Mother's story to several studios. Angelica appeared regularly on national talk shows, and the nuns of Our Lady of the Angels Monastery had just cut an album in Nashville. All the buzz attracted celebrities to

Mother and her new program. The guest roster for the shows included Pat Boone, Chuck Colson, Betty Hutton, and others.

The format, like the host, was straightforward. Mother began the program by chatting with "the family"; then, after a break, she reappeared in an aluminum folding chair surrounded by her audience for a quick Bible study. Back on the brown couch, she interviewed that night's guest and fielded viewers' calls: dispensing spiritual solutions to real-world problems. With few exceptions, the format of *Mother Angelica Live* would remain unchanged for twenty years. There were no scripts, no preplanned questions—no preparations at all, in fact. Mother Angelica would simply join hands with her crew, pronounce a prayer, and then march onto the set for a one-hour high-wire act unparalleled in television.

"The providence of God helps me, 'cause I don't know what to do next," Angelica said of her television technique. "Sometimes I am so dumb-witted or worried or frustrated about something, or just plain sick, that I don't know what to say until that light goes on. And I'll do the whole hour program and they'll laugh and they'll cry . . . and I had nothing to do with it."

On October 19, money had again dried up. For the first time in two years, Mother broke her own rule and asked viewers for funds. After explaining her dependence on divine providence, she said, "You the people are part of that Providence. If you want to see these programs continue, we need help this week to go on."

Days later, Harry John agreed to send her $120,000 to meet transponder payments for the month. But unknown to Mother Angelica, her benefactor was planning to mount his own challenge to EWTN: Harry John was building his own Catholic television network.

On October 27, the night of her final live program pilot, Mother Angelica had yet to decide if the live show would continue. "She wasn't sure if she wanted to give up that much of her time," Matt Scalici recalled. "I think her sisters were needing more of her at that point."

In the last half hour of the broadcast, Mother took a call from a boy threatening suicide. His mother dead, his father in the hospital, the boy saw no reason to go on. He claimed to have a pistol pointed at his head. "Put the gun down," Angelica pleaded.

"No," he said.

Mother renewed her plea. She sympathetically counseled the youth and instructed her viewers to pray for the boy's welfare. Through the static of the phone line, the audience heard the gun drop. Sister Raphael's notes provide the only evidence of the suicide call, as the program was subsequently edited. All that remains on tape is a worried Angelica throwing to a station break and then an emotional conclusion. In the show's final moments, Mother reported that a priest, recognizing the boy's voice on TV, had rushed to his home, broken down the door, and restrained the youth as he again attempted suicide. In a prayer of thanksgiving on air, she said, "We just thank you, Lord, that you have used us in some small way. . . . We thank you that we were here in this time of great need for our brother."

The program demonstrated the power of the live show—its ability to reach the spiritually impoverished in the midst of their struggles, and the lifeline it could be to those who were hurting. Angelica and her staff were convinced that *Mother Angelica Live* had to continue.

The Blessing of Money

WILLING TO BET what was left of his stake in the Miller Brewing Company fortune, Harry John impetuously founded Santa Fe Communications, a twenty-four-hour state-of-the-art Catholic cable network. Never mind that he knew virtually nothing about television. Inspired by the example of Pat Robertson, Jim Bakker, and, yes, Mother Angelica, Harry John believed he could improve the Christian TV genre. He immediately purchased the Gower Studios in Hollywood and a chain of satellite studios in Paris, New York, San Francisco, El Paso, and Steubenville, Ohio. Top-flight writers, producers, directors, and technical staff were recruited to man the facilities. The very best equipment lined Santa Fe's control rooms.

Harry John would eventually spend more than $2 million a week on his television colossus. In professional and financial terms, Santa Fe would eclipse anything Mother Angelica or the bishops could devise. John only needed on-air personalities to front his network. Having already invested so much in her, he turned to Mother Angelica.

Always on the lookout for an infusion of cash, Mother struck a deal with John. He could reair her live shows at a cost of two hundred dollars a minute; taped broadcasts for one hundred and fifty dollars per minute. On Mother's order, the EWTN crew worked day and night dubbing the shows, shuttling them to California, "before Harry said stop." Within weeks, Santa Fe was awash in Mother's product.

In January 1984, Harry John stopped the dubbing. By that time, he owed Mother Angelica as much as she owed him. John offered to apply his outstanding payments toward Mother's loan debt and call it even. She accepted. Though Santa Fe was no longer interested in the nun's archive, it would continue to pay for her live broadcasts— a good thing, since Angelica had expansion on her mind.

EWTN was quickly outgrowing its garage-size studio. Mother's permanent set dominated the space, limiting audience capacity and forbidding the production of other programs. "That's when I knew we needed a bigger studio," she said.

In December 1983, Mother told Nelson Campbell, her in-house carpenter, to mark off a fifty- by seventy-foot perimeter, where she envisioned a new studio and attached office space. She suggested he tie white rags around the pine trees to clearly delineate the site.

Days later, a group of bishops recording programs at the network inquired about the ninety white-sashed trees. "We need a new studio and we don't have the money," Mother told them forthrightly. "So I put the rags there to remind the Lord that that's where it should be."

The bishops checked one another's reactions and then one spoke up. "Don't you think He knows where it should be?"

"Yeah, but it doesn't hurt to remind Him," Mother replied.

An old friend, Jack Ledger, also asked about the tree flags. He returned later that same day with the first fifty thousand dollars for the project.

In August 1984, an elderly couple visiting the monastery for the first time toured the grounds and quizzed Mother about the new studio. Feeling sorry for the couple, she filled a shoe box with bananas and sandwiches for them to eat on their trip home. She patiently answered their questions, then sent them on their way.

Upon their return to Gainesville, Florida, the couple Mother pitied, the Bombergers, called an emergency board meeting of the philanthropic foundation they led. At their insistence, the foundation awarded Mother $150,000 to complete her studio. A generous donation from the Knights of Columbus and a $25,000 grant secured by Archbishop Bernard Law of Boston completed the funding for the entire studio complex. The EWTN staff split its time between television duties and working at the building site while Mother Angelica personally oversaw all aspects of the construction.

Touted as "the Catholic voice in America," Harry John's Santa Fe Communications began broadcasting in the spring of 1984. Buoyed by the deep pockets of its founder, the for-profit network sailed toward a triumphant future just as EWTN's fortunes ran aground. By June 28, Mother Angelica was two months behind on transponder payments and in danger of losing her satellite time. Two hundred and sixty thousand dollars would not come easily. With his resources committed to Santa Fe, Harry John rejected Mother's request for financial aid. Her string of emergency donors responded in kind. This time, the money failed to materialize, and God seemed very far off.

Darkness Falls

"PERHAPS THE GREATEST interior suffering is the kind that strikes us when we thirst for God and then find ourselves deprived of the awareness of His presence," Mother Angelica wrote in her mini-book *The Healing Power of Suffering*. In 1984, she faced this miserable reality.

Starting on July 7, 1984, and lasting for more than three months, Mother Angelica underwent what the community history calls "the experience." The death of her mother, the pressures of the monastery, and the real possibility of losing the network coalesced into a spiritual deprivation akin to Saint John of the Cross's "dark night of the senses." When it began, she was in Virginia Beach for an appearance on *The 700 Club*. In a never-before-published diary entry, she described something like a vision:

> Lord, unbelievable darkness enveloped me. It was as if people from every corner came into view. There were so many. I seemed so small—so empty—so alone. My soul seemed suddenly drained of every ounce of love—my capacity to love was shattered, my strength overcome by weakness. Everyone I love was snatched away from me by some unknown force and I stood before You, Lord God, broken alone and empty. . . . What everyone thought I possessed I did not, so I thought I must be a hypocrite. All the demands made upon me were impossible to fulfill. Then a chasm opened up before me and I knew my place forever if I did not love. . . . The ones I always felt loved me were nowhere to be seen—they were gone. I looked right and left but the only ones I could see were those who needed me— the lonely, the sick, those who live in vacuums, friends and enemies, children, and the elderly. Everyone looked to me with pleading eyes. My hands were empty, my soul dried up.

Mother Angelica's interior loneliness and the grief over Mae's passing is all over the page. Yet to the outside world, nothing appeared out of order. Jean Morris, who was with Mother on the trip to Virginia Beach, can remember no difference in her demeanor or conversation. Angelica continued her live show, cracked jokes, interacted with the public, and shared spiritual insight with callers, but privately she felt the approach of death.

Angelica's description of her inner turmoil and her estrangement from God reads, on the surface, like a textbook "dark night" experience. On July 9, she wrote to her Spouse: "You emptied Yourself so totally. Are you asking me to do the same? I am afraid. It seems like a living death. I do not possess the strength—help me Oh God." The following day, she was even more anguished:

The struggle continues Lord. Am I fighting whatever You are trying to do in my soul? . . . I cling to everything and as I do I feel it slip through my fingers. What or who is there that will not pass from me sooner or later anyway? . . . My weakness blocks the vision of your face. My struggles push away the inner longings of my soul, my sins loom up as phantoms of the night to haunt me and make me step back from your awesome holiness. . . . Everything around me seems to be falling apart. Everything I hold dear is getting further and further away. . . .

Perhaps nothing was drifting away faster than the network. On more than one occasion, before her community and in front of network employees, Mother broke down in tears over the two unpaid transponder bills, which she knew portended EWTN's extinction.

On July 13, in her monastery office, Mother Angelica dialed a reliable donor in a last-ditch effort for funds. Watching her reaction, Sister Raphael could tell that help would not be forthcoming. When the call ended, Raphael proposed a way out, even though she knew Mother would probably veto it. Raphael thought the family of viewers should be informed of the network's dire state and given a chance to save it through a telethon. Believing that airtime should be spent spreading the Gospel, Angelica loathed what she had seen of telethons on the Evangelical networks. But given the gravity of the moment, she acquiesced to the plan.

"I can't now, I'm too emotionally upset," she told Raphael. "I'll do it tomorrow night."

Mother pulled herself together and for six nights, starting July 14, 1984, begged for dollars. Jabbing her Italian hands at the camera, she spelled out the crisis and approached the audience with subtle lines like: "All right, cough it up, kids." Coming from a sixty-one-year-old chortling nun, with a crucifix dangling from her neck; who could resist?

Like everything else at EWTN, the telethon was a family affair. Seven employees and six nuns manned the phones while Mother, Matt Scalici, and visiting priests drummed up donations.

Father Mitch Pacwa, a Jesuit living in Nashville, sang the Polish

national anthem for five grand. Mother even waltzed across the studio floor with a visiting priest to secure donations. During one of
the telethon interviews, Angelica asked Sister Regina how she decided to join a Franciscan order. Regina stared dumbly at the camera and proudly announced, "I didn't know it was Franciscan for
two years." The abbess was speechless. Gaffes aside, the telethon
procured the needed funds, and accomplished something more: "It
was a major shift in the relationship between Mother, EWTN as an
entity, and the viewing public," Sister Antoinette, a violinist who
entered the monastery in the spring of 1984, said of the telethon. "It
really intensified the sense of family, which Mother spoke of from
the beginning." From that time forward, donations became personal: The viewers weren't sending their checks to the network;
they were sending them to Mother Angelica. Years later, she'd coin
a phrase that would become her live show sign-off, and the sum total of her fund-raising efforts: "Remember to keep us between your
gas and electric bill. This network is brought to you by you." Viewers believed her and would religiously send their donations in each
month to keep their network up and running.

Before the telethon, on July 12, 1984, Father Bruce Ritter of
Covenant House in New York sent his young fund-raiser Jim Kelly
to offer EWTN guidance in the depths of its financial shortfall.
Kelly was handsome, cosmopolitan, and acquainted with the
movers and shakers of the Catholic Church. Ginny Dominick, the
network's vice president, was his main point of contact. In time,
Dominick found Jim Kelly irresistible. She told coworkers, "What if
I marry him? He lives in New York."

During subsequent trips to Manhattan with Dominick, Mother
witnessed the attraction firsthand. Back in Birmingham, the nun
and her vice president would confer intensely about the relationship.

"We would wait for Mother to come home for supper before the
show and she'd be in the office talking to Ginny," one of the nuns,
who asked not to be identified, recalled with some annoyance. "I
mean hour after hour after hour."

Sources close to the principals said the discussions touched on

Dominick's relationship with Jim Kelly, network jealousies, and spirituality. Matt Scalici, Chris Harrington, and Marynell Ford described these private conferences as "tearful" and "emotional" encounters—occasions that provided Angelica with a clear understanding of where things were headed.

Any lingering hope she harbored that Ginny might enter contemplative life disintegrated during those conversations. Sister Mary David had gone, and now it felt as if Ginny was leaving her, as well. The perceived rupturing of this mother-daughter relationship hit the nun hard. This unexpected pain may account in part for her diary entry of July 18, 1984. Once more, Mother addressed Jesus Christ:

> I always felt and thought that if I love You intensely I would not be affected by the presence or absence of human love, possessions, success and all those things in daily life that make it livable and bearable . . . to love as You loved in this life is to be open, vulnerable, ready to love so intensely that one's heart ceaselessly gives as an overflowing fountain, vulnerable enough to feel the least absence of love but generous enough to stand beneath the Cross of separation, misunderstanding, hostility, and loneliness and never closing the flood gates of love. Is it to be able to feel the numbness of heartache and never surrender to self-pity, to long and thirst for infinite love and struggle with the attachments that seem so much a part of us?

Mother Angelica's attachment to Ginny Dominick could not be quickly dismissed. She loved Ginny like a daughter. And though she had told the young woman just months earlier, "If you love somebody and they love you, you marry them whether I approve or not," Mother hardly expected to have her dictum tested so soon. She wanted the best for Ginny. But she also wanted their relationship to continue unaltered.

Over the next few months Angelica's internal purgatory dragged on. She wrote of a barrier between herself and God: "Will I cross over the invisible wall that stands between us? I wonder if my own selfishness is the wall?" A pronounced spiritual confusion, a common feature of the "dark night" experience, was evident. "I feel somehow I do not belong—I am in a foreign land," she wrote on July 20. "The language I want to share no one understands. The trials I undergo I cannot express." By the end of the month, her torment was in full flower: "My soul is in such turmoil. My imperfections and weaknesses seem to be bursting within me. . . . I fight for the least good thought. I struggle to pray—every prayer is separated by tons of aggravating thoughts, turmoil and distress. It is like picking roses amidst a garbage heap."

That fall, Harry John faced his own ordeal, though it was decidedly temporal in nature: a restraining order issued in October 1984. Santa Fe Communications had seriously drained John's financial wellspring by that point. In little more than a year, $100 million of his De Rance Foundation assets were gone. Hard up for cash, John borrowed against his home and raided his children's education funds, until his wife had had enough. Concerned about his judgment, to say nothing of the wild spending, Erica John petitioned the court for a restraining order, essentially removing Harry from the board of De Rance.

Peter Grace was called in to liquidate Santa Fe Communications' assets, including a mahogany-encased editing bay and switcher worth $2.5 million. It was later sold to EWTN for a mere $800,000.

On October 23, Angelica thanked God for revealing the "depths of her misery." Her "dark night" experience appears to have receded. At least the entries terminate, though her troubles were far from over.

Days later, on November 7, 1984, a notice arrived from Peter Grace's foundation calling in the three-year-old $650,000 loan, with interest. The loan, which included a mortgage of the satellite dish and transmission equipment, had actually been due in 1983. Though some saw this as an attempt by Grace to take control of the network, Dick De Graff, who worked for Grace, disputed this interpretation.

"Peter eventually saw this as an empty pit and he didn't know where the money was going. Grace had spreadsheets and budgets for toilet paper . . . and EWTN had no budget," De Graff said. "The foundation called the note in because they were under legal pressure; they couldn't write it off and retain their 501c3 status. Peter did not want the television network; we had 168 companies we were already trying to run."

Records indicate that Grace personally gave Mother a $100,000 donation in 1983 to pay down a portion of the outstanding loan. If he wanted control of the network, it is doubtful he would have offered any financial assistance, and it seems strange that he didn't call the loan in a year earlier, when it was technically due. According to DeGraff and the OLAM History, it was the treasurer of the Grace Foundation who convinced Peter that the law required EWTN to repay the loan. Mother put out a dragnet for funds.

On November 9, Angelica, Bill Steltemeier, and Ginny Dominick flew to Florida to visit a retired lawyer and his wife. The wife had been on retreat at the monastery earlier that year and had invited Mother to contact her should she ever need anything. The need was now major. Before Angelica left their home, the couple promised to advance her $700,000 to pay off the Grace Foundation loan.

"In New York, Peter Grace's people were shocked out of their minds because all of a sudden here's a check paid in full," Mother said later, shaking with laughter. "These are the kinds of things, honey, that prove God's providence. We never know where the next penny's coming from. That's what I'm trying to get through people's heads: This is an act of God." Mother Angelica knit her brow as she considered the sustenance of her network. "Our witness is the total providence of God. He led us; He provided for us; He protected us. Nobody can say these nuns, any of us, could have accomplished this—we couldn't. Everything evolved, and it evolved as long as we kept up with Him."

Keeping up with Him as she stepped into the late 1980s would try Mother Angelica on a deeply personal level and plunge her into the very depths of spiritual despair.

13
The Abbess of the Airwaves

A WENDY'S AD featuring a shrunken old woman with hound-dog jowls asking, "Where's the Beef?" probably started the trend. Within months, lovable Angela Lansbury chasing murderers through Cabot Cove and a quartet of retirees living in Miami known as *The Golden Girls* led the Nielsen ratings, confirming the shift. By late 1984, spunky, sharp-tongued grandmothers had come into vogue, and Mother Angelica found herself well positioned to capitalize on this geriatric cultural mood.

Slouching on the brown sofa each week, her braced legs crossed at the ankle, Mother was like no one else on television. She coughed when her asthma acted up, chomped on lozenges, unleashed explosive sneezes that drew tears from her eyes, and regularly collapsed into fits of laughter. This purposely unvarnished approach endeared her to the audience. In the gaffes and imperfections, they saw themselves.

For many Angelica became a surrogate grandmother; a trusted friend the confused, the bruised, and the elderly could rely upon for spiritual counsel and comfort. More than any other Catholic figure in the late twentieth century, she seemed accessible. The Pope, though beloved by Catholics of all stripes, remained a distant icon of holiness: the father guiding the faith in another part of the world, removed from their daily existence. Mother Teresa, already regarded as "the saint of the slums," had achieved an almost mythic level of sanctity few in suburbia felt capable of imitating. And though people knew their bishops by name, personal encounters were rare. Only Mother Angelica peered into the daily lives of the laity—into their living rooms, their bedrooms, their kitchens. As familiar as a morning cup of steaming java, she popped in with an inspired word just when they needed it. Evincing humanity, poking fun at her flaws, she made holiness attractive and feasible for the masses.

Mother Angelica conversed in the idiom of the people, using lingo sooner found in a barbershop than a cathedral.

"If you're close to Jesus in your daily life, you can explain Jesus in a very simple way because you're attuned to the living Jesus, the living Gospel," Angelica said of her approach. "Jesus spoke the language of the people—you could understand; children could understand. Too often, we in the Church talk to ourselves."

Applying spiritual balm to the wounds of the common man, her program tackled drug addiction, alcoholism, the pain of divorce, and loneliness. The "people that hurt" were hers. They were people like Rita Rizzo.

When a caller informed Mother that her husband had brought another woman home to live with them, Angelica's advice was typical: "Well, kick him out!"

"Oh, I can't," the caller said.

"What do you mean, you can't?"

"They have no place to go."

"I could tell them where to go," Mother purred. "They're headed for hell. Tell 'em to go there."

"I can't judge them," the caller whimpered.

"Are you nuts? Another woman is sleeping with your husband under your roof, and you can't judge!"

On another occasion, Mother lectured her audience about dressing modestly, not sparing the senior citizens: "Nobody tells you because they're afraid to hurt your feelings. But some of you old gals—believe me—cover it up! Whatever was there is gone."

There were serious moments, too. Abandoned by her children and her spouse, suffering with multiple sclerosis, a woman called

Mother Angelica one evening in despair. "I know how you feel. My mother used to feel that way," Angelica counseled. "Don't blame God for what your husband or your children did. . . . You have a great cross there, but don't put the cross of bitterness on top of it, because that's when you get hopeless. I want you to take that cross and give it to Mary. . . . She knows what it means to be abandoned. . . . Now I'm going to say a prayer for you."

"She tends to be earthy and biblical," Ben Armstrong of the National Religious Broadcasters Association said in 1985. "She's the Bishop Fulton Sheen of this generation, and there's room for her voice." The cable industry agreed.

Mother Angelica's spiritually enhanced straight talk garnered the attention of her peers, who in 1984 nominated *Mother Angelica Live* for an ACE (Award for Cable Excellence), conferred by the industry. Mother's would be the only religious program nominated. Catholic broadcasters and communicators similarly recognized her impact, awarding Angelica their highest honor, the Gabriel Personal Achievement Award, in December 1984.

Even her blunders attracted notice. At the close of 1984, Mother Angelica received the Golden Blooper Award from Dick Clark and Ed McMahon. During the presentation on NBC's *Bloopers and Practical Jokes,* she guffawed at her own less-than-perfect takes and reveled in the lunacy of the honor. Like her Spouse, she went where people could see her and fearlessly ventured into places where no bishop would be caught dead.

Her secular approach worked. By early 1985, EWTN was carried on more than 220 cable systems, and could be seen in nearly 2 million homes. *Broadcasting* magazine, a television-industry publication, tagged EWTN as the fastest-growing cable network in the country. That growth could be directly attributed to Mother Angelica and her common touch.

Growing Pains

MORE THAN FOUR HUNDRED people gathered outside the chapel of Our Lady of the Angels Monastery on April 14, 1985, for the dedication of the new studio facility. In place of the white-ragged pine trees, a 6,500-square-foot brown brick edifice stood adjacent to the monastery. Providence and tenacity had granted Angelica yet another favor.

Benefactors and friends wandered wide-eyed through the $375,000 production headquarters. They viewed the office space, the new conference room, a set shop, and, most important, the fifty- by seventy-foot studio, capable of holding up to four sets. Few visitors appreciated the significance of what they were seeing. Suddenly capable of generating up to 50 percent of its own programming, the new studio space meant independence for EWTN. The network would be far less reliant on material acquired from outside sources. Mother could now create programming to suit her tastes and thereby ensure the orthodoxy of the content. This was no small matter, considering her new understanding of the network's national import.

"EWTN is the key to restoring the Roman Catholic Church in America," the Pope reportedly told Cardinal Silvio Oddi during a private meeting. Oddi shared the observation with Angelica on June 19, 1985, while visiting the network for a live appearance. Whether the papal quote is accurate or not is immaterial. It influenced Mother's thinking at the time, inspiring her to use the network to buttress "the Catholicism of the simple, the poor, and the elderly."

In less than a year, more overtly religious programs predominated on EWTN. *The Bill Cosby Show* and *Wok with Yan* disappeared from the lineup, replaced by shows like *Glory to God* and *Life in the Holy Spirit*. Though a few old secular movies ran in the *EWTN Family Theater* slot, the network was becoming explicitly Catholic in tone. Angelica even instituted a Rosary program, over the objections of some senior staff, who believed such repetitious fare would never catch on. It quickly became a viewer favorite and confirmed Angelica's knack for anticipating the desires of her audience.

In the summer of 1985, in order to accommodate network growth, Angelica restructured management, sharply defining duties for the first time. Marynell Ford was named VP of marketing, Dick Stephens VP of programming, Chris Harrington VP of operations and production, Matt Scalici VP of engineering and satellite operations, and Ginny Dominick executive VP of religious affairs and program-concept development. For all the apparent delegation of responsibility, Mother Angelica had no intention of pulling away. In a memo to her associates, she underscored her oneness with the network and her role as guiding light: "The changes, turns, directions, and risks have been placed on my shoulders by the Lord. It is a lonely task to see what others do not see and so it is imperative that each one of you work closely with me in a cooperative effort to carry out His will. To be able to discern when to take a risk, when to stand still and when to pull back on a day to day basis takes confidence in God and in each other."

To facilitate that cooperation, Angelica treated the network as an extension of her religious community. She taught an employee lesson each Monday from one of her minibooks, roamed through the work areas, casually conversing with employees, and maintained an open-door policy in her office, which was situated just off the network reception area.

"She had a huge candy jar, and we would get candy, stop in, and see her. It was a real family then," Father Joseph Wolfe remembered. Wolfe came to the network in 1985, when technical glitches were routine. As he watched Mother's show in Dubuque, Iowa, one night, the program vanished from the air without notice. After a prolonged black hole, Mother reappeared, looked into the camera, and said, "As you can see, we need an engineer." Wolfe, a General Electric Medical Systems engineer, responded to the call and was eventually hired.

"We were still a mom-and-pop organization," Chris Harrington recalled wistfully. "It was a manageable reality and it was fun. It was really truly what you would call a family."

The folks in televisionland must have had similar feelings. In 1985, donations exceeded expenditures by more than $1.5 million. And though EWTN carried a debt load of $3.2 million, growth was not hampered. In less than a year the network would expand its broadcasting day from four to six hours.

According to a memo issued in 1985, Mother's most trusted collaborator at the network had a job description that permitted maximum flexibility. Ginny Dominick "interpret[ed] company policy in the absence of the Chairman of the board or President." She was to ensure that the "spirit of the network [was] kept intact in all series and other programming" and became the network "trouble shooter to handle political and ecclesiastical authorities." The revamped position allowed Ginny to be in the network but not of it. In mid-1985, with Mother's blessing, Dominick spent more time in New York getting to know Jim Kelly. During her sabbatical, the pair developed a true bond.

In Birmingham the remaining EWTN vice presidents felt slighted by what they construed to be Dominick's growing power within the organization at a time when she was apparently disengaging from network affairs. One senior manager claimed, "Mother was willing to give Ginny as much authority as she could," most likely to demonstrate her confidence in Dominick, and to preserve their friendship. But Ginny didn't see it that way. Unaware of the memo defining her new position, and with no one now reporting to her, Dominick felt pushed aside.

The misunderstandings and mixed signals were part of a thorny relationship truly understood only by the participants. What is known is that Mother envisioned Ginny as a natural successor to run EWTN: a loyal, competent, spiritual woman capable of protecting the network in her absence. Their personal relationship complicated matters.

As Ginny's trusted adviser, Mother thought it her place to offer a judgment on the man Dominick intended to marry. For whatever reason, Jim Kelly did not meet with Angelica's approval. Given Mother's background, it is questionable whether any man would have been considered good enough for her adored surrogate daughter. This core disagreement over the suitability of Ginny's fiancé would fracture and strain their friendship.

"Ginny wanted to get married and Mother really didn't want Ginny to get married," Jean Morris said of the relationship. "She thought Ginny was called to work at the network." But Ginny had found love.

Despite Mother's opposition, Ginny Dominick married Jim Kelly in January 1986. After the wedding, Ginny moved to New Orleans, but, at Mother's invitation, she continued to serve as EWTN's executive vice president and a member of the board. Even as life took Ginny elsewhere, Angelica attempted to hold on to her "daughter." From New Orleans, Ginny wrote Mother's monthly newsletter and helped construct the nun's book for Harper & Row, *Mother Angelica's Answers Not Promises*. A compendium of Angelica's no-nonsense wisdom mined from the live show, the book was transcribed and reworked into a readable format by a hired writer, revised by Angelica, and polished by Ginny. Mother "lovingly dedicated" the 1987 publication "to Ginny Dominick Kelly, without whom it would not have been conceived or completed."

Over distance and time, the pair maintained an on-again, off-again friendship. Angelica was the godmother of Ginny's first child, and in 1990, Jim Kelly joined the network to streamline the fundraising apparatus.

"She was very determined that her husband was the only one who could make the network go," Mother Angelica told me. About six weeks later, following professional disagreements, Jim Kelly had to leave. And though she would not resign from the EWTN board until April 1991, Ginny Dominick Kelly was gone, as well. The hasty departure of Jim Kelly from the network definitively severed the friendship between Mother and Ginny, but in-house resentments and shattered expectations were also contributing factors.

In the wake of the parting, Mother Angelica came to a personal decision: Never again would she attach herself emotionally to a layman or permit such a deep friendship to develop outside the cloister. While giving spiritual direction to one of the sisters in 1998, Mother reportedly said:

> I've given my love and friendship to lay people only to find them turn on me if I didn't agree with them. I have forgiven them and would greet them warmly if they came to see me, but to give them my love? I'm no punching bag—I stay at arm's length. I've been hurt by those I've loved the most. I've

finally made a decision: that's enough! Jesus is always faithful. I have my Jesus, my mission, my sisters, and my work—that's enough for me.

But Mother knew that part of fulfilling her mission was to pass the network on to a spiritual heir who could sustain it without her. Bill Steltemeier could tend to the business concerns of the network, but she needed a successor to "insure that the spirit of the network [remained] intact." With Ginny's departure, the position lay vacant.

In October 1986, Mother lost something else very dear to her: EWTN's satellite and transponder lease. The satellite provider refused to renew EWTN's contract for 1987, and their competitors were only interested in accommodating twenty-four-hour cable networks. To keep her network on the air, Angelica could secure another six-hour deal on a secondary satellite or expand EWTN's broadcasting day to twenty-four hours, and move to Galaxy III: a new satellite, which few cable systems could (or wanted to) look at. No matter which choice she made, Matt Scalici told Mother, EWTN would "lose all of its affiliates and have to start from zero."

Angelica prayed for guidance. "When the Lord acts with me, there's always a leap of faith," Mother explained, "the leap of faith that says yes or no. And at that point, the question is: Do you recognize the Providence of God?"

On the morning of October 24, 1986, Angelica gathered all forty-five employees in the studio, informed them of the options she was weighing, warned them of the massive challenges and benefits that awaited them should they enter the twenty-four-hour cable arena, and awaited their response. Each employee would voice an opinion and make a choice: either to keep the six-hour feed or to take the twenty-four-hour plunge. Enormous amounts of programming would be required to sustain a continuous feed, the financial strain would intensify, and an already taxed workforce would be expected to put in more time. One by one the employees spoke up, unanimously encouraging Mother to "go for it."

"It was the most edifying, wonderful day of our lives because they knew that we were going to go back to nothing and start over." Mother's face flushed with excitement as she relived the decision to broadcast twenty-four hours a day. "I told them they'd probably have to work without pay for a while. They didn't care; they were challenged, and we did it."

Shortly after EWTN signed onto Galaxy III, a formidable lineup of cable networks bought out the satellite. They provided reception dishes to the nation's seven thousand cable systems, turning Galaxy III into the most popular satellite in cable television—home to Nickelodeon, C-SPAN, and EWTN.

During the frenzied preparations for the twenty-four-hour launch, the Vatican announced a ten-day papal visit to America in the fall of 1987.

"Suddenly, the best marketing tool a Catholic network could have comes to town," Matt Scalici recalled. "It was like God saying, 'You are willing to start from zero. I'm going to send my guy to do some live TV.' "

Mother Angelica committed the network to complete coverage of the papal visit. A marquee event to kick off her twenty-four-hour launch had fallen from the heavens, but there was to be a price. The day after Christmas, Mother was rushed to the hospital with heart pains. Four days of testing revealed ulcer complications and a hiatal hernia pushing on her enlarged heart. Undeterred, Mother and her sisters considered the physical hardship a spiritual prepara-tion for some impending good.

Giving Orders

FOR A WOMAN so committed to the teachings and traditions of the past, Mother Angelica never lost sight of the future. Lacking a lay successor and determined that her contemplative nuns should not be directly involved in the life of the network, Angelica birthed a pair of active religious orders in May 1987. Fed by her charisma, these spiritual sons and daughters would protect the mission of EWTN in perpetuity and continue her fervent devotion to the Eucharist. "It's just being practical," she said of the new orders in 1987; "things have to go on."

She had two groups in mind: the Order of the Eternal Word, a community of priests and brothers, and the Sister Servants of the Eternal Word, an active extension of Angelica's contemplative order. Their joint work, according to Mother, was to "ensure that the Word of God and the teachings of the Church are proclaimed faithfully through EWTN."

To head up the Sister Servants, Mother turned to Sister Gabriel Long. This strong-willed thirty-five-year veteran of the Dominican order had the build of a stevedore and an uproarious sense of humor. Gabriel first met Angelica during her tenure as principal at St. Rose Academy, a Dominican school in Birmingham. After running another school and serving as a superior in her order, Sister Gabriel needed some personal time.

"Her mother prioress asked me if I would let her come here for a year, to take some time off," Mother said. "I thought, Since she's here, she would be perfect to start this thing with me."

Together, Angelica and Gabriel would gamely cofound the Sister Servants of the Eternal Word.

To lead the Order of the Eternal Word, Mother tapped Father Donat McDonagh, a pastor from Clearwater, Florida, and director of the diocesan Charismatic Renewal. The lean canon lawyer with the dynamic preaching style hungered for the contemplative life. In early 1987 that life became a possibility. But there were troubles from the start.

Mother wanted the order to be Franciscan and active while Father McDonagh had visions of a monastic community immersed in prayer and penance.

"Mike was a person who wanted it his way, and he had more of an Augustinian manner," Father Richard Mataconis, a later member of the order, said of its superior.

Mother foresaw her religious sons and daughters expanding her mission: "In these two new orders we'll have engineers, script writers, and camera people, everything we need to promote, and produce, and build entities in other cities." But in an interview at about the same time, Father McDonagh sounded a contrary note: "I don't envision that we will all work here at the network. God will lead us in different directions. I'm sure there will be activity in the area of mass communications, but maybe not restricted to that."

Competing visions and all, Father McDonagh joined Mother as the on-air cohost of her thrice-weekly live show. If they disagreed on the nature of the religious order, their on-air chemistry and shared charismatic approach to prayer became a source of unity.

"Father Michael was very charismatic and he convinced Mother that we should have these weekly prayer services with the sisters," Father Joseph Wolfe recollected. "We could close the doors of the chapel and sing praise music. Some people would have a word of prophecy. Mother and the sisters prayed in tongues."

While her brothers and sisters strummed guitars or sang, Mother kept time on a snare drum in the corner. Afterward, overwhelmed by the Holy Spirit, she would occasionally go limp while in prayer, experiencing what she called "the sleep of the powers." "She would be unresponsive for hours," Sister Margaret Mary recalled.

Along with the prayer services, the communities shared meals in common and lots of laughs. "People asked me if I entered a cloister, and I said it was a semicloister," Sister Mary Agnes, who arrived in 1986, observed. "We had no silence, no wall; we had a family spirit."

Whether due to the family spirit or the prayer, all three orders thrived. By 1988 there were nine members of the Order of the Eternal Word, six Sister Servants, and fifteen contemplative Poor Clares. Television afforded Mother an unrivaled opportunity to attract more vocations to the orders. But even great advertising could not overcome the personality clashes and disparate visions that threatened both of her new communities.

The Sheep Bite the Shepherd

IN THREE SEPARATE LETTERS, Mother Angelica tried to persuade the Pope to add a Birmingham stopover to his American itinerary in

1987. Though the personal visit never materialized, Angelica would make the Pope's September pilgrimage to the United States personal for millions. During the ten-day visit, EWTN would do what no broadcaster in the nation had ever attempted: complete and unedited live coverage of a papal trip from touchdown to liftoff, morning to night.

Mother began beaming twenty-four hours of programming coast to coast just days before the papal jet pierced the sweltering heat and landed in Miami on September 10. As she threw the switch launching the twenty-four-hour feed at the top of the month, she told those assembled in the control room, "This is for all time, until Gabriel blows his horn. And maybe we'll get him on camera blowing it." EWTN could now be seen continuously. The fledging cable network had entered the major leagues.

Acutely aware of Mother Angelica's newfound reach, the Bishops' Communications Committee proposed that EWTN and the bishops' conference collaborate on the broadcast of the papal pilgrimage. The effort would accomplish the dual task of showing a unified Catholic presence on television while bolstering the bishops' troubled Catholic Telecommunications Network of America (CTNA). As incentive, the bishops offered to pay most of the production costs associated with the visit. Mother had only to make her twenty-four-hour satellite available and pick up half of any additional expenses. The partnership would put CTNA on the cable map for the first time in its existence. Viewers nationwide would finally be able to see that the bishops indeed had a television operation. To Angelica, the joint coverage meant great publicity for her network and gave EWTN credibility within the cable industry.

To contain costs, team coverage originated out of WRAL, a CBS affiliate in Raleigh, North Carolina. Father Bob Bonnot, president and CEO of CTNA, and Mother Angelica would host the coverage, providing papal play-by-play. "I've never been an anchor before, so I hope I don't fumble all over myself," Angelica told a reporter before the start of the coverage. "But it'll be fun. I plan on being a homey anchor. I think most anchors are too serious and too sophisticated."

With plenty of secular buzz and heavy promotion by the bishops conference, the EWTN signal was picked up by some seven hundred cable systems in forty-four states, reaching 20 million homes. "Suddenly, there was a lot of interest in our signal," Matt Scalici said. "Cable operators gave us a week, and we went from ten million to twenty million–plus."

Before he left the comfort of his Alitalia jet, *Shepherd One*, to kiss the sizzling tarmac in thanksgiving, bless the adoring crowd at the Miami airport, and greet President Reagan, Pope John Paul prepared himself for the heavy task that lay ahead. On his second American pilgrimage, the Universal Shepherd had to lead an unruly flock back into the fold. A growing minority of loud Catholic voices had been lobbying for a more democratic Church, one liberated from the doctrines and authority they considered restrictive.

The year before had been a rocky one for the Church in America. In Seattle, Washington, Archbishop Raymond G. Hunthausen openly defied Church discipline and practice. According to complaints by the faithful, he assigned ex-priests to parish work, allowed a national gay organization of Catholics to use his cathedral for Mass, permitted non-Catholics to take communion illicitly, and carelessly chose candidates for the seminary. Following an investigation, the Holy See took the extraordinary step of stripping the archbishop of key powers and deputizing Bishop Donald Wuerl to run parts of the archdiocese. The chagrined archbishop called the arrangement "unworkable" in the press. In the ensuing months, the *National Catholic Reporter* and others decried the "repression" of Hunthausen by Rome, arguing that it violated the collegiality of the Second Vatican Council, and the archbishop was eventually reinstated.

At Catholic University in Washington, D.C., Father Charles Curran's dissenting views on sexual morality differed little from those of much of the theological establishment in the late 1980s. But Curran was a moral theologian at the only pontifical university in the United States, and his brazen teachings soon drew the eye of officials in Rome. Curran believed "artificial contraception, divorce, sterilization, premarital sex, homosexuality, masturbation, and abortion"—all practices strictly forbidden by traditional Catholic teaching—could be considered morally acceptable under certain conditions. The Vatican's Congregation for the Doctrine of Faith disagreed and, on August 18, 1986, definitively forbade Curran to teach in a Catholic institution, citing his dissent from the Magisterium (the Church's teaching authority). Seven hundred and fifty theologians and nine former presidents of the Catholic Theological Association would stand with the recalcitrant theologian.

Using political rhetoric, the press described both the Hunthausen and Curran cases as raging battles between "progressives" and "conservatives," with the Pope cast as the villainous conservative, and all dissenting parties as freedom-loving progressives.

By 1987, challenges to Rome's authority had become routine, and dissent commonplace. As Pope John Paul began to move among his American flock, some of the sheep bore sharp teeth, and they were not averse to biting if necessary.

The stifling air of Miami surrounded the Pope as he entered St. Martha's Church for a meeting with U.S. priests on the first day of his visit. The gathering was one of several structured dialogues with the Pope, a chance for representatives to share the concerns of a specific Church group with the man in charge.

Father Frank McNulty, vicar of priests for the Archdiocese of Newark, New Jersey, was chosen by the bishops conference to address the Pope on behalf of U.S. priests. McNulty quickly raised "the celibacy question." "Its value has eroded and continues to erode in the minds of many," the priest said. "This is of great concern for us because it has serious implications for the Church."

The Pope, who sat impassively through McNulty's speech, adlibbed the opening of his response. "I remember a song," the Pope said wryly. "It's a long way to Tipperary." Translation: Don't hold your breath. In his planned remarks, the Pope reaffirmed priestly celibacy and requested prayers for priestly vocations.

Mother Angelica was distressed by what she saw, and probably embarrassed. After all, it was her network broadcasting the public challenge to the Pontiff's authority. Propagating dissent and planting doubt in the minds of her viewers were not what she had bargained for. So whenever the opportunity presented itself, she offered her own brand of balance in the form of homey orthodox commentary.

"I think Mother Angelica had a perspective that she asserted," Father Bob Bonnot said of Mother's contribution to the coverage. But his most vivid memory, which the priest insisted was "symptomatic of the whole situation," occurred when the Pope visited Phoenix on September 14. "It was the feast of the Holy Cross, and the Pope venerated a huge cross there. And Mother Angelica took off on how inappropriate it was that it was a cross and not a crucifix. She said, 'I want my Jesus on that cross.' And she picked up the crucifix around her neck and kissed it. It was bad theology then and it's bad theology now," Bonnot said of Mother's comments. "Some of the tension and conflict that ensued came from this disposition that Mother felt she could let loose and be very critical of events within the Church, even the veneration of a cross."

But to Mother Angelica, the bare cross ignored the sacrifice of her Spouse. She felt that to leave the body of Christ off the cross made it appear as if those assembled were venerating an instrument of torture rather than the specific cross and sacrifice of Christ. The infraction would seem minor compared to what was about to unfold two days later in Los Angeles.

After a wearying journey that took him to Miami, New Orleans, San Antonio, and Phoenix, the Pope arrived in the City of the Angels for a closed-door meeting with his bishops on Wednesday, September 16. The mounting dissent that had greeted the Pope sporadically throughout his American sojourn would reach its zenith in L.A.

Rather than allow the bishops to communicate individually with the Pope, the conference preselected four representatives to speak for all the shepherds. This "dialogue," like those before it, would be totally controlled by the conference, with predictable results. The four appointed bishops constituted the progressive vanguard of the Church in America. They would subject the Pope to artful tongue-lashings on a host of progressive pet issues.

Cardinal Joseph Bernardin of Chicago, one of the most influential and powerful bishops in the conference, spoke first, discussing the relationship between the Universal Church and the local Church. "We live in an open society where everyone prizes freedom to speak his or her mind." the cardinal said in his soothing way. "Many tend to question things, especially those matters which are as important to them as religion is." He warned the Pope that Americans "almost instinctively react negatively when they are told that they must do something." Bernardin was merely the warm-up act for what was to come.

Archbishop John Quinn of San Francisco advised the Pope that traditional moral teaching would not do in these modern times. He told the Pope, "We cannot fulfill our task simply by an uncritical application of solutions designed in past ages for problems which have qualitatively changed or which did not exist in the past."

Next came the *capo di capi* of progressives, a man regarded as a "maverick" in Vatican circles; the Benedictine, Juilliard-trained musician, Milwaukee archbishop Rembert Weakland, rose to address the pontiff. A few years earlier, Weakland had ended an "inappropriate relationship" with another man, a liaison that had begun in 1977. News of the romance, handwritten letters, and an archdiocesan payment of $450,000 to buy the man's silence would shamefully drive the archbishop from office in 2002. But the relationship was still a secret when Weakland faced off with the Pope in 1987.

"The faithful," due to education, wealth, and other factors, would no longer accept Church teaching on the "basis of the authority itself," Weakland threatened. "An authoritarian style is counterproductive, and such authority for the most part then becomes ignored." This clear shot at Vatican governance perhaps also referenced the Hunthausen affair.

Weakland then pressed the case for the ordination of women. "Women," Weakland explained, "seek to be equal partners in sharing the mission of the Church . . . that teaches and shows by example the co-discipleship of the sexes as instruments of God's kingdom. They seek a church where the gifts of women are equally accepted and appreciated . . . where the feminine is no longer subordinate but seen in a holistic mutuality with the masculine as forming the full image of the Divine."

Finally, the vice president of the bishops conference, Archbishop Daniel Pilarczyk, offered a grim appraisal of priestly and religious vocations. He claimed that the Church was experiencing a "broadening of the concept of the church vocation and ministry." Through "participation and collaboration," the laity could fill the gaps left by absent clergy, he seemed to imply. But the laity were developing their own notions of what it meant to be a part of the Church: "We are increasingly a Catholic community that realizes that external conformity to rites and rules, important as that is, is not enough," Pilarczyk concluded.

"It was unprecedented to have the Holy Father challenged and addressed in that manner," said Cardinal J. Francis Stafford, a participant at the Los Angeles meeting. "One left those meetings feeling very empty because the tensions provoked in the previous years were amplified in that moment."

Mother Angelica was infuriated, particularly by the veiled pleas for female ordination. "Women in the priesthood, that's just a power play, that's ridiculous," Angelica said a day after the meeting in L.A. "As it is women have more power in the Church than anybody. They built and run the schools. God has designed that men be priests, and we can't afford to deny God his sovereign rights."

For all the controversy, the EWTN/CTNA coverage of the papal trip was a runaway success. *USA Today* proclaimed, "Secular coverage second to nun's." EWTN picked up twelve new cable affiliates following the papal visit, and despite their concerns with Mother's commentary, CTNA officials rhapsodized about future collaborations. The CTNA programming director, Father Gerald Burr, told the Catholic News Service that the collaboration proved CTNA and EWTN didn't "need to compete" and that the networks were already discussing joint coverage of the annual bishops conference meeting in November. But Mother Angelica wasn't so sure. If reform-minded bishops felt free to boldly challenge Church teaching in front of the Pope, what might they do before her live cameras?

Dancing with the Bishops

THE IDEOLOGICAL DIVISIONS manifest in the Church and the reactions to Vatican authority during the period in some ways became personified in the rivalry between EWTN and CTNA. Both broadcasters vied to advance their own vision of the future Church. Where CTNA broadcast mainline Judeo-Christian fare, open to new and ever-changing realities, EWTN gave viewers traditional Catholic spirituality and time-tested devotions.

"I don't want to be conservative and I don't want to be liberal. I want to be Catholic," Mother said of the network programming and emphasis. "Now if that offends the liberals, tough. If it offends the ultraconservatives, tough. I can't be influenced by any of them. I want to know what the Church teaches."

Many bishops interviewed blamed CTNA's overly broad programming for its failure and eventual demise. As early as 1983, Catholics in Rhode Island and elsewhere began protesting CTNA's programming, convinced it presented a mix of "modernism and liberal politics" injurious to their faith. The program *Spirituality in the Eighties,* a series of interviews with dissenting theologians Hans Kung, Edward Schillebeeckx, and others explaining their "faith experience," was mentioned by name. Even enthusiastic clients lost faith in CTNA over time. One bishop, speaking on the condition of anonymity, said, "Nobody could watch it. They had stuff on how to form your ushers! It was crowded with a liberal agenda. The bureaucrats were running that thing, not the conference."

Bewildering programs and waning interest pushed CTNA to the brink of bankruptcy. Only 100 of the more than 180 dioceses were clients. Communications directors in places such as Delaware openly dismissed CTNA as "a disaster," an "example of the Church throwing good money after bad." In the Catholic press, it became known as the "bishops' big white elephant."

To salvage the sinking network, Father Bob Bonnot and other officials at the bishops conference seriously considered an invitation by TCI, the country's largest cable provider, to become part of a new interfaith network. Vision Interfaith Satellite Network (VISN) was to be the one-stop shop for religious programming. Mainline Protestants, Jews, Muslims, and, it was hoped, Catholics would air generic religious fare, free of doctrinal disagreement or fundraising. CTNA's programming seemed to fit the bill. If VISN

launched, CTNA would have a reason to justify its continued existence, and a means to reach cable audiences without having to go
through Mother Angelica. Dick Hirsh, secretary of communications for the bishops conference, joined the VISN board to assist in
shaping the network, but formal cooperation would require the as-
sent of the entire body of bishops.

Mother Angelica opposed VISN from the outset. At a meeting of
Catholic communicators in Tampa, Florida, in November 1987, she
cautioned that participation in VISN would lead to "watered down"
Catholic teaching and limit Catholic programming on cable. Angelica, Father John Catoir of the Christophers, and others feared that
once cable operators embraced VISN, they would consider their
religious-broadcast obligations fulfilled and would begin eliminating individual religious networks from their lineups.

"If there was strong Catholic participation in VISN, then it was
clear to EWTN that the cable industry would go very strongly to
carriage of VISN, and any dream that EWTN had of being a stand-
alone, fully carried network would proportionately vanish," Father
Bob Bonnot noted.

Father Bonnot and Mother Angelica disagreed on more than
VISN. In the middle of November, EWTN notified CTNA that it
would not participate in joint coverage of the bishops conference
meeting from Washington as previously discussed. The network
would produce its own coverage, including orthodox commentary
to acquaint viewers with magisterial teaching as they watched.
There would be no repeat of the papal-visit experience: Recreant
bishops and theologians were not welcome on Angelica's network.
But CTNA needed the coproduction to raise its profile in the cable
industry and thought a compromise might be possible.

On the afternoon of November 10, 1987, the phone rang in the
hallway of Our Lady of the Angels Monastery as Mother and her
sisters finished lunch in the refectory. "Father Bob Bonnot is on the
line, Reverend Mother," one of the sisters informed her. She
walked into the hallway, pulled the accordion door closed for privacy, and lifted the receiver. In her recollection, Father Bonnot
pressed for joint coverage during the call. He also tried to convince

her to air interviews with any and all bishops, regardless of their point of view, out of respect for their teaching office.

Though Father Bonnot didn't recollect the exact nature of the conversation, he told me, "If her stance was being selective about which bishops could be allowed to speak, I am quite confident that our stance and policy was: We see the bishops as entrusted with leadership in the Church and no bishop on principle should be excluded."

As the phone call continued, Mother Angelica got "louder and louder," according to her sisters. One by one, the nuns gravitated into the hall, listening to the conversation as if awaiting the final twist of a radio drama. Though Mother respected the office of the bishops, she could not bring herself in good conscience to relinquish her network to individuals or ideas opposed to the Magisterium—bishops or no.

"And who are you to decide which bishop should be aired?" Father Bonnot asked.

"I happen to own the network," Angelica responded curtly.

"Well, you won't always be there."

"I'll blow the damn thing up before you get your hands on it," Angelica shouted, as if speaking to the deaf. "I've chosen my Magisterium; you choose yours!" Slamming down the receiver, to the delight of her nuns, she terminated the conversation.

Two days later in a letter to Mother Angelica, Father Bonnot renewed his case for partnership and reiterated his opposition to censoring bishops. Mother wrote the nuncio on November 16 to justify her position. After recounting the heated phone conversation, she told the papal representative that Father Bonnot's "idea of television is to allow everyone to voice his own opinion about faith, morals, doctrines and dogma. . . . Our Holy Father delineated the truths we are to live by and dissent on those issues is not appropriate on national television." The OLAM History later noted that "Rome knew what she was doing and approved."

CTNA and EWTN offered separate and independent coverage of the November meeting of the bishops conference that year.

Before the close of 1987, the usually discreet adversarial forces within the bishops conference crossed swords in public. In December the administrative committee of the conference released a thirty-page policy document on AIDS without the consent of the full body of bishops. Drafted by Cardinal Bernardin and three other bishops, the statement noted the Church's sexual teaching and then, in deference to America's "pluralistic society," said condom education could be permitted as a means of preventing the dreaded disease. "Educational efforts, if grounded in the broader moral vision outlined above, could include accurate information about prophylactic devices," the statement read. The document suggested a radical reversal of Church teaching and tacit approval of condom use.

Soon, a slew of bishops across the United States were denouncing the document, demanding reconsideration of its contents and forbidding its implementation in their respective dioceses. Here were the approved interpreters of Catholic doctrine warring publicly over moral teaching.

"We did not have a unified vision for the Church," is how one high-ranking American churchman described the late 1980s to me. "There were differences between the leadership of the conference and the Holy See and the bishops. The Church in America was divided in its message."

In this moral haze, Mother Angelica began to see EWTN as a beacon of theological clarity, a safe port for the average Catholic. As a matter of conscience, only individuals reflecting the magisterial teachings of Rome would traffic her airwaves. "Our mission is to portray the truth, to just put it out there as the Catholic Church gives it to whoever wants it," Mother said. "Now they have to judge by that picture. I'm not judging them; I'm not criticizing them. I'm only saying, Here's the truth." Angelica had indeed chosen her Magisterium.

Bishops gathered in Atlanta on May 5 for a meeting to discuss future cooperation with EWTN were annoyed by Mother's intransigence. As the discussion turned to establishing a formal relationship between EWTN and the bishops, Mother laid out her terms.

"She was a tough negotiator," Cardinal Edmund Szoka, the second president of CTNA, recalled. "In effect, she was saying she would review and censor the programming in terms of what she judged to be in keeping with the Magisterium. I don't blame her. There were some bishops I wouldn't have wanted on my programming, either. But she was wrong to set herself up as the lone arbiter of orthodoxy."

Bishop Robert Lynch, then associate general secretary of the conference, recounted an exchange between Cardinal Szoka and Mother that is indicative of the "rather tense meeting." The cardinal allegedly said, "Are there good bishops and bad bishops?"

"Yes," Angelica responded.

"Like my auxiliary?" (the very progressive Gumbleton of Detroit).

"Yes, that's a good example," Mother said, brightening. "I don't want those bishops on my network."

That sentiment would be reflected in the final proposal she offered to the bishops in the spring of 1988. The proposal committed EWTN to air conference programming free of charge for several hours a day. Any program with a bishop on-camera would unconditionally air. All other programs would be subject to the discretion of EWTN. To protect its position in cable and kill the possibility of the bishops joining the VISN interfaith network, Bill Steltemeier and Mother insisted on an exclusive contract. If the bishops accepted the deal, the conference would be restricted from taking its programming elsewhere. Even rejected programming could not be aired on another outlet.

The bishops had a decision to make: either to enter into a pact with their hard-nosed sister or join an interfaith network that could possibly destroy her. The showdown began on Friday, June 24, the first day of the bishops' spring meeting in Collegeville, Minnesota.

Going into the vote, VISN enjoyed wide support. UNDA and the Bishops Communications Committee, chaired by Bishop Anthony Bosco, urged the body of bishops to support membership in VISN. The board of CTNA also endorsed the idea of partnering with VISN. EWTN's fortunes turned when Cardinal Edmund Szoka, as chairman of CTNA, stood to personally oppose the VISN offer.

"My intervention was decisive. I did it to protect EWTN," Szoka said later. "The cable people came up with this idea to have one channel that all the religions would share, but it would have killed EWTN and reduced CTNA's time to maybe an hour a day. Every cable system would have had reason to take EWTN off their lineup had VISN been successful."

Though Szoka may have had EWTN's best interest at heart, during his speech he exhorted his brothers to unscramble CTNA's signal and allow him to take it directly to cable operators. Had they consented, CTNA would have been in direct competition with EWTN, endangering the very network Szoka wished to protect.

Archbishop Francis Stafford of Denver, who had spent nearly a year conducting a study of the bishops' communications efforts, opposed the VISN deal as well.

"The catechetical vision in the United States was so weakened after the Second Vatican Council by a reliance on experience as a matter of faith that a radical statement of Catholic faith was needed, on television, not an interfaith effort," Stafford maintained. "It would have been a misuse of Catholic resources."

The day of the vote, Bishop Thomas Daily of Brooklyn and Bill Steltemeier, running his rosary beads through his hands, presented the EWTN proposal to the conference. Bishop Bosco was the advocate for the VISN proposal.

"I think Bishop Daily was very persuasive on the platform as he spoke on the EWTN position: Dance with us and nobody else or don't dance with us at all," Father Bonnot said. "Bishop Bosco was more playful. He did not successfully make the case for going with VISN."

Transcripts and coverage of the Collegeville meeting show an uncertain group of bishops torn over how to proceed.

"What happens to Eternal Word? Do we kill Mother Angelica?" Bishop Cletus O'Donnell of Madison asked before the vote.

"I don't think anyone could kill Mother Angelica—not if you know her," Bishop Bosco said dryly. "She won't let anyone kill her."

During the debate, the bishops fretted over the VISN proposal. The undefined time slots available to them, advertising that might contradict Catholic teaching, and hidden costs were all concerns.

On the other hand, some bishops were vexed by EWTN's theological approach and objected to Mother Angelica censoring their programming.

To break the stalemate, Angelica, at the urging of Archbishop Phillip Hannan of New Orleans, an EWTN ally, agreed to submit any disputed programming to a review board of five bishops. If a majority of the board found the program free of doctrinal error, she would air it. This eleventh-hour concession, along with a motion by Bishop Rene Gracida of Corpus Christi to conduct the vote by secret ballot, cinched the deal. The anonymity of the vote gave Mother's friends the freedom to support her without suffering the scorn of their opposed brethren. By a'vote of 122 to 93, the bishops agreed to sign a two-year pact with EWTN.

The decision seriouly "hobbled" VISN's plans and dealt a lethal blow to the leadership of CTNA. "It was highly regrettable, in my opinion, a failure in leadership on the part of the bishops," Father Bonnot told me. "The conference accepted EWTN's conditions . . . and they were subjected to an ideological sieve."

In the end, neither Mother Angelica nor the bishops were entirely comfortable with the agreement struck, but it had saved EWTN from another potential threat and the bishops had amassed some free airtime. No longer a pariah, EWTN left the Collegeville meeting with the imprimatur of the bishops conference. The question was, Could Mother keep it? Cooperation or no, Angelica would continue to blaze her own trail.

By midsummer of 1988, Mother Angelica was the undisputed matriarch of Catholic communications. On the seventh anniversary of her network, further evidence of her supremacy rolled out in the form a thirty-five-foot state-of-the-art production vehicle christened Gabriel I. Donated by Joe and Lee Bruno, the traveling production facility and $600,000 worth of onboard equipment could broadcast live events from anywhere in the country. By the end of 1988, 12 million households could see EWTN, and Cablevision named it the fastest-growing religious network in the industry.

With the network on firm footing and with the passing of her dear friend of forty-four years, Sister Veronica, Angelica began to evaluate her life. She considered retiring from the network, or at least withdrawing from active duty. As was her routine, she discussed it with her Lord. They shared everything: tough decisions, money woes, pains, joys, and sorrows. Even a new pair of shoes would be trotted into the chapel to "show Him," according to the sisters. In the fall of 1988, during one of her prayerful conversations, she told the Lord of her plan "to pull back a little" from EWTN.

" 'No,' He says to me. 'I want you to begin a shortwave-radio network.' I said, 'Lord, I don't know anything about shortwave.' He said, 'I know. Begin.' "

Confused, she picked up the phone, called Bill Steltemeier to the monastery, and resolved to begin, as instructed.

14

A Witness to the Nations: WEWN

SHE CHASED INSPIRATIONS the way lesser mortals pursue fame, titles, and riches. Inspiration was Mother Angelica's lifeblood, the fleeting elixir that fed her vision and fueled her actions. Her rational mind intruded only once momentum had been firmly established.

"She instantly follows every inspiration. She never tests them," Bill Steltemeier said, almost bragging about Mother's spiritual daring. "The Lord seems to show a specific picture, not a big picture, just a little something. And she will instantly do it; whether it makes sense or not doesn't have anything to do with it."

The shortwave radio inspiration made no sense—not to Mother Angelica. Or to any of her intimates. So she prayed over the thing, tending it like a grapevine in her grandfather's backyard vineyard, straining for the light to see what was required of her.

Perhaps it would be another stillborn inspiration, like the unrealized "large farm with homes for single parent families and unwed mothers" that she had vowed to build, according to *USA Today*.

In the monastery parlor, feeling her way through the haze of her latest prompting, Mother told Bill Steltemeier, "The Lord said, 'Go to Rome.'"

"Why?" Steltemeier asked.

"I'm not sure."

"Well, He's talking to you, not me. Just pray," Steltemeier advised, ending the meeting. Steltemeier could put flesh on an inspiration, but Mother had to birth it first. She returned to praying.

The following day, Angelica called a VP meeting in the network conference room. Like Moses coming down from Sinai, it was a solemn moment. "The Lord spoke to me last night and I saw the world," Mother began. "And He said, 'Angelica, I've trusted you with the small things; now I want you to do something big.' "

"Talk about humility: small things? These were the biggest things I had done in my life," Matt Scalici said, tears welling up in his eyes. "That's when she revealed her idea for radio. The United States wasn't our only market. Catholicism was aching to be released in other parts of the world, she said."

"In blind obedience," the VPs accepted Mother's vision, though none really understood or endorsed the project. Worse, they had qualms about its necessity. But Mother Angelica would not be deterred. No matter how cloudy the marching orders, she was obliged to fulfill them. It was not a question of whether the shortwave operation would be built, but when and how.

"The key to her success is: She relied on inspiration," said Father Benedict Groeschel, a Franciscan Friar of the Renewal and a New York psychologist who has known Angelica for more than twenty years. "Mother Teresa was like that. I worked closely with both of them—they were intuitive women. Saint Thomas said the highest form of intelligence is intuition. And she has succeeded by the inspirations of the Holy Spirit."

Weeks later, Mother Angelica called Steltemeier back to the monastery parlor. She excitedly told him of a breakthrough she had had during her meditation. She had found a Scripture passage: Revelation 14:6. It read, "And I saw another angel flying through the midst of heaven, having the eternal gospel, to preach unto them that sit upon the earth and over every nation and tribe and tongue and people."

Emboldened by those words, and certain that she was being called to preach the Gospel to all nations, Angelica told Steltemeier, "I guess the best thing to do is to go to Italy."

"Why do that?" Steltemeier asked.

"That's where all the languages are. Don't you need languages in shortwave?"

"I don't know anything about shortwave, let alone languages."

"We've got to go to Rome tomorrow," Angelica said with new surety.

A Home in Rome

ON JANUARY 28, 1989, Mother Angelica, Bill Steltemeier, and Sisters Michael and Regina arrived in Rome for what would be a peculiar visit. There were no appointments, no plans, no nothing. The only meeting on the schedule was in Holland (later in the week), with a millionaire Bill Steltemeier hoped could finance the amorphous venture. In the meantime, the nuns and Steltemeier dejectedly stared at one another in the hotel room.

"I never wanted to turn back as bad as I did then. I thought, What are we doing here? Where are we going? What are we going to do?" Mother recalled. "So we started looking for land. What else could we do?"

A real estate agent recommended by a bishop in Rome helped them scout the countryside for a suitable location to plant a shortwave antenna.

Seeking a blessing on her confused efforts, Mother and her entourage attended the Pope's private Mass on January 31. After Mass, the Pope caught sight of the abbess at the end of the receiving line. "Mother Angelica, you are a strong woman," John Paul rumbled. From his greeting, one can assume the Pope had heard tell of Mother's exploits during his America sojourn in 1987 and probably knew something of her run-ins with the bishops conference. The nun told him of her plans to broadcast Catholic programming via shortwave radio into Russia and the Eastern Bloc, which received an ecstatic Papal reaction. Mother interpreted the response as permission to proceed.

The Pope's regard for Angelica was obvious a little more than a month later when he spotted her in the crowd at the conclusion of a general audience in Paul VI Hall at the Vatican. He reached over the barricades, holding her face in his hands. "Ah, Mother Angelica, the grand chief," he announced over the din. "Mother Angelica, the grand chief!" he repeated, laughing.

On the afternoon of February 1, Angelica met a man pivotal to the future of the shortwave endeavor. The Dutch Catholic millionaire and philanthropist Piet Derksen had canceled their scheduled meeting in Holland and opted instead to fly to Rome.

Derksen was the founder of a chain of sports shops in Holland, an enterprise that had made him comfortably wealthy. But a revolutionary idea he had in 1967 had made him one of the richest men in the Netherlands. He envisioned "a holiday the weather couldn't spoil, with every imaginable facility built in, combining the flavor of the country club, the health farm, the sports complex and the villa holiday." His ecoconscious vacation villages built around huge transparent domes (to regulate the temperature for water recreation) became a European sensation. In time, Derksen would open twelve Center Parcs throughout Europe. In 1982, after recovering from a protracted illness, he had funneled his money into a foundation called Witness To God's Love and started bankrolling religious projects. Missionary work, television start-ups, radio efforts—any evangelistic activity—could rely on Derksen's foundation for funding. "My wealth has been like a stone around my neck," Derksen told a reporter in 1984. "I'm glad to get rid of it."

Mother Angelica was only too happy to assist him. The stately, slightly hunched gentleman with the swollen eyes of a mole slowly approached Angelica in the coffee shop of the Rome hotel that first day of February. He had high cheekbones and a broad pate fringed by wavy gray locks, lending him a fatherly aspect.

"You're the one," Derksen told the nun in a heavy Dutch accent. "What do you need?"

The suddenness of the question threw Mother Angelica. "Maybe two million dollars," she said.

"I'll get it for you," Derksen promised. He would chat with Mother for less than a half hour, leaving as quickly as he had come. By the end of the week, Derksen wired the entire $2 million to EWTN's account. The shortwave project had definitely begun.

Mother imaged seminarians studying in Rome would drop by her studio to record devotions, prayers, catechesis, and Scripture readings in their native tongues. She would broadcast their labors via shortwave, reaching every nation and tribe. To ensure success, Angelica would replicate the Birmingham model, establishing the production and broadcast facility next to a house of comtemplative prayer.

A villa purchased in April 1989 suited her purposes. It was located in the suburb of Olgiata, an hour north of Rome. The left side of the villa housed radio equipment, visiting clergy, and members of the Order of the Eternal Word studying for the priesthood. Four brothers would relocate to Rome in September 1989. The sisters' cloister occupied the right side of the villa. Every few months three sisters rotated in from the Birmingham foundation to maintain the convent and pray for the radio work.

By April, Angelica had purchased a mountaintop seemingly made to carry a shortwave antenna. Piet Derksen committed more money to the effort and the German-based Aid To the Church in Need donated $600,000 of radio equipment and $400,000 in funds. Everything was falling into place, save for a broadcast license and permission to build.

Repeated attempts to secure the authorizations from the Italian government were frustrated. "The government had passed a law two years earlier that no foreign entity could ever own a license," Mother Angelica recollected. "But every two months, I'd go to Rome and they'd say, 'Well we're talking about it and it looks favorable.' "

Matt Scalici, who relocated to Rome with his family to construct the technical aspects of the shortwave operation, has his own perspective on the bureaucratic setbacks. "The corruption in Italy was unbelievable. Everyone wanted a kickback. We found sites but couldn't get the power out there. The lead time was three to five years, and Mother never committed to a project that far out. If it didn't happen now, forget it. So she said, 'Let's find something in Alabama.' "

Though she continued pursuing the shortwave production and broadcast facility in Rome, by September 1989, Mother had begun work on a parallel shortwave project based in the United States.

Whether this station was intended to relay the Roman signal to the Americas or to serve as a backup in case the European venture failed is unclear. A study commissioned by Mother found Alabama to be the ideal spot for transmitting a shortwave signal capable of blanketing the Americas and beyond. Her gaze turned homeward. With Piet Derksen's funds tied up in the Roman initiative, Angelica needed money to pursue her American-based project.

As she had throughout her religious life, she went to a fellow Italian. Joseph Canizaro, a self-made real estate developer from New Orleans, who had guaranteed the Galaxy satellite for EWTN in 1987, took Mother's call in the autumn of 1989.

The nun was very direct, as Canizaro remembered it: "Joseph, what can I pray for to get you to give me a million dollars?"

"Mother, I've never given away a million dollars in my life, and I can't make payroll," Canizaro quickly told her, skimming past the request the way a pirogue glides over bayou waters. Unbeknownst to Angelica, a real estate recession had struck and Canizaro's finances were ensnared in a piece of property drenched in toxic waste. The necessary cleanup was projected to cost $100 million.

"Call me back and tell me what I can pray for," Mother said, ending the conversation before she got a definite no. After some thought, Canizaro phoned the nun with a prayer request.

"I told her if I could sell my Crown Plaza Hotel for enough money, I could give her a million. I thought she was nuts," Canizaro said. Still, he asked her to urge God to hasten the sale of his hotel.

Mother Angelica prayed in earnest for the New Orleans businessman, estimating her radio operation would cost $11 million. As a spiritual sign of her need, she and the sisters filled a small bag with eleven copper coins. The bag was tied to the fingers of a small plaster Jesus held aloft by a Saint Joseph statue in the monastery hallway. The way Jesus turned water to wine, Saint Joseph was expected to turn copper to gold. The nuns began a simple prayer petition to the saint.

Mother Angelica's focus on the radio apostolate and the extensive renovation of her monastery chapel (under way since the summer) increasingly separated her from the network.

"She said, 'I'm going to renovate the chapel; I'll be back in two weeks,' " Chris Harrington, then VP of operations and production recalled. "For all intents and purposes, she never came back."

Her time consumed by travel to Europe, the responsibilities of her community, and the ongoing renovations, Mother spent only a few hours a week at the network. Matt Scalici, VP of engineering, was dividing his time between Rome and Birmingham, while Bill Steltemeier jetted back and forth to Europe, trying to keep the Roman adventure afloat. The scattering of the management team and Mother's absence took a noticeable toll on EWTN, according to Marynell Ford, VP of marketing. "Within twenty-four hours, all the spiritual direction—everything—was gone; the backbiting and stuff started. The world entered in. Chris and I sat out on the curb in front of the network, just alarmed about the future." Harrington and Ford would for the most part shoulder day-to-day operations for the next two years.

For all the distractions, network programming did not escape Mother's attention, particularly those programs submitted under the contract with the bishops conference. Mother Gabriel Long and some of the Sister Servants screened anything submitted.

"The programming, qualitywise, was so bad," Angelica admitted later. "Like I remember a nun talking about the Holy Father, something about him being too old and not aware of what he was doing, so I wouldn't air that."

A 1989 report by the Bishops Communications Committee claimed EWTN rejected "one out of every three programs submitted" by the conference. EWTN disputed the figure, insisting they refused only one program for content reasons under the contract.

But other conference programming was officially rejected by EWTN for another reason. As Bishop Robert Lynch, who was a liaison between the network and the bishops conference, told me, "The reason given for denying programming was technical. Mother Angelica was bitten by a fox; she was no one's dummy."

"We were told that the programming did not meet technical standards," Bishop Anthony Bosco said with a smile. "Frankly, I believe that Mother believed that some of the bishops were not orthodox. In a way, I don't blame her."

The situation led to a "fruitless exchange of recrimination" between the two sides, in the estimation of Bishop Edward O'Donnell, chairman of the Bishops Communications Committee. Barred by the contract from shopping even rejected programs to other outlets, the bishops voted in November to overhaul their agreement with EWTN. They hoped to segue into a less exclusive deal. But Bill Steltemeier would save them the trouble.

Before the two-year term of the contract had expired, Steltemeier viewed a submitted show featuring a cleric promising female ordination under the next pontificate. "It was the last straw" for Steltemeier. In response, he sent the bishops conference a letter, terminating their agreement. Though some press reports credited the bishops with ending the contract, Steltemeier said, "That's a lie from the word go." Whoever stopped the music, Mother's dance with the bishops conference had ended.

The beginning of 1990 brought an answer from Saint Joseph and a reward for Angelica's faith. Joseph Canizaro's hotel deal did not submit to Mother's tenacious prayers, but a separate court settlement exceeded his expectations. A parcel of polluted land purchased in the early 1980s threatened to bankrupt Canizaro. To try to recoup something, he sued the original landowner, an oil company, for $15 million.

"I walked out of court with thirty-five million dollars," Canizaro crowed in a loud voice. "There is no doubt in my mind that it was Mother Angelica's prayers that got that for me. That was her million dollars. It was the miracle of my life, which allowed me to buy land along the riverfront in downtown New Orleans. It's what made me. I knew it was an answer to prayer."

In Birmingham, Mother and her community offered a tearful thanksgiving to Saint Joseph in the monastery hall. Canizaro and Archbishop Phillip Hannan of New Orleans hand-delivered the million-dollar check to Angelica on February 15, 1990. It would be the financial genesis of the U.S. shortwave network. A week later, providence extracted personal payment from Mother Angelica.

She was leaving the Galleria Mall outside of Birmingham on February 22, a pillow under her arm, when it happened. Sisters

Rizzo and her mother, Mae, in a studio photo from the early 1920s. *(OLAM)*

The wandering father, John Rizzo. *(OLAM)*

Rita and Mae in one of their many storefront apartments. *(OLAM)*

Sass and spunk. The first female drum majorette at McKinley High. Rita Rizzo in 1939. *(OLAM)*

Rita, Grandma Gianfrancesco, Mae Rizzo, and Aunt June Francis before the Gianfrancesco home on Liberty Street in the early 1940s. *(OLAM)*

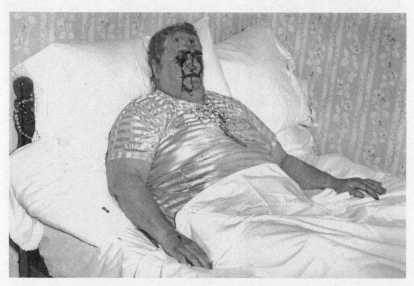

The mystic: Rhoda Wise enduring Christ's passion on a Friday in the 1940s. *(OLAM)*

The first solemn profession of Sister Mary Angelica of the Annunciation. The thorns were fitting that day, January 2, 1947. *(OLAM)*

The Angler: Mother Angelica and her fishing lures, 1961. *(OLAM)*

Presenting the inspired monastery in cardboard to Bishop Thomas Toolen of Birmingham. Mother Veronica looks on, February 30, 1961. *(OLAM)*

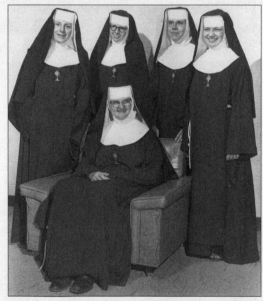

The Sisters of Birmingham Foundation: *From the left*: Sr. M. Joseph, Sr. M. Raphael, Sr. M. Assumpta, Sr. M. Michael, and Mother M. Angelica *(seated)*, 1962. *(OLAM)*

The community in the late 1970s.
Angelica's mother, Sr. Mary David, is seated in the wheelchair. *(OLAM)*

The confidant and the guardian: with Ginny Dominick and Bill Steltemeier in the mid-1980s. *(OLAM)*

The builder: overseeing construction of EWTN's new studio, 1985. *(OLAM)*

Hamming it up with Tom Monaghan on *Mother Angelica Live!* (EWTN)

"I'm so tired of you, liberal Church in America." World Youth Day, August 14, 1993. (Author/OLAM)

The Crutch and the Crozier: with Bishop David Foley on the day of his installation, 1993. (OLAM)

"Mother Angelica, weak in body, strong in spirit." With Pope
John Paul II, 1996. *(L'Osservatore Romano)*

With the author in the
monastery garden, 2004.
(Author/OLAM)

Flights of Angelicas: the Abbess of Our Lady of the Angels and her nuns, 2004. *(OLAM)*

In Lourdes, October 16, 2003. *(OLAM)*

Joseph and Regina walked ahead of Mother, loaded down with the items they had just purchased. As they approached the parking lot, Mother felt "somebody" thrust her forward. She lost her balance and threw her left arm out to break the fall. A loud crack ricocheted off the asphalt. Because she was unable to get up on her own, two passersby and the nuns helped Angelica to her feet and into the car.

"Go to St. Vincent's Hospital," Mother instructed. "I broke my wrist."

"No, you sprained it," the perpetually jovial Sister Regina told her.

"No, honey, I broke it." For emphasis, Mother raised her limp wrist; a pair of bones protruded through the flesh at opposing angles. "Go easy; you don't have to drive fast."

The shattered wrist caused Mother the "worst physical pain" of her life. Four pins attached to a metal framework penetrated her flesh, holding the broken bones in place. Sanctifying the setback, Angelica told Sister Raphael she was offering the pain up "for the continuation of God's blessing on the work He has given me to do." Mother would bear the discomfort of the metal contraption for a month, but she never regained full mobility in her left wrist. Where healing evaded her, God's blessing was less bashful, tangibly appearing later that spring.

Matt Scalici consulted with shortwave pioneer George Jacobs to assemble a list of possible Alabama locations for the radio network. On inspection, none of these sites proved suitable. A 180-acre mountaintop property an hour outside of Birmingham was similarly discarded as being too difficult to build on and not appropriate for shortwave transmission. But Mother insisted on seeing the place personally.

They drove up the mountain's rocky incline through a slim cavern of trees on May 31, 1990. At the summit, beyond the dense woods, Mother and Scalici found an old peach orchard and cannery. Angelica's eyes fixed on something outside the window.

"Here. Right here," she said, stepping from the car. "We're going to buy it."

"You can't buy this; it's no good," Scalici counseled, even though the land belonged to a friend. "It's rocky."

"Do you see Saint Michael up there?" Mother asked.

"Where? *Where?*" Scalici studied the surroundings. "Do you see him?"

"Right there." Angelica pointed in the distance. "Do *you* see him?"

"I don't see anything."

"Well, I do, and we're buying it."

Mother Angelica claimed she saw Saint Michael the Archangel, "a handsome, strong, manly looking six-foot-tall warrior," atop the Vandiver, Alabama, mountain. It was not her first acquaintance with such phenomena. In 1989, while praying at Italy's Mount Gargano, where, tradition holds, Saint Michael impressed his footprint upon an altar, Mother felt the angel's sword touch her shoulders. "I will ever be at your side, and we will fight together," Saint Michael told Angelica, according to the OLAM History. She maintained that the archangel appeared to her repeatedly over the years.

"On the one hand, I don't think these are imaginary phenomena, but on the other hand, I would not put them in the category of apparition," Father Benedict Groeschel, an expert on spirituality and private revelations, said of Mother's experiences. "They fall into the realm of imaginative visions, where the inspiration takes on a sensible form to that person; it's not a hallucination. A hallucination is a pathological phenomenon, which is accompanied by a disintegration of the personality. This is integrated with the personality. It makes her successful."

A skeptical Matt Scalici went to the county courthouse to research the boundaries of the mountaintop property. He was stunned to learn that the land straddled Shelby and St. Clair counties. Scalici knew Saint Clare was the patron saint of television and founder of the Poor Clares. What were the chances of Mother Angelica deciding out of the blue to purchase property located in the very county named after her order's foundress? And in the Bible Belt no less? The confluence of events could not be dismissed as coincidental. To Scalici, it was assurance that someone other than Mother was leading the acquisition.

Angelica bought the Vandiver property in mid-June, just as

foreign-language production commenced at the villa in Olgiata. Lithuanians, Belorussians, and Romanians clandestinely recorded prayers outlawed in their native countries. Although she was pleased by the reports of new programming, the Italian bureaucratic delays gnawed at Mother. Perhaps every "nation and tribe" could be reached just as easily from Alabama, Angelica thought. Piet Derksen would need convincing.

A letter of October 30, 1990, from Archbishop John Foley of the Pontifical Council for Social Communications would change everything. The letter, apparently written at the behest of the Vatican secretariat of state, discouraged Mother Angelica from pursuing a radio operation in Europe, as it could sap monies from other efforts. The shortwave operation was considered unnecessary, since Vatican Radio was already broadcasting internationally. A copy of the letter was sent to Piet Derksen.

Angelica felt obliged to respond to Foley's letter, considering it unjust. On November 14, she wrote the archbishop, informing him that she was in possession of a separate note sent to Piet Derksen by Foley, which "impl[ied] that Mr. Derksen should not fund this project." "Mr. Derksen has spoken to the Holy Father several times about this project and I was called by the Holy Father's secretary a few months ago to go to Castel Gandolfo," Angelica explained. "The Holy Father encouraged the project and has given both it and Mr. Derksen His personal blessing." She regretted that any cardinal or bishop would object to "evangelizing the poorest of the poor" and ended with: "I do not understand politics, nor do I wish to. I merely wish to accomplish the mission the Lord has given me to do."

Annoyed by the resistance from some in the Vatican, the mounting expense, and the ponderous legal progress in Italy, Piet Derksen placed an angry call to Mother on April 29, 1991. She says he "raved and ranted," questioning her use of funds and the bureaucratic stasis. Blaming Italy for the expense and the slowdown, Mother raised the possibility of building the shortwave network near Birmingham. The ranting stopped. "Well do it," Derksen told her. "Do it!"

Mother's shortwave dream was still alive.

Broken Orders

FROM THE VERY INCEPTION, Mother Angelica and Father Michael McDonagh could not agree on a trajectory for the Order of the Eternal Word. Like two parents in a tug-of-war over their child's future, the cofounders forcefully pulled in opposing directions: McDonagh clinging to his ascetic visions, Angelica determined that the priests and brothers should be working outside the monastery, serving the network and evangelizing the public.

On April 27, 1991, Mother invited Father McDonagh into her parlor for the "come home to Jesus" meeting. Beneath the thick salt-and-pepper hair climbing up under her veil, Angelica wore the fixed expression of one who had long ruminated on a problem and, having arrived at a painful solution, was determined to carry it out. The departure of twelve brothers from the community (some having gone to Mother with allegations of cruelty against Father McDonagh) and the demand that she build the brothers a monastery behind the network, troubled the abbess. She told McDonagh that the "penances, fasting, and contemplative prayer" were keeping the brothers from the service they could be providing to the network and that some modification of their life was needed. The Irish priest stood firm. He would continue training the brothers in the contemplative Augustinian manner to which they had become accustomed—and as long as everyone was coming clean, he announced that he no longer enjoyed being part of her live show. The friendship and the collaboration quickly terminated.

"Father and I have been friends for many years, and this is a very hard time for me," Angelica said to the nuns following the meeting. "I thought the Order would be otherwise, but it isn't. I released the Order, and leave Father Michael the freedom to see what the brothers want to do."

In May 1991, Mother traveled to Rome to offer her brothers studying at seminary a choice.

"The split was announced in Olgiata," Father Philip (Richard) Mataconis, a transfer from the Salesian Order, recalled. "She said that Father Michael wanted to found his own order but that we were free to do what we wanted. 'Stay with him or come with us,' she said."

Three men either left the order or followed Father McDonagh. Father Philip and five brothers remained with Mother Angelica. From this small remnant would spring a renewal of the Order of the Eternal Word, closer in practice and vision to Mother's initial inspiration.

Just days before their return to Birmingham, she sought to reclaim the order and remind the men of their Franciscan roots. In a letter dated June 13, she told the brothers that God had called them to bring "back the stray sheep" by "serving them in every spiritual need, [through] direction, teaching, retreats, radio, television, and the printed word." She advised them to read the Rule of Saint Francis and to allow it to seep into their community life.

Angelica adopted a hands-on approach with the order. She regularly visited the friary and offered the brothers mid-week lectures that affectionately became known as "the Wednesday audiences."

A new devotion to the foundress arose in the friary. "Mother was the icon of orthodoxy for us and we wanted to protect her," Father Francis Mary Stone told me.

Convinced that the sisters needed to reestablish an enclosure without breach, Mother Angelica instructed the nuns to venture no farther than the new cedar fence going up around the monastery.

"Why are you putting up this wall?" a sister asked the abbess one day, mournfully looking out Mother's office window.

"Because the Lord told me, 'This is the time,' " Angelica answered.

The days of the nuns mingling with pilgrims and workers on the extended property had come to an end. Mother's prime intention was to stem network gossip about the Order of the Eternal Word and the Sister Servants by limiting access to the community. But interviews suggest there may have been deeper spiritual motives at play.

Over the years, Mother had grown increasingly concerned about a coming spiritual chastisement: a moment when God might permit his people to undergo a period of trial for the sins of the age. In preparation, she recalled her sisters from Rome and drew the community into a formal cloister. Restoring the monastic traditions of the order, she shielded the nuns from even a passing acquaintance with the world. Network business, once shared freely at table, was now confined to the ears of a few intimates. The sisters were to focus on their calling and to avoid becoming "preoccupied" with external affairs.

In the summer of 1992, Mother learned that the bishops conference planned to tinker with the English translation of the Mass. The acclamation after the Scripture readings—"This is the Word of the Lord"—would be changed to "The Word of the Lord." A subtle change, to be sure, but one Mother Angelica saw as symptomatic of the ever-shifting translations threatening the stability of the Mass. To protect her sisters from the liturgical novelties of the day, the abbess asked three nuns to pore over the documents of Vatican II and related official writings in order to see what options were available to them. The nuns discovered that the Second Vatican Council had never intended a wholesale abandonment of Latin in the new Mass. Quite the contrary, the official council and papal documents encouraged the retention of Latin and the use of Gregorian chant in the renewed liturgy. Immune to the changeable whims of translators, Mother saw Latin as a refuge.

No longer would her sisters or her audience be subjected to what she called the "electric Church" ("Every time you go, you get a shock"). On July 5, 1992, Mother announced that the televised conventual Mass of Our Lady of the Angels Monastery would be celebrated in Latin. The homily, readings, and certain prayers would remain in the vernacular.

The nun's repertoire of folksy guitar tunes from the 1960s and 1970s were gradually phased out, replaced with violin-backed harmonized arrangements of the Pater Noster, the Gloria, and the Agnus Dei. Though the monastery celebrated the new Mass of Vatican II, the priest with his back to the people, the sounds of the service, and the old devotions were often mistaken as a throwback to a bygone era. In point of fact, it was much closer to the renewal foreseen by the Second Vatican Council—and it was beaming into nearly every diocese in America.

"To show the power of EWTN and Mother Angelica: When I first came here people were saying, 'Why are they doing the Kyrie? Nobody understands that anymore. Why are they doing the Lamb of God as Agnus Dei?'," Bishop David Foley, the bishop of Birmingham, recalled. "But if you go into a lot of churches today, they are singing the Agnus Dei and the Kyrie now. They would never have done that if it hadn't been for EWTN."

In their white Dominican habits draped with the brown scapular of Saint Francis, the Sister Servants looked nothing like their cloistered counterparts. The wardrobe differences only underscored the disunity in the cloister. Mother Gabriel could not help acting like the superior she had once been as a Dominican. Through habit, the Sister Servants deferred to Gabriel in matters large and small. They even developed their own devotions, privately retreating to the small apartment off the carport to recite the rosary as a group, thus excluding the cloistered nuns. Beneath Angelica's nose a distinct order had taken shape, an order unto itself.

The Sister Servants' independent streak was also evident at the network. EWTN employees remember the Servants directly intervening in programming decisions. On one occasion a show supposedly vetted by Mother Angelica vanished from the EWTN shelves.

"It turned out that one of the Sister Servants didn't agree with the program, so she hid it," Chris Harrington recalled. "That was the end of the Sister Servants' participation in the network."

On May 5, 1992, matters came to a head. Mother called a Sister Servant into her office, aware that the woman had been struggling with her vows. In the course of their conversation, the nun revealed that she was not at peace in the monastery, and neither were the other externs. Angelica "grieved." Following a conversation, Mothers Angelica and Gabriel decided that the Sister Servants would build their own retreat house in Birmingham and establish a separate community there. "They couldn't be forced to do what was not in their hearts," Sister Raphael wrote of that day.

Angelica conceded that the choice of Mother Gabriel to lead the Sister Servants may have been a rash one. "She never got the gist of what she was supposed to do," Mother Angelica told me. She then grew quiet—thoughtful. "I came to the conclusion that I'm not a very good foundress. I'm sure I'm at fault all the way somewhere . . . I don't know."

Mother Gabriel and the Sister Servants refused to be interviewed for this book, so their perspective on the community founding and the eventual breakup can only be surmised. But from the short communications I shared with them, it is obvious they would prefer to leave this unpleasant chapter of their history in the past.

Today the Sister Servants offer retreats led by EWTN personalities and provide lodging to visitors, though they have no formal ties to Mother Angelica or her order.

Global Radio

ON THE third-tallest mountain in Alabama, ten acres of trees lay scattered like matchsticks, torn from the earth to make way for the only privately owned shortwave network in the world. Locals fumed over the environmental damage and the fresh power lines zigzagging through their property. Others sued the network for trespassing and expanding the only dirt road to the mountain summit. Then the local utility provider estimated that it would cost roughly a million dollars a year just to power up the station.

"It was a time when you wondered, Did I make the right decision? Did the Lord really tell me to do this?" Mother said of the challenges. "From the very start, it was a heartache, a question, a doubt—but we kept on going."

Like a metallic phoenix spreading its wings above the Alabama brush by sheer will, WEWN's curtain antennas shrouded the mountaintop. Powered by four 500-kilowatt transmitters and backed up by double generators in case of a power failure, or a prolonged chastisement, the station was built to last. Unforeseen excavation, blasting, weather delays, and technological expenses bloated the budget to $23 million.

On December 28, 1992, Piet Derksen flew to Alabama to launch WEWN at Mother's side. Thick fog wreathed the mountain, obscuring what his $23 million had purchased.

Before more than one hundred onlookers inside the sparkling facility, Derksen and Mother tripped the switch, sending the shortwave signal rippling through the valley and far beyond. In a speech at the launch, Angelica underscored the unique service the radio operation would provide to humanity and praised Piet and Trude Derksen for their unflagging commitment to the project.

"Their faith throughout the years of building WEWN, and the thought of the millions of souls that will be saved as a result of the daily broadcasts gave everyone the courage to persevere. . . . It is exciting for all of us to realize that wherever there is an earthquake or any other tragedy, that by this wonderful medium, we will have the ability to reach people immediately."

England, Russia, Japan, India, and other countries soon confirmed reception of the signal. So did some Alabama residents, who, even without the aid of a shortwave radio, could hear WEWN resonating in their dental work and brass beds!

Initially, the shortwave network broadcast Scripture readings, catechesis, and devotions in twenty-six separate languages. But in two years' time, the programming was heavy with rebroadcasts of radio-friendly TV series and Mother Angelica's live shows.

Following his termination in 1993, an employee at the shortwave network sent a letter to Piet Derksen, charging Mother Angelica with financial impropriety. Though the claims were never substantiated—and vehemently denied by Matt Scalici, Bill Steltemeier, and Mother Angelica in interviews—Derksen called the abbess in an accusatory rage. In Mother's reconstruction of the conversation, he called her "a crook" and refused to hear any explanation. "If this is God's will, let Him finish it," Derksen told the nun. After spending an estimated $35 million between the projects in Rome and Alabama, Piet Derksen cut off all financial support. Before Derksen's death, he and Mother would reconcile, but at the time, the nun was crestfallen.

"I can't tell you how I felt. It was beyond brokenhearted, beyond failure," Mother said of that moment. "We were scared about how we were going to make payments every month."

Angelica dragged herself to the chapel and asked her Spouse to prove that the shortwave operation was part of His will by sustaining it. She instructed Bill Steltemeier to fold the shortwave expenses into the operating costs of the network and trusted that God would somehow provide.

Following instructions, she had built a thing capable of reaching "every nation and tribe." In the contentious struggle over doctrine and practice within the Catholic Church, Mother Angelica would soon discover a new purpose for the shortwave network, and for her entire media empire.

15
The Defender of the Faith

IT WAS AN INTERVENTION by Cardinal Bernard Law of Boston at an extraordinary Synod of bishops in 1985 that would give birth to the first universal catechism of the Catholic Church in more than four hundred years. Law, voicing a widely held episcopal wish, called for a single volume that would codify exactly what the Church believed and taught in the fractious post–Vatican II period. Embracing the idea, Pope John Paul II authorized a draft committee in 1986.

The original French edition of this catechism, promulgated by the Pope in October 1992, sold more than a million copies. International public demand intensified, necessitating the release of Spanish, Asian, Italian, and African editions. But the English edition, caught in a linguistic and theological morass, was nowhere to be found. Mother Angelica was partly responsible for the delay.

Owing to his seminal role in the creation of the catechism, it was only natural that Cardinal Law should oversee the translation of the English edition. Under his leadership, the translators adopted an inclusive approach, systematically expunging gender-specific terms from the catechism, leaving behind neutral alternatives. References to "men" were translated as "humanity"; "men and women" became "people and family." Jesus' words "As you did it to one of the least of my brethren" read in the new translation "As you did it to one of the least of these who are members of my family."

In a letter of December 1992 accompanying the final English

draft, Cardinal Law described the translation to his brother bishops as a "moderate approach" toward inclusive language. The American bishops ratified the draft and sent it to Rome for final approval. A firestorm of criticism ensued.

"They're not changing the language for organic reasons, but because some pressure groups say, 'We're offended,'" Father Joseph Fessio, editor of the traditional Ignatius Press, charged in the media. Fessio believed that the translation capitulated to progressives and feminists, who wished to adjust Catholic teaching to accommodate their own agendas. "There are other Catholics who don't want the change, and they are being ignored," Fessio said.

In his archdiocesan paper, Cardinal Law defended the translation on cultural grounds. "There was a time when the word 'man' would generally be understood . . . as meaning all human beings," he wrote. "This is not always the case today, given the cultural shift concerning inclusivity."

Mother Angelica's sisters had already ordered 150 English catechisms to sell in their gift shop when word of the controversy reached the cloister. The spirited Sister Agnes, a nun graced with beauty and spunk, phoned the vendor to determine which edition they could expect to receive. When she learned that they had reserved copies of the "inclusive language translation" of the catechism, Agnes canceled the order, assuming Mother Angelica would approve. Had it been any other group of sisters, the incident would have passed without notice, but a cloister with a direct pipeline to millions of Catholics merited close scrutiny.

The monastery phone rang on January 8, 1993. It was Cardinal Law, purportedly calling Mother Angelica to discuss the cancellation of the book orders and to share a message from the papal nuncio. Hoarse from a severe asthma attack, Angelica refused the call. According to the OLAM History, the nuncio himself then called the network, and he was similarly informed that Mother could not speak.

Late in the day, Bishop Raymond Boland of Birmingham rang to assure Angelica that the inclusive language translation of the catechism would be approved by Rome and that public opposition would be seen as hostile to the will of the Church. Mother took the call. In a rasp, she told the bishop she didn't appreciate inclusive language and asked a rhetorical question: "[Was] Jesus . . . conceived of the Holy Spirit and born a human or an individual? You don't ask a mother if the baby is a human, you ask if it's a boy or a girl!" Though she was not directly responsible for canceling the book order that provoked the call, Mother was only too happy to express her opinion. The battle was joined.

After reviewing the English draft of the catechism, the Vatican summoned Cardinal Law to Rome in February. At the same moment, Mother Angelica had her own business in the Eternal City. As she approached the Congregation for the Doctrine of Faith next to St. Peter's Basilica, Cardinal Law exited the palazzo, his fleshy face plastered with a smile.

"Oh, hello, Mother. I hear you have an appointment with Cardinal Ratzinger. Now you push that inclusive language. That's very important in America," Angelica remembered the cardinal telling her. "And I thought, boy, you ought to know why I'm going in."

Mother Angelica met with Cardinal Joseph Ratzinger, the Vatican's doctrinal authority and the man ultimately responsible for the catechism. In his parlor, they chatted intensely. Sitting uncomfortably in a gold-and-red velvet-upholstered chair that could have easily passed for Napoleon's coronation throne, Angelica explained the reach of her twenty-four-hour TV operation and the shortwave network. "I want to put the Church all over the world, and we can do it. But I can't if it's in inclusive language," Mother told the cardinal, boldly referencing the American version of the catechism. "It's terrible; it changes doctrine, and it changes everything." After trading cordialities, Mother thanked the cardinal for his time and left.

The Vatican rejected the gender-neutral draft, suspending publication of the English catechism for nearly a year and a half. In the interim the Holy See commandeered its own translation, one faithful to the French original, replete with masculine pronouns and gender-specific terminology. While it is impossible to gauge Mother Angelica's influence on this turn of events, more than a decade later Cardinal Law is still stung by the rejection and mindful of Angelica's hand in it.

"I think our final product was better than what was formally re-leased, and she had some pretty tough things to say about me. The reaction to the project was, I felt, very unjust," he told me. Law ob-jected to the characterizations of his ideological position and the motives ascribed to his actions. "I think I was marginalized perhaps after that—because I know I wasn't invited to appear on EWTN af-terward."

Congestion and coughing fits regularly sidelined Mother Angel-ica in the early part of 1993. The seventy-year-old abbess routinely fought laryngitis and wheezing spells during her live show. At home, she sucked on inhalers and relied on oxygen tanks for survival. On May 5, her taxed lungs required professional attention.

Diagnosed with a severe bronchial infection, she was confined to the hospital for two weeks. One evening during her stay, a ferocious cough, which caused her portly frame to shudder and turned her cheeks hot pink, smashed a vertebra in her spine. The shattered bone damaged a nerve running to Mother's right leg—her good one. Like ink-stained porcelain, the leg turned an ugly purple and re-fused to move. The pain was excruciating. To compensate for the spinal damage, she wore a new back and leg brace. She dedicated the back brace to God the Father, the right leg brace to the Son, and her old left one to the Holy Spirit. To walk even short distances, a pair of crutches was now required.

Looking back, Mother saw the hand of providence in the pain: "It kept me dependent on the Lord to do anything and everything. It was a safety because I could never give myself credit for any accom-plishment. It's a protection; it's like a shield for me. I think that's true for everybody; they just don't see it, or they're not told about it."

After a seven-week absence from the airwaves, she shared her painful experience with her family, saying, "One of the lessons I've learned is that suffering and old age are most precious. You know why? Because at that point in our lives we're powerful."

Weeks later the old abbess would show just how powerful she was at a World Youth Day celebration in Denver, Colorado.

The Gender Bender in Denver

THE POPE'S MEETING with the youth of the world was to EWTN what the Olympics were to a secular network. Bringing the Pope live and unedited to the 32 million homes receiving the signal had now become almost expected. Father Timothy Dolan of St. Louis and Stephanie Claudy, a student, were slated to anchor the visit. Mother Angelica offered special commentary in a half-hour daily segment entitled *Mother's Corner.*

On the evening of Friday, August 13, EWTN aired a Way of the Cross from Mile High Stadium at 7:30 P.M. Mother had hyped the event the day before, encouraging her audience to join the Pope and the world's youth to contemplate Christ's passion.

But that night at Mile High Stadium, nothing went according to schedule. Cardinal Eduardo Pironio of the Pontifical Council on the Laity, not the Holy Father, presided over the Way of the Cross. And when the Cincinnati-based mime troupe, the Fountain Square Fools, stepped into the arena to reenact Christ's passion, shock rippled through the country.

A new producer, Michael Warsaw, once responsible for publicity at the Shrine of the Immaculate Conception in Washington, D.C., sat in the EWTN truck, a puzzled look on his face as he watched the Way of the Cross come down on the feed. There was something odd about one of the mimes performing the passion. When Warsaw stepped away for a break, Chris Harrington took his place before the bank of TV monitors. She was mortified by what she saw, and certain that Mother Angelica would have a similar reaction. On screen, swathed in a white chiffon garment, the attractive Christina Brown, looking every inch a woman, appeared before 70,000 teens and millions of households in the role of Jesus Christ.

Harrington abandoned the truck to find Mother Angelica. Seated in a hotel restaurant with Bill Steltemeier and Sister Margaret Mary, the nun was staring down a white-chocolate dessert when Harrington charged in.

"Mother, I've got something I need to tell you," Harrington

heaved. "They're doing the Stations of the Cross and they have a woman portraying Christ."

"You're kidding," Mother Angelica said, placing her fork alongside the untouched dessert. She got to her feet and hobbled out to the production truck to see for herself. "That's a woman," she exclaimed indignantly, peering at the monitors. "This is it. I've had all I'm going to take."

Mother Angelica dispatched Steltemeier to the offices of the bishops conference to get an explanation. She was hurt and angry. From her perspective, EWTN had been roped into what amounted to an agitprop for female ordination. If a woman could play Jesus before millions at an official Papal event, why should women be denied the right to stand in *persona Christi* at the altar?

Steltemeier's room adjoined Mother Angelica's. He said the abbess was up most of the night, crying and praying. Anguished over how to respond to what she considered a politically loaded presentation, Mother felt she had to defend the Church and the Pope.

"Lord, I'm angry. I'm upset," she prayed. "I don't want to say what I'm thinking. I want to say what you want me to say." Without planning anything definite, she resolved to make a statement the following day.

Reacting to Steltemeier's unrelenting inquiries and hoping to diffuse a developing controversy, the bishops conference issued a terse statement on August 14. "Mime never is an historical representation," the statement read. "The organizers never intended the portrayal of the Stations of the Cross to be a historical representation. Anyone, even a child, could have played any of the roles."

Lacking the subtle interpretive skills of the conference's staff, the *Denver Post* in its morning edition viewed the transgendered Way of the Cross differently. The story noted that "Jesus was portrayed by a woman, a fact some found ironic since the Catholic Church will not ordain women as priests."

The organizers admitted that the choice of a female to play the lead role was premeditated. Salli Lovelarkin, executive director of the Fountain Square Fools, told the Catholic News Service on September 8 that Christina Brown was chosen specifically because she "looked very much like the standard Renaissance portrayals of Jesus" and that every attempt had been made to "separate gender from the portrayal altogether."

That separation was lost on Sister Maureen Fiedler, a fierce advocate of female ordination. "The whole reason the Vatican claims women can't be priests is that we do not image Christ," Fiedler told a reporter following the Way of the Cross. "But obviously if they're imaging Christ as a woman, somebody in there thinks that we can image Jesus. If they're using a woman in the Stations of the Cross . . . by their own hand they have demolished one of their major arguments."

A high-ranking Vatican official present while the Pope viewed the Way of the Cross on television told me in an interview that His Holiness, "being an actor, could put it in context. But he certainly got the intended message." The archdiocese of Denver launched an investigation to uncover who was responsible for the performance. But the staff of the bishops conference closed ranks. Sister Mary Ann Walsh, the communications director for World Youth Day, said the Fountain Square Fools had been endorsed by the archdiocese of Cincinnati—a claim the Cincinnati archdiocese would later deny.

Surveying the reportage at breakfast, Mother Angelica announced her plan for the day. "I'm going to blast them. What do you think?" Mother asked Bill Steltemeier.

"Let's go for it, Mother."

Angelica phoned Sister Raphael and told her to be sure the sisters watched the midday broadcast.

On that Saturday, the *Mother's Corner* segment was titled "The Hidden Agenda." Seated on a stool before a TV screen bearing the World Youth Day emblem, Mother Angelica appeared miffed from the start. Like a dam holding back a torrent, her chin pressed to her chest, her eyes like two BBs, Angelica was ready to rumble.

"Yesterday I made a mistake when I was talking to you. I asked you to watch the Holy Father as he made the Stations, but he didn't make the Stations. So I'm sorry for that error. I'm very happy he wasn't there. The Stations were beautiful. The Prayers were beautiful. But they depicted Our Lord as a woman, an abomination to the Eternal Father!"

Like a mother defending her young, this time she lobbed something far sharper than a bread knife at her adversaries. The result was no less visceral or impassioned. As she continued, the pace quickened.

"It's blasphemous that you dare to portray Jesus as a woman. You know, as Catholics we've been quiet all these years. After the Vatican Council—those beautiful documents inspired by the Holy Spirit . . . they were misrepresented and misportrayed and misinterpreted all these years, and every excuse, like this mime, has been blamed on the Vatican documents. . . . I'm tired, I'm tired of being pushed in corners. I'm tired of your inclusive language that refuses to admit that the Son of God is a man! I'm tired of your tricks. I'm tired of your deceit. I'm tired of you making a crack, and the first thing you know there's a hole, and all of us fall in. No, this was deliberate. . . . You made a statement that was not accidental." She drew a deep breath, cutting her eyes. "I am so tired of you, liberal church in America."

Reciting a litany of outrages, including disrespect for the Eucharist, centering prayer, and mandatory sex education in the schools, Angelica finally exploded. "You're sick. . . . You have nothing to offer. You do nothing but destroy," she said, seething.

"You don't have vocations and you don't even care—your whole purpose is to destroy." Mother crossed her arms, her voice rising. "This Holy Father *is* a holy father. His whole duty is to portray the truth and . . . you destroy it before it appears in the papers. You speak against it. You call him an old man . . . you plant this mime, this woman as Jesus. You can't stand Catholicity at its height, so you spoil it, as you've spoiled so many things in these thirty years. . . . Try it with Martin Luther King. Put a white woman in his place and see what happens. Try it with Moses and Mohammed. No, we're the only ones who can be bashed to the ground and we say nothing."

She hissed to quell the hurt, her eyes turning moist. Defending the person of Christ and his Church, she roused herself to full fury. Biting at each syllable, clutching the Crucifix at her chest as if it were the source of the oratory, she continued, "You see this collar. We had this little modern collar so that we could appeal to this modern world, this pagan society. . . . We're going to change it. We're going to look very Roman because I'm making a statement!"

A cheer erupted from within Our Lady of the Angels Monastery. At least most of the sisters gathered in Saint Joseph's Room cheered.

"You've hidden your agenda with a mime. My agenda's not hidden," she said. "I have yet to hear anyone contradict you or cross you or say anything to distress you. Well I'm saying it. . . . I resent you pushing your anti-Catholic, ungodly ways upon the masses of this country. . . . Live your life, live your falsehood, live your lies— leave us alone . . . don't pour your poison, your venom on all the Church." Suddenly, her voice fell quiet. "In spite of what I've said I love you and I feel very sorry it has to be like this, but it has to be."

Mother's public challenge to the progressive wing of the Catholic Church reverberated far beyond World Youth Day, totally eclipsing the mime act that had inspired it.

"Clearly, her message resonated with a large portion of our audience," Michael Warsaw revealed. "She said what so many people had been thinking and mumbling to themselves privately for so long. It was their 'We're mad as hell, and we're not going to take it anymore.' "

"World Youth Day was *the* turning point for the network and for Mother," Chris Harrington opined. In that short half hour in Denver, Mother Angelica had summoned an orthodox crusade, challenging those who felt disenfranchised and confused by the continuing changes within the Church to stand firm and to cede no further ground.

The official response to Mother's outburst was swift. During a phone call on August 15, the president of the National Conference of Catholic Bishops, Archbishop William Keeler, told Mother she had "overreacted." Days later he would urge EWTN to shelve the editorial and suspend reruns so as not to fan the flames of controversy. But flames had already been fanned.

In a blistering editorial, Archbishop Rembert Weakland wrote that the "senseless and heartless condemning of one another" had to stop. He then proceeded to condemn Mother Angelica's "vitriolic" commentary: "For a half hour she ranted and raved about all the abuses since Vatican II, according to her own personal judgment which, of course, she equates with that of the Holy Father,"

Weakland wrote. "It was one of the most disgraceful, un-Christian, offensive, and divisive diatribes I have ever heard."

"He didn't think a woman playing Jesus was offensive," Mother said of Weakland's criticism. "He can go put his head in the back toilet as far as I am concerned."

The *National Catholic Reporter* branded Angelica a fundamentalist, who, in her World Youth Day appearance, had spread "darkness and fear." Relations with the bishops conference deteriorated. "At that moment, she threw down the gauntlet as the arbiter of orthodoxy and art forms," Bishop Robert Lynch, then a bishops conference official, said. "From 1988 to 1993, we danced at a distance; after 1993, she went over the edge."

But to a growing cadre of traditional Catholics, Mother Angelica had given voice to their frustrations and earned her stripes as their spokesperson. In a joint statement, a group of prominent Catholics, including writer and theologian Ralph McInerny; Father Joseph Fessio, publisher of Ignatius Press; and Helen Hull Hitchcock of Women for Faith and Family, saluted Angelica for her outspokenness and echoed her concerns.

"I was just being bold," Mother said of her World Youth Day commentary. "To me, that was a sacrilege, and it showed me just how far the liberal church had gone, and how they intended to reduce the faith to nothing."

Angelica's boldness was reported by National Public Radio, the *Washington Post, Newsday,* and papers all over the country. The general public, many seeing her in Denver for the first time, were fascinated by the "zinging nun," and they wanted more. Cable systems took notice. In the year following World Youth Day, EWTN picked up more than two hundred cable affiliates, thereby reaching at least 2 million new households in the United States and another 2 million—plus abroad. Mother Angelica's one-woman show in Denver was a demonstrable hit, one that would leave lasting marks on the nun and her community.

Back to the Future

NOTHING ADVERTISED Mother's newly revived orthodoxy like the traditional Franciscan habit she and her sisters were to adopt. Delivering on her promise to "look very Roman," Mother dispensed with the abbreviated tan veil her sisters had worn since the sixties and instituted the black veil and wimple she had known in her early religious life. The new headwear completely surrounded the face, covering the neck and ears. A thick band of material ran across the forehead, blocking off the hairline. Atop the nun's head, the black veil, like a flat overhang, jutted out in front and cascaded down the back into a neat pleat. The design took months to perfect and replicate.

Though Mother's Denver pronouncement introduced the wardrobe change, a small group of nuns, including Sister Antoinette and Sister Margaret Mary, had been agitating for a return to the old habit since 1988. When their redesign ideas were rebuffed by Mother, who thought viewers would perceive the community as being "pre–Vatican II," the group of nuns began a private novena. To remind one another of their intention, they would silently run a finger across their foreheads while passing in the hallways. The high sign indicated the place where the white band of the headwear would sit when their prayers were answered. On Christmas Eve in 1993, they got their wish. At the televised midnight Mass, all the nuns of Our Lady of the Angels Monastery wore the traditional headgear. The older sisters resisted the change of habit more than their younger counterparts. "I didn't like it," Sister Joseph told me in an interview. "I didn't find it really comfortable."

Her diminished peripheral vision made one former nun feel as if she were "in a box" while wearing the headgear. Even Sister Raphael, the vicar, was not comfortable with the change; but, in obedience, she and the other sisters wore the habit proudly.

"The old face is the same. You just don't see the old chin hanging down. There's one good thing about a full habit," Mother said, joking with her television audience on January 4, 1994. She explained that the habit change was a needed witness, a symbol that conveyed a "constant and understandable sermon of the Gospel."

Inside the cloister, Mother made her intentions even plainer, telling her nuns, "This is a risk we take, because we do not foresee all its effects. We may lose or gain viewers and benefactors, but nothing matters—only to do His Will. We must witness perhaps in an exaggerated form. Perhaps other sisters will gain courage and resume wearing habits. We have to go that extra mile—it is a witness to our total commitment to the Lord, to each other, to obedience to the Church."

She did not stop with externals. In-house, Angelica restored cloister practices she had derided in her earlier days. The stating of faults, or *culpas,* returned, and strict silence was imposed on the cloister. There would be no more reading of papers or watching TV news in the community. Mother would tell the nuns what they needed to know. To focus the sisters on adoration of the Blessed Sacrament, she reinstated long-abandoned pious acts. The nuns would prostrate themselves during the Consecration at Mass, and a mandatory prayer of thanksgiving would be pronounced at the start of their private hours of adoration. Mother herself began to spend three hours in undisturbed prayer before her Spouse each day for the "conversion of the world." She would do her first hour from 5:00 to 6:00 A.M., the second stint from 12:30 to 1:30 P.M., and the last hour after the live program before retiring to bed.

"At that point she made a decision: To heck with the Vatican II misinterpretation, we are going back to the core," Father Joseph Wolfe said. "She had to be what she professed to be: a cloistered nun. Part of it was to protect against criticism, to keep her own nose clean."

In the post-Denver period, the teachings of Mother Angelica evolved as well. Her sisters and brothers noted a righteous indignation in her approach after World Youth Day—a Mother less nurturing and more corrective. The times were getting too serious and the stakes too high for frivolity. Where she had once emphasized divine providence, submission to God's will, and the power of suffering, now talk of a coming chastisement, and the dire warnings of mystics seeped into her on- and off-air monologues.

Having first experienced God's presence at the hands of the stigmatist Rhoda Wise, Mother Angelica had a soft spot for visionaries and mystics. She was receptive if not attached to their claims and purported revelations, maintaining contact with several private seers over the years. Some claimed to receive messages from the Virgin Mary; others believed they heard from Christ Himself. In general terms, they agreed that a coming chastisement, a divine purging of man's sin, was imminent. Fire would fall from the sky and unspeakable anguish awaited those on earth. Some, like the visionaries of Garabandal, Spain, claimed a warning would precede the chastisement, a chance for mankind to recognize its sins and repent before the fiery trial. Mother found comfort in the warning and previewed this coming attraction on the air.

"[The] warning. It will be an act of God's mercy if it occurs. Which means at some point for some reason, nobody knows, we will all suddenly know ourselves as God knows us. . . . We're like the people in Noah's time. We don't see the signs because we've been waiting a hundred years." She then pointed the audience toward hope and the need to love one another more deeply.

On another occasion, springboarding off a recent rash of floods, Mother made the connection between natural disasters and the "satanic cruelty" of abortion. After a long moment of reflection, she looked up from the floor and, wetting her lips, said, "This flood my poor friends is nothing compared to what the Lord is going to do if this country does not go down on its knees and repent. Repent! The good and the bad are going to suffer together." She raised a hand, keeping time with each successive word. "And that's a sign. Don't miss this sign."

Mother Angelica could see the signs and she prepared accordingly. Father Mitch Pacwa remembered seeing food and water stockpiled in the monastery basement during the March blizzard of 1993. A pump was installed over a natural well behind the rock garden, across from the monastery chapel. If deprivation were coming, the sisters would not be caught short. Mother used the airwaves to prepare her audience spiritually.

"Many of you listening tonight, you listen because I am earthy and rather saucy. You're right . . . but I don't want you to listen to me for that," Mother said, yanking the ribbon markers of her Bible during the broadcast of July 27. "I want you to listen to this network because you want to get closer to the Lord. I want you to listen to this network because we have our serious times and people all over the world are suffering."

Mother Angelica Live lost its frothiness in 1993. The program had become very serious, and it would be used by its host for serious ends.

Avenging Angelica

IN HER MIND, Mother was fighting a public and private war for the future of the Catholic Church. "War is long overdue," she told viewers shortly after Denver. "I think we've needed the war we've begun a long time ago."

"She was stronger, almost like an activist," Chris Harrington, Mother's longtime producer, said of the nun's stylistic change on air. "She was the orthodox Catholic's activist."

In the fall of 1993, Mother fixed her sights on familiar targets: inclusive language, altar girls, and the breakdown of Catholic education. During a program with Bishop Robert Banks of Green Bay, a question came in about the closing of a Catholic school in Hartford, Connecticut. Bishop Banks avoided commenting since the archbishop of Hartford was a friend and classmate. "I have to stick up for my friend," the bishop told his host.

"I've got to stick up for those people," Angelica retorted, pointing toward the lens. "They keep the network going you know. . . . I think, unfortunately, since I don't have any friends in the hierarchy I can say what I think. And what I think is that we need to really get back to that wondrous teaching of the Magisterium."

When it was rumored that Pope John Paul II was about to permit girls to serve at the altar, Mother went on the defensive. Describing it as a "prelude" to women's ordination, she told her audience, "I think it's unfair to a girl, because what happens if she's serving Mass day after day and week after week, and she gets the same idea that this boy has: 'I think I'd like to be a priest'? And she can't. Isn't that kind of a letdown? Why would they even expose a girl to that?" She encouraged her troops to write a letter a week to the Vatican opposing the altar girl innovation. "If you don't, then shut up and don't be griping about anything," she told her flock. "Put up or shut up."

But in April 1994, when the Vatican formally allowed female altar servers, Angelica submitted to Rome's authority and comically accepted the defeat: "The Vatican has approved altar girls . . . for the first time in 30 years all the liberals were obedient." She would never again publicly criticize female altar servers.

During the broadcast of November 2, 1993, Mother Angelica and Father Joseph Fessio informed viewers of an upcoming vote by the bishops conference, which might have serious effects on the Scripture readings and prayers of the Mass. The inclusive-language translation under consideration by the bishops threatened to change the theology of the readings as well as their gender. It was the catechism battle all over again.

Flashing the address of Bishop Wilton Gregory, chairman of the bishops' liturgy committee, Mother mused, "I think when this program's over I want you to send a postcard or a letter. You don't have to say anything except: 'I for one do not want inclusive language anywhere, anytime.' Now that's not hard to remember. I think that would be a big help." Her viewers heard the call.

Mindless of scorn and of the mitered fire she was drawing, Angelica went where angels feared to tread. "My enemies don't know something about me," Mother confided to me in 2001. "I don't care. I don't care whether you love me or you don't. But if I think God's honor and glory and awesome gifts are being jeopardized for another agenda, then that to me is reason for just anger: That's legitimate."

Mother's "just anger" and the continuing "war" created casualties. If the officials couldn't get to Angelica due to her pontifical protection, they could strike the priests around her. Father Philip Mataconis, superior of the Brothers of the Eternal Word, was recalled by the Salesian order, to which he still owed obedience, on November 9, 1993. Other priests—from guests to series hosts— were no longer permitted to appear on EWTN's airwaves in an effort to deprive the network of a clerical presence.

Mother had become a nuisance to the establishment and a

threat to some bishops, but her influence was undeniable. Thousands of letters and postcards deluged the National Conference of Catholic Bishops in response to Mother's on-air plea. The postal campaign ultimately derailed the inclusive-language translation of the Mass, giving traditionally minded bishops the support they needed to throw the vote their way.

"Something needs to be done" about Mother Angelica, Archbishop Weakland fumed after the vote. A few of his brothers snapped into action. On Long Island, Bishop Emil Wcela campaigned to remove EWTN from local cable affiliates. The new bishop of Birmingham received complaints from some in the episcopacy, who demanded changes in Mother's on-air Mass.

But Bishop David Foley did not cotton to outside intrusions into the affairs of his diocese. A former auxiliary from Richmond, Foley became bishop of Birmingham in May 1994. Looking like a middle-aged hobbit, with a voice borrowed from Mr. Magoo, the bald, diminutive prelate could be formidable under pressure. In the face of mounting criticism, he steadfastly defended Mother Angelica's liturgical choices. "I said, 'Everything done at that Mass, I like.' And so they could not do anything," Bishop Foley revealed, spinning the chunky ring of his office. "They would complain to me, but I said, 'What they are doing are all options.' They didn't like the interspersing of the Latin. But to any bishop who objected, I would say, 'I don't care. I like it.'"

For his loyalty and friendship, Mother made Bishop Foley an offer he gladly accepted. With the publication of the English edition of the catechism of the Catholic Church in June 1993, EWTN rolled out a new live program, *Pillars of Faith,* a systematic explanation of the catechism's contents. As host of the program, Bishop Foley became one of the most recognized bishops in the world.

With her bishop protector and a stack of victories, Mother Angelica seemed invincible. But she had made more enemies among the episcopacy than she realized; enemies who would be watching for a misstep and waiting for the first opportunity to level the playing field.

16
Hammer of the Heretics

DURING A LIVE SHOW in January 1995, Mother Angelica attributed all her accomplishments to the "foundation of pain" God had laid in her life. "Why? Well, because that's how God works," she explained. "See, it sometimes takes more than prayer. . . . It takes great suffering."

In fifty years of religious life, Angelica had learned to embrace suffering and had come to believe that God "talked to [her] in pain and tragedy." In March, an asthma attack hit the nun with such severity, she knew the voice of God could not be far off. While desperately gasping for air, Angelica had an experience that would leave a deep impression. In a note to her employees written at 1:00 A.M. on March 3, she explained the events of the preceding night:

> . . . my head was wet with perspiration and I cried out to Jesus—"Hold me." I stopped gasping and love surrounded me and slowly I began to breathe.
>
> In the midst of this awesome experience and after it was over I saw Jesus on the cross—His head was tossing back and forth—His eyes and mouth were wide open—His hair was wet with blood and perspiration—
>
> His chest rose and fell as he gasped for breath. He was close to death. I realized He had allowed me to experience

some of His agony. I remember thinking that His heart broke from our sins of indifference and lack of love for Him.

For hours my body felt like a shell—empty and alone.

Whatever the spiritual benefit of the pain, Mother was not to be alone in her trials. Her vicar at Our Lady of the Angels, Sister Mary Raphael, after months of bleeding, was diagnosed with uterine cancer in June 1995. Angelica and the sisters were devastated by the news. Doctors assumed that a speedy hysterectomy would arrest the cancer and Raphael acceded to the surgery. But she refused an experimental follow-up treatment, leaving her fate to God.

On June 7, days after Sister Raphael's diagnosis, Mother Angelica announced a satellite deal that would globalize her homespun TV network. The Intelsat satellite would carry EWTN to forty-two countries in Europe, Africa, and Central and South America. As the bishops of the United States voted to liquidate their Catholic Telecommunications Network of America, having lost in excess of $14 million on the project, the seventy-two-year-old nun was going global in multimedia. Soon she would have the ability to broadcast internationally on radio and television, something no Christian entity in the world could claim. With a ring of prophecy, Mother said before the launch, "Conditions around the world are so serious— wars, earthquakes, floods—that we need to reach people everywhere. In the coming years their faith is going to be tested—they are going to need hope. EWTN offers great hope and great teaching."

On August 15, EWTN's international signal could be seen in 40 million households worldwide. Two days later, propelled by the same mind-set that hastened the international launch, Mother began searching for land to build a new monastery. In part motivated by the conviction that the sisters needed "protection" during the coming chastisement, and concerned that the noise surrounding the Birmingham foundation was not conducive to a contemplative life, Mother scoured the Alabama countryside for an appropriate locale. She thought of turning the old monastery into a novitiate to train the younger nuns and reserving the new place for professed sisters. The land search continued until October 12, 1995.

Mother's real estate agent drove her to see a piece of property in Hanceville, Alabama, an hour north of Birmingham. They drove past a run-down convenience store, a salmon-colored house with a cinder-block front porch, and the Center Hill Baptist Church. Gentle rolling hills led to an expansive tree-dotted valley. "I got out of the car and I knew; I felt the Lord's presence so strongly," Mother said of that day. "I knew this is where He wanted us."

The two-hundred-acre plot was situated in the bow of Mulberry Fork, a tributary of the Black Warrior River. At the end of the property, a natural plateau rose up from the river's bend: an ideal spot for a new monastery. Seemingly rendered in watercolors, a surreal backdrop of blue mountaintops hovered in the distance. Mother made an offer on the property on October 15.

Inspired to purchase adjoining land in order to keep hotels and eateries away from her monastery, she would eventually accrue 403 acres. Not only could Mother Angelica broadcast farther than the Pope; she now owned a homestead nearly three hundred acres larger than Vatican City.

"Mother wanted a thirteenth-century monastery and the grandest thing that had ever been," Walter Anderton, the Baptist architect of the new monastery, said of the design. "She knew what she wanted from day one. She wanted to grow all of her own food, have cattle; we even have a slaughterhouse over there." So as not to attract unwanted attention, Mother privately referred to the project as a "farm" with an attached "small farm chapel." Aside from the stipulation that it should look like the Basilica of St. Francis in Assisi and have a thirteenth-century character, Mother gave no other orders to the architect. He would travel to Europe for several months, studying the great cathedrals of the world as he drafted plans. True to form, there were no funds for the project and, aside from the scope of the thing, no definite plans for the interior.

And a Child Shall Lead Them

TO TOUT EWTN'S international signal, Mother Angelica traveled to South America in early 1996. A grueling European tour followed in May, commencing with a visit to the Vatican.

The Pope's personal secretary placed Mother, Sister Margaret Mary, and Chris Wegemer, the VP of marketing, at the end of the Papal receiving line on May 1. After routinely tracing a cross in the air before each pilgrim and leaving a rosary keepsake behind, the swollen-backed Pope paused before the nun, who teetered on aluminum crutches.

"Mother Angelica, strong woman, courageous woman, charismatic woman," the Pope announced for all to hear. For the first time anyone could remember Angelica blushed and looked away from the Pope. Like a little girl presenting her father with a homemade gift, she handed him a portfolio detailing the network's international expansion.

"Your Holiness, this is a footprint of the satellites. It shows where we are going to broadcast throughout the world," Mother said. "We're in South America, and soon we'll be going to Europe—"

"And then?" the Pope asked.

"Then we go to Russia."

"And then?"

"Then we go to China."

"And then?" The Pope smiled, fully realizing Mother had run out of lands to conquer. He laughingly took the portfolio and headed toward his private quarters. At the doorway, he turned for one last look. Observing the crutches, the braces, and the visible weakness of his plump daughter, he walked back to her. Placing one hand atop her veil, he drew a cross on her forehead with the other.

"Mother Angelica, weak in body, strong in spirit," he said. "Charismatic woman, charismatic woman."

Chris Wegemer shook visibly as the Pontiff shuffled away. Feeling she could "take on the world," Mother's face glowed a bright pink. For a woman rejected by her natural father, this validation from the great paternal figure of her life marked an important milestone. His blessing would be a source of refreshment in the trying days to come.

On her return to Birmingham, Mother found a check for $1 million, earmarked for the construction of her new monastery. She had made no mention of the project on the air, but when a couple called to ask if the nuns needed money, Angelica had shared her plans. In March they had vowed to send her a million dollars if they could sell their business. By May the business had been sold, and Mother had the first of the many millions it would take to build her monastery.

On June 20, 1996, Mother Angelica headed to Colombia, Peru, Ecuador, and Bolivia to publicize her new Spanish channel. Thousands poured into the streets and churches to glimpse the broadcasting nun.

In Bogotá, Colombia, Father Juan Pablo Rodriguez, Mother's host, whisked the nun and her entourage to his parish. He thought it important that she see a small shrine dedicated to the Divino Niño, the Divine Child.

Established in 1935 by Father John Rizzo, an Italian Salesian missionary, the shrine featured a thirty-nine-inch statue of the baby Jesus: pink-clad with outstretched arms. The statue had originally been attached to a cross, but Father Rizzo disliked the implications of a child Jesus nailed to the wood, so he had the figure removed. Since 1935, thousands had visited the shrine, attributing miraculous powers to the image of the Holy Infant.

As she entered the chapel, Mother spotted a bronze plaque bearing Father John Rizzo's name. Referencing her father, she quipped, "Well, there is a good John Rizzo!"

Locals jammed the aisle of the chapel, blocking Angelica's view of the Divino Niño. To see the object of devotion, she stood to the left of the elevated glass box covering the statue. Hands turned heavenward, she began to pray. Tears suddenly wet her cheeks. Only later did Angelica reveal what had happened. While standing before the Divino Niño, she said, the statue appeared to move.

"All of a sudden, He turns to me," Angelica recounted, "and He says, 'Build me a temple and I will help those who help you.' That's all he said." She claimed the voice was audible and that of a child.

The sisters saw nothing but the tears streaming down their abbess's face. Rushing to her side, they asked what was wrong. "Nothing," Mother told them. She needed time to discern the meaning of the message.

"I didn't know what a temple was. I had only heard of Jewish temples and Masonic temples. And I didn't like the idea of Him helping people who helped me. All I could think of was Jim Bakker, who said, 'If you give me a hundred dollars, God will give you a thousand.' I never mentioned that part of the command for a couple of years," Mother told me. "The whole message to me was questionable."

Months later, on her way out of St. Peter's in Rome, Angelica read an inscription in stone that began with the words: "This temple." The penny dropped. The Christ Child wanted an elaborate shrine, Mother realized. There *was* such a thing as a Catholic temple, and her Lord desired a new one.

Contrary to information found in the book *Come and See,* published by Our Lady of the Angels Monastery, the Divino Niño's inspiration did *not* provide the first impetus for the monastery project. Excavation on the Hanceville property had been under way for nearly six months prior to the Bogotá trip. What the encounter with the infant Jesus did was to crystallize Mother's vision for the Hanceville monastery, radically altering the original plans. In the wake of what she considered a divine command, the "simple farm chapel" would be anything but.

The Second Founding

THE INTERNATIONAL TRANSPONDER contracts lay on the altar of Our Lady of the Angels chapel for a full twenty-four hours before Mother Angelica would sign them. With a stroke of her pen, her network catapulted onto the most popular satellite in Latin America—PanAmSat—on June 14, 1996. The twenty-four-hour Spanish channel would be the first in a barrage of initiatives that would place EWTN at the forefront of Christian communications.

EWTN appeared on the World Wide Web in 1996 with an impressive site featuring news, Church documents, apologetics, program schedules, and more. The network, started an on-air news operation, a satellite delivery AM/FM service, a QVC-style *Religious Catalogue* program, and by year's end, began broadcasting to the Pacific Rim, reaching Australia, New Zealand, China, Japan, and the Philippines. Fifty million homes could now view Mother Angelica, and for the first time in the history of the Christian faith, the entire planet could participate simultaneously in the events of the Universal Church. In retrospect, the year was "like a second founding of EWTN" for Mother.

In Hanceville, the monastery "farm" was expanding exponentially. "It's like a woman making a patch quilt," Mother said of her building approach. "It got bigger on demand, because every time I'd go up there, I didn't like this, or we didn't like that."

Sister Margaret Mary and Mother approved each phase of the construction, and if something did not meet expectations—no matter the cost or state of progress—they would demand redesigns or a reversal of direction. Mother justified her perfectionism in an interview with a local paper: "[God] was very fussy about the Temple in Jerusalem. I'm not sure God wants these pre-fab things we just clunk together. I don't think it's austere. I think it's stupid. . . . If you worship in a church made like a garage, you come out feeling like you've been in a garage. We need to see beauty or we don't know what beauty is. Did you ever get inspired by a warehouse?"

Mother estimated the monastery would cost $3 million, but following her custom, there was no budget. Her donors were incredibly understanding. Though she never raised funds for the monastery on the air, five separate families and a foundation came forward, donating upward of $48.6 million to the project. They underwrote all aspects of the monastery, sparing no expense; one family paid for the crypt church and sacristy, another for the chapel and furnishings, a third for the cloister, another for the bell tower, and so on. In some cases the families, who insisted on anonymity, encouraged Mother to purchase materials and artwork far beyond her imaginings. When the bills arrived, she forwarded them to her benefactors and payment was made, no questions asked.

Bishop David Foley of Birmingham did have questions, however—not so much about the funding of the project as about its scope. He personally surveyed the site in April 1997, with Mother Angelica acting as tour guide. Not long afterward, Foley requested a "visitation" of the monastery—a chance to meet individually with each sister, share the Mass, and teach the nuns about their constitutions. After Mother's withdrawal from what she considered a liberal association of Poor Clare monasteries, the bishop may have thought the community's pontifical status had changed.

Mother Angelica refused his visitation request, telling the bishop, via Bill Steltemeier, that it could impair her status and create an impression that there were internal problems requiring the intervention of the local bishop. Without an invitation from the abbess, Bishop Foley could not enter the papal enclosure. Although convinced that he had an oversight role, Foley dropped the subject for the time being.

Startled by the bishop's unwanted attentions, Mother Angelica and Bill Steltemeier worried about the autonomy of the network and its property once the nuns moved to their new home. The sisters' vow of poverty might not permit them to retain concurrent ownership of the Birmingham compound, the Vandiver mountaintop, and the Hanceville farm. To simplify matters, or so Mother thought, the nuns of Our Lady of the Angels voted on May 20, 1997, to donate much of their property (excessively appraised at $14,683,259) in three Alabama counties to EWTN. When the bishop notified Bill Steltemeier that any alienation of Church property totaling more than $3 million required the consent of the Vatican, Steltemeier returned some of the land to the monastery and had the entire package reappraised at a lower value. But the bishop was watching, and he was taking notes.

Hoping to appeal to international and domestic audiences, EWTN diversified its offerings in the second half of 1997. They debuted a slate of original programming geared to every Catholic taste: *The World Over,* an international newsmagazine; *Life on the Rock,* a program for teens and young adults; *The Journey Home,* a talk show featuring converts to the Catholic faith; and, later, *Nuestro Fe en Vivo,* a Spanish-language live show. Targeting international markets with tailor-made programming, EWTN became the first broadcaster in the world to utilize a state-of-the-art Hewlett-Packard video-file server. The technology allowed the network to simultaneously transmit seven independent feeds of distinct programming to its various clients around the globe.

In April 1997, EWTN petitioned cable officials in Canada for a license to broadcast in that country. And though the license was refused (it went to the Playboy Channel), letters of support streamed in from members of the church hierarchy, among them Cardinal Anthony Bevilacqua, archbishop of Philadelphia; Cardinal John O'Connor of New York; and the cardinal archbishop of Los Angeles, Roger Mahony. A year later, Mahony would still be penning letters about EWTN, though they would be of a markedly different character.

The Mahony Affair

WELL INTO HER November 12, 1997, live show, Mother Angelica rattled off a familiar complaint. [The average layperson is being told] "there's no need for confession, there's no need for Baptism, there's not really a Body, Blood, Soul, and Divinity," she said to her guest, Father C. John McCloskey, a priest of Opus Dei. Then, moving toward the conclusion of her thought, she threw out a bit of evidence and unknowingly crossed a canonical line. It was little more than a side comment, a throwaway, part of an evolving question lasting less than seventeen seconds—seconds that would cost Mother Angelica dearly.

Rearing back in her chair, waving her right hand in the air for emphasis, she said, "In fact the cardinal of California is teaching that it's bread and wine before the Eucharist and after the Eucharist. I'm afraid my obedience in that diocese would be absolutely zero." She touched her index finger to her thumb, making an O for effect, then delivered the clincher. "And I hope everybody else's in that diocese is zero. But I mean you just kind of have to ask yourself . . ." And she continued on as if nothing extraordinary had happened. But it had.

At the Franciscan Missionaries of the Eternal Word Friary in Birmingham, Father Nevin Hammon, a canon lawyer teaching courses to the brothers, was listening to Mother's program on the radio that night. He was lying down when he heard her speak of "zero" obedience. The priest told me, "I jumped off my bed and said to my radio—and I am not used to talking to radios—'Oh Mother, you shouldn't have said that. You are going to be in a lot of trouble.' "

Three e-mails sailed into Cardinal Roger Mahony's laptop at the North American College in Rome, alerting him to Mother's comments. He was attending a special Synod of bishops from the Americas at the time. Being the only cardinal in California, Mahony seethed as he read the quotes attributed to Mother Angelica.

Bishops and others in residence at the North American College remember a cardinal totally preoccupied with the nun. Mahony would coolly flash the "Angelica" e-mails to any bishop he could corner, trying to win allies. One bishop quoted Mahony as saying, "Did you see what she did to me? Don't you think she shouldn't have done it?"

Mahony's audience was less than receptive. "He was driven to be the punisher, and he wanted me to be on his side," another bishop who attended the Synod told me. "I don't know why he was investing so much anger in it."

Yet another Synod participant recalled "a conversation where Mahony was quite upset, the source of which seemed to be that Mother Angelica was releasing people from ecclesial obedience." From Rome, Cardinal Mahony repeatedly phoned Bishop Foley of Birmingham, demanding he do something about the outspoken abbess.

Angelica would very likely have known nothing of Mahony's pastoral letter on the liturgy had not one of the nuns given her a copy of the document before her live show on November 12. During dinner, Mother casually leafed through the pastoral, "Gather Faithfully Together: A Guide for Sunday Mass," promulgated in L.A. the previous September. Unlike the meal, the pastoral letter was hard for Angelica to swallow. What she considered its soft-pedaling of transubstantiation—the teaching that the bread and wine of the altar, once consecrated, become the actual Body and Blood of Jesus Christ—angered Angelica. She carried her reaction to the letter like a grudge onto the live show that night. While running through a litany of outrages, Mahony's letter popped into her mind, and the commentary flew out of her mouth. Implying that the cardinal taught heresy was impolitic, but the apparent call for zero obedience in the diocese violated canon law. As Cardinal Mahony studied his options, he faxed a letter to Mother Angelica on November 14.

"For you to state publicly on television that I do not believe in the Real Presence is astounding and reprehensible and calls for an immediate clarification and apology from you," the outraged Mahony wrote. "For you to call into question my own belief in the Real Presence is without precedence. To compound the matter, your call for my people to offer zero obedience to their shepherd is unheard of and shocking."

Michael Warsaw, then senior vice president of production for EWTN, insisted that Mother's comments were not "premeditated." "I think she took offense at what she saw as a weakness on doctrine, and because it was about the Eucharist, I think it was very personal for her," Warsaw said. "Had Cardinal Mahony not raised such a fuss, she probably would not have done a critique of his pastoral letter, and never directly commented on it. But when challenged by him, I think she felt that she had to step up and defend the teaching of the Church. I remember her saying at the time, 'I have to say what I believe, and I can't back down. What's the worst they can do to me, send me back to my monastery?' "

On November 18, sitting on her live show set, staring into the camera, Mother attempted to comply with the cardinal's "clarification and apology."

She read a transcript of her November 12 show and then quoted extensively from Cardinal Mahony's letter: "I must insist you issue a formal retraction of your statement and that you assure your viewers that the cardinal archbishop of Los Angeles does indeed fully believe in the Real Presence and fosters devotion to this great mystery of our faith."

"So I do want to apologize to the cardinal for my remark, which I'm sure seemed excessive. But he's asked me for a clarification. And this is what I would like to do this evening. This is my opinion and this is how I saw it when I read it."

For the remainder of the hour, Mother served up a point-by-point critique of the pastoral letter: "What came through to me was the principal focus in the letter on assembly, the concentration on assembly by the people in the Church rather than the Eucharist. So, I felt the letter was unclear as to what the Church teaches about the Real Presence, Body, Blood, Soul and Divinity of Jesus . . . , "Angelica said.

The only clear explanation of transubstantiation was in "a very small footnote," she maintained. "I don't know about you, but I don't read footnotes, unfortunately. I read big print," Mother squeaked. "So I missed the footnote . . . and if I overlooked it, I imagine a lot of other people overlooked it."

Mother pressed the point further, questioning Mahony's "confusing" teaching that Jesus' presence is "*in* the simple gifts of bread and wine," as he had written. "I'm a member of the masses; I'm a simple woman and I don't understand this," she admitted to her audience. "Does that mean Christ is present before the consecration, in the bread and wine . . . ? Or does it mean that He is present after the consecration? . . . Does He just kind of hop into the bread and wine, but it's still bread and wine? Or does it become His Body and Blood? . . . If there is still bread and wine, why would I adore Him? Why would I kneel and prostrate myself to bread and wine?

"Last week, I said if somebody taught me that, I would not obey. Well, the canons tell me I can't say that, that's a no-no: to tell anybody they should not obey their bishop or cardinal. For that I apologize." She repositioned herself, heaving a sigh. "It is very confusing to people when leaders seem to ignore the real problems in the Church that need to be addressed, seem to tolerate and encourage liturgical fuzziness and practices that don't, to me, show or manifest the holiness of the Sacrifice of the Mass.

"His Eminence asked for a public clarification. And I want to say to him I don't mean to cause you any problem. I don't mean to deny the Church or cause anything. I'm just confused because I don't understand." Mother was measured and careful. "I'm not here to correct anybody. . . . I'm not here to teach in place of anybody either. I know my place and I try to keep it. But it is my duty, because the Lord has asked me to enlighten the people, not to give them my ideas and theories but just to say, Here, this is what the Church teaches. . . . I hope I satisfied the cardinal's request. I will pray for him, and I hope he will pray for me." She was nearly finished. "So Your Eminence, if I have mistaken your letter I'm very sorry, but I still find it confusing. . . ."

Mother bundled up a tape of the live show, along with a letter stating her compliance with the cardinal's request and sent it to Los Angeles. She imagined the controversy was behind her.

Progressive and orthodox Catholics began to take sides. Adoremus, the Society for the Renewal of the Sacred Liturgy, condemned the Mahony pastoral as a "strikingly truncated theology of the Eucharist," while the National Catholic Reporter hailed Mahony's "pastoral leadership" and breaking of "ecclesiastical taboos."

With the death of Cardinal Joseph Bernardin of Chicago in 1996, Cardinal Mahony had assumed the mantle of leadership for the Catholic left. In fact, during Bernardin's last days, Mahony sat by the elder cardinal's bedside mesmerized by the dying man's heroic struggle. Bernardin's choice of Mahony as principal celebrant for his funeral Mass was widely interpreted by progressives as a passing of the torch. In time, Mahony would prove his worth.

The annual Los Angeles Religious Education Congress, sponsored by the archdiocese, featured a cavalcade of dissenters and anti-Vatican agitators. Advocates of female ordination, critics of the papacy, discredited theologians, and others found safe haven at the gathering. Judging from the roster of invited speakers, the cardinal's indulgence of dissent and criticism of Church officials was considerable—which made his reaction to Mother Angelica all the more peculiar. When laymen questioned the heterodox voices featured at the Religious Education Congress in 1997, Cardinal Mahony stood firm, declaring his "profound commitment" to the event. During his scuffle with Mother Angelica, progressives showed their profound commitment to Cardinal Mahony.

In a November 19 letter, Bishop Robert Lynch of St. Petersburg, Florida, denounced Mother Angelica's on-air display as "the latest example of the absolute contempt in which you hold the bishops of the United States, with few exceptions." He continued, "I pray that you cease these personal and vicious attacks on those whom the Successor of Peter has chosen to lead the Church in this country at this time. . . . You and your network are not helping me in my office as Shepherd, Pastor, and Leader."

In the meantime, Cardinal Mahony sat with an invited group of bishops in Rome to screen Mother's "apology and public clarification." The viewing only deepened his outrage.

According to one cleric, "Mahony threw a snit" during a dinner in the Red Room of the North American College. "He was obsessed by the question," the clergyman remembered, "talking to everyone about it and what it meant to be Catholic, and that Mother Angelica was doing this totally without sanction or permission."

Mahony scheduled appointments at the Vatican with those who had authority over Mother Angelica, intending to register his complaint.

"It was kind of the talk of Rome those days that every dicastery had received a message from Mahony demanding that they act," one Synod participant told me. "He was bombarding the congregations."

The cardinal visited the Pontifical Council for Social Communications, the Congregation for the Doctrine of Faith, and, sometime before November 27, the Congregation for the Institutes of Consecrated Life and Societies of Apostolic Life [CICLSAL], which had direct control over Mother and all religious.

After learning of the situation, one elderly curial cardinal was heard to comment, "Mother Angelica has the guts to tell him what we do not."

"I must respectfully state that your November 18th program could not be termed a public clarification and apology," Cardinal Mahony wrote to Angelica on December 1, 1997. "Had you simply read the two parts in which you did, indeed, offer that apology, and went on to other subjects, I would have been quite satisfied.

"I believe that your apology was so diluted by your continuing commentary, that any ordinary viewer would have found my pastoral to be at best confusing, and at worse [sic], somehow a dangerous teaching document. You yourself used the words 'confused or confusing' at least 30 times during the course of that segment, leaving no doubt that you disapproved of the Pastoral Letter."

Canon law then made an appearance. Pointing to Canon 753, Mahony wrote that only the Pope and the Holy See have a right to correct "the teaching of [a] diocesan bishop." As he considered his rights violated, he informed Mother of the complaint lodged against her with the congregation responsible for religious and issued one final demand: She would read a new apology, on-air, before Christmas. The statement would affirm the cardinal's belief in the Eucharist, admit Mother's incorrect reading of his pastoral, and inform viewers that she lacked the authority to criticize bishops. Mahony recommended that Bishop David Foley compose the mea culpa and that it be read publicly on four separate occasions—free of the taint of additional criticisms. Otherwise, he would pursue a case in Rome.

"I gave him his apology and clarification. This is blackmail. Why can everybody critique the Pastoral but me?" Mother asked Bishop Foley during a phone conversation on December 3. She was in Europe at the time, reviewing the progress on the monstrance, stained-glass windows, and other appointments for her monastery.

Angelica apologized to the bishop for any trouble she might have caused, but said she saw no reason to retract her statement or to issue an endorsement of the cardinal's pastoral. "I have dedicated my life to the Eucharist and I cannot deny Jesus," she told Foley. "I'm willing to give up my position at the network, and give up the 'Live' show and live my contemplative life, but I cannot deny Jesus." Foley supported her position, but he had to try to appease the aggrieved cardinal. He asked Mother to pray for him.

Foley and a visiting theologian, Father Don Deitz, worked on a retraction statement that would meet the cardinal's conditions but was nuanced enough to gain Mother's acceptance. The draft appears to have been a group effort. One draft acquired by the author bears the fax imprint of the USCC, suggesting that individuals at the bishops conference massaged the wording.

Intent on achieving his goal, Cardinal Mahony pursued Mother

Angelica from every angle. At his insistence, the grand knight of the Knights of Columbus, Virgil Dechant, in a December 10 letter, pressed Mother to meet the cardinal's demands and issue a retraction. On the same day, the auxiliary bishops of Los Angeles wrote the Congregation for the Institutes of Consecrated Life and Societies of Apostolic Life, urging that Mother Angelica be compelled to retract her comments. Meanwhile, Bishop Donald Trautman of Erie, Pennsylvania, and Bishop Lynch of St. Petersburg, two bishops close to Mahony, filed complaints against the abbess with the CICLSAL. The chickens had come home to roost.

Bishop Foley bore the unenviable task of presenting the Mahony-approved retraction statement to Mother at her monastery on December 15. She studied the copy for a moment, then, looking up at the bishop, adamantly refused to read the statement on-air. The bishop tried to persuade her otherwise. "No," Mother announced deliberately, "I'm seventy-four years old. I'm not about to deny Our Lord when I'm so close to facing him in judgment."

For Mother Angelica, this was not a battle of wills, or a matter of courtesy, but it was about belief in the Eucharist. "With all the stress and everything else, I was going to stand tall in God's grace. And I know Our Lord was giving me strength, 'cause I was quoting what He said. I was not quoting my opinion," Mother reflected. "I didn't feel stubborn about it; I didn't feel disobedient. I felt this is what my Church teaches."

Bishop Foley returned home to a series of faxes and phone messages from Cardinal Mahony, who was no doubt eager to learn Mother's reaction to the statement. "So I phoned Mahony," Foley recalled. "I said, 'I don't think she is going to do it.' 'So what are you going to do as the local bishop?' he asked. 'I'm not going to do anything about it,' I said. And he was mad at me for a time, but he got over it. It was being played in the secular media as the nun versus the cardinal. Mother loves a fight, and she was in the middle of it."

On repeated occasions, I sought to interview Cardinal Mahony, both in writing and in person, to better understand his perspective on the controversy. All my requests were denied.

My final attempt was in November 2003, at the bishops conference meeting in Washington. After forwarding several interview requests to his room, I spied Cardinal Mahony in the hotel lobby. Pursuing him en route to the elevators, I asked him about Mother Angelica and their disagreement. Without making eye contact, he brushed past me saying, "That's all ancient history."

But in late December 1997, Mother Angelica's obdurate stance seemed to totally absorb Cardinal Mahony—and he grew testy. Having heard nothing from the nun, he fired off a letter on December 23, demanding compliance with his request and extending the deadline to January. Five days later, Mother responded.

A retraction would "amount to a denial of" her "belief in the Doctrine of Transubstantiation," she wrote to Mahony. Angelica refused to budge. "I apologize again for any hurt and pain that you have felt because of my statement. But I too feel great pain and hurt over the many slanderous articles about me and EWTN in diocesan newspapers. I am hoping and praying that this matter is now resolved."

But it was not to be.

Mahony craved satisfaction and was not about to be outmaneuvered by a populist nun in Birmingham, Alabama. The public battle, and Rome's involvement, made the stakes too high to retreat. In January 1998, the cardinal widened his plan of attack. In discussions with Vatican officials, he voiced concerns about EWTN as a network—its programming, governance, and management. According to reports, he consulted with canon lawyers to discover what ecclesial tethers wound round Mother Angelica and her network, hoping to ensure an outcome favorable to him.

"The cardinal wants the Holy See to do something about Mother Angelica's whole attitude that she is not responsible to the National Conference of Catholic Bishops or to any of the individual bishops," Father Gregory Coiro, director of media relations for the L.A. archdiocese, told the *National Catholic Reporter*. "It goes beyond her criticism of the cardinal—it's about how the network operates and to whom it is accountable."

The network needed to be "reoriented," in Cardinal Mahony's estimation, and his spokesman unveiled a possible instrument to ensure that it happened. Father Coiro mentioned Canon 1373, a law forbidding individuals from inciting disobedience against the Pope or bishops. Among the "just penalties" attached to the canon was "interdiction." This severe punishment, akin to excommunication, excludes the individual or entity from the sacraments and is meted out by the Church for "grave crimes."

"Is Mahony looking for Rome to slap an interdict on EWTN, which technically would be justified under the circumstances?" Father Coiro mused in an interview. "Probably not, though I wouldn't rule it out."

The threat was dismissed within EWTN as a desperate attempt to draw Mother out of her silence. Network obligations and the slowly rising monastery in Hanceville consumed Angelica's attention, making it easy for her to overlook the Los Angeles tough talk. But something about the threat of interdiction caused her to pause. Could she be deprived access to the very sacrament she lived to protect and defend? Could the Church oblige her to relinquish control of the network to individuals, even authorities, who might use it to undermine the Pope and Catholic teaching? For the moment these thoughts were passing phantoms; but over the next two years, she would return to them again and again.

17
Miracles and Chastisements

CLOSING IN on her seventy-fifth year, encased in a growing metal framework of braces, weakened by severe asthma attacks, and wrangling by writ with the "Cardinal in California," Mother Angelica strained to stay on task. She put in time at the network, sat through long meetings with the vice presidents, authorized expensive wall-to-wall live coverage of the Pope's historic visit to Cuba in late January 1998 (without the benefit of funds), and somehow managed to get through her twice-weekly live shows and *Religious Catalog* taping sessions. But around the edges, she was fraying. Her collaborators found her edgy, distracted, and "not herself."

The building delays at the new monastery became a source of frustration for Angelica, who frequently rambled up to Hanceville to check on the work site. At the Birmingham monastery, she continued teaching lessons to her nuns, kept tabs on the friars, and never missed her private adoration time. But no amount of activity could help her escape the festering Mahony conflict.

A letter from Cardinal Mahony, written on January 2, 1998, reignited the quarrel. He could not put the matter behind him and called once more for a broadcast apology, preferably the one drafted by Bishop Foley.

For good reason, Mother did not respond. According to the OLAM History and several bishops interviewed by the author, certain Vatican officials privately supported Angelica's position, advising her to remain silent. They probably shared her reservations about Mahony's teachings, but could not be seen as publicly crossing a cardinal. Mother notified her direct superior, Cardinal Eduardo Martinez Somalo, prefect at the Congregation for the Institutes of Consecrated Life and Societies of Apostolic Life, of the Mahony letter and returned to planning coverage of the papal visit to Cuba.

The Healing

PAUL'S SECOND LETTER to the Corinthians reads, "My grace is sufficient for thee: for power is made perfect in infirmity. Gladly therefore will I glory in my infirmities, that the power of Christ may dwell in me." For Mother Angelica, this was not mere instruction, but dogma to be lived and exemplified daily. In her personal theology, her bloated heart, her diabetes, and her stumplike legs were providential mysteries, gifts to be embraced, not evils to be cast off or delivered from. Thus, she never asked God to remove her handicaps, and she harbored no bitterness about their presence in her life. They were, by the late nineties, a part of Angelica and served to deepen her "reliance on God."

On the evening of January 28, 1998, Mother trudged to the studio, as she had hundreds of times before, passing through the corridor connecting the monastery to the network. The rosary dangling from her waist clanged against the aluminum crutches and thudded dully on the leg braces beneath her habit as she moved. Even the short walk from the cloister to the live-show set was a challenge for the nun, owing to a nerve-damaged withered right leg, the result of muscle atrophy, according to Dr. David Patton, her general practitioner.

Mother's advance ended at the elevated, live-show platform. Planting her crutches on the stage, the security guard grabbed her waist and hoisted her onto the riser. Getting up there on her own was out of the question. She carefully stepped to her padded seat, relinquished her crutches, and plopped down to start the show. For the next hour, Mother Angelica and Father John Corapi had an energetic, if perfunctory, conversation about the power of the rosary. Under normal circumstances, at the show's conclusion she would wave to the busloads of adoring pilgrims in the studio audience and return to the cloister. But this night, she had an appointment to keep in her office.

Paola Albertini, a small, pugish Italian woman with a pageboy haircut and an odd countenance, had been demanding to meet Mother Angelica for days. The former music teacher had supposedly been receiving visions of the Virgin Mary since 1986. These mystical visitations purportedly occurred whenever Albertini prayed the rosary—usually during the recitation of the fourth decade, according to reports. Hoping to persuade Mother Angelica to spread the secrets entrusted to her, Albertini, a translator, and a pair of disciples had trekked down to Birmingham in late January. Wielding a "special message from Our Lady," Albertini had tried to gain access to the renowned abbess, with little success.

"We get a lot of these mystics, and Mother resisted her," Sister Agnes told me. Leery of the claims, and simply busy, Mother had no time for the mystic. Then on January 27, she'd agreed to a brief meeting in her parlor. In Italian, Albertini said the Virgin Mary had asked her to come, and she insisted that Mother pray the rosary with her the following day. Reluctantly, Angelica consented to join the mystic in prayer at 8:00 P.M. the next evening, after her live show.

Mother Angelica hobbled past the applauding crowd and headed into her office at the conclusion of the program. Paola Albertini waited inside, her rosary at the ready. Lacking a common language, Albertini recited the "Glorious Mysteries" in Italian while Mother prayed along in Latin. At the start of the fourth decade, the Assumption of Mary, Albertini lifted her head, locking her eyes on a portrait hanging above Mother's desk. Sister Mary Clare, one of the nuns in the office, said a "bright glow" surrounded the painting of Saint Francis reaching up to the crucified Christ. "Our Lady is here," Albertini announced. She then proclaimed a message the Virgin ostensibly wished to share with Mother Angelica:

"What joy you give to the heart of Jesus, your beloved spouse. . . . Defend the Holy Eucharist even with your own life. Yes, Jesus still today is being made a fool of and sneered at. . . . I bless this location, I bless you my daughter, and with so much love

I tell you: Don't stop! Go forward for the love of Jesus unperturbed along the way that Jesus traced for you since you were in your maternal womb. . . ."

At some point during the fourth decade of the rosary, Mother Angelica had "a feeling" that God wished to heal her. "Lord, all these years You've used me as a comfort and an example for all the handicapped and crippled," she thought. "If You want to change it, it's okay with me."

Moments later, Albertini asked if she could pray for Mother. When Angelica consented, the mystic fell to her knees, muttering a prayer in Italian. After several minutes, Albertini requested that Mother remove her braces. Complying, the abbess bent to unfasten the metal rods running up the sides of her legs, then motioned to Sister Agnes to release her worn shoes. Agnes did so, but she worried that Mother would fall without the braces. "I had seen her try to walk. The foot was just floppy; it would drag," Sister Agnes said.

The dwarfish mystic took Mother Angelica by the hands, leading her across the floor as one would a toddler taking her first steps. The nuns nervously stood on either side of their Mother, in case she should lose her balance. Then Mother faltered. Her feet lifelessly mashed on their sides with each step.

"Come. Don't be afraid," Albertini barked.

"I walked to the door," Mother recalled, "and had a hard time turning around, because both legs were going every which way." The tottering nun inched toward the mystic, flanked by her sisters.

"Let her be," Albertini shouted, trying to shoo the nuns away.

"Mother, let's not do this," Sister Agnes pleaded.

"Agnes, I feel this warmth in my ankles," Mother said, continuing to move toward Albertini. "Don't be afraid."

Imperceptibly, the legs became more stable as she crossed the room. Her feet slowly moved into position and straightened. When she paused, Albertini pressed a crucifix to Mother's back and legs.

"Let's walk," the small woman ordered. "Now, lift your legs." Angelica raised the formerly disabled limbs. Balance returned and the unsteadiness vanished. She bounced like a child showing off a new dance step.

Throwing wide the door to her office, Mother yelled to the security guards, "Look, no crutches and no braces."

"Well, glory be to God," Johnny Laurence, one of the guards, blurted out, as if he had just seen a ghost blow through the door. In exhilaration, Mother Angelica took the hands of a visiting guest, who happened to be passing through at the time, and spun about the studio kitchen with him.

To test the legs she had not commanded for forty-two years, Angelica walked the length of the studio. She then bounded up the live-show platform that only an hour earlier had been impossible to mount without assistance. In the monastery, the nuns were ecstatic at the sight of their abbess. As if some new feast day had been proclaimed, Mother waltzed the night away with the younger sisters and chattered into the early-morning hours.

The next day, crowds gathered outside the carport grille for a glimpse of Mother Angelica's miracle. Obliging the throng, she exited the cloister, to an explosion of tears and laughter. Before publicly announcing the healing that night on the EWTN youth program, *Life on the Rock,* Mother again met and prayed with Paola Albertini. This time, Albertini told the nun to remove her back brace, which she did. Later, she would put it back on. "I have to be honest; it wasn't healed," Mother told me. "I can go without it for a couple of hours, but it's hard. Why should I fake something for somebody else?"

Three physicians who independently examined Mother Angelica following Paola Albertini's visit insist that the healing of her legs was anything but fake. Dr. Stan Faulkner, Angelica's orthopedist, described the physical change as "pretty miraculous." And he believed the healing extended beyond her limbs. "Mother suffered from a narrowing of the spinal canal, where it strangled the nerves," Faulkner said. "I honestly thought she needed surgery. But it went away and went back to normal. It healed better than it would have with surgery. You don't see many miracles nowadays, and that's what I assumed it was."

Dr. David Patton, chief of medicine at Healthsouth in Birmingham and Mother's general practitioner, examined her legs as well. "I am a skeptic by nature, and she told me about the healing and I looked," Dr. Patton said, grinning. "I have never seen anything like it. Physically, I saw a withered leg visibly better. When muscle is atrophied for a long period of time, it usually doesn't come back."

Dr. Richard May, a Birmingham internist, examined Angelica's legs on the sly after hearing stories from his colleagues. During one of Mother's hospitalizations, he crept into her room and took a look for himself. "What I saw were muscular legs with rounded calves, and not the legs as they should have been," Dr. May said. "Her legs were better than they should have been at her age and activity level. These were the legs of someone who had walked a lot." To lend credibility to their accounts, May described himself and Dr. Patton as "cynical curmudgeons: a Methodist and an Episcopalian not given to rush after miracles."

The purpose of the healing was to increase the faith of viewers and employees at the network, Mother told *Life on the Rock* host Jeff Cavins on the live January 29 broadcast. Though elated by the healing, Mother couldn't resist a subtle allusion to her doctrinal tussle with Cardinal Mahony: "Never in the history of the world has there been so much blasphemy, disbelief, error, schism, and cruelty towards the Body and Blood of Jesus. The Father is going to make up for that, and Our Lady is going to make up for that in a brand-new way."

The spokesman for the Los Angeles archdiocese, Father Gregory Coiro, told the *National Catholic Reporter* that he heard about the miraculous event on the Internet "from people suggesting that Mother Angelica was healed because she took on Cardinal Mahony." Coiro said, "I've been telling people in jest that the healing was for my benefit, so I can't be accused anymore of criticizing a crippled nun."

With no mention of the healing, Cardinal Mahony wrote Mother on February 5, lamenting her non-response to his repeated overtures. For the betterment of EWTN, he informed her, he would be meeting with Vatican officials at the Congregation for the

Institutes of Consecrated Life and Societies of Apostolic Life, though he still hoped some mutual resolution to their conflict could be reached.

Mother did not reply immediately, and, would twice refuse Mahony's phone calls. But her tersely worded fax to the cardinal on February 26 left little doubt as to where she stood: "Nothing further can be gained from our discussing this matter, since the issue is a doctrinal one," she wrote.

Mother's constant deferring to doctrine and her refusal to back away from her on-air comments incensed the cardinal. In a letter of February 28, Mahony relayed details of his meeting with the CICLSAL. Officials there recommended that he pursue new national norms and guidelines for media—in-house regulations created by the National Conference of Catholic Bishops—which Mother's network would be bound to accept. In this case, the body of bishops could compel her to do what an individual bishop could not. The cardinal promised that a request for such norms was already on its way to the NCCB. At the conclusion of his letter, he invited Angelica to a face-to-face meeting on March 21 in Orlando, Florida, where they could air their differences and work out a solution.

Archbishop Oscar Libscomb of Mobile and Cardinal Martinez Somalo urged Mother in separate missives to accept the invitation and meet with Mahony.

"Silence is my weapon," Mother said of her strategy. "I think silence is in order many, many times when you know people are after you and that no matter what you do or what you say, it will be unacceptable and will just make it worse. You just add fuel to the fire. So at that point, I just drop everything: I don't talk. I don't write. I don't do anything." Which is practically what she did on this occasion, informing Cardinal Martinez in writing that "it would be highly inappropriate" to meet with Cardinal Mahony, since she was filing a petition with the Vatican's doctrinal office, requesting a formal ruling on the teaching contained in Mahony's pastoral letter. The showdown was getting serious.

In her petition to the Congregation for the Doctrine of the Faith, Mother spelled out the theological flaws of the document and begged then cardinal Joseph Ratzinger to "cast out the confusion of the Pastoral letter of Cardinal Mahony regarding the Doctrine of Transubstantiation. If not the Church in America will be lost."

Both sides had now appealed to separate Roman congregations for relief. Before issuing a judgment, the Vatican made one last run at an informal solution. They appointed Cardinal John O'Connor of New York a delegate of the CICLSAL on March 13 and sent him to Birmingham. He was charged with the formidable task of brokering a peace plan to end the Mahony/Angelica dispute.

A feverish Cardinal O'Connor, battling a bacterial infection, emerged from a car outside of Our Lady of the Angels Monastery on March 21, 1998. "I don't believe this," he said, catching his first glimpse of the crutch-free Angelica. The two warmly embraced and retired to the St. Francis room of the monastery for an hour-and-a-half conference. Mother Angelica, Cardinal O'Connor, and Bill Steltemeier were the only participants.

O'Connor began gingerly, assuring Mother of the Holy Father's support, though he confessed that even the Pope was uncertain how to extricate Mother from her current snare. He underscored the critical nature of the situation and bemoaned the scandal it had caused. O'Connor suggested that Mother Angelica create a series on the Eucharist, featuring leading curial figures. This would demonstrate her devotion to the sacrament and inoculate her viewers against the deficient teaching she dreaded.

She should produce the television series, O'Connor advised, and issue some gentle brief statement that would not violate her conscience but would concede that Cardinal Mahony accepted Church teaching on the Eucharist. She would also need to apologize. As incentive, Cardinal O'Connor ran through the possibilities should Angelica maintain her position: The Holy See could remove her from television; Mahony could demand interdiction, restricting her from the sacraments, or he could sufficiently rile up the bishops to make a play for the network.

Mother Angelica was back to square one. The cardinal archbishop of the largest archdiocese in the country still sought *her* imprimatur.

Mother politely refused. "I couldn't walk into that chapel and face the Lord if I gave in just because he's a cardinal," she said. "I can't."

"You must," O'Connor demanded, beating the tabletop.

She stared at the cardinal. "I won't."

O'Connor had made the trip of his own accord, he told her. He had come to help. His voice rose, but Mother was unmovable. After a tour of the network, the cardinal embraced Angelica, said "I love you," and sped off to the airport.

In a series of faxes, Cardinal O'Connor offered modified statements for Mother to read on the air, one merely restating bits of her initial "apology broadcast." Still, Angelica could not bring herself to speak another word publicly about Cardinal Mahony or his pastoral letter. Promising to remain silent, she told O'Connor in a fax on April 7, "I find it extremely beneath the dignity of a Prince of the Church to continue bringing this subject up before the public, both here and abroad, over a 15 second remark. Why is it that such a brief remark should have such long-lasting repercussions? I now realize there is no end to His Eminence's demands." At the close of the fax, she wrote, "I will not be made a pawn or tool in the hands of American liberals who have done such great harm to so many people."

If she gave in this time, where would it end? Mother wondered. Would every statement uttered during seventeen years of broadcasting be dredged up and challenged? What else would she be forced to recant publicly if she repudiated this statement?

A frustrated Cardinal O'Connor, judging from his correspondence, finally requested that Mother send him an edited transcript of the broadcast apology of November 18, indicating the places where she had satisfied Mahony's request. This would constitute her statement. In late April, O'Connor included the material in a report to the Holy See, along with some personal recommendations.

On April 23, three days after her seventy-fifth birthday, Mother Angelica's asthma returned, necessitating a hospital stay. From the midnineties on, Mother had been hospitalized several times a year to control the asthma attacks, attacks Dr. Patton said were severe and "worse than average." To break the assault on her lungs, Patton

resorted to high doses of injected steroids. And though these injections eased Mother's breathing, unintended side effects of the
steroids would complicate her life in other ways. The regular intake
brought on diabetes and weakened her bones. Nevertheless, the attacks were so frightening for Mother and her community, they
gladly accepted the consequences. Breathing was not optional.

A letter from the CICLSAL in late June practically took her
breath away. Acting on the advice of Cardinal O'Connor, the congregation said it had elected to do nothing concerning the Cardinal
Mahony situation. The letter of June 27 merely requested an
EWTN mission statement so that the connection between the
monastery and the network could be studied.

Mother Angelica had seemingly escaped penalty for her broadcast review of Mahony's pastoral. But buried in the request from
the congregation was the seed that would shake her community,
the network she had founded, and her very person. Floating in the
minds of the episcopacy were new questions: Who owned EWTN?
Who controlled EWTN? And what would happen in the absence of
Mother Angelica?

In a July 17 letter of response, Angelica told Cardinal Martinez
Somalo that the "Eternal Word Television Network is neither
owned nor operated by Our Lady of the Angels Monastery. EWTN
is a civil entity incorporated under the non-profit statutes of the
State of Alabama." Bill Steltemeier, then president of EWTN, was
even more blunt in his letter to the CICLSAL: "The real issue
raised by your letter is the future control of EWTN and its programming, either directly or indirectly. This is an issue which only
EWTN's board of governors can decide." A copy of the mission
statement was included.

In spite of the congregation's ruling, Cardinal Mahony spent
part of his *ad limina* visit to Rome in September again discussing
Mother Angelica with Cardinal Martinez Somalo. He groused to
reporters about "programming attacking bishops," and at successive
meetings of the bishops conference, led the charge to regulate
Catholic media outlets. As late as November 2003, Mahony was
still at it: amending a bishops' document on popular devotions to

ensure that any materials broadcast or placed on the Web conformed to the "theological and ecumenical developments of the contemporary" Church.

As the curtain fell on the Mahony crisis, Mother dedicated herself to fulfilling the destiny of her shortwave radio network. Since 1996, EWTN had been offering its shortwave programming free of charge to any Catholic radio station in the country. Only fourteen Catholic frequencies existed in the United States at the time. In 1998, Mother Angelica attempted to inspire the laity to establish even more Catholic AM/FM stations, in their own communities. "Some of you Catholics are loaded—with money, I mean," her pitch would normally begin. During the September 2, 1998, live show she told viewers that radio stations were needed to reach the "average person in the hubbub of the city" and challenged CEOs and board chairmen of major corporations: "I've got a whole list of you and you're not very generous," she said. "We're not very evangelistic and I think it's because we don't love God enough. So please if you have more than you'll ever need . . . you ought to do something for Jesus. You could buy ten radio stations." A Buffalo-based millionaire heard the call and contacted EWTN the next morning. He was put in touch with Jim Wright, a local businessman who had been trying to bring a Catholic radio station into upstate New York. In 1999, Wright and his benefactor purchased WLOF—an FM station in Buffalo—which remains on the air today. As of this writing, there are more than eighty independent AM/FM Catholic radio affiliates of EWTN. Most remain viable due to the free programming offered by Angelica's network.

Raising the Temple

THROUGHOUT MUCH of 1998, Mother Angelica lavished attention on the building of the Hanceville monastery. "Mother changed walls the way most women change wallpaper," Sister Agnes said of the building process. The abbess attended to every detail—overseeing three versions of the chapel ceiling, adding forty feet to the church after the foundation had already been poured, and traversing the globe to find the best artisans and materials that money could buy.

"This is a big building and that chapel didn't come cheap," Mother said in retrospect. "It's not a sale at Kmart, if you know what I mean."

It would be a "farm chapel" like no other. The raw materials used in the construction would correspond with those of King Solomon's temple: red jasper on the floors, rare cedar for the confessionals, and gold for the eye-popping eight-foot monstrance. The Gustav van Treeck studios in Munich fashioned thirty-five stained-glass windows bearing images of Jesus, the Virgin Mary, assorted saints, and the nine choirs of angels. Sister Margaret Mary and Sister Agnes greatly influenced the window designs, spending months locating appropriate images to replicate in glass. Spanish craftsmen at Talleres de Arte Granda in Madrid assembled the forty-five-foot brass communion rail, the fifty-five-foot gold-leaf reredos, the monstrance, and the other chapel appointments.

To set the place off, Mother added a piazza to the front of the chapel, complete with a colonnade. For the centerpiece of the square, she chose a snow-white marble statue of the Christ Child extending His red jasper heart to visitors. "I felt with the heart out, it would be more appealing to women who were considering abortions," Angelica said of the sculpture. "Maybe it will get them to reconsider."

Even though the sisters designed their own work spaces within the monastery and marveled at the grandeur of the place, there was a hesitancy about moving to the new digs. Some had grown attached to the cramped coziness of the Birmingham monastery, and they worried that the sheer size of the new cloister would loosen the familial bonds of community. Addressing those concerns, Mother told the nuns, "The new monastery will enhance our contemplative life. The silence will be awesome. . . . You can't live with one leg in the world and one leg in the cloister. It's one or the other, so make your choice." Then she finished on a prophetic note. "Sisters, if you knew what was coming none of you would be complaining of any sacrifice. Get your souls ready for what is coming."

At the EWTN board meeting on October 17, only one of the three bishop members showed up: Bishop David Foley. Both Bishop Thomas Daily of Brooklyn and Archbishop Charles Chaput of Denver could not attend due to prior commitments. Minutes of the meeting show that Bishop Foley repeatedly asked one question, posing it in various guises. "Who owns EWTN?" the bishop inquired good-naturedly. Sister Raphael, the community vicar and a member of the board, noted that Foley "had an obsession" with the topic. He opined that Mother and the sisters should "own the network." Bill Steltemeier argued that EWTN was not Church property, and he reminded the bishop of the board's independence. But Foley was not persuaded, creating a tense moment at the table. Much was at stake.

IRS records reveal that EWTN possessed more than $49 million in assets and collected upward of $19 million in annual contributions in 1998. Combined with the network's reach and market penetration, estimated to be worth billions, it was an empire too big to ignore, and too valuable to let slip away.

18
The Last Things

BISHOP DAVID FOLEY was well known by his peers, and teased with regularity. During the annual bishops meeting in Washington, old friends would rib him with introductions like: "This is David Foley. He's from Mother's diocese." Foley took the chuckles in stride, speaking well of Mother Angelica and even defending her on occasion.

But deep down, the subtext of the familiar "Mother's diocese" jab had to sting. The perception was that the licit authority in Birmingham, a successor to the apostles, had become the wisecracking nun's dupe. Conventional wisdom held that Mother called the shots in Birmingham and that no bishop, not even her own, could control her.

Foley knew better. He knew how tenuous Angelica's position had been. He faced the angry calls and letters from brother bishops. Unwillingly drafted into every one of the nun's controversies, he was obliged to play the role of peacekeeper. They were so close that Mother confided in Foley, sharing with him her distrust of certain bishops and her particular distaste for bishops conference intrigues. Yet for all that, he could still not get her to allow him the right to officially visit her monastery. Nobody said shepherding in "Mother's diocese" would be easy.

So it could have been expected that sooner or later Bishop Foley would flex his ecclesial muscle as a demonstration of his authority, a public witness to his independence, and just to show Mother Angelica who was boss in Birmingham. The liturgy would be his instrument of emancipation.

Since the establishment of Our Lady of the Angels Monastery in 1962, the priest celebrating the Conventual Mass had always faced the nuns, with his back to the rest of the congregation. The posture of the priest, officially known as *ad orientem* ("to the East") was the established norm in Catholic worship for centuries. After the Second Vatican Council, most priests turned to the faithful, becoming the focal point of the "communal supper." Still, the council documents and the Roman Missal indicated a preference for the *ad orientem* posture. Clinging to that preference, the first televised Mass from Our Lady of the Angels Monastery in 1991 featured the priest offering Mass with his back to the people.

Hoping to retain the nun's liturgical custom after their move to Hanceville, Bill Steltemeier, in a meeting on May 20, 1999, told Bishop Foley that he foresaw the televised Mass from Birmingham continuing unaltered—right down to the priest facing east.

In a written response of June 3, 1999, Bishop Foley made no mention of the celebration of the Mass. Instead, he was interested in a clear definition of the relationship among four entities: Mother, the monastery, EWTN, and himself. Aside from declaring his authority over the Birmingham chapel after the sisters' departure, the letter contained little else.

In public, the bishop and Mother Angelica continued their cordial relationship. On August 6, he presided over a two-hour blessing of the nearly completed Hanceville monastery, kicking off a series of open houses and special walk-through tours for employees, priests, benefactors, and the public. One open house drew as many as thirty thousand people in one day. The largely Protestant visitors gawked in amazement at what had risen in their backyard. Mother personally greeted each guest, wearing a perpetual smile as she stood at the side entrance for hours. Only Sister Raphael broke her happy mood.

For weeks, the seventy-one-year-old nun had been experiencing shooting stomach pains whenever she ate. A CAT scan revealed a thickness just below Raphael's abdomen. Subsequent biopsies of the tumor determined it to be an aggressive form of cancer, most likely a reoccurrence of the cancer she had battled in 1995. Angelica wept as she announced the news to the community. The ever-faithful Sister Raphael was there to console her.

Mother Angelica knew she could do little to halt the inevitable. She made sure her friend had constant attention, and she offered prayers for her recovery, but Angelica's focus was divided. European shipments of the chapel furnishings were snagged in transit, threatening delay of the long-planned consecration ceremony, scheduled for November 21. But shipping delays would seem pleasant distractions compared to the challenges that awaited the abbess.

Facing East

THE CHIEF LITURGIST for the Birmingham diocese met with Father Joseph Wolfe in August 1999 to finalize the protocol for the chapel consecration. Joseph was told that the bishop had approved all aspects of the ceremony, but he would not grant the request to celebrate the Mass *ad orientem*. Even though he had personally celebrated the Mass on-camera at Mother's monastery since 1994, standing with his back to the people, Foley now asserted his authority and shunned the posture. To Bishop Foley, the rationale for turning away from the assembly was gone. In the old monastery the celebrant had to give his back to the congregation in order to face the nuns who sat behind the reredos. But in the new monastery, the direction the priest faced mattered little, since the sisters would not be situated behind the altar, but in a Mass choir on the right side of the sanctuary.

Mother was outraged that the bishop would use the occasion of her chapel's consecration to make a point. She learned of his decision on August 24, the same day Sister Raphael decided against chemotherapy treatments. Feeling it would not prolong her life significantly, the nun even cancelled some of her doctor visits. She could feel her passing, and the sisters could see it.

The spread of the cancer to the lymph nodes drained Raphael's once rosy complexion and lulled the vicar into long midday naps. Medication became difficult to swallow, and though Sister Michael slaved over soft foods like mashed potatoes and stewed chicken, Raphael could keep none of it down.

Her vicar's deterioration underscored the brevity of life and turned Mother's thoughts to the last things. Indicative of her mindset, Angelica spent the first half of 1999 preparing for the dreaded Y2K bug: the much-ballyhooed computer glitch that on January 1, 2000, threatened to shut down the power grid and everything else attached to a hard drive. Mother installed windmills at the Hanceville monastery to pump water, purchased two tons of dried, ready-to-eat dinners, ordered wood-burning stoves, and made sure her sisters had warm clothes just in case the heat failed.

Angelica's actions were reserved compared to those of other Catholic and Protestant leaders across the country. Swept up in the Y2K craze, some notable figures invested in wilderness retreats, where they saw themselves living off the land. Others took up the crossbow for hunting (due to its reusable ammunition) and wrote pious manuals on the finer points of burying human waste and purifying contaminated water. Pools were converted into private water reservoirs while mountains of soup cans and barrels of grits appeared in the garages of the enlightened.

In Hanceville, construction ground on slowly. The contractors had already built and demolished two versions of the staircase leading to the lower church and were on their third attempt when Mother called a powwow. In September, she begged the construction team to finish the job. Time was of the essence, she told them, and the monastery had to be completed before Y2K struck. Whatever was coming, the sisters would be ready, and in the new monastery when it happened.

In a letter written on September 13, Mother protested Bishop Foley's decision to face the people during the consecration. That orientation would offend the architectural design of the chapel and break the 145-year tradition of her order, she insisted. The letter ended: "I appreciate and honor your authority as the Bishop of this Diocese. I humbly ask that you honor my authority as Abbess of this Monastery and its particular lawful customs and traditions."

After a consultation with the liturgy office of the National Conference of Catholic Bishops, Foley wrote to Angelica on September 29. He asserted his authority over the Mass, even in Mother's monastery, and flatly forbade the use of the *ad orientem* posture, explaining that it was not the norm for the Pope, the bishops, or the priests of Birmingham.

Mother disagreed, and she told the bishop he had been "misinformed by his consulting canonists." In her letter of October 10, she argued that the universal law of the Church permitted the priest to face either the people or east during Mass, but neither orientation was considered normative. She also noted that the Pope "in fact celebrates [the Mass] *ad orientem*" in his private chapel, which she had witnessed herself.

But to Foley the entire matter was an "obedience issue," a point of honor that defined his office and power. "I see it as a defiance of my authority—or any bishop's authority," he said of Mother's challenge to his decision. "I am the chief liturgist of this diocese. Mother isn't. I am."

The bishop had a choice to make: He could either back down and concede he had stretched the law with his demand or push forward, using his office to raise the ante. Cheered on by his canonist, Father Gregory Bittner, Foley explored the legal possibilities and consulted once more with canonists "beyond Birmingham," according to public remarks made by Bittner. Those comments indicate that the bishop again turned to the National Conference of Catholic Bishops in Washington for help.

The stress of the Foley intervention, the building delays, and Sister Raphael's worsening condition may have contributed to Mother Angelica's asthma attack on October 6. A double dose of steroids eased her breathing, but the frequency of the injections began to take their toll. Mother's face appeared swollen and red during broadcasts, and her temperament changed.

"She was taking a lot of steroids, and the steroids would make her very adamant about things, very aggressive," Sister Mary Catherine said. "She couldn't help it, but she would get angry." Mary Catherine paused apologetically. "It wasn't Mother," she said.

Her tough edge periodically surfaced on-air, especially when discussing the coming chastisement or the fallout that Y2K promised. When a tornado touched down in Oklahoma one night, destroying lives and property, Mother saw it as a sign.

"I think, my friends, that we're going to see more tragedies because even the world is shaking at the evil upon it. Shaking!" Mother said on her broadcast of May 4, 1999. "We deserve whatever we get, whether we're guilty or not. . . . So when a nation approves abortion, promotes abortion in other countries, allows murder in the worst ways—its awesome huh? . . . When abortion stops in this country maybe the weather will improve. I don't know, maybe it won't. But if you feel angry about this tornado, there are other things coming. I am sure. But in all things we must praise God."

Some viewers were disturbed by Mother's new approach. "I never saw viewers back away until she started on the end-of-the-world stuff, straighten up and fly right," Mother's producer Chris Harrington told me. "That's when I started getting calls saying, 'She's harsh.'"

"Because of the hurt, she lost some of her hope, and that allowed the chastisement stuff to come to the fore," Father Mitch Pacwa, a network regular, said. "With all the hurt, some of her humor went out."

As far as Mother was concerned, she was responding to the mission God had given her in that present moment. "I think what He wants me to do is to increase the remnant in the Church. To keep the Church in the Church. . . . The people have to prepare themselves and change their way of living to a deeper spirituality—to prepare themselves for the next world, not this world only," she told me at the time.

In a move akin to setting off a neutron bomb to kill a gnat, Bishop Foley promulgated a particular law in the diocese of Birmingham, outlawing the *ad orientem* option on October 18, 1999. Describing the orientation in a cover letter to his priests as a "political statement . . . dividing the people," Foley argued that local custom somehow invalidated the universal law permitting the priestly posture. To protect Birmingham's faithful from the "illicit innovation or sacrilege" of the priest turning his back to them, Foley decreed that all Masses would henceforth be celebrated at a freestanding altar, and, consistent with local tradition, the priest would face the people. Clerics challenging the decree risked "suspension or removal of faculties." The law would become effective three days before the consecration of Mother's chapel.

During her live show on October 19, Angelica cracked open the Bible and taught on the hypocrisy of the Pharisees, repeating the seven woes Jesus delivered upon them. For anyone who knew the back story, the commentary was obvious. Five days later, Mother dispatched Bill Steltemeier and Michael Warsaw to Rome to hand-deliver letters requesting the intervention of the Vatican congregations responsible for the Mass and for Church doctrine.

Mother knew she had an ally in Cardinal Joseph Ratzinger (the future Pope Benedict XVI), the Vatican's doctrinal authority and the most powerful man in Rome after the Pope. Cardinal Ratzinger had long espoused the virtues of the *ad orientem* priestly posture, saluting its theological emphasis—principally, the unified orientation of priest and people offering sacrifice to God rather than to one another.

Angelica's letters and her powerful advocate triggered an almost immediate response. A fax from the Congregation for Divine Worship and the Discipline of the Sacraments to Bishop Foley on November 8 condemned his decree, ruling that:

1. No custom presumed or otherwise could intervene against the liberty of the celebrant to celebrate the Sacred Liturgy in accord with the rubrics of the *Missale Romanum*.

2. . . . After having heard the opinion of the Congregation for the Doctrine of the Faith, which has expressed to this Congregation its own serious concerns, this Dicastry has concluded that individual Diocesan Bishops may not prohibit celebration of the Sacred Liturgy facing the apse (*ad orientem*), and therefore, it must respectfully ask that Your Excellency withdraw this Decree because it is contrary to the *ius commune* with regard to liturgical matters.

But Mother Angelica knew nothing of the Vatican ruling, and Bishop Foley kept it to himself. The only Vatican communication with Angelica came from Cardinal Martinez Somalo of the CICLSAL, responsible for religious. That letter of November 12 commanded Mother "As abbess of a Monastery within [Foley's] diocese, you will conform to the decrees of said diocese."

Meanwhile, the Congregation for Divine Worship and Discipline of the Sacraments recruited Archbishop Oscar Libscomb of Mobile, Foley's metropolitan bishop, to try to convince the Birmingham shepherd to turn course. The congregation even alerted Foley by letter that the ruling sapped his decree of all strength, and implored its rescission.

Running out of options, Bishop Foley attempted to leverage the bishops of the United States against the Vatican. He again found aid and comfort in the arms of the National Conference of Catholic Bishops.

In private talks at the fall meeting of the bishops conference, Foley and his liturgist, Father Richard E. Donohoe, met with NCCB liturgy officials to craft a solution to the stalemate.

Bishop Foley shared the content of those conversations. He said, "I explained the matter to the president of the conference, Joe Fiorenza, and he saw the problem. I said, 'I'm not speaking against Mother, but she has an instrument that is more powerful than anything else in the world. I mean, it's television. That is the problem, not Mother.' So I said, 'I do not need [that *ad orientem* Mass] to be on television.' So he said that I was representing the National Conference of Catholic Bishops and the contention was that this caused confusion in the U.S. when broadcast on television."

With that, Bishop Foley became the official representative of the NCCB, free to press his point in Rome, not as the bishop of Birmingham but as the voice of the bishops of the United States. The conference apparatus fully participated in the effort.

Sources I talked to remember draft copies of Foley's letters circulating among bishops and NCCB staff at the November 1999 meeting. Father Bittner, Foley's canonist, admitted, "Many meetings and discussions ensued with members of the Secretariat for liturgy of the NCCB as well as other liturgists and canonists." This

was a national effort and perhaps a final chance to gain some ecclesial control over Mother Angelica.

To shield her friars from "suspension or removal of faculties,"
and to avoid a possible trap, Mother told the priests to comply with
the bishop's decree and to celebrate Mass facing the people. She
instructed the nuns to leave the reredos screen closed during Mass
so that the public could not see their participation in the liturgy.
The nuns would not sing or pray aloud during their remaining days
in Birmingham.

Unbeknownst to Mother Angelica, Bishop Foley wrote the Vatican on December 14, promising to withdraw his decree, if a new
"suitable decree could be promulgated," and a private meeting
arranged with Cardinal Medina Estevez at the Congregation for Divine Worship.

"In my farming way, but with a foxy mind, I told Rome I would
not withdraw the decree until I was satisfied. So my purpose was
that Rome satisfy me," Bishop Foley said later.

The question remains: Why? Why would a bishop engage in a
tug-of-war with Rome over a decree that he knew was untenable?
Motives are hard to discern. Observers in Rome and the United
States speculated that Foley had fallen under the influence of Cardinal Mahony, who was trying to settle a not-so-old score. Foley dismissed this scenario, telling me that he and Mahony had not been
in contact "since the faxes he sent over his pastoral letter."

So what did drive Bishop Foley to provoke a public debate over a
licit form of the Mass? And why, knowing it would put him on a col-
lision course with the Vatican, did he continue to threaten priests
with such draconian penalties?

"The threat of suspension was to get the attention of Rome,"
Bishop Foley told me.

Obviously, getting the Vatican to focus on the *ad orientem* posture would force a definitive pronouncement on that issue. But
there may have been a side benefit to the controversy: Only a year
after the Mahony fracas, Mother Angelica was back in the public
spotlight, locking horns with another bishop. This image took on
great importance at the time.

Since 1997, Bishop Foley had been relentlessly questioning his relationship with Mother, the monastery, and the network. The crux of his inquiries seemed to be how much control the local ordinary could exercise over the monastery and, by association, EWTN. Dissatisfied with the answers provided, and denied the right to visit the monastery, Foley petitioned Rome for relief sometime between 1997 and 1999. He wanted the Vatican to authorize an apostolic visitation of Mother's monastery, to determine where things stood. This was a bit like calling the FBI in to investigate a domestic disturbance.

Where the Cardinal Mahony conflict threw Mother onto Rome's radar, the sparring match with Bishop Foley may have convinced officials there that Our Lady of the Angels and its abbess warranted a closer look. Whether by design or unintentionally, Bishop Foley had gotten Rome's attention.

On December 4, a day after Mother and her sisters drove to Hanceville, permanently vacating the Birmingham monastery, Cardinal Martinez Somalo wrote to inform the abbess that an apostolic visitator had been appointed by the Congregation for the Institutes of Consecrated Life and Societies of Apostolic Life. A comprehensive Church probe into the life and affairs of Our Lady of the Angels Monastery would begin shortly.

Going Home

AFTER SPENDING more than $50 million and expending countless hours approving and planning every detail of the temple, Mother Angelica, like millions around the world, watched its consecration on television.

The Consecration of the Shrine of the Most Blessed Sacrament had to be moved to December 19, 1999, due to shipping delays of chapel furnishings from Germany and Spain. As a result, many who had hoped to attend had to cancel. Bishop Foley was not among them. As main celebrant he anointed the altar, straining to rub oil across the marble expanse; drew slick crosses onto each column supporting the vaulted ceiling; smoked the interior of the chapel with fragrant incense; and celebrated Mass facing the people.

In silent protest, Mother and the cloistered nuns did not appear on the public side of the chapel during the ceremony. They viewed the entire consecration on two Jumbotrons behind the gold reredos. Even Sister Raphael, looking gray and listless in her wheelchair, gazed in amazement as the elaborate event unfolded.

For the public, it was a first glimpse of the Romanesque-Gothic temple Mother had talked about for years. Her intention to "overwhelm everybody, should they forget the reality that this is God's presence—God's House—" was more than fulfilled.

The cameras homed in on the twenty-four-karat-gold-leaf reredos rising like a castle from the chapel's sanctuary. Behind the altar, the tabernacle: a resplendent cathedral of glittering spires and hand-carved gold arresting the eye. Mother had ordered that the interior back wall of the tabernacle—home to the monastery's most precious possession, the Eucharist—be encrusted with diamonds, visible only to the Occupant. Jesus deserved the very best. As she viewed the image of her labors on the big screen, Angelica's mind must have wandered back with satisfaction to her promise made in 1956 to "build God a monastery in the South."

Near the end of the ceremony there was one uncomfortable moment. Originally, Mother had been scheduled to offer a few words to the congregation, before she and the sisters processed into the cloister. The bishop would then bless the enclosure door and lock them away. But with the *ad orientem* issue still raging and Bishop Foley showing no sign of retreat, Mother made a decision: "I didn't want him to bless that door, I didn't want him to do anything. Calling me sacrilegious . . ."

Not only was the procession off; Mother would not address the congregation, either. A misinformed Bishop Foley called Mother Angelica to the podium for her reflections. Applause rang out, followed by a long, awkward silence. Behind the reredos, Mother, motionless, stared at the screen.

Sister Antoinette touched the abbess's arm. "Reverend Mother, I think they are waiting for you to go out there and say a few words."

"I'm not going out there," Mother whispered, staring at the screen, her feet firmly planted.

After waiting several minutes, a visibly nervous Bishop Foley, his eyes fluttering, intoned, "I suppose Mother Angelica is *not* going to say a few words after all." He commended Angelica's faithfulness to the Eucharist, then climbed to the top of the reredos, and encased the Host in the eight-foot monstrance, to the thunderous outburst of Handel's "Hallelujah Chorus."

In their cavernous monastery, the thirty-one nuns adjusted to their new life of rustic solitude. They silently baked bread in the bakery, bottled fruit in the canning room, and sorted through baskets of EWTN correspondence in the immense mail room. It was a back-to-basics, fully contained, contemplative existence.

Living an hour from the network solidified Mother's personal withdrawal from EWTN. With the permission of the Holy See and Bishop Foley's blessing, she and one of the sisters continued to travel to EWTN on Tuesdays and Wednesdays for the live show, and saw to other business. Her focus was now on preparing for the future. She coached her vice presidents in her unique brand of decision-making and advised them on how to proceed without her. It must have been a difficult mentorship. Management techniques and cost-cutting measures are easy things to impart, but how does one teach radical responsiveness to God's inspiration and a steadfast faith in divine providence? Luckily for Mother, the VPs had witnessed her in action for years, so there was no wasting time convincing anyone of the legitimacy of her methods.

Sister Raphael's gastric system spasmed on December 22. She was rushed to the emergency room of the Cullman Regional Medical Center where physicians quickly identified a large tumor as the source of her problems. Tests confirmed that the cancer was "everywhere." Raphael again refused surgery or even a mild form of chemotherapy. To make her more comfortable, she was fitted with a nasal-gastric tube. A morphine drip helped dull the pain. "I know I am dying," she serenely told the doctors.

Pope John Paul II's Great Jubilee of the Year 2000, a year set aside by the Church to celebrate the anniversary of Christ's coming, arrived without incident at Our Lady of the Angels Monastery. Without power outages or the predicted pandemonium, the Jubilee

Year swept in while the nuns were attending Mass in the chapel. Days later, Mother told the sisters, "Don't say just because January 1st and Y2K are past nothing will happen. I assure you, sisters, something is coming." And in a way, she was right.

If Mother believed that some tribulation awaited mankind, she can be forgiven. Ceaseless tribulation had assailed her community for the better part of two years, and the future didn't look too bright, either. The pending apostolic visitation, the Foley imbroglio, and Sister Raphael's downward spiral visibly taxed Mother Angelica. Her blood pressure spiked and she could no longer check her emotions. Each time she tried to make funeral arrangements or plan the election to replace Raphael as vicar, tears flowed. Burying her face in a handkerchief, she would conceal her personal grief from the others. "Mother Vicar's death will be very hard on me," she confided to the nuns. "She's been a loyal friend all these years."

On January 5, Angelica's confidante and support for almost forty-nine years returned home to die. Emaciated and panting for air, Sister Raphael dozed in the infirmary under the watch of a hospice nurse. When Mother Angelica stopped by the room, she broke down, weeping. Somewhere within the shriveled gray woman, her mouth slack from morphine, was the sensitive Canton novice Angelica had liberated from sorrow so long ago. Her chief consoler became the source of her grief.

A minor improvement occurred on January 6, when Sister Raphael began to speak. She smiled, showing her long teeth, and happily sang the Ave Maria with the sisters. Then panic moved over her. She tearfully begged Mother: "Don't leave me. I want to die in your arms."

"I'll always be with you," Mother said soothingly.

A tumor protruded from Raphael's lower back, intensifying her pain. For weeks leading up to her hospitalization, she made repeated comments about the recliner's lumpy cushion, not realizing the lump was on her person.

"She accepted it all; she never complained," Sister Michael recalled. "You knew she was suffering a lot, but she never said a word, never complained."

From January 7 through January 9, Raphael claimed to have seen Sister Mary David, the saints, and Jesus. There was a radiance about her in those final days. Lapsing in and out of consciousness, she conversed with Christ: "O yes my love, oh yes," she cried as her blood slid down the nasal-gastric tube, into an attached receptacle.

Many times, the sisters thought they had lost her. Raphael would say, "Jesus is coming," closing her eyes. Moments later, they would snap open. After a few false alarms, Mother joked, "He's coming, but He's slow."

Mother's arms surrounded her friend on the afternoon of January 9. For nearly two hours, she held that pose, embracing Raphael as she approached death. The sisters gathered around the bed, praying quietly. Glancing out the window, Angelica could see Gabriel, the EWTN production truck, gliding into position for the broadcast of Sister Raphael's funeral Mass.

"I love you, I love you," Raphael gurgled to Mother.

"I love you, too," Angelica said, tenderly stroking the nun's head. "Go to Jesus now." Mother pressed her forehead against Raphael's, resisting a deluge of tears, and offered a silent good-bye. At 4:43 P.M., cradled in the arms of Mother Angelica and gripping her profession crucifix, Sister Mary Raphael went to God.

"If you ever had two people who were like one, it was those two. Almost like a marriage, where you have the husband and wife. They were always together in spirit, mind, thoughts," Sister Regina said. "Sister Raphael would defend Mother even to the point of getting mad at another sister. She'd lay right into us."

Sister Raphael's rapid decline and death left Mother feeling beaten and concerned. "It was a premonition that things were not going well, and they didn't," Angelica said.

The televised morning Mass from the Shrine of the Most Blessed Sacrament drew negative reviews from a large segment of the EWTN audience. Letters of complaint swamped the network. Viewers missed seeing the nuns and felt removed from the worship. Some expressed dismay over the ostentatious chapel and accused Mother of using their money to pay for it. After a monthlong absence from the live show, Mother Angelica returned on January 18, 2000, to set them straight.

She started gently, talking about the "packs of nasty letters" she had received. "Some people are criticizing the gold, the silver, the marble." She was more disappointed than angry. "You know what I think? I think you've lost it. Because you don't object to big houses for kings and queens. You don't object to the White House, which is much too big for two people. And sometimes there are more than two people, and those people shouldn't be there," she said, alluding to the Clinton sex scandal. "What bothers me is we're satisfied with the very least for God, but only the best for us."

Raising her forearm across her body as if to block an attacker with an open palm, she continued. "Not one penny you gave went into the building of that church. Five people. One, two, three, four, five—in case you can't count. Five people built that church and that whole monastery. . . ."

Breathing hard, she let her Italian temper flare. "To some of you I am a mother. To some of you I am a grandmother. To some of you I am a father. Well tonight, I am a father. My humble answer to your questions is: enjoy it and shut up." She flipped her veil back to punctuate the line and then glanced off-camera. Wandering into talk of Sister Raphael's death, tears intruded. She thrust her fingers at her eyes to stop them, but it was too late. In silence, expressions of hurt and anger warred on her face. She struggled for composure, disgusted at breaking down on live television, and finished the hour, telling viewers she "had to get it off her chest."

Moved to pity by the program, letters and calls of support came in from all over the world, and so did donations.

In Rome on February 4, the representative of the National Conference of Catholic Bishops, the Most Rev. David E. Foley, and his entourage arrived for their appointment at the Congregation for Divine Worship and the Discipline of the Sacraments. Before Cardinal Medina, Foley identified the *ad orientem* posture as a "problem" in the United States and a sign of "disunity." Cardinal Medina listened patiently, then suggested that the bishop's real gripe seemed to be the broadcasting of the *ad orientem* Mass. Foley agreed. The congregation instructed the bishop to draw up norms prescribing the direction of televised Masses, and again insisted that he rescind his decree.

According to sources in the Apostolic Palace, members of the Papal household were irritated by Bishop Foley's decree and his hostile stance toward the nun they called "the miracle woman." At the time, a curial official with access to the Pope referred to Foley in this author's presence as *"el obisbo loco"*—"the crazy bishop"— leaving little doubt as to how the situation was perceived in the upper echelons of the Vatican.

A large white satin box bearing the Papal insignia landed in the EWTN mail room on Valentine's Day. There was no note, just the box and a Vatican postmark. A phone call later informed Mother that the box contained a gift from the Holy Father, "in appreciation for the work being done by EWTN around the world" and for the sisters' dedication to the Eucharist.

The following night on her live show, she and the EWTN vice presidents fanned out around the mysterious box as if it were the Ark of the Covenant. "I know the Holy Father gives gifts, but I never saw one this big," Mother said. Before the end of the program, she broke the seal on the box, exposing a monstrance given to His Holiness by the people of Nowa Huta during his 1999 pilgrimage to Poland. A gleeful Angelica thanked the Pope and her VPs for their hard work. "Somebody, somewhere has to say, 'You're doing a good job. Just keep on.' And that's what I think this says to all of us," she declared. The bishops conference would later ask that the program not be rebroadcast.

The Pope's gesture spoke volumes. A high-ranking Vatican archbishop, who was in a position to know, told me the gift was a "sign of the Pope's solidarity with Mother Angelica."

"It was a big boost for the people here," Michael Warsaw, the network president, said. "But most of all, it brightened Mother's spirits." The Papal encouragement could not have come at a more propitious moment. The apostolic visitation was only days away, and on February 22, Bishop Foley unveiled his "Norms for Televising the Mass in the Diocese of Birmingham in Alabama."

With the release of the norms, Foley withdrew his decree of October 18, 1999, "in its entirety," including the severe penalties. A letter of February 8 from Cardinal Medina unambiguously stated that whether the priest faced the people during Mass or turned his back to them, "the two options carry with them no theological or disciplinary stigma of any kind." Unable to outlaw the *ad orientem* Mass, Bishop Foley simply forbade its broadcast. "All televised Masses will be celebrated in such a way that when the priest is standing at the altar he is facing the faithful," Foley wrote. At a time of continuing liturgical abuse and innovation, the perfectly licit *ad orientem* posture was banned from the airwaves in Birmingham, presumably to prevent its replication.

Citing "technical issues" at the Hanceville chapel, EWTN shut down broadcast of the sisters' Mass on March 12, and returned production to Birmingham in full compliance with the bishop's norms. As of this writing, Mass continues to be celebrated each morning *ad orientem* at Our Lady of the Angels Monastery, sans the cameras.

The Visitation

THE OFFICIAL Vatican visitor, Archbishop Roberto Gonzalez, of San Juan, Puerto Rico, had been studying the financial records of EWTN, Our Lady of the Angels Monastery, the Franciscan Missionaries of the Eternal Word, the EWTN *Religious Catalogue*, and all related enterprises for several weeks prior to his arrival in Birmingham on February 29. His would be a far-reaching and thorough inquiry.

The Vatican investigation would focus mostly on life at the monastery: the liturgy, prayer, maintenance of enclosure, administration, and the relationship with the diocesan bishop. Any inquiry into EWTN or its affairs was to be limited. In its guidelines for the visitor, the CICLSAL clearly stated that EWTN was not "central" to the visitation but that "it seems necessary to consider to what extent if any it has an impact on the living of the contemplative life of Our Lady of the Angels Monastery and whether its governance and financial administration are fully distinct from those of the Order."

There were several questions to be explored, but three were paramount to Gonzalez: First, who owned EWTN? Second, was Our Lady of the Angels Monastery within its rights when it deeded lands and property to EWTN? And, finally, was Mother Angelica, who had been superior for thirty-nine years without having been elected to the position, truly an abbess?

Archbishop Gonzalez, a trim, olive-complexioned man with huge black eyes and a timid manner, jetted to Birmingham accompanied by a canon lawyer, a civil lawyer, an accountant, and a religious sister. At forty-nine, Gonzalez was a rising episcopal star and the youngest archbishop in the country. Cardinal O'Connor had plucked the Franciscan priest from a Bronx parish in the 1980s, recommending him to Cardinal Bernard Law. Law had been looking to name a Hispanic auxiliary in Boston, and Gonzalez fit the bill. Ordained a bishop in 1988, he was installed as coadjutor bishop of Corpus Christi, Texas, in 1995, during a tempestuous period. Within a year of his arrival, the Texas attorney general sued the bishop of Corpus Christi, Rene Gracida, to remove him as president of the Kenedy Foundation, a charitable trust, charging impropriety. In a case eerily reminiscent of Mother Angelica's, it is reported that bishops from outlying dioceses instigated the lawsuit against their brother, hoping to route Kenedy Foundation dollars toward their own projects. In the end, Gracida was vindicated. The final settlement expanded lay control of the Kenedy board, marginalizing the influence of future participating bishops.

Roberto Gonzalez had witnessed firsthand an ugly, high-stakes episcopal takeover attempt. As he undertook his probe into Mother's affairs, balance sheets and the requirements of Church law were familiar terrain to the young archbishop.

Mother girded herself for the visitation with a simple faith. On Monday, February 28, the day before it was to begin, she received an Italian statue of the baby Jesus seated in a chair. Indulging her favorite devotion before the sisters, she repeated Father John Rizzo's line to the Divino Niño: "You're going to fix this, aren't You? If You don't they're going to kill me and smash You."

The first stop for the visitators was a meeting with as many

EWTN board members as could be assembled on short notice. The investigators questioned Angelica's status as abbess, provoking an immediate reaction from Bill Steltemeier and certain members of the board. There were peripheral discussions about EWTN's programming policy, and the use of the word *Catholic* in the network's title. Gonzalez also explored the financial connection between EWTN and the monastery.

"They were on a fishing expedition to find information that would help support somebody's ends," Michael Warsaw, then an EWTN vice president, said. "You never got the sense that this was to be supportive, or helpful to EWTN."

"It seems to me the line of questioning was aimed at finding out whether EWTN belonged to the order. And if so, they could just take it over," Helen Hull Hitchcock, a member of the board, recalled. Still, Hitchcock believed that Archbishop Gonzalez acted fairly. "I thought he had to ask the questions and be hard, but he was sympathetic to us. Gonzalez was not in sympathy with Mother's tormentors."

A major concern for the visitator was the degree of control Mother exercised over the network. According to the EWTN articles of incorporation, the abbess of Our Lady of the Angels Monastery and her vicar were entitled to serve ex officio as permanent members of the board. A subsequent bylaw designated the abbess as chairman of the board in perpetuity, with veto power over any vote. Even if the entire board were to vote for a given action, without the consent of the abbess, it couldn't pass. This meant that the woman who ran the monastery ran the network.

The questioning of Mother Angelica's validity as abbess concerned Steltemeier. If the visitator came to the conclusion that she was not abbess of the monastery, control of the network and its assets could be up for grabs. And if the visitator brushed aside Steltemeier's claim that EWTN was a civil entity, as opposed to Bishop Foley's contention that the network was the apostolate of the monastery, a case could be made that the entire corporation was Church property, and thus subject to the bishop and the Holy See. Bill Steltemeier was worried.

On the evening of March 2, 2000, Archbishop Gonzalez had a private meeting with Mother Angelica in the monastery parlor. For several hours, they conversed, interrupted only by dinner.

"We want you to remain doing what you're doing," he told her. "We just want to be sure the sisters are okay, have plenty of room, and are not affected by the network."

Mother liked him. She liked the way he listened, and she respected the strength of his positions even when she disagreed with them. And there were disagreements. Of note was Gonzalez's observation that everything Angelica did was invalid, due to her failure to secure appropriate permissions.

"Are you saying when I had two hundred dollars, no knowledge, and I got that inspiration to build a television studio that I should have written to Rome—and they would have said yes?" Mother asked incredulously.

"No, they wouldn't have," the archbishop answered. "But you didn't do it."

"Well, I'm sorry," Mother replied.

"And this temple?" the archbishop asked. "This monastery? Who gave you permission to build this?"

"The Lord, He asked me to build Him a temple. And after that, I didn't think I needed anybody else's permission."

"The Holy See will have to forgive you for all you've done."

"Well, leave a little room, because I'll probably do the same thing again," Mother said.

Particularly galling to Angelica was the presumption that she had siphoned money from the network to pay for the monastery.

"All they saw was money," Mother told me. "It's just so hard to make people understand that this place is the fruit of God's providence." She leaned back for a typical Mother Angelica explanation. "If I say the Lord spoke to me and He wanted me to build this building and nothing ever happened and it turned out to be a shack—obviously it was not the Lord. I mean, the test is not believing me; the test is that it happened! And how did it happen? I never went out; I never made one petition for funds for this place."

The nuns produced copies of the donor checks, some in million-dollar increments, to substantiate Mother's account. This evidence definitively killed the charges of financial malfeasance related to the Shrine. •

Before leaving, Archbishop Gonzalez firmly advised Mother that she should not think of giving up her position as CEO and chairman of the board at EWTN. To surrender the network to lay hands was far too risky, and the veto power too precious to forfeit, he told her.

On the morning of March 3, the visitators inspected the cloister and met with Mother and four of her nuns. Archbishop Gonzalez told them he would recommend that the Congregation (CICLSAL) sanate (meaning "to heal at the root" or retroactively forgive) the failure to obtain written permission for building projects, expenditures, and the donation of property to EWTN. Once again, the archbishop warned Mother against resigning her position at the network, as this could constitute another alienation of property and compound her troubles. Without the permission of the local bishop and the Holy See, such a severing of the apostolate from the monastery would be invalid, he said. Mother listened apprehensively.

Sister Catherine attended the meeting. "It was almost like they were trying to take over EWTN at that point," she told me. "They were trying to say that this was our apostolate and we were trying to prove that it was not our apostolate. We only open the mail. We weren't actively involved. Mother was the only one actively involved."

Individual interviews with the nuns on March 4 shocked the visitators. Probably expecting whispers and reluctant witnesses, they found fire and spunk in Mother Angelica's daughters. "The novices just laid them out like pizzelle," Mother recalled.

Word that Archbishop Gonzales had questioned Angelica's legitimacy as abbess had already penetrated the cloister walls. Naturally, her daughters took offense.

"The interrogation, I call it," Sister Joseph said. "It was a personal investigation of Mother and the network, particularly the finances."

"We had a visitation in Canton, but it was nothing like this," Sister Michael said, concurring. "This was more of an investigation of the network rather than a visitation of the monastery."

Even the reserved Sister Bernadette got her two cents in: "Archbishop Gonzalez was nice, but he didn't get to first base, because I told him, 'You are trying to fight something God has his hand in.' And he just looked at me."

On March 4, following her final afternoon meeting with Archbishop Gonzalez, the scales fell from Mother's eyes and her next step became clear. Angelica told me she had asked Gonzalez why certain bishops were intent on controlling the network. "They don't want to control you, Mother. They want to destroy you," the archbishop allegedly said. Sources close to Gonzalez dispute the comment. Nevertheless, it became Gospel to Mother—a final confirmation that she must do the unthinkable. The archbishop pronounced the apostolic blessing and officially ended the visitation at 7:30 that evening. Later that night, Bishop Foley drove from Birmingham to the guest house to confer with the investigators.

Before day's end, Mother ordered Bill Steltemeier to draft resolutions overhauling EWTN's articles of incorporation and bylaws.

Burning the Bridge

TRUE TO HER consensus-building style, Mother shared her plan with Bill Steltemeier, the sisters, and Michael Warsaw before presenting it to all the network VPs on March 6.

"I had never seen her so obviously burdened by something. She looked tired, thoughtful, preoccupied," Michael Warsaw recalled. "She told me what she was thinking of doing. I remember initially saying surely there must be another option, somebody we could go to in Rome to stop this."

At the VP meeting in her office, Mother provided a summary of recent events peppered with her own perceptions. Then, corporately, the VPs debated the pros and cons of her proposed solution. It was Doug Keck, the vice president of production, who delivered an uncharacteristic opinion, which proved to be decisive. For twenty years Keck had headed up operations at Rainbow, the conglomerate responsible for a host of cable networks, including Bravo, American Movie Classics, and the Playboy Channel. A rediscovery of his faith had led Keck to EWTN, where he would be instrumental in transforming the on-air look and content of the network. The tall, slouching VP with blond hair like a Fuller brush usually let others take the lead, but on this occasion he felt compelled to speak his mind.

"I surprised myself and something told me to say, 'Mother, I think you're right. I think you need to step back to protect the network.' She was floating the idea," Keck said. "I usually don't think about plots, but something was absolutely happening."

The VPs had feared an episcopal coup against Mother since the run-in with Cardinal Mahony. The visitation only deepened their sense of danger. The data gleaned from the investigation could be used to justify some future action. They believed the congregation or Bishop Foley could compel Mother to institute changes at the network; reconfigure the board; or—worst-case scenario—appoint a progressive successor armed with the veto power. Angelica might have to make a choice between her obedience to Rome and her responsibility to EWTN and its viewers. By March 6, the VPs unanimously agreed with Mother: Her continuing leadership at EWTN placed the organization and her community at great risk.

Perversely, the very thing that had protected the network from so many assaults—Mother's position as abbess of a pontifical order—now jeopardized its future. She herself had become the bridge church leaders could use to invade the organization and distort its message. Disregarding the personal risks and believing resolutely that the network should remain an autonomous, lay-run, civil entity, Angelica decided to use the escape hatch before any demands could be made of her. A man might have stayed and fought. But a mother would do almost anything to protect her offspring.

Mother Angelica signed a letter of resignation at that meeting, and Bill Steltemeier accepted it. The second paragraph of the letter asserted "that the only apostolate of the Poor Clares of Perpetual Adoration in Hanceville, Alabama is to keep adoration of the Most Blessed Sacrament and to pray for the salvation of souls. The Monastery has never had any other apostolate than this." Mother's resignation wouldn't take effect until March 17, 2000, following an emergency board meeting scheduled for that same day.

Members of the board were notified of the special emergency teleconference by mail and told that they would consider ending the ex officio board memberships and dissolving the veto power of the chairman. No mention of Mother's resignation was made.

In one of her final acts as CEO, Mother symbolically surrendered the network to the vice presidents during a videoconference. "Take this network," she told them. "Treat it as if it were your only child." Marynell Ford, the vice president of marketing, turned to another VP and openly sobbed.

Tipped off by a board member, one of the apostolic visitators called Angelica on March 13. He objected to the rush to amend the network bylaws and informed Mother that the visitation was not yet completed. More information was needed, he said, and Archbishop Gonzalez and company would be back in Hanceville the first week of April.

The next night, Mother's plans were further complicated by heavy congestion in her chest, thought to be a cold. It was actually pneumonia, which landed her in the hospital for nine days. Undeterred, Angelica would proceed with the resignation from her hospital bed.

On March 16, a day before the board meeting, Archbishop Gonzalez appeared at Our Lady of the Angels Monastery, demanding to see Mother Angelica. His personal mission was to kill the emergency meeting and dissuade Mother from relinquishing her permanent slot on the network board and her veto power. The nuns told Gonzalez that the abbess was unavailable. Bill Steltemeier later confessed she was in the hospital, although he refused to identify which hospital. Left without a choice, the archbishop penned a note to Mother Angelica, begging her to delay the board vote until his report was filed and Rome had had a chance to review the contents.

Sitting on the edge of a mechanized bed in a hospital gown, an oxygen tube dangling from her nose, Mother Angelica prepared to abandon the media empire she had worked nearly twenty years to build. Her swan song would be as contentious, dramatic, and comic as anything in her life had been. Bill Steltemeier, a few of the sisters, and a lawyer clustered around the bed. The members of the board were electronically ushered into the room via speakerphone.

Like the ringmaster at an unruly circus, Steltemeier strove to keep attention on the resolutions in the center ring, but the side acts created their own distractions. Almost immediately, the three bishop board members—Archbishop Charles Chaput of Denver, Bishop Thomas Daily of Brooklyn, and Bishop David Foley of Birmingham—protested the meeting and the items under consideration. Archbishop Chaput moved for a postponement, in deference to the apostolic visitator, with whom he had spoken the night before. Rebuffing him, Bill Steltemeier said a religious matter had no bearing on the board meeting of a civil entity, and he hastened to proceed with the business at hand. Bishop Foley interjected that the monastery and EWTN were inseparable in the eyes of the Church. Steltemeier ruled him out of order.

Seeing the direction things were going, Bishop Daily excused himself from the meeting and hung up. The bickering stopped just long enough for Mother Angelica to take the floor, her voice thick and hoarse. She recounted the providential founding of the network and offered the board a historical retrospective. She recalled Bishop Vath, who had suggested giving up the habit to pursue television in 1981; the contentious relationship with CTNA; the joy of her repeated visits with the Holy Father; the inspiration to build the Shrine; and the violation she felt throughout the visitation process. She then dropped the bombshell, reading her letter of resignation, followed by a few comments:

> I'm an obedient daughter of the Church. I have cried for it, bled for it, laughed for it, spread it around the world. And now I'm in suspicion. Now my sisters' life and Order and vocation are in question. We're contemplatives, and we're going to stay contemplatives. . . . I don't understand this power struggle in the Church for this network. Nobody bothered about it when we were struggling. Nobody bothered about it except to criti-

cize and try to control and control. . . . God has upheld this network. It's not mine. It doesn't matter whether I'm there or not. You're dealing with Him. You're not dealing with me. You're dealing with God. . . . Maybe I do need forgiveness for doing what we've done. I'd be happy for it. And then get off my back! I'd be happy for it. But then get off my back and leave us to do what the Lord wants us to do. I don't understand this suspicion. I'm sorry. But I don't think I have to apologize for doing God's work! 'Under a law.' The Pharisees said that. The Pharisees who are everywhere. 'Ah, but no you can't heal on Sunday!' You can't build an $800 million network! You can't build a $50 million Church paid for by five families! You're not in the law! You're not in the rule! Well, I didn't do it purposely."

Steltemeier literally wailed, choking on tears at the conclusion of her soliloquy. After taking a breather for prayer, he moaned, "I've been with Mother twenty-one years! She's been crucified upside down! . . . All the conniving and compromising makes me sick!"

For two hours, tempers flared, theatrics flourished, and threats flew. The bishops were "trying to filibuster" the proceedings according to Steltemeier, Chaput complaining that his rights were being violated, worried that the monastery's property was being alienated without appropriate compensation from EWTN. Foley asked for endless clarifications. In between, Steltemeier tried to cover his legal bases while Mother urged the vote.

"The Lord gave it to me to do. I've done it," she said. "I'm seventy-seven pretty soon. My asthma's bad. I can't leave this network hanging in the air for anybody to grab it."

"We must proceed," Steltemeier cried. "We've had all this discussion; there's no sense fooling around." Steltemeier called the question, and just before the vote, Bishop Foley cut in once more, requesting additional discussion. "We've been talking about it now for one hour and fifty minutes," an exasperated Steltemeier huffed.

"Bishop," Mother said, leaning toward the speakerphone on her bed, "I'm not changing my mind, and I think we need to get on with this."

Over the objections of Archbishop Chaput, who felt "railroaded" by the process, and Bishop Foley, who worried that the veto power and ex officio positions could not "be easily gotten back," Mother and Steltemeier prevailed. The board voted to alter the bylaws and accepted Angelica's resignation. Only the two bishops registered dissenting votes.

At 5:00 P.M. on March 17, 2000, Mother Angelica rested comfortably in her hospital room, officially separated from the network she would forever be identified with. She had silently burned the bridge behind her. No religious, cleric, or bishop could ever exercise complete control over EWTN again. Relying on divine providence, she was confident the board and vice presidents could perpetuate her vision and keep the network steadfastly loyal to the Magisterium in Rome. The network now belonged to the laity and God. The coup had been beaten back and routed.

On the face of it, an organized plot to take control of EWTN seems far-fetched. There is no doubt that some bishops were preoccupied, perhaps even obsessed, with Mother's authority over the network and were obviously on a hunt to discover any misstep. But was there a master plan to take possession of the network? Every bishop I interviewed who was familiar with the case dismissed the idea. This author was similarly unconvinced.

Then in October 2003, Bishop Foley's canonist, Father Gregory Bittner, at the end of a long speech to the Canon Law Society of America, revealed his own final solution for EWTN. Reacting to the board's acceptance of Mother Angelica's resignation, he posited in a speech that "the Holy See . . . could have authorized a civil lawsuit against the board of governors of EWTN, Inc." to have their actions "declared invalid and illegal." Additionally, Bittner suggested, the Holy See could have sanctioned another lawsuit "for the dissolution of the corporation and then its reincorporation, ensuring the role of the sponsoring institution and the mission of the Roman Catholic Church in the field of communications media. The moving parties would be the three bishops who are/were members of the Board of Governors." In other words, take the civil corporation to court, gut the board, and rebuild the thing with the bishops calling the tune.

Beyond revealing a mischievous mind, Bittner's suggestions prove little in themselves. But they do lend credence to Angelica's belief that stratagems were fermenting and plans were afoot to capture her network. As these remarks came from the canonical adviser to Bishop Foley, it is hard to imagine that the bishop himself was not at least partially familiar with such musings.

A year after resigning, Mother Angelica had no regrets about her decision. "I had to retire because it was the only way to save the network, and I had to prove that it could continue on its own," she said.

Archbishop Gonzalez returned to the monastery on April 5 to peruse additional financial records and resolve some final questions. It would take the congregation (CICLSAL) in Rome more than a year to react to the findings of the Gonzalez report. In a letter of June 26, 2001, Cardinal Somalo sanated the donation of properties and Mother's long, unelected term as abbess. He granted her permission to continue hosting the live show in Birmingham, asked that she attempt to heal the shattered relationship with Bishop Foley, and, almost as an afterthought, ruled that the network had no negative impact on the lives of the nuns.

In a separate letter to Bishop Foley, the congregation washed its hands of anything to do with the network, claiming it was "beyond our competency." It did, however, defend the EWTN board's right to abolish offices, rescind powers, and appoint board members as it saw fit. Rome had diplomatically come down in Mother's favor.

Bishop Foley was removed from EWTN's board of governors and his live show, *Pillars of Faith,* was canceled. The notice came in a letter of June 16, 2000, from EWTN's newly elected chairman and CEO, Bill Steltemeier.

The fights behind her, Mother Angelica settled into community life and relished the time away from the network. She spent days studying the Scripture on her back porch, planning the construction of a castlelike gift shop and pilgrimage center near the monastery, and found rest in prayer before the Blessed Sacrament.

The morning of July 3, 2000, she almost found perpetual rest. Returning her breviary to a choir stall after Mass, Mother sensed the onset of a headache. As she reached into her habit for a Tylenol tablet, a sensation of numbness ran from the top of her head downward. The pillbox fell from her hand, drawing the attention of the sisters. Suddenly shaking, Angelica clutched the stall to steady herself. A nun caught the abbess by the waist and, with assistance, maneuvered her into a wheelchair. "Jesus help me. Jesus help me," Mother said. The next moment, she was unresponsive.

"She was turning blue. Her lips were set," Sister Antoinette said. "It looked like she was dying."

Fearing the worst, the nuns called 911 and a young friar administered last rites. As the emergency crew whisked her away, Antoinette whispered in her ear, "Reverend Mother, you can't die yet—we're not ready." Angelica could hear nothing.

"Oh God," Dr. James Hoover, Mother's physician, said when they wheeled her into the Cullman Regional emergency room. "She arrived at the hospital unresponsive. It was as if she was in a deep coma," Hoover recalled. Angelica was so limp, the nurses had to slit her habit open to prepare her for testing. The CAT scan, EKG, and lab work were all deemed unremarkable by Dr. Hoover.

"But in a relatively short amount of time, she awoke and was fine," Hoover said. "Medically, it was an extraordinary event. There was no evidence of stroke or seizure. The dramatic turn from an unresponsive state to an awakened state was like nothing I have seen in a patient."

Shortly after waking, Mother told her new vicar, Sister Mary Catherine, of the strange experience she had had while comatose.

"I was in a dark room. I could feel Our Lord's presence on the right side. I thought, Well, I'm dying. I better say my ejaculation for the Poor Souls: 'Jesus and Mary, I love you, save souls!' " Mother recounted. Sensing time was short, she said, "Lord, I don't think I'm ready yet, but it's okay." She told me, "At that instant, I saw my soul leave my body. It went out and came back three times."

A couple of days later, Mother returned to the monastery, trying to make sense of the episode. "In my heart I really feel I died and came back," she told the nuns on July 7. "I have no more fear of death, no more fear of bishops or of what is going to happen . . . nothing matters but God, and how we are to express that love to the world."

A renewed Mother Angelica shared her near-death experience on her live program of July 11. She assured the terminally ill and elderly members of her family that they had nothing to fear. "I don't know how long our Dear Lord will leave me here," she said. "I hope it's a long time. But I know for sure that I won't be afraid. There's no need to fear being called by an awesome, loving, compassionate and merciful Father. There is no reason to be afraid."

During an interview session at the end of 2000, Mother shared with me a prayer that she had been offering to God since the near-death experience: "Lord, I want you to use me in any way you want. I don't care what it is. Just don't let me see the fruit."

In 2001, God would accept her offer.

19

Purification

ON THE EVENING of December 12, 2000, the world caught a glimpse of what Rita Rizzo must have been like as a drum majorette. Waddling and waltzing, shimmying and cackling, Mother Angelica celebrated the feast of the Virgin of Guadalupe in the company of a mariachi band. The unsuspecting that night might have mistaken EWTN for Univision. Her live show had not been so live in years. For old friends, who were seated down front, like Jean Morris, Tom Swatek, and Gene McLane it was to be a last hurrah—a final chance to savor the Mother Angelica of old: carefree, spontaneous, and utterly unpredictable. Donning a Mexican sombrero atop her veil, she faked Spanish lyrics and swayed with the mariachis in a rollicking display that reminded some of her charismatic days. But it was not to last.

Out of obligation to the audience, Mother continued hosting the live show, making the pilgrimage from Hanceville to Birmingham each week. But the travel became a "physical strain," which showed itself on the air. In the first half of 2001, Mother's Tuesday night teaching show seemed more random and repetitive than ever before. Though her spiritual insight and advice to the suffering was undiminished, Chris Harrington said, "Her delivery was disjointed. There was no train of thought, and the old stories were cropping up over and over."

Lay cohosts shouldered the content of the Wednesday night interview program, freeing Mother to comment at her leisure without the responsibility of carrying the load alone. For the most part she enjoyed the interplay, and the audience loved having her there.

On August 15, 2001, sitting before the packed studio audience, she looked distracted, tired, and strangely resigned to the twentieth anniversary of her network. To celebrate the occasion, and her fifty-seventh year in religious life, EWTN broadcast a day of special programming, including an *ad orientem* liturgy from Hanceville, in defiance of the NCCB norms. The capstone of the day was a live on-air celebration featuring EWTN's foundress and leading icon.

Mother laughed at the impromptu serenades, retold old stories of the network's founding, tossed off a few jokes, and patiently answered the questions of international well-wishers. But reminiscence held little allure for her, and the old fire had waned. At certain moments, Mother stared impassively at the camera. As the program wore on, she had difficulty completing thoughts. Shifting in her chair, she occasionally turned to the audience for words or facts that escaped her.

Five days later, Mother felt achy all over. After the Mass of August 20, in the middle of reciting her breviary, she found it impossible to make sense of the words on the page. Perspiring profusely, she called for help. But hard as she tried, she could not recall Sister Margaret Mary's name.

This was not the first time Mother had had problems reading. While driving to Birmingham with Sister Agnes to do the live show, she'd had a similar experience. But fearing a stroke and not wanting to provoke alarm, she kept the event to herself. This time, Margaret Mary was informed and a nurse was called to the monastery.

Shivering in her bedroom, Mother wanted to test her reading ability. Sister Faustina randomly chose a book from the shelf—the Navarre edition of the Gospel of John—and handed it to the abbess. Angelica flipped the book open and read aloud the first verse she happened upon, John 11:4: "This illness is not unto death; it is for the glory of God, so that the Son of God may be glorified by means of it."

A blood test later revealed that she was suffering from a kidney infection. Antibiotics and a period of rest were prescribed. But days later she still felt weak and lethargic. During a bright spot in her convalescence, Mother claims to have seen the child Jesus dashing down the halls of the monastery. This was by no means an isolated event. Again and again, the OLAM History cites instances where the Divino Niño not only appeared to Mother but spoke to her in the "voice of a child." Though the sisters saw nothing, they believe their Mother did. As the saying goes, For those with faith, no evidence is necessary; for those without it, no evidence will suffice.

Pirate of Souls

WHATEVER THE STRENGTH of Mother Angelica's mystical perceptions, she was clearly aware of something at the start of her September 4, 2001, live show. She informed the audience that the family prayer intention was "to pray for those who experience unexpected tragedies."

She talked of heaven's wonder, and the reality of hell and Satan. The extern nuns watching the program at home thought they saw Mother's eyelids fluttering out of sync, but they couldn't be sure.

The next morning at breakfast with Sister Margaret Mary, Mother started to laugh at a joke, but her face failed to cooperate. The left side of her mouth stretched downward, as if yanked by some unseen hand. Her unblinking left eye froze in a macabre stare. Sister Margaret Mary urged a visit to the hospital.

"Why?" Mother slurred. "I don't feel anything."

An MRI showed the facial paralysis to be the result of a series of "recurrent bihemispheric strokes," according to Dr. David Patton. The ministrokes had apparently been afflicting the abbess for some time. To ward off any future attacks, the doctor prescribed Coumadin, a blood thinner.

On the morning of September 11, Mother called me from the hospital. "I had a mild stroke," she said, sounding as if her mouth was full of vermicelli. "Everything's working except half my face. They tell me I should have been completely paralyzed on one side. But I'm doing great—I just look like Apple Annie." As we talked, a second plane piled into the World Trade Center on national television. The devil she had denounced only a week earlier had shown his face, and one of many "unexpected tragedies" had befallen the nation.

To preserve Mother's left eye, salve had to be applied at regular intervals and a patch worn to protect it from ulcerating. Why has God permitted this? Angelica wondered. She turned inward for answers, contemplating the faults she felt had blocked her way: her quick temper, her impatience. "Please don't allow me to frustrate your plans because of my own weaknesses and imperfections," she begged God in prayer. Eventually, Mother discovered a purpose in the pain.

"I've never had in all my life such an awareness that God was choosing me to help people," she said after the stroke. "This is to bring people to a new reality that suffering is brought by God to make us holy. I am so aware of that." Mother Angelica felt compelled to return to the airwaves.

"I didn't think initially that it was a good thing," Michael Warsaw said of Angelica's TV homecoming. "I was afraid that people would see her in a weakened state and her enemies would try to take advantage of that and her audience would feel that Mother or the network was in decline. I think she had a sense that she wasn't going to have much more time."

The familiar *Mother Angelica Live* theme music sounded in homes across the globe on September 25, 2001, but the image to follow was anything but familiar. Her mouth twisted in a cruel contortion, a black patch under her glasses, Mother returned to her people looking like an icon of redemptive suffering. "Hi, be not afraid. It's me," she chirped, breaking the ice. "With all these little handicaps I need to be with you as long as God wills."

The tone of the program quickly turned serious. Angelica thought the hunt for terrorists after the attacks of September 11 ironic, since the United States continued to coddle what she called "social terrorists" on its own shores. Offenders included drug dealers, pornographers, and especially abortionists—"the worst," according to Mother, "because they destroy innocents, and life, and populations." Worried that the terrorist attacks might provoke gen-

eral hatred of Muslims, Mother begged for tolerance, and she recalled the Islamic doctor who had operated on her back more than
fifty years earlier.

Even in deformity, Mother had lost none of her bite or appeal.

Sixty-five thousand pieces of mail came in reaction to the broadcast, most of them expressing concern about Mother's visage. At a
time when the cult of perfection dominated the airwaves, when
youth and beauty were television's most venerated values, here was
a striking countercultural statement: a disfigured old woman
shamelessly and without vanity proclaiming what she believed to
be the truth.

Stroke victims and the deformed, living in shadows of shame,
wrote to offer their thanks. Mother had given them permission to
come out of hiding and had inspired them to return to life. "One
woman said, 'I listen to you, Mother, I see all your programs, and I
love you, but now you're one of us,'" Angelica told me. "It took me a
while to kind of understand that. I hope I understand it."

By November, Mother Angelica was losing muscle tone in her
face. Despite the setback, she continued her television work. And
though no cross in her life had been "as good as this one," in her estimation, Mother could sense the finality of the time. One evening
in November, while waiting for her ride back to Hanceville in the
sloped network parking lot after the live show, she soberly observed
to Michael Warsaw, "In my life, there has always been a very definite beginning and a very definite end to everything God gave me to
do. I feel like I'm coming to the end of my time with the network."

On December 5, Mother recruited Father Mitch Pacwa, a Jesuit
Scripture scholar and an EWTN staple since 1984, to fill in as permanent guest host when she found it impossible to appear on the
live program. His superiors would later accept the arrangement,
though Mother showed no signs of slowing down that day.

In the morning, she recorded a *Catalogue* program, attended an afternoon VP meeting, shot a Christmas special, and then joined me
in the evening for her live program. In a rare quiet moment before
going to the studio, I posed a difficult question. Taking into consideration her steady withdrawal from EWTN, the current manage-

ment, and the precarious state of world affairs, I asked her what she believed would happen to the network. She took both my hands, stared hard with her red-rimmed right eye, and said, "Nothing lasts forever, sweetheart. You remember that. Nothing lasts forever. Ha-ha." By the end of 2001, Mother Angelica's detachment from EWTN was complete.

The following Tuesday, December 11, before her live show, she ate Chinese food in Birmingham with Sister Margaret Mary, Sister Michael, and their driver. While snapping open fortune cookies, it was decided they would stop by Books-A-Million on the way to the studio to collect a cookbook ordered by one of the nuns.

The driver ran in to retrieve the volume, but it could not be located. To find a suitable alternative, Sister Margaret Mary and the driver returned to the store, leaving Mother and Sister Michael in the car. Time passed. Angelica wondered what was taking so long and worried about missing her live show. Annoyed by the delay, she opened the car door and told Sister Michael, "Let's go in."

Inside the bookstore, Mother and Michael split up to search for Sister Margaret Mary. The one-eyed abbess spotted her stray daughter on the far side of the store and moved in her direction. Unaware of the raised platform blocking her path, she took a headlong plunge, her face slamming to the ground, her left arm cracking above the elbow.

At the hospital, an X-ray confirmed that Mother had broken her arm, but her blood was so thin due to the Coumadin that surgery had to be delayed. To thicken her blood for the surgery, Angelica was injected with frozen plasma on December 12th. All went well until she reached the holding area outside the operating room. Suddenly Angelica began to shudder, "her face like a basketball, her lips purple." The violent reaction mystified the doctors, who scrambled to stabilize the abbess.

Later, while brushing her teeth in Mother's hospital suite, Sister Margaret Mary found a deflated plasma bag marked "O-positive" on the counter next to the sink. Mother's blood type was O-negative! The panicked nun alerted Angelica's physicians. To this day, Margaret Mary believes the accidental transfusion of two units of

O-positive blood could have killed Mother, and had certainly contributed to her perilous condition. Dr. Patton said in an interview that the frozen plasma may have been a factor, but the cause of Angelica's trauma was "never totally clear."

A pin and two screws were used to set Mother's fractured arm on December 14. Two days after the surgery, Dr. Richard May vividly remembered entering the ICU during rounds to check on Mother Angelica. The abbess was lying in bed, grimacing, her right eye tightly shut while Sisters Margaret Mary and Michael hovered nearby.

"Dr. May, you have to help her," Margaret Mary pleaded. "She says the devil is after her and he is showing her the tormented souls in hell. She doesn't want to be left there."

Lacking a prescription for such a malady, the doctor offered comforting words "in Presbyterian fashion" at the bedside, then returned to writing his orders. Dr. May later said, "There was an oppressive feeling in the room." Glancing back at Angelica, he saw she was still "tight-eyed and battling." Having heard something of the Catholic devotion to Saint Michael the Archangel as a means of warding off evil, the doctor offered a silent "mental prayer," something he had never done before for a patient. "Lord, if the devil is really after this woman, I can't help her. You'd better send Michael now," he prayed. Telling no one of his petition to God, he resumed his paperwork.

Minutes later, Angelica brightened. "Everything's okay now," she said.

"What's wrong?" Margaret Mary asked nervously.

"Everything's fine now. Michael's here."

"Sister Michael?"

"Oh no. Michael the Archangel's here." Angelica turned over and went to sleep.

"I was pale, but there was a palpable difference in that room," Dr. May recalled, his eyes pink with moisture. "Something happened."

Whatever it was, and whatever she saw, would remain Mother's secret. She would only tell the nuns, afterward, "We must suffer . . . to keep souls from going to hell. People don't understand what it means to go to hell."

A battered Mother Angelica returned home in a wheelchair, wearing a blue arm cast and a patch to conceal her gaping right eye. For all her miseries, she was looking forward to Christmas: her favorite day of the year. Over breakfast on December 20, two days after her return home, she gave the nuns some "points to ponder" in anticipation of Jesus' birthday. Seated behind a solitary table at the front of the refectory, under the carved high wood ceiling, she told them, "This Christmas we will have a lot of surprises." Mother then shared a prayer she had been offering to God: "Lord, here I am— not very bright—a wreck. Take what I have and make it beautiful for God." She hoped they would make the prayer their own. "Get ready for anything He gives," she instructed.

The Christmas Surprise

ON THE MORNING of Christmas Eve, Mother's body again submitted to the will of her Eucharistic Lord. Sitting in the chapel before Him, she collapsed in her wheelchair. Finding her unresponsive and immobile, the sisters shifted into a familiar emergency mode, scrambling for oxygen, orange juice, and Sister Margaret Mary.

When she arrived at Cullman Regional Medical Center, Mother was unable to communicate. The paralysis on the right side of her body indicated a "brain event" to Dr. Hoover. A CAT scan confirmed his diagnosis. The left side of Mother's seventy-eight-year-old brain had been traumatized by a lethal stroke accompanied by a cerebral hemorrhage. "After I saw that, I really felt like she would probably die from the bleed," Hoover said.

Mother's only chance of survival, the doctor reckoned, was to undergo immediate brain surgery. But based on the CAT scan and Mother Angelica's age, no hospital would accept her. Then Dr. J. Finley McRae, a neurosurgeon at St. Vincent's Hospital in Birmingham who had appeared on one of Mother's early live programs, agreed to operate—assuming she survived the hour-long drive. The nuns crawled into an ambulance with their foundress and sped to Birmingham, some fearing it would be their last trip together.

Already catatonic, Mother faced another challenge in the ambulance. She began aspirating the orange juice the sisters had given her that morning to equalize what they assumed was imbalanced blood sugar. Emergency personnel labored to keep Mother alive. Sister Margaret Mary was in the front of the ambulance at the time. She recalled: "The man working on Mother looked through the peephole and said, 'Did anybody tell you how serious this is? She's vomiting everything up and sucking it back in.' The acid should have destroyed her lungs."

Mother Angelica reached St. Vincent's sometime after two o'clock. Dr. David Patton, standing at the entryway, instantly assessed her condition. "It was bleak," he said later. "Statistically, I knew the odds were grim. I knew truly it would be in God's hands."

Even the surgeon remained skeptical about the chances of success. "It was a risky situation in the face of the blood thinner and her age," Dr. McRae recalled. "We had to give her a reversal so the blood would clot, and with the multiple medical problems, there was a 50 percent chance that she would survive. It had to be done at that time or not at all. She could not have survived with that pressure on the brain."

In the OR, the surgeon immobilized Mother's head, made a crescentlike incision from her forehead to her left ear, and then chiseled several openings in her skull with a bone saw. Using forceps and suction, McRae extracted the clot, permitting blood to circulate freely through the left hemisphere of her brain. But the hemorrhage had already done serious damage: The part of the brain responsible for speech and comprehension had been deprived of oxygen.

In the days immediately following the surgery, Mother's elegant hands, snaked with raised veins, were her only recognizable features. The swelling consumed her physical characteristics. Aside from her hands, she could have been anybody. Red and bloated, her engorged head covered by a surgical cap, Mother rested fitfully in the ICU. Lying there, she could have passed for her spiritual mother, Rhoda Wise, in one of those yellowed photographs—enduring Christ's passion on Fridays in Canton.

She occasionally grunted and grimaced, her gray eyes blankly roving across the ceiling, her legs pitching indiscriminately. The doctors wrote off the movements to involuntary reflexes; they were certain she would be paralyzed, if she survived at all.

Joining the procession of sisters, brothers, and old friends passing through the room, I was told to say my good-byes. On December 29, a nurse in the hall told me Mother would "be a vegetable at best," and might "not last the week." That nurse didn't know Mother Angelica or her legions of spiritual children.

On the EWTN Web site, hundreds of thousands promised to offer Masses and prayers for her recuperation. The nuns prayed for the complete healing of their leader. Outfitted with a relic of Blessed Francis Xavier Seelos of New Orleans and the crucifix that had once belonged to Rhoda Wise, Angelica made a remarkable recovery.

By the end of 2001, a week after the surgery, Mother could move both legs. The paralysis that had held her mouth and left eye captive since September had vanished. Her comprehension also seemed to be returning.

When Bishop David Foley crept into the ICU for a visit on December 29, alarms squealed and twittered on the monitoring equipment. Mother's vitals went haywire as her blood pressure went through the roof. In this raucous response to the visitor, the nuns saw hope. Mother's memory was functioning and the predicted vegetative state had not materialized. Undeterred by the reception, the bishop later returned to pray with Mother and spoke fondly of her to the sisters. In the January 4 edition of the diocesan newspaper, he wrote, "Mother Angelica has been a star for our time leading us to Bethlehem to see wondrous things and to discover again in our lives Jesus Christ the Son of God. The Epiphany goes on. And may Mother continue to be the star for all of us."

Asked by a nun on January 7 if she had offered herself as a victim soul, to suffer for the good of others, Mother puckered her lips. "No," she said clearly, rolling her eyes.

Informed on January 25 that she could return home, Mother Angelica eagerly swung her legs to the side of the hospital bed and began to move her right arm, which everyone had assumed would be paralyzed. Later that day, the abbess reentered the monastery. To an a cappella rendition of "Adoremus in Aeternum" the nuns processed with their Mother to the chapel, where the Christ Child had come for her.

Lying on a stretcher that day, mutedly singing along beneath the monstrance holding her Spouse, Mother Angelica returned to her first vow—her first calling. After so many divided years, she would again be a fully cloistered nun, accessible to God alone.

The Lonely Place

THE COFFEE-TABLE BOOK *Come and See,* which illustrates the art and architecture of the Shrine of the Most Blessed Sacrament, opens with a quote from the Gospel of Mark. "You must come away to some lonely place and rest awhile," it says. For Mother Angelica, that line could have been the advertisement for her new life.

Prayer and the sacraments occupied Mother's days in the cloister. She made an earnest effort to participate in community activities, even music practice, from which she had exempted herself in days gone by. The monastic routine was broken only for half-hour sessions with speech, occupational, and physical therapists. The results were striking. By February, Mother Angelica could read aloud and stroll the length of the monastery with only the aid of a walker.

"I can't think of anyone who recovered like Mother Angelica," Dr. Patton said, shaking his head. "To me, the functionality is incredulous and incredible."

Though the improvement was astounding, Mother craved independence beyond her capabilities. To the abbess's great annoyance a team of sisters, terrified she might fall, shadowed her as she traversed the hallways. One day, to evade her cautious attendants, she ducked into Sister Mary Catherine's office, slamming the door behind her. "I want to get rid of those creeping characters," she said, wagging a finger at the door.

The therapists fared no better. During one therapy session, Mother was told to lie down in bed and then demonstrate her technique of rising. "That's not necessary," the old nun snapped. "I've already done that today." By March she reduced her physical therapist's hours and cut the speech coach loose altogether, citing frustration with the sessions.

Her inability to perform certain tasks and her medications brought tears and depression. Visits to the bathroom, bathing, and just getting about were no longer solitary activities. For an independent woman like Angelica, the adjustment was difficult, but she slowly surrendered to the situation, offering no resistance.

"Mother is such a woman of the present moment, she was very abandoned—she wasn't trying to push us away like some would," Sister Margaret Mary, Mother's prime caregiver, said. "I never felt that she was struggling with us, never."

Throughout 2002 and 2003 Mother Angelica experienced seizures of varying intensity. Though not lethal, the frightening episodes sapped her energy and confined her to bed for long stretches.

"This has been hellish for her," Sister Mary Agnes confided. "It's so hard to watch her suffer, and when she wants to say something and can't get it out, it's agonizing."

Save for rapid-fire quips, Angelica experienced communication problems following the stroke. One evening at supper the nuns were fussing over her meal, shuffling a series of rare to well-done steaks before the abbess. Observing the pageant of plates, she did a take to the room and in exasperation announced, "Why don't we go out for dinner?" But more thoughtful expressions eluded her.

Meetings in the parlor, where she had once dominated the conversation, became bittersweet exercises for the abbess.

"She used to do all the talking. Now I have to do all the talking," Father Joseph Wolfe said.

Using facial expressions, Mother could react to a visitor's chatter, but the verbal art—her great gift—had fled. She would begin in fine form, snag on a word, stumble into painful silence, and finally frown at the ideas she could contemplate but not disclose. With an apologetic shrug, she waited for the other party to continue.

The loss of communication, of independence, Father Wolfe believed, transformed Angelica: "She is now like her old fun-loving self, like in the early days when I came. She seems very happy. That's how I remember her—no one was intimidated by her presence."

The stroke and recovery hewed Mother Angelica into a different woman. The fighting spirit, once so evident in her personality, dissolved into a serene acceptance. The tough, indignant, at times wrathful edge that had thrilled her followers and frightened her enemies was no more. A sweet, almost childlike radiance now shone from the abbess.

At the first opportunity, I sought Mother Angelica's assessment of her latest trial. On February 13, 2002, I found her in the monastery infirmary, planted in a recliner. She wore a thin pastel robe, her shorn head covered by a handkerchief. The brown scar of the brain surgery was still faintly visible.

"Is there a reason for the stroke, a reason for your limited speech?" I asked her.

"Purification. My purification," she answered without hesitating.

It reminded me of something she had written in the 1970s: "[God] has a definite plan in mind, a purification in view—one that is necessary if we are to live with Him in the Kingdom."

I moved on to another question. While the stroke was happening, before she lapsed into unconsciousness, was she aware of anything? I asked. She drew a breath, released it past her lips, and then answered: "Yes, I was aware, aware—Jesus came and testified to me—testified—for testimony that I would suffer much and suffer plenty, plenty, plenty." She hummed, searching for the next word. "Suffer anguish for Jesus' sake . . ." Her thought trailed off into a tangle of words she could not unravel.

Before I left that day, Sister Margaret Mary asked Mother if she foresaw a return to television. Without missing a beat, she responded, "I doubt it."

But by October 2002, Mother was again before the cameras. On a solitary morning, EWTN recorded Angelica leading the rosary in the monastery chapel. Though the final result is seamless, Mother had a hard time getting through the mysteries: dropping words, repeating others, and at times going silent. Heavy editing and a loop of Mother's best takes salvaged the shoot, creating a devotional experience her family could savor again and again. They've been praying the new rosary with her nightly since March 2003.

Angelica's next attempt at TV revealed her waning powers of communication. In December 2002 she appeared in a pretaped segment on a live program. "Merry Christmas and Happy New Year," she pronounced with the old aplomb. But when her producer, Chris Harrington, suggested adding the tag line "Keep us between your gas and electric bill," Mother faltered. Eager to please, she excitedly took a stab at the line: "Merry Christmas, and remember—" The tag line never came, only copious tears. Drenched in sorrow, she stared into the camera and haltingly sobbed "Happy New Year" in a manner far from happy. To acquaint the audience with her condition, EWTN aired the botched attempt at holiday cheer in its entirety.

Of all the afflictions suffered in her eighty years of life, the loss of speech may have been the heaviest cross for Angelica and her community. The deprivation of language, the inability to release the thoughts racing through her still-active mind, became a supreme purgatory. So when Christina Akl, a Swissair employee and a member of EWTN's board of governors, expressed her dream to take Mother to Lourdes—one of the few pilgrimage sites the nun had not visited—she was more than receptive. As the manager of VIP services at Swissair, Akl promised to arrange the trip at the appropriate time. In August 2003, Akl imagined that the time would come much later, once Angelica had regained more of her strength.

"When do we go?" Mother challenged, accepting the invitation on the spot.

Given the abbess's enthusiasm, plans were immediately made to travel to Lourdes, France, before the year was out.

Healing at Lourdes

MOTHER WAS RESTLESS for one more miracle.

On the eve of the greatest crisis in the history of the Catholic Church in America, she had been stifled—struck dumb just when the faithful needed her most. Near the end of 2001, she had told me, "I believe next year will be one of our worst. The devil wants his own people."

The clerical sex-abuse scandal broke like a dam in early 2002, sinking negligent bishops, errant clergy, and the faith of many in the U.S. Church. In the aftermath, the credibility of Catholic clerics, particularly bishops, was at an all-time low. The people hungered for spiritual leadership.

By 2003, Angelica probably felt the old evangelistic tug. If she could recapture her voice, she could call the faithful back, acknowledge their pain, and lead them to the suffering Christ, whom she knew better than most.

Perhaps Lourdes could resurrect her mission. Perhaps one final healing awaited Rita Rizzo in the miraculous spring promised to the peasant girl Bernadette Soubirous in 1858.

On October 12, 2003, Mother Angelica, four sisters, Lisa Gould (an EWTN vice president), the Akls, a doctor, and the author boarded a G-5 jet to Lourdes for a secret six-day pilgrimage.

The secret lasted until we reached the hotel. A busload of American tourists spotted Mother in the lobby and, like a flame moving from candle to candle in the square outside the basilica in Lourdes, word of Angelica's presence soon spread all over town.

On the afternoon of October 14, protected by security, Mother was wheeled to the renowned baths of Lourdes. Millions of ill and suffering had gone before her, heeding the Virgin Mary's call to Bernadette: "Go drink of the water and wash yourself there." Angelica would do likewise, joining the people of last resort, pleading the Virgin's intercession for a miracle.

They ushered Mother into bath number nine. As a concession to her handicaps, the attendant said it was not necessary to submerge in the tub, that a washing of the face would suffice. "I wish to walk in the water," Mother said, rising from her wheelchair.

Coming up from the marbled bath's icy pool after repeating the prescribed prayers, she bubbled with joy. Maybe it was that glow, or perhaps the habit, that drew the attention of the crowds as she left. African priests choked by bright yellow scarves, mezzo-sopranos from the Philippines, gnarled Italian women clutching their rosaries, a bearded Spaniard with a creased picture of his dead son, and a tour group from Chicago pressed in to touch their Mother. Coming in on all sides, they slowed the progress of the wheelchair to a standstill, throwing themselves on the concrete at her feet. They yanked at her frail arms, sang religious songs in her honor, kissed the brown habit, and wept uncontrollably. After being away from them for almost two years, Mother relished every moment.

Forsaking the advice of the sisters, she reached out to the multitude, obliging their prayer requests and touching each bead and prayer card as the rest of us locked arms to try to keep the throng from crushing her. But Mother was unconcerned. She was again among her people.

Moving through the frenzied adulation, Mother Angelica seemed to be taking her victory lap. Viewers from Britain, France, Spain, the United States, Africa, Asia, and elsewhere pressed forward to thank her for the spiritual encouragement, the guidance, the wounded love, and the hope she had given them for years. Without counting the cost, the unwanted girl from Canton had touched many lives and accomplished much.

FOR THE CHURCH, she had established a thriving community of Poor Clare Nuns of Perpetual Adoration and given birth to two religious orders: the Franciscan Friars of the Eternal Word and the Sister Servants of the Eternal Word. And though her Sister Servants had gone their own way, operating an independent retreat center in Birmingham, the ghost of their absent Mother has never been far off. It is her network that attracts most of the retreat masters and clients that keep them in business. The Sister Servants' departure and their inability to fulfill their founding inspiration proved to be one of the great disappointments of Angelica's religious life.

Her friars, on the other hand, realized Mother's vision for them in time. After years of setbacks, the Franciscan Missionaries of the Eternal Word now attend to the spiritual needs of network visitors and are more actively involved in the work of EWTN than ever before. In addition to hearing confessions and celebrating the Mass, they host programs, shoot and edit video, produce, floor direct, and are today the presence among the lay staff that Mother long hoped they would be. A few of the eighteen friars have taken up residence on the grounds of Our Lady of the Angels Monastery in Hanceville, regularly providing the sacraments to their contemplative sisters and their Mother.

Secluded in the Alabama countryside, the forty-plus Poor Clare Nuns of Our Lady of the Angels Monastery live out their hidden existence in the spirit of their foundress. For all their amazing diversity, each of Angelica's daughters carries a piece of the abbess within them: her spunk, her joy, her infectious orthodoxy, and her unrestrained love of Christ in the Blessed Sacrament. A few of the community members recently relocated to Portsmouth, Ohio, to save a foundation that was experiencing difficulties attracting vocations. Mother Angelica's group has never had such troubles. The novice mistress says that on average they receive seven inquiries a week from young women considering the religious life. To accommodate their new members, a wing of bedrooms was recently added to the Hanceville monastery. As of this writing, the sisters plan to establish a new foundation in Phoenix, Arizona.

For the laity throughout the world, both Catholic and non-Catholic, Mother Angelica will be most remembered for the inspired things she built: the Shrine of the Most Blessed Sacrament and the broadcast empire now firmly established worldwide. In 2003, Mother was named a Cable TV Pioneer, and by any measure she was that. When cable was still in its infancy, she raised the world's first Catholic satellite network and kept it on the air for more than twenty years. At the same time she built the largest privately held shortwave network in the world, a satellite-delivered AM/FM service, and the premier Web site in Catholicism. Those in the Church marvel at her contributions.

"Her importance is like the founding of the parochial school system. She founded a Catholic network as a means of teaching," Bishop David Foley reflected. "Who founded the New Evangelization in the United States? Mother Angelica did."

Bishop Macram Gassis of Sudan agreed. "Her contribution to the Church internationally is incredible—I see her program in Germany! This network is vital because it is restoring the Church to its foundation, to its roots."

But EWTN and all its offspring were merely a means to an end for Angelica.

"What impresses me most about Mother is her love of souls," Sister Mary Catherine, her vicar, revealed. "She said that if that whole network, with all the money it cost—millions and millions—saved one soul, then it was worth it. Her main interest was to save souls, whether it was one soul or a million."

Sitting in her cushioned chair, running her hands over the Bible with the crocheted "Word of God" cover, Mother Angelica eventually reached millions of souls. Her everyman spirituality caught the attention of channel surfers and the hurting alike. While their mouths opened with laughter, she fed them digestible bits of Church doctrine to be consumed and lived. In the confusion of the post–Vatican II Church, Angelica's network became an immovable rock of assurance, anchored to the Pope in Rome.

Author and religious expert Father Richard John Neuhaus said, "The greatest thing John Paul II did was constructing and putting in place the authoritative interpretation of Vatican II. And though we are still in a state of confusion and enormous damage, I think one can say the tide has turned, and Mother Angelica played a significant part in that."

"Mother Angelica represented the plain Catholic, who is 90 percent of the Church," Cardinal J. Francis Stafford, the Major Penitentiary of the Apostolic Penitentiary in Rome, observed. "Without her, the plain Catholic would have been further confused, but with her they had a clear vision of the beauty, glory, and truth of the Church."

More than preaching at them, Mother gave her flock things to do. She used television to teach and popularize pious devotions thought lost to modernity. It can be safely said that no one in America, and perhaps in the world, did more than Mother Angelica to perpetuate and stoke interest in the rosary, eucharistic adoration, Latin in the liturgy, the Divine Mercy Chaplet, litanies, and traditional prayers. She wove a thread of devotion into the hearts of the young that will not quickly loosen and dropped seeds that sprouted a generation that author Colleen Carroll has tagged "the New Faithful."

Among young Catholics in their twenties and thirties, Angelica's influence is profound. Generation X absorbed more television than any group before it. For the spiritual seekers of that generation, Mother offered an alternative to *Beverly Hills, 90210* and *Melrose Place:* the time-tested faith through her personal prism. Look at the new crop of seminarians, young priests, religious, and the families sitting in the pews wrestling with their young children. They are informed, gutsy, traditional in their practice, and, if pushed, can get in your face. Angelica's reflection is hard to miss.

"We wouldn't have this new generation of good and faithful Catholics if it wasn't for the Holy Spirit working through Mother Angelica," Beverly Sottile-Molana, a former diocesan official in Buffalo, New York, told me. "She saved our children and their hippie mothers."

Despite her absence from live television, Mother remains a vital and beloved figure for countless people.

Listen to the woman in a New Orleans coffee shop: "Since she's been off her show, I often ask myself, What would Mother say about this or that in the world?"

A Southern Baptist pastor, unaware that he has been watching reruns, sends an e-mail, thanking Mother for the powerful spiritual insight she gave him last Tuesday. A Methodist minister orders tapes of *Mother Angelica Live* for his congregation and writes that he never misses the program.

In Rome, a priest chases me down Borgo Pio, near the Vatican, booming, "I'm a son of Mother Angelica! She is the reason for my vocation, you know."

A middle-aged businessman, with stooped shoulders and wounded eyes, wanders up to me in a New York restaurant to reveal his encounter with Mother. "Something she said one night changed my life forever." He leans in, lowering his voice, "I haven't had a drink or touched a drug in eight years. She gave me back my family. Tell her I love her."

EVEN BY CANDLELIGHT, she drew their affection. As I pushed Mother into that train of placid misery known as the "Procession of the Sick" in Lourdes, they were all watching her. From the sidelines, people waved, but they dared not disturb the solemnity of the occasion by crying out. Like all the others, she held aloft a glowing candle topped by a paper shade.

Standing in front of us on the steps of the basilica, priests and bishops took turns at the microphone, reciting the rosary in foreign tongues. As the procession terminated, we moved to the front area reserved for the wheelchair-bound. There was something sad about seeing Mother in the ranks of these terribly sick people. In front of us, a woman with matted hair spasmodically trembled, her arms contorted like the broken wings of a sparrow. A few rows up, lifeless babies lay on stretchers attached to machines while their parents purposefully mouthed prayers. Five wheelchairs down from us, a boy of eight or nine frantically brushed the nappy hair of a plastic doll, his tongue jutting in and out as he repeated a comfort ritual he had obviously performed thousands of times before. And in between each Hail Mary, during the transitional silences, guttural moans and uncontrolled bleats rose up from the afflicted crowd.

Mother took them in, looking at each soul around her. She hung her head and prayed, holding the candle high. She didn't pray for herself. It was for them. She had fully entered into their suffering without the consolation of miracles. She was truly one of them now.

Ten years earlier, Mother Angelica had commented to a caller on her live show, "I'm glad you're going to Lourdes. You'll get something in Lourdes. Whether it's physical healing I don't know—but you'll get something very spiritual in Lourdes and you'll understand what you don't understand now."

Waking from a nap in the early evening of October 17, her last day in Lourdes, Mother had a flat black look in her eyes. "I'm disappointed," she told Sisters Catherine and Gabriel. "I wanted a miracle. I have lost hope." Her old eyes clenched with emotion. The nuns tried to cheer her, but after so long a journey, and a lifetime of supernatural interventions, maybe she had come to expect miracles. Then she got one.

In the elevator on our way to supper, the shrill yell of a baby from downstairs faintly filled the car. When the metal doors slid open, we saw the source of the clamor: a small Italian child, maybe a year old, with puffy yellowed eyes, wriggling in her father's arms. The parents from Naples looked much older than they were. They approached Mother's wheelchair, explaining their plight in Italian, worry lines and smudges of gray circling their eyes. The baby, they said, cried incessantly; and as if the challenge of Down's syndrome were not enough, the child refused to sleep or go to anyone else. A loud shriek, like a commentary, flew from the toddler. Lourdes was their last hope. They begged Mother for her prayers.

The crossed eyes of the retarded child flickered with fear as she was lowered to the dejected abbess. Mother Angelica lightly trailed her fingers over the lopsided forehead, and the child quieted. "Blessing, blessing," Mother whispered like a prayer. With her eyes shut, she prayed over the girl, then opened her arms, inviting the baby into her lap.

The child uttered no peep. Lying peacefully, she reached for the fleshy face cinched by the wimple. As if made of whipped cream, Angelica's cheek submitted to the pressure of the tiny hand. Mother chuckled at the touch and light returned to her eyes. "Awww," she said, petting the child.

For several minutes, they continued like that, the two of them exchanging blessings, sharing a type of healing between them. In that moment, Mother Angelica recovered her mission and gained a tiny miracle in return.

Lourdes had distilled the essence of Mother's mission: to bring hope to the forgotten through personal suffering. She discovered she was still needed, still wanted, and could do much good, even in silence. She understood what she hadn't understood before.

At this writing, Mother Angelica continues her work: embracing the present moment, interceding for others, and listening for her Lord in a grand silence.

TO DELAY taking her nap on February 2, 2004, Mother Angelica finds refuge in her monastery office. She sits at the huge, bare, cherry desk and stares longingly out the window toward some distant vista. She is pensive, far away. "What are you looking at, Mother?" one of her nuns asks, trying to break the spell.

The abbess, gazing out the window, wets her flaccid lips. "Heaven," she says almost to herself. Pointing into the luminous whitewash of light in the cloister yard, she repeats, "Heaven. Heaven. Heaven."

Later, in her cell, surrounded by armies of baby Jesus statues and images of the Savior, she is again transfixed by the heaven outside her window. The nuns encourage her to rest. Totally absorbed by the vision, she refuses. The sisters noiselessly stand aside, hoping she'll reconsider. An expectant hush hangs in the air. Suddenly startled, Mother tilts her face upward. Her glance travels above the bed to a painting that once hung in Rhoda Wise's house: a crude mustard-colored portrait of the wounded Christ. Angelica's eyes widen.

She whispers, "Listen!"

NOTES

For the sake of brevity, author interview citations have been largely omitted from the notes that follow; particularly those relating to Mother Angelica. If a quote is not listed below, assume it came from an author interview with the respective party conducted between 1999 and 2004. Similarly, EWTN's *Mother Angelica Live* program is noted only in those instances where the broadcast date is absent from the text. Unabridged notes can be found at raymondarroyo.com.

PROLOGUE

1   *"Jesus is coming today"*: Author interview (hereafter A.I.) with Sister Mary Antoinette, 2003.

2   *Description of Mother Angelica in chapel and subsequent hospital treatment*: A.I. with Sister Margaret Mary, Sister Mary Agnes, Sister Mary Catherine, Sister Mary Faustina, 2003.

3   *"There is nothing we can"*: A.I. with Sister Margaret Mary and Dr. L. James Hoover, 2004.

CHAPTER 1: ONE MISERABLE LIFE

5   *Birth date*: Canton public records, Canton, Ohio.

5   *Aside from being the birthplace*: Stark County Bicentennial Story Committee, *The Stark County Bicentennial Story* (Stark County, Ohio: privately published, 1979), pp. 166–243.

5   *"the slums"*: A.I. with Dr. Norma Marcere, 2001.

6   *Black Hand and details of life in southeast Canton*: A.I. with Sabatino Pentello, Steven Zaleski, and others, 2003.

7   *"flew into a rage"*: Sister Mary Raphael, "Mother Angelica and Her Mother" (unpublished ms.), p. 14. Our Lady of the Angels Monastery Archives, Hanceville, Ala. (hereafter referred to as OLAMA).

7   *Oversized hats, billowing dresses:* A.I. with Margaret Santilli, 2003.

7   *during a fire drill:* A.I. with Mother Angelica, 2000.

8   *"never liked him":* ibid.

8   *"Why didn't you wait":* ibid.

8   *"She didn't have enough foresight":* Sister Mary Raphael, "Mother Angelica and Her Mother," p. 14.

9   *"If my father's mother":* ibid., 15.

10 *Prohibition, which hit Canton:* Edward T. Heald, *The Suburban Era in Stark County, Ohio, 1917–1958* (Canton: Stark County Historical Society, 1958).

11 *"I couldn't have been more than":* A.I. with Mother Angelica, 2000.

12 *"The stage looked gigantic":* ibid.

12 *Background on Don Mellett's slaying:* "$11,000 Offered for the Slayers of Don R. Mellett," *Canton Daily News,* July 16, 1926.

13 *St. Anthony's would be relocated:* "Woman Slayer Held Without Bail," *Evening Repository* (Canton, Ohio), March 11, 1929.

13 *"Father Riccardi was fighting for":* ibid.

13 *Father Riccardi's slaying:* ibid.

13 *"not guilty of murder":* Ohio v. Maime Guerrieri, Case # 9020, Stark County Clerk of Courts Archives (May 30, 1929).

14 *"extreme cruelty": Mayme Gianfrancesco Rizzo v. John Rizzo,* divorce petition, Stark County Clerk of Courts Archives (September 24, 1930).

15 *"I asked him for alimony":* A.I. with Mother Angelica, 2000.

15 *When Rita and her mother:* A.I. with Lisa Hayes, Victoria Addams's great-niece, 2002.

16 *"Oh, you just take one":* Sister Mary Raphael, "Mother Angelica and Her Mother," p. 18.

17 *"She was always threatening suicide":* A.I. with Mother Angelica, 2000; see also Sister Mary Raphael, "Mother Angelica and Her Mother, p. 17.

18 *"All of a sudden, it felt":* A.I. with Mother Angelica, 2000.

18 *"a miracle . . . somebody jump":* Sister Mary Raphael, "Mother Angelica and Her Mother," p. 17.

19 *"You know I was talking about you":* A.I. with Mother Angelica, 2000.

20 *Rita's condition:* testimony of Rita Francis (Rizzo), undated (probably from 1943), OLAMA.

20 *"not herself . . . total fatigue":* A.I. with Mother Angelica, 2000.

CHAPTER 2: THE GIFT OF PAIN

22 *Details of Gianfrancesco home and occupants*: A.I. with Joanne Simia, 2001; A.I. with June Peterson Francis, 2003.

23 *"When's your mother coming home?" and knife-throwing incident*: A.I. with Mother Angelica, 2001.

23 *whose tears Rita dreaded*: ibid.

24 *"My mother has worked in the precincts"*: ibid.; see also Sister Mary Raphael, "Mother Angelica and Her Mother" (unpublished ms.), OLAMA, p. 22.

25 *Description of Rita's stomach troubles*: testimony of Rita Francis (Rizzo), undated (probably from 1943), OLAMA.

25 *Mae Rizzo's second nervous breakdown*: Sister Mary Raphael, "Mother Angelica and Her Mother," p. 22.

25 *petitioned the Stark County Court*: Mayme Gianfrancesco Rizzo v. John Rizzo, D.R. 1385, Stark County Clerk of Courts Archives (May 22, 1941).

26 *Rita's stomach condition and treatment*: testimony of Rita Francis (Rizzo), undated (probably from 1943), OLAMA.

26 *fifteen thousand Canton women*: Stark County Bicentennial Committee, *The Stark County Bicentennial Story* (Stark County, Ohio: privately published, 1979), p. 274.

26 *Timken was a powerhouse*: ibid., p. 223.

26 *Rita's duties at Timken*: A.I. with Mother Angelica, 2000; A.I. with Joanne Simia, 2001; A.I. with Mary Murphy, 2003.

26 *"Mr. Poss thought" and memory of ladies' lounge*: A.I. with Elsie Machuga Johnston, 2003.

27 *Diagnosis of Dr. Wiley Scott*: testimony of Rita Francis (Rizzo), undated (probably from 1943), OLAMA; see also letter from Dr. Wiley Scott to Msgr. George Habig, March 19, 1943, OLAMA.

27 *"nerves were worse than ever" and "I couldn't sleep"*: testimony of Rita Francis (Rizzo), undated (probably from 1943), OLAMA; A.I. with Mother Angelica, 2000.

CHAPTER 3: THE HEALING AND THE CALL

28 *Events of January 8, 1943*: A.I. with Mother Angelica, 2000.

28 *"Why don't you take Rita to Mrs. Wise?"*: ibid.

28 *Background on Rhoda Wise*: Karen Sigler, *Her Name Means Rose* (Birmingham, Ala.: EWTN Catholic Publisher, 2000).

30 *"You doubted me before" and "was astonished to find"*: ibid., p. 58.

30 *instrument of countless miracles*: "Stigmatic Baffling Medical Science," *Columbus Star*, October 6, 1945.

31 *"prayers to the Little Flower and told"*: ibid.

31 *"the sharpest pains"*: Sister Mary Raphael, "Mother Angelica and Her Mother" (unpublished ms.), OLAMA, p. 28.

32 *"It was like a rock, completely healed"*: A.I. with Joanne Simia, 2001.

32 *"neurotic female"*: letter from Dr. Wiley Scott to Msgr. George Habig, March 19, 1943, OLAMA.

33 *"little stool"*: A.I. with Mother Angelica, 2000.

33 *"before I was cured"*: letter from Rita Rizzo to Fr. F. C. Soisson, September 18, 1943, OLAMA.

33 *Rita's devotional practices*: A.I. with Mother Angelica, 2000.

34 *"If you have a picture of a movie star"*: A.I. with Steven Zaleski, 2003.

34 *"going together" and "She was attractive"*: A.I. with "Adolph" Gordon Schulte, 2003.

35 *"overly pious"*: A.I. with Mother Angelica, 2001.

35 *"She doesn't belong to us anymore"*: Sister Mary Raphael, "Mother Angelica and Her Mother," p. 28.

35 *John Rizzo married a second time*: John M. Rizzo and Winsome M. Girt, application for marriage license, #63436, Stark County Clerk of Courts Archives (July 22, 1943).

35 *"deep awareness" and subsequent text*: A.I. with Mother Angelica, 2000.

35 *Rita's calling*: It would seem from the evidence and the testimony of Mother Angelica and Elsie Machuga that Rita's call to religious life occurred in 1943, not the summer of 1944, as advanced in another biography: Dan O'Neill, *Mother Angelica: Her Life Story* (New York: Crossroad Publishing, 1986). There would not have been enough time to test the call, investigate religious orders, and decide on a course of action had the vocational call occurred in 1944. Rita would flee to the convent in August 1944.

36 *Description of occurrences in the Wise home*: A.I. with Mother Angelica, 2000; A.I. with Steven Zaleski, "Adolph" Gordon Schulte, and Elsie Machuga Johnston, 2003.

37 *"Where is Rita?" and extended conversation*: A.I. with Elsie Machuga Johnston, 2001, 2003.

37 *"Someday I'll build a castle"*: A.I. with Steven Zaleski, 2003.

38 *"No, you can't go there" and description of visit with Msgr. Habig*: A.I. with Mother Angelica, 2000.

38 *Rita's first visit to St. Paul's Shrine*: A.I. with Mother Angelica, 2000.

39 *"Rita? My Rita?"*: Karen Sigler interview with Catherine Barthel (undated), Rhoda Wise House Archives; see also Sigler, *Her Name Means Rose*, p. 136.

40 *"would do great things for the Church"*: Sophia David testimony, Rhoda Wise House Archives (September 28, 1997); also A.I. with Mother Angelica, 2000.

CHAPTER 4: BRIDE OF CHRIST

41 *"My own dearest Mother"*: letter from Rita Rizzo to Mae Francis, August 14, 1944, OLAMA.

42 *"My only child is gone"*: A.I. with Joanne Simia, 2001.

42 *"It was like I died"*: Sister Mary Raphael, "Mother Angelica and Her Mother" (unpublished ms.), OLAMA, p. 30.

43 *Rita was "ungrateful"*: A.I. with Dr. Norma Marcere, 2003.

44 *History of Franciscan Nuns of the Most Blessed Sacrament*: Father Constant of Craon, O.F.M. Cap., *Perpetual and Reparative Thanksgiving* (Troyes, France: privately published, 1946).

46 *"permission to go to the hospital"*: A.I. with Mother James, the abbess of St. Paul Shrine, who consulted the monastery records, 2003.

46 *"a big fuss over her"*: Sister Mary Raphael, "Mother Angelica and Her Mother," p. 30.

47 *"a very regimented kind of life"*: A.I. with Mother Angelica, 2000.

47 *"My, you're quiet"; "two puffy water-filled grapefruit"; and "In those days"*: ibid., 2001.

48 *Conversation with Mother Agnes about Rhoda Wise*: ibid., 2000; A.I. with Karen Sigler, 2003.

48 *"To the King of Kings"*: diary of Mae Rizzo, April 20, 1945, OLAMA.

50 *Chapter vote for Rita to enter novitiate*: A.I. with Mother James, the abbess of St. Paul Shrine, who verified the vote in monastery records, 2003.

51 *"To the mother in law of Jesus"*: letter from Sister Angelica to Mae Francis, November 8, 1945, OLAMA.

52 *"One time I said to the Lord"*: *Mother Angelica Live*, EWTN, June 9, 1992.

52 *Call from Bishop McFadden*: *25 Years Living in Light* (Canton: Poor Clares of Perpetual Adoration, 1971); see also *The Voice of Sancta Clara* (Canton: Poor Clares of Perpetual Adoration, Summer 1954), p. 9.

52 *"Mother Clare and I have made a decision"*: A.I. with Mother Angelica, 2000.

CHAPTER 5: SANCTA CLARA

54 *Departure and first day at O'Dea house*: *25 Years Living in Light* (Canton: Poor Clares of Perpetual Adoration, 1971).

54 *Sisters sent to Canton*: Sancta Clara Protocol, October 1, 1946, Sancta Clara Archives (hereafter referred to as SCA).

54 *Background on O'Dea house*: Charita M. Goshay, "Gift of Faith: Diocese Marks 50 Years, Recalls Late Industrial's Generosity," *Repository*, May 13, 1993.

56 *Broken faucet handle and culpas*: A.I. with Mother Angelica, 2000.

56 *Description of Sister Mary of the Cross*: A.I. with Joan Frank, 2003.

57 *"A lot of times I was on edge"*: Dan O'Neill, *Mother Angelica: Her Life Story* (New York: Crossroad Publishing, 1986), p. 51.

58 *Interaction between organist and Sister Mary of the Cross*: A.I. with Mother Angelica, 2001.

59 *"the espoused" and subsequent quotes*: letter from Sister Angelica to Mae Francis, 1947, OLAMA.

59 *"Don't be lonesome sweet heart"*: letter from Sister Angelica to Mae Francis, undated, OLAMA.

59 *"Dearest Mother"*: letter from Sister Angelica to Mae Francis, undated, OLAMA.

60 *Number of sisters at Sancta Clara: 25 Years Living in Light.*

60 *Sewer-main break:* 1950 calendar, March 15, 1950, SCA.

60 *Interracial Day: 25 Years Living in Light;* see also 1950 calendar, August 20, 1950, SCA.

61 *Sister Mary Joseph:* A.I. with Sister Mary Joseph, 2001.

61 *Kathleen Myers:* Sister Mary Raphael, "Behind the Wall and Over the Hill" (unpublished ms.), OLAMA, p. 7. See also Sister Mary Raphael, *My Life with Mother Angelica* (Birmingham, Ala.: EWTN Catholic Publishers, 1982), p. 20.

61 *Sister Mary Michael:* A.I. with Sister Mary Michael, 2001.

62 *"Mother, we've got to fix this place up" and subsequent quotes*: A.I. with Mother Angelica, 2000.

62 *Angelica's "Tonys"*: A.I. with Joan Frank, 2002.

63 *Positions held by Sister Angelica:* A.I. with Mother Angelica, 2001; see also Sancta Clara Protocol, SCA.

63 *Appraisals of Mother Mary of the Cross:* A.I. with Joan Frank, 2002; A.I. with Sister Mary Michael, 2003; A.I. with Mother Angelica, 2000.

63 *"Received the worst public"*: Sister Mary of the Cross's entry in 1950 calendar, May 22, 1950, SCA.

63 *John Rizzo's visit to the monastery:* A.I. with Mother Angelica, 2000; see also Sister Mary Raphael, "Mother Angelica and Her Mother" (unpublished ms.), OLAMA, p. 33.

64 *John Rizzo's death: Canton Repository,* October 29, 1952.

65 *"those who are going to lead"*: A.I. with Joan Frank, 2003.

66 *Sister Angelica's solemn vows: Canton Repository,* January 1953.

67 *Mother Veronica's departure:* Sancta Clara Protocol, August 12, 1953, SCA.

67 *Descriptions of Mother Mary Immaculate:* A.I. with Sisters Mary Michael, Mary Joseph, and Mary Bernadette, 2003; A.I. with Joan Frank, 2003; and A.I. with Mother Angelica, 2000.

68   *Date of Mother Angelica's fall:* For the first time, we definitively know the date of this pivotal event in Mother Angelica's life. For years, the timing of the incident had been an open question; both in the order's history and in the extensive reportage of Mother Angelica. The only surviving medical records from the period track Sister Angelica's back and leg treatments from April 27, 1959, to May 7, 1959. As all her Mercy Hospital and orthopedic records have been destroyed, the Cleveland Clinic report of 1959 is the only source of a credible date. It establishes the year of the fall as 1953 and notes a back surgery that occurred three years later. A 1956 calendar I located at Sancta Clara notes that Angelica underwent surgery in the summer of that year—which would seem to confirm the accuracy of the Cleveland Clinic report.

68   *Mother Clare's heart attacks:* Sancta Clara Protocol, November–December 1953, SCA.

68   *Symptoms of novices:* A.I. with Joan Frank, Sisters Mary Michael and Mary Assumpta, 2003; and A.I. with Mother Angelica, 2001.

68   *"It was like a kind of bondage":* O'Neill, *Mother Angelica,* p. 59.

69   *Date of Sister Angelica's taking charge of the novices:* The date is hard to pin down. In an unpublished manuscript, Sister Mary Raphael gives the date as November 14, 1954, but in the community archive she mentions November 8, 1953, as the day. Judging from interviews and the dates of professions, the event most likely occurred in November 1953.

69   *"Leave me alone":* A.I. with Sister Regina, 2001.

69   *"complete abandonment to God":* Brother Lawrence of the Resurrection, *The Practice of the Presence of God* (New York: Doubleday, 1977).

69   *"didn't break the rules":* A.I. with Joan Frank, 2002.

70   *"a minor breakdown":* A.I. with Mother Angelica, 2000.

70   *"pitfalls that had trapped":* Sister Mary Raphael, "Behind the Wall and Over the Hill," p. 9.

70   *"chime in, saying,":* A.I. with Joan Frank, 2002.

71   *"had turned on her" and "for some reason God":* ibid.

CHAPTER 6: PROVIDENCE IN PAIN

72   *Mother Angelica's inspection of the paint job:* A.I. with Mother Angelica, 2001.

73   *Mother Veronica's return to Canton:* Sancta Clara Protocol, May 1955, SCA.

73   *"Dear Sr. M. Angelica returned home":* 1955 calendar, June 13, 1955, SCA.

73   *Medical techniques to aid spinal alignment:* Sister Mary Raphael, *My Life with Mother Angelica* (Birmingham, Ala.: EWTN Catholic Publishers, 1982), p. 8; A.I. with Mother Angelica, 2000.

74   *Background on Dr. Charles Houck:* obituary, *Canton Repository,* December 15, 1975.

75   *"Having worked with the Negros* [sic]": letter from Sister Angelica to Bishop Emmet Walsh, March 27, 1957, OLAMA.

76   *Discoveries during surgery:* Cleveland Clinic records of Sister Mary Angelica Francis, April 27, 1959.

76   *Jewish blood donors:* Sister Mary Raphael, *My Life with Mother Angelica,* p. 16.

76   *"I've never been the same since":* Mother Angelica Live, EWTN, June 23, 1998.

76   *Infirmary details:* A.I. with Joan Frank, 2003; A.I. with Sisters Mary Joseph, Mary Anthony, and Mary Bernadette, 2003.

77   *"No":* letter from Mother Veronica to Bishop Emmet Walsh, March 7, 1957, OLAMA.

77   *"a genius":* A.I. with Joan Frank, 2003.

77   *Florida bishop first approached about foundation:* A.I. with Sister Mary Joseph, 2003; A.I. with Mother Angelica, 2001.

78   *"Our great desire":* letter from Mother Veronica to Archbishop Thomas Toolen, January 8, 1957, OLAMA.

79   *On February 28, 1957:* letter from Bishop Emmet Walsh to Mother Veronica, February 28, 1957, Diocese of Youngstown.

79   *"To her it is a mission":* letter from Mother Veronica to Bishop Emmet Walsh, March 7, 1957, OLAMA.

80   *"Your Excellency":* letter from Sister Angelica to Bishop Emmet Walsh, March 25, 1957, OLAMA.

81   *"your soul is beautiful":* letter from Sister Angelica to Mae Francis (undated), OLAMA.

82   *"every good, pious Catholic" and conversation with Mother Veronica:* A.I. with Mother Angelica, 2000.

82   *Sixty-two workmen: The Voice of Sancta Clara,* Spring 1959, p. 5.

82   *a "contract job":* Santa Clara Protocol, March 14, 1958, SCA.

82   *"bizarre gait":* Cleveland Clinic records of Sister Mary Angelica Francis, April 27, 1959.

83   *Conversations with syndicate boss and Uncle Nick:* A.I. with Mother Angelica, 2000.

84   *Background on John XXIII:* Eric John, *The Popes: A Concise Biographical History* (New York: Hawthorn Books, 1964).

84   *Vision of architectural plans:* A.I. with Mother Angelica, 2000; see also model preserved at OLAMA.

85   *"About three years ago":* letter from Sister Angelica to Bishop Emmet Walsh, August 7, 1959, OLAMA.

86   *Bishop Walsh approved the general concept:* letter from Bishop Emmet Walsh to Mother Veronica, November 6, 1959, Diocese of Youngstown.

86   Popular Mechanics *as source of lure parts:* John Wright, "Franciscan Nuns to Build Birmingham Monastery by Selling Fishing Lures," *Catholic Week,* March 10, 1961.

87   *Sisters assembling lures for first time:* A.I. with Mother Angelica and Sister Mary Joseph, 2000.

87   *Repairman story:* Wright, "Franciscan Nuns"; also A.I. with Mother Angelica, 2000.

87   *"It seemed the only name":* Henry F. Unger, "Something Fishy in the Cloister," *Extension Magazine,* October 1960, p. 22.

88   *"The purpose of the course":* St. Peter's Fishing Lures mailer, OLAMA.

88   *"Mother Angelica and Jesus were not":* Dan O'Neill, *Mother Angelica: Her Life Story* (New York: Crossroad Publishing, 1986), p. 73.

88   *Media response to lures:* Dale Francis, "The Convent of Double Trouble," *Our Sunday Visitor,* April 10, 1960; see also Chuck Such, "Local Cloistered Nuns Making Fishing Lures," *Canton Repository,* April 10, 1960; and "Bait for St. Peter," *Sports Illustrated,* May 22, 1961.

89   *"special contribution to a sport":* "Artificial Bait Wins Plaque for Nuns in Canton," *Cleveland Plain Dealer,* June 22, 1961.

89   *"Dear Family":* St. Peter's Fishing Lures mailer, Christmas 1961, OLAMA.

90   *On October 29, 1960:* letter from Mother Veronica to Bishop Emmet Walsh, October 29, 1960, OLAMA.

90   *"Rome granted the Alabama Foundation":* Sancta Clara Protocol, February 19, 1961, SCA.

CHAPTER 7: THE FOUNDATION

91   *Uncle Nick and nuns departing Canton:* Our Lady of the Angels Monastery History, February 26, 1961 (located in OLAMA and hereafter referred to as OLAM History).

91   *Background on Birmingham:* Leah Rawls Atkins, *The Valley and Hills: An Illustrated History of Birmingham and Jefferson Counties* (Woodland Hills, Calif.: Windsor Publications, 1981); see also Kris Axtman, "In Birmingham a Chance for Justice Long Delayed," *Christian Science Monitor,* April 20, 2001; Leah Rawls Atkins, "Birmingham Magic City," www.archivists.org/so camericarchivists.

92   *Statistics on order's foundations:* John Wright, Jr., "Nuns Will Not Witness Blessing of Monastery," *Catholic Week,* May 1962.

94   *Land search:* OLAM History, March 11, 1961; A.I. with Bishop Dermott Malloy, 2002.

95   *"I could have crowned her":* OLAM History, March 16, 1961.

95   Sister Was a Sport: "Veteran of Local Stage Writes Guild Play," *Canton*

Repository, April 5, 1961; see also "Plain Dealer Series Inspires Drury Play," *Cleveland Plain Dealer*, January 7, 1962. Copy of the play provided to author by Margaret Glazer.

96 *"Oh, they got that wrong"*: A.I. with Joan Frank, 2002.

96 *Size of Birmingham property*: OLAM History, 1961; see also "Ground Broken for $100,000 Franciscan Monastery," *Catholic Week*, July 28, 1961.

96 *"God is good."*: OLAM History, 1961.

97 *"We were so deep in it all"*: ibid.

97 *Archbishop Toolen breaking ground*: ibid.

97 *"You better see Mother"*: ibid.

98 *"We'll find a hill around here" and hole story*: A.I. with Mother Angelica, 2000.

98 *Donations*: OLAM History, August 27, 1961; A.I. with Cossette Stephenson, 2004.

98 *Schedule during building*: OLAM History, July 30, 1961.

98 *"When I take off my gimp"*: ibid.

99 *"For a couple of days"*: OLAM History, September 17, 1961.

99 *"I had to tell the bricklayers off"*: ibid., October 14, 1961.

100 *"When I read the life of St. Teresa"*: ibid., November 9, 1961.

100 *Mae Francis's visit to Birmingham*: ibid., September 18, 1961.

101 *"the biggest beggar this city" and details of speech*: *Kiwanian Bulletin* (Kiwanis Club of Birmingham), March 6, 1962; see also *Birmingham Post Herald*, March 3, 1962.

101 *"Don't worry, the Lord will provide"*: OLAM History, October 8, 1961.

101 *Archbishop Toolen's concern*: letter from Archbishop Toolen to Mother Angelica, November 3, 1961, OLAMA.

102 *"But Your Excellency, the bedrooms" and details of Archbishop Toolen's visit*: A.I. with Mother Angelica, 2000.

102 *Sancta Clara loan*: Sancta Clara Protocol, November 8, 1961, and December 26, 1961, SCA.

102 *"Sister spine gets to yelling" and subsequent quotes*: OLAM History, 1961.

CHAPTER 8: A FAMILY MONASTERY

104 *Incident at the small house*: OLAM History, February 25, 1962; A.I. with Mother Angelica, 2000; A.I. with Sister Mary Joseph, 2001.

104 *"could smell the gunpowder"*: Jerry McCloy, "Nuns Say Prayer for Terrorists," *Birmingham Post-Herald*, February 23, 1962.

105 *"It was as close to hell"*: OLAM History, February 25, 1962.

105 *"not typical of Birmingham"*: "Holy Ghost Descended on Nuns with Bang," *Catholic Week,* March 3, 1962.

105 *"If it happens a third time"*: OLAM History, March 11, 1962.

105 *Nuns depart Sancta Clara*: Sister Mary Raphael, "Behind the Wall and Over the Hill" (unpublished ms.), OLAMA, p. 1.

105 *"brought the cream of the crop"*: A.I. with Joan Frank, 2002.

106 *Description of monastery interior*: John Wright, Jr., "Nuns Will Not Witness Blessing of Monastery," *Catholic Week,* May 1962.

106 *"The entire project was planned"*: James Perry, "Monastery's Main Feature Is Love," *Birmingham Post-Herald,* May 26, 1962.

107 *"Sisters, you can never go overboard"*: Sister Mary Raphael, Notebook of First Lessons, October 23, 1962, OLAMA.

107 *"powerhouse of grace and prayer"*: "Nuns Wave Farewell," *Birmingham News,* May 21, 1962.

108 *"no longer an isolated individual"*: Mother Angelica, *The Family Spirit* (Birmingham, Ala.: EWTN Catholic Publisher, 1976), p. 3.

109 *"little heart to heart"*: OLAM History, August 1962.

109 *Details of "God's Love for You"*: "Mother Angelica Releases Record," *Birmingham Post-Herald,* December 22, 1962.

110 *Inauguration of the Second Vatican Council*: George Weigel, *Witness To Hope* (New York: HarperCollins, 1999); see also Carl Bernstein and Marco Politi, *His Holiness* (New York: Doubleday, 1996).

110 *"felt pushed"*: OLAM History, September 1963.

110 *Background on Sixteenth Street Baptist Church*: Kris Axtman, "In Birmingham a Chance for Justice Long Delayed," *Christian Science Monitor,* April 20, 2001.

111 *Jo Ann Magro enters OLAM*: OLAM History, August 15, 1964.

111 *"packed with some 50 stones"*: ibid., October 21, 1964.

112 *periti previews*: A.I. with Archbishop Phillip Hannan and Cardinal Avery Dulles, 2004.

112 *"directives and changes promoted by the Holy See"*: Mother Angelica, "One Heart, One Soul," *Review for Religious* 24 (1965), pp. 543–47.

113 *"Why are so many of our monasteries"*: Mother Angelica, "Contemplatives and Change," *Review for Religious* 25 (1966), pp. 68–72.

113 *"exchange ideas"*: OLAM History, September 17, 1965.

114 *"help them update"*: ibid., October 19, 1965.

114 *"Oh, you're just like your father"*: Sister Mary Raphael, "Mother Angelica and Her Mother" (unpublished ms.), OLAMA, p. 37.

114 *"adequate and prudent experimentation" and subsequent quotes:* Second Vatican Council, *Perfectae Caritatis,* October 21, 1965.

114 *Renewal of Our Lady of the Angels Monastery:* OLAM History, 1965–68.

115 *"good public relations":* ibid., July 23, 1966.

115 *"an old habit cut short":* ibid., May 3, 1967.

115 *"We found out these Southern fish don't bite":* "Where Christmas Lives," *Birmingham Magazine,* December 1968.

116 *Inspiration and planning of peanut business:* OLAM History, December 5–8, 1967.

116 *On Ash Wednesday:* ibid., February 19, 1969.

118 *"missionary activity" and "You will have a long":* ibid., March 22, 1969.

CHAPTER 9: THE SPIRIT MOVES

119 *Father DeGrandis's visit:* A.I. with Mother Angelica, Father Robert DeGrandis, and Sister Regina, 2001.

120 *"This Holy Spirit is really wonderful" and subsequent conversation:* A.I. with Father Robert DeGrandis, 2001; A.I. with Mother Angelica, 2000.

120 *Barbara Schlemon and Father DeGrandis visit to monastery:* OLAM History, February 11, 1971.

120 *compressed fracture of the vertebrae:* ibid., April 5, 1970.

122 *Details of Bible study:* A.I. with Jean Morris, 2002; A.I. with Phyllis Scalici, 2003; and A.I. with Mother Angelica, 2000.

123 *"speaking in tongues":* OLAM History, April 11, 1971.

123 *getting on radio:* A.I. with Father DeGrandis, 2001.

123 *WBRC program:* "Monastery Begins Tape Ministry," *Birmingham Post-Herald,* June 1972.

124 *"You mean a kickback?":* OLAM History, April 13, 1972.

125 *"prayer formats" and "a closer relationship":* Mother Angelica, *Journey into Prayer* (Birmingham, Ala.: EWTN Catholic Publishers, 1972), introduction.

125 *"This will be the second phase":* A.I. with Mother Angelica, 2001.

126 *"on the other side of the railroad tracks":* A.I. with Jean Morris, 2001.

126 *"It's like a mystery story":* Teresa Gernazian, "Invitation to Holiness," *Georgia Bulletin,* November 20, 1975.

127 *"We use the talents we possess":* Mother Angelica, *Three Keys To the Kingdom* (Birmingham, Ala.: EWTN Catholic Publishers, 1977), p. 9.

128 *"The Christian should be":* Leonard Chamblee, "Bumper Stickers Fight Mind Pollution," *Birmingham Post-Herald,* June 22, 1973.

129 *"Where will you get the money?"*: Sister Mary Raphael, *My Life with Mother Angelica* (Birmingham, Ala.: EWTN Catholic Publishers, 1982), p. 27.

129 *"Money is His problem"*: Gernazian, "Invitation to Holiness."

129 *"Want to lend us $10,000?"*: OLAM History, October 16, 1975.

129 *"Did you think to measure"*: ibid., January 25, 1976.

130 *"Ten thousand books!" and subsequent quotes*: A.I. with Mother Angelica, 2000.

131 *"[Sister David] never felt"*: Sister Mary Raphael, "Mother Angelica and Her Mother" (unpublished ms.), OLAMA, p. 4.

132 *Minibook inspiration*: OLAM History, January 28, 1976.

132 *Cost of print shop*: ibid., July 3, 1976.

133 *Mother Angelica's heart problem*: ibid., July 15, 1976.

133 *"Give me ten Jehovah Witness type Catholics"*: Sharon Hollis Sutter, "New Pamphleteer Proclaims God's Love," *Florida Catholic,* January 21, 1977.

133 *"The books, and minibooks are mustard seeds"*: Sonya LaRussa, "An Interview with Mother Angelica," private newsletter, May 1977, p. 13.

134 *Eight hundred people distributed thirteen thousand books*: "Contemplative Nun and Evangelizer," *Florida Catholic,* January 21, 1977.

134 *"a disease called 'healingitus'"*: Henry Libersat, "Nun Calls Catholics 'Deadheads,'" *Florida Catholic,* February 4, 1977.

134 *Background on Ron Lee*: "Ron Lee—His Product Is Jesus," *Florida Catholic,* June 30, 1978.

134 *"regional guardians"*: OLAM History, July 3, 1977.

135 *"forming a human seal" and details of first CFMA summit*: ibid., December 2, 1977.

136 *"Lord, I gotta have one of these"*: *Mother Angelica Live,* EWTN, July 27, 1993.

136 *"Tom, how much does something like this cost?"*: A.I. with Tom Kennedy, 2003.

136 *"Boy, it don't take much to reach the masses"*: A.I. with Sister Mary Joseph, 2001.

137 *"the Lord spoke"*: A.I. with Tom Kennedy, 2003.

138 *"Do you know where we can make a tape?"*: A.I. with Jean Morris, 2002.

139 *"Grandma Moses with an Andy Gump profile"*: Sister Mary Raphael, *My Life with Mother Angelica* (Birmingham, Ala.: EWTN Catholic Publishers, 1982), p. 35.

139 *"Katherine Cullman style event"*: OLAM History, May 21, 1978.

140 *"Have you ever wondered what happened"*: *Our Hermitage,* EWTN, June 1978.

141 *"Roman Catholic program" and subsequent quotes:* A.I. with Tom Rogeberg, 2003.

142 *"For too long the TV tube has been":* OLAM History, July 13, 1978.

143 *"I'm going to pray.":* A.I. with Matt Scalici, 2003.

143 *Watching the new Pope on television:* OLAM History, October 16, 1978.

144 *"blasphemy" and background on* The Word: Leonard Chamblee, "Mother Angelica Too Busy to Make Speeches," *Birmingham Post-Herald,* November 4, 1978.

144 *Conversation between Mother Angelica and Hugh Smith:* A.I. with Hugh Smith, 2003; OLAM History, November 2, 1978.

145 *"very calm":* A.I. with Hugh Smith, 2003.

145 *"I blew it":* Sister Mary Raphael, *My Life with Mother Angelica,* p. 38.

145 *"television studio" and "I don't know anything":* Mother Angelica Live, EWTN, July 27, 1993.

146 *"Go back and sharpen your pencil":* Sister Mary Raphael, *My Life with Mother Angelica,* p. 40.

147 *"food poisoning and no love gift":* OLAM History, June 1, 1979.

147 *"I go through hell worrying":* Sister Mary Raphael, "Mother Angelica and Her Mother" (unpublished ms.), p. 40.

148 *Conversation with engineer:* Mother Angelica Live, EWTN, July 27, 1993.

148 *Conversation with Robert Corazzini:* A.I. with Robert Corazzini, 2003; A.I. with Mother Angelica, 2001.

149 *"I am convinced God":* transcript of a 1979 PTL program, possibly aired January 22.

149 *"We're after the man in the pew":* New York Times, August 15, 1981.

150 *$380,000 debt:* OLAM History, May 7–8, 1980.

150 *Background on Harry John and De Rance:* Paul Wilkes, "Harry John Was Not Your Average American Catholic," *National Catholic Reporter,* September 17, 1993; Gretchen Schuldt, "De Rance Dispersal Is Ruled Legitimate," *Milwaukee Journal-Sentinel,* June 21, 1997.

150 *"didn't appear clean":* A.I. with Chris Harrington, 2002.

150 *"a beret, suspenders,":* A.I. with Monsignor Michael Wrenn, 2003.

151 *MA's conversation with Harry John:* A.I. with Dick DeGraff, 2003.

151 *"You want to do something for the Lord":* Christopher Close-Up, March 20, 1983.

151 *"You really expect me to approve this contract?":* A.I. with Bill Steltemeier, 2003.

152 *"chubby guy," "The Lord said to me," and meeting with Lloyd Skinner:* A.I. with Mother Angelica, 2001.

CHAPTER 11: CATHEDRAL IN THE SKY:
THE ETERNAL WORD TELEVISION NETWORK

154   *Arrival of FCC license:* OLAM History, January 27, 1981. Though granted on January 19, the license didn't arrive at the monastery until January 27.

154   *"A spiritual growth network":* Carolynne Scott, "Cloistered Nuns Receive Satellite TV License," *One Voice,* January 31, 1981.

155   *Visit with Peter Grace:* OLAM History, February 15, 1981.

155   *"No one will be able to extinguish this flame":* A.I. with Sister Regina, 2001.

155   *EWTN board and advisers:* letter from Mother Angelica to Bishop Joseph Vath, January 19, 1981, OLAMA.

156   *Father John Hardon speaks to Vatican official:* A.I. with Sister Mary Catherine, 2003.

156   *But on February 27, Vath revoked:* letter from Bishop Joseph Vath to Mother Angelica, February 27, 1981.

156   *"to see to the work of EWTN":* letter from Mother Angelica to Bishop Joseph Vath, March 7, 1981, OLAMA.

156   *Bishop Vath phoned Mother Angelica:* OLAM History, March 10, 1981.

156   *"Your Excellency, I have all these talks":* A.I. with Mother Angelica, 2001. A letter from Bishop Vath to Mother Angelica on March 13, 1981, confirms her memory of the phone conversation, which is referenced therein.

157   *"destroy the network":* OLAM History, March 2, 1981.

157   *"He can't do that" and subsequent quotes:* A.I. with Sister Regina, 2001.

158   *Mother Angelica wrote the nuncio:* letter from Mother Angelica to Archbishop Pio Laghi, March 6, 1981, OLAMA.

158   *Arrival of satellite dish:* OLAM History, March 5–6, 1981.

158   *Deliveryman and Mother's reaction:* A.I. with Bill Steltemeier, 2003.

158   *Assembly of satellite:* OLAM History, March 18, 1981.

159   *secretary of the Papal representative:* OLAM History, March 19, 1981.

159   *Peter Grace loan:* ibid.

160   *"Your Eminence, Mother Angelica" and subsequent conversation:* A.I. with Bill Steltemeier, 2003.

160   *DeGraff dispatched to Rome:* OLAM History, May 17, 1981.

161   *"I am happy to bless":* Monastery guest book, May, 21, 1981, OLAMA.

161   *"What do you want?" and conversation with Cardinal Oddi:* A.I. with Bill Steltemeier, 2003; and A.I. with Mother Angelica, 2001.

161   *Permission to leave the monastery:* letter from Archbishop Mayer, prefect of the Congregation for Religious, to Mother Angelica, June 10, 1981, OLAMA.

162   *"to the advancement of truth" and subsequent quotes:* EWTN mission state-
       ment.

162   *"I feel in my heart":* Judy Gillespie, "The Coaxial Congregation," *Cable Mar-
       keting,* November 1981.

162   *Description of launch day:* A.I. with Tom Kennedy, Matt Scalici, Jean Mor-
       ris, and others, 2003.

163   *"O God, Lord of heaven and earth":* program of EWTN dedication cere-
       mony, August 15, 1981, OLAMA.

164   *only six cable systems:* Dr. Sammy R. Danna, "From Cloisters To Cable by
       Satellite," *EITV,* January 1983.

164   *Mother and Ginny Dominick ran the network:* A.I. with Marynell Ford,
       Chris Harrington, Matt Scalici, and others, 2003.

165   *"What I demand of the crew":* Patrick E. Brennan, "Catholic Television
       Comes of Age," *Columbia Magazine,* January 1988.

167   *Squeezed into the corner of the Southern:* Donna Plesh, "Religious View of
       TV Business," *The Register,* June 4, 1981.

167   *Praying at the* Playboy *booth:* A.I. with Mother Angelica and Bill Steltemeier,
       2001.

168   *"a proud and disobedient nun":* "Communications Controversy," *Florida
       Catholic,* June 12, 1981.

168   *Background on CTNA:* Joe Michael Feist, "Dream for Quality, Profitable
       CTNA, Is Elusive," *Catholic Sun,* April 23, 1986; Monsignor Noel C. Burten-
       shaw, "Cable Television Rage across America," *Georgia Bulletin,* July 1, 1982.

169   *"[CTNA] is a diocesan network":* Russell Chandler, "Religious Groups Plan
       Major Use of Video Technology," *Los Angeles Times,* December 25, 1983.

169   *"needless duplication":* "Communications Controversy."

169   *"I have absolutely no problem with the bishops":* ibid.

169   *"Cloistered nuns should stay in their monasteries":* ibid.

170   *Visit of Richard Hirsh and Father John Geaney to EWTN:* OLAM History,
       September 10, 1981.

170   *"At the time, it was":* A.I. with Father John Geaney, 2003.

170   *CTNA meeting:* OLAM History, February 7, 1982.

170   *"Well, Bishop, I don't have a budget" and subsequent conversation:* A.I. with
       Bill Steltemeier, 2003.

171   *Wold contract:* OLAM History, January 14, 1982; A.I. with Matt Scalici and
       Bill Steltemeier, 2003.

171   *She told the nuns:* OLAM History, March 1, 1982.

171   *"stunned and starry eyed" and "several small strokes":* ibid., May 6, 1982.

172   *"Now that's providence"*: Jack Hawn, "Nun Looks To the Heavens—For Satcom TV Service," *Los Angeles Times,* July 21, 1982.

172   *Satcom statistics:* Danna, "From Cloister To Cable by Satellite."

172   *fee of $132,000:* OLAM History, October 1, 1982.

172   *breaching the Wold contract:* EWTN Five Year Business Plan, Touche Ross & Company, December 4, 1982, p. 39.

173   *spit her food:* A.I. with Sister Mary Catherine, 2003.

173   *"As she grew to depend on me":* Sister Mary Raphael, "Mother Angelica and Her Mother," p. 4.

173   *"Oh, Raphael, you're going to lose your David":* ibid., p. 5.

173   *"Why did you leave me":* Sister Mary Raphael, "Behind the Wall and Over the Hill" (unpublished ms.), OLAMA, p. 7.

CHAPTER 12: DEATH AND THE DARK NIGHT

174   *Details of Mother Angelica at Sister Mary David's bedside:* A.I. with Dr. Rex Harris, 2003.

174   *"[David's] dead of heart failure":* Sister Mary Raphael, "Mother Angelica and Her Mother" (unpublished ms.), OLAMA, p. 7.

174   *"Sister don't go—oh David!":* ibid.

174   *"Lord, You can't take her now" and subsequent quotes:* A.I. with Mother Angelica, 2000.

175   *"Oh David. Jesus loves you":* Sister Mary Raphael, "Mother Angelica and Her Mother," p. 9.

176   *"absorb" and "take it over":* OLAM History, October 1, 1982.

177   *"Whoever has the media":* ibid.

177   *"present the Eternal Word Television Network":* EWTN Family Newsletter, December 1982.

178   *"I have heard about you.":* Sister Raphael's Chronology, November 12, 1982. OLAMA.

178   *"Don't air it":* OLAM History, November 29, 1982.

178   *Background on liaison meeting:* ibid., December 15, 1982; A.I. with Bill Steltemeier and anonymous sources, 2003.

178   *"CTNA was undercapitalized":* A.I. with Bishop Robert Lynch, 2003.

179   *In early December, Bill Steltemeier:* OLAM History, December 5, 1982.

179   *"I'll lose the network Monday":* ibid., December 21, 1982.

179   *"Every month we agonize":* ibid., January 25, 1983.

179   *Background on Wold lawsuit:* A.I. with Mother Angelica 2001; A.I. with Matt Scalici and Bill Steltemeier, 2003; OLAM History, May 11, 1983.

180   *"You go."*: A.I. with Bill Steltemeier, 2003.

180   *"A miracle took place"*: ibid.; the previously cited five-year plan by Touche Ross & Company gives a projected Wold payout of $240,000, but this was written months before the deal was consummated.

181   *"This is our first live"*: EWTN 2nd Anniversary Show, EWTN, August 15, 1983.

181   *ninety-five cable systems:* John Stickney, "Pay TV's Flying Nun," *TV Cableweek,* August 14–20, 1983.

182   *Harry John agreed to send her $120,000:* OLAM History, October 21, 1983.

183   *Background on Santa Fe Communications:* Frank Trippett, "Harry's Holy War," *Time,* May 26, 1986; Paul Wilkes, "Harry John Was Not Your Average American Catholic," *National Catholic Reporter,* September 17, 1993.

184   *Deal with Harry John:* OLAM History, November 21, 1983.

184   *"before Harry said stop"*: ibid., January 27, 1984.

184   *"We need a new studio"*: ibid., December 7, 1983; A.I. with Mother Angelica, 2000.

185   *Bombergers' visit and contribution:* OLAM History, August 11, 1983; A.I. with Mother Angelica, 2001.

185   *"the Catholic voice in America"*: Russell Chandler, "Religious Groups Plan Major Use of Video Technology," *Los Angeles Times,* December 25, 1983.

185   *"Perhaps the greatest interior suffering"*: Mother Angelica, *The Healing Power of Suffering* (Birmingham, Ala.: EWTN Catholic Publishers, 1976), p. 22.

186   *"Lord, unbelievable darkness enveloped me"*: Mother Angelica's diary entry, July 7, 1984, OLAMA.

186   *"You emptied Yourself so totally"*: Mother Angelica's diary entry, July 9, 1984, OLAMA.

187   *"The struggle continues"*: Mother Angelica's diary entry, July 10, 1984, OLAMA.

187   *"I can't now"*: Sister Mary Raphael, "Behind the Wall and Over the Hill" (unpublished ms.), OLAMA, p. 13.

187   *"All right, cough it up, kids."*: telethon tape, July 1984, OLAMA.

187   *Background on telethon:* A.I. with Matt Scalici, Father Mitch Pacwa, Chris Harrington, Marynell Ford, and others, 2003.

188   *"I didn't know it was Franciscan"*: A.I. with Mother Angelica, 2001.

188   *"What if I marry him?"*: A.I. with former EWTN employee, 2003.

189   *"I always felt"*: Mother Angelica's diary entry, July 18, 1984, OLAMA.

190   *"I feel somehow I do not belong"*: Mother Angelica's diary entry, July 20, 1984.

190   *"My soul is in such turmoil"*: Mother Angelica's diary entry, July 26, 1984, OLAMA.

190   *Harry John's troubles:* Paul Wilkes, "Harry John Was Not Your Average American Catholic."

190   the "depths of her misery": Mother Angelica's diary entry, October 23, 1984, OLAMA.

190   a notice arrived from Peter Grace's foundation: OLAM History, November 7, 1984.

191   Grace personally gave Mother: ibid., December 20, 1983.

CHAPTER 13: THE ABBESS OF THE AIRWAVES

193   "people that hurt": Barbranda Lumpkins, "TV Nun's a Novice No Longer," Akron Beacon Journal, February 27, 1985.

194   "She tends to be earthy": Michael D'Antonio, "Mother Angelica Live," Newsday, September 6, 1985.

194   ACE nomination: Private Cable, 1985.

194   Golden Blooper Award: Birmingham Post-Herald, November 12, 1984.

194   EWTN Carriage Figures: Lumpkins, "TV Nun's a Novice No Longer."

194   Broadcasting magazine citation: AP story, Selma Times Journal, July 30, 1984.

195   Statistics on new studio: "EWTN's New Studio Is 'Prayer Come True,'" Catholic Voice, April 12, 1985.

195   "EWTN is the key to restoring": OLAM History, June 19, 1985.

196   "The changes, turns, directions, and risks": memo from Mother Angelica to the vice presidents, August 5, 1985.

196   EWTN donations for 1985: EWTN Annual Report, 1985.

197   "interpret[ed] company policy": memo from Mother Angelica to the vice presidents, August 5, 1985.

198   "lovingly dedicated": Mother Angelica, Mother Angelica's Answers Not Promises (New York: Harper & Row, 1987), dedication page.

198   "I've given my love": OLAM History, November 2, 1998.

199   "insure that that spirit": memo from Mother Angelica to the vice presidents, August 5, 1985.

199   Background on Galaxy deal: A.I. with Matt Scalici, 2003; Patrick E. Brennan, "Catholic Television Comes of Age," Columbia Magazine, January 1988.

199   Meeting with employees: OLAM History, October 24, 1986.

200   Galaxy III turnaround: Brennan, "Catholic Television Comes of Age."

201   "It's just being practical; things have to go on": Greg Garrison, "Mother Angelica's Orders to Carry on Her Video Visions," Birmingham News, July 3, 1987.

201   "ensure that the Word of God": Brennan, "Catholic Television Comes of Age."

201   Background on Sister Gabriel Long: A.I. with Mother Angelica, Sister Mary Catherine, and others, 2001; Lou Jacquet, "Preparing New Servants for the Lord," Our Sunday Visitor, October 16, 1988.

201 *Background on Father Donat McDonagh*: Brennan, "Catholic Television Comes of Age"; Lou Jacquet "Preparing New Servants for the Lord"; A.I. with Mother Angelica, 2001.

201 *"In these two new orders we'll have"*: Brennan, "Catholic Television Comes of Age."

202 *"I don't envision that we will all work"*: Jacquet, "Preparing New Servants for the Lord."

202 *"the sleep of the powers" and "She would be unresponsive"*: A.I. with Sister Margaret Mary, 2003.

202 *Membership in Mother Angelica's orders*: OLAM History, November 25, 1988.

202 *Letters to Pope John Paul II*: "As Scandals Rock Televangelism, Nun's Network Tells It 'Like It Is,' " *Miami Herald,* July 7, 1987.

203 *"This is for all time"*: OLAM History, September 1, 1987.

203 *CTNA/EWTN joint coverage*: memo of agreement between EWTN and CTNA, June 1, 1987.

203 *"I've never been an anchor before"*: Bill Lohmann, "EWTN Will Have Its Eye on the Pope," UPI, September 1987.

204 *Background on Hunthausen and Curran cases*: Kenneth Briggs, *Holy Siege: The Year That Shook Catholic America* (New York: HarperCollins, 1992).

204 *"unworkable"*: Timothy Egan, "Seattle's Prelate Says Fight with Vatican Is Over," *New York Times,* April 13, 1989.

204 *"artificial contraception, divorce, sterilization"*: Briggs, *Holy Siege,* p. 9.

205 *citing his dissent from the Magisterium*: ibid.

205 *"the celibacy question" and "Its value has eroded"*: Susan Yoachum, Knight-Ridder News Service, July 10, 1987.

205 *"I remember a song"*: David Anderson, "Pope Meets with Priests," UPI, September 11, 1987.

206 *"We live in an open society"*: Joseph Berger, "The Papal Visit," *New York Times,* September 17, 1987.

207 *"We cannot fulfill our task simply"*: statement of Archbishop John Quinn, AP, September 16, 1987.

207 *"maverick" and "inappropriate relationship" and background on Archbishop Weakland*: Rod Dreher, "Weakland's Exit," *National Review,* May 24, 2002; "Archbishop Makes Apology," *Newsday,* June 2, 2002.

207 *"The faithful" and subsequent quotes*: statement of archbishop Rembert Weakland, AP, September 16, 1987.

208 *"broadening of the concept" and subsequent quotes*: statement of Archbishop Daniel Pilarczyk, AP, September 16, 1987.

208 *"Women in the priesthood"*: Cornelia Grumman, "Nun on the News," *News and Observer*, September 18, 1987.

208 *"need to compete"*: Sister Mary Ann Walsh, "Live Coverage of Papal Visit," Catholic News Service, September 28, 1987.

209 *"I don't want to be conservative"*: Lou Jacquet, "Preparing New Servants for the Lord."

209 *The program* Spirituality in the Eighties: James Sterling Corum, "CTNA: A Disaster Waiting to Happen," *The Wanderer*, April 7, 1983.

209 *"a disaster" and "an example of the Church throwing"*: Lou Baldwin, "Communications Director Says Evangelists Forget TV Is Mostly a Business," *Catholic Standard and Times*, October 8, 1987.

209 *the "bishops' big white elephant"*: *National Catholic Register*, March 6, 1988.

209 *VISN network*: CTNA, *The Link*, September 1987.

210 *"watered down"*: Ed Wojcicki, "Catholic Presence on Television," *Catholic Times*, November 22, 1987.

210 *Father Bonnot's phone call*: OLAM History, November 10, 1987.

211 *"louder and louder"*: A.I. with Sister Antoinette, 2001.

211 *"And who are you to decide" and subsequent comments*: A.I. with Mother Angelica and Sister Antoinette, 2001.

211 *in a letter*: letter from Father Bonnot to Mother Angelica, November 12, 1987, OLAMA.

211 *"idea of television is to allow everyone"*: letter from Mother Angelica to Archbishop Pio Laghi, November 16, 1987, OLAMA.

211 *"Rome knew what she was doing"*: OLAM History, December 10, 1987.

212 *"pluralistic society" and "Educational efforts"*: John Dart, "Catholics OK Condom Data as AIDS Safeguard," *Los Angeles Times*, December 11, 1987.

213 *"rather tense meeting" and conversation at meeting*: A.I. with Bishop Robert Lynch, 2003.

214 *"The catechetical vision"*: A.I. with Cardinal Francis Stafford, 2003.

214 *"What happens to Eternal Word?"*: NCCB transcript, June 24, 1988.

215 *This eleventh-hour concession*: A.I. with Chris Harrington, Marynell Ford, and Bishop Rene Gracida, 2003.

215 *"hobbled" and "It was highly regrettable"*: A.I. with Father Bob Bonnot, 2003.

215 *Gabriel I statistics*: "EWTN Dedicated New Production Vehicle," *One Voice*, August 12, 1988.

216 *"to pull back a little"*: A.I. with Mother Angelica, 2001.

CHAPTER 14: A WITNESS TO THE NATIONS: WEWN

217   *"large farm with homes"*: Barbara Reynolds, "Topic: 1987 Resolutions," *USA Today*, January 2, 1987.

217   *"The Lord said, 'Go to Rome' "*: A.I. with Mother Angelica, 2001; and A.I. with Bill Steltemeier, 2003.

218   *"The Lord spoke to me last night"*: A.I. with Matt Scalici, 2003.

218   *"In blind obedience"*: ibid.

219   *"Mother Angelica, you are a strong woman"*: OLAM History, January 31, 1989.

220   *"Ah, Mother Angelica, the grand chief"*: A.I. with Sister Margaret Mary, 2003.

220   *Background on Piet Derksen*: Richard Gilbert, "Welcome To the Pleasure Dome," *Financial Times*, April 4, 1992; Jennifer Clark, "Beaming a Holy Message," *Times* (London), November 30, 1988; George Armstrong, "The Media: Now God's Anchorman," *Guardian*, October 10, 1988.

220   *"My wealth has been like a stone"*: "Personalities," *Washington Post*, March 3, 1984.

220   *Description of Piet Derksen and meeting*: A.I. with Mother Angelica, 2001; and A.I. with Bill Steltemeier, 2003.

220   *"You're the one"*: ibid.

221   *Description of villa*: OLAM History, March 17, 1989.

221   *Donations to shortwave project*: ibid., April 14, 1989.

221   *Mother had begun work on a parallel shortwave*: ibid., September 12, 1989.

222   *Mother's conversation with Joseph Canizaro*: A.I. with Joseph Canizaro, 2003.

222   *she and the sisters filled a small bag*: OLAM History, January 1, 1990.

223   *"one out of every three programs submitted"*: Liz Schevtchuk, "Bishops Approve Step toward Renegotiating EWTN Contract," Catholic News Service, November 18, 1989.

224   *a "fruitless exchange of recrimination"*: "After Hearing Complaints, Catholic Bishops Vote to Renegotiate TV Pact," *St. Petersburg Times*, November 18, 1989.

224   *Canizaro and Archbishop Phillip Hannan of New Orleans hand-delivered*: OLAM History, February 15, 1990.

225   *Mother's fall in Birmingham*: A.I. with Mother Angelica, 2001.

225   *"for the continuation of God's blessing"*: OLAM History, October 8, 1990.

225   *Conversation on the mountaintop*: A.I. with Mother Angelica, 2000; and A.I. with Matt Scalici, 2003.

226   *"a handsome, strong, manly looking"*: A.I. with Mother Angelica, 2001.

226   *"I will ever be at your side, and we will . . ."*: OLAM History, March 5, 1989.

226   *Scalici researching property*: A.I. with Matt Scalici, 2003.

227 *Letter that would change everything:* letter from Archbishop John Foley to Mother Angelica, October 30, 1990, OLAMA.

227 *"impl[ied] that Mr. Derksen should not fund":* letter from Mother Angelica to Archbishop John Foley, November 14, 1990, OLAMA.

227 *Piet Derksen placed an angry call:* OLAM History, April 29, 1991.

227 *"raved and ranted" and "Well do it":* A.I. with Mother Angelica, 2003.

228 *"penances, fasting, and contemplative prayer":* ibid., April 28, 1991.

228 *"Father and I have been friends for many years":* ibid.

229 *"back the stray sheep":* letter from Mother Angelica to the brothers, June 13, 1991, OLAMA.

229 *"Why are you putting up this wall?" and "Because the Lord":* A.I. with Sister Agnes, 2003.

229 *Stemming network gossip:* OLAM History, June 15, 1991.

230 *"preoccupied":* A.I. with Sister Mary Catherine, 2003.

230 *Mother announced that the televised conventual Mass:* OLAM History, July 5, 1992.

231 *"To show the power of EWTN and Mother":* A.I. with Bishop David Foley, 2003.

231 *"grieved" and "They couldn't be forced":* OLAM History, May 5, 1992.

232 *Reaction to construction of shortwave facility:* Greg Garrison, "Mother Angelica's Radio Towers Rouse Static," *National Catholic Reporter,* January 8, 1993.

232 *Details on shortwave station:* Mike Brezonick, *Diesel and Gas Turbine Publications,* June 1993.

232 *Description of launch day:* OLAM History, December 28, 1992.

233 *"Their faith throughout the years":* Dan O'Neill, *Mother Angelica: Her Life Story* (New York: Crossroad Publishing Company, 1986), p. 160.

CHAPTER 15: THE DEFENDER OF THE FAITH

235 *Background on the new catechism:* Lawrence Cunningham, "The New Catechism," *Commonweal,* March 12, 1993; Gerald Renner, "Catholic Catechism Available in English," *Hartford Courant,* June 22, 1994.

236 *"moderate approach":* Cunningham, "The New Catechism."

236 *"They're not changing the language":* Larry Witham, "Gender-Neutral Catechism on Hold," *Washington Times,* March 26, 1993.

236 *"There was a time when the word 'man'":* ibid.

236 *When she learned that they:* OLAM History, January 8, 1993; A.I. with Sister Agnes, 2003.

237   *"[Was] Jesus . . . conceived of the Holy Spirit"*: OLAM History, January 8, 1993.

237   *"Oh, hello, Mother"*: A.I. with Mother Angelica, 2001; Larry Witham's *Washington Times* story of March 26 confirms that Cardinal Law was in Rome in February 1993.

238   *"I think our final product was better"*: A.I. with Cardinal Bernard Law, 2003.

238   *Bronchial infection and shattered vertebra*: OLAM History, May 5–14, 1993.

238   *"One of the lessons I've learned"*: *Mother Angelica Live*, EWTN, June 22, 1993.

239   *Detail of Fountain Square Fools performance*: "Mother Angelica Sounds Off," *Catholic World News*, October 1993.

239   *"Mother, I've got something I need to tell you"*: A.I. with Chris Harrington, 2002.

240   *"You're kidding"*: A.I. with Mother Angelica, 2001.

240   *"Lord, I'm angry"*: ibid.

240   *"Mime never is an historical representation"*: World Youth Day/Bishops Conference press release, August 14, 1993.

240   *"Jesus was portrayed by a woman"*: *Denver Post*, August 14, 1993.

240   *"looked very much like the standard"*: Carol Zimmerman, "Group Outraged That Woman Depicted Christ at World Youth Day," Catholic News Service, September 16, 1993.

241   *"The whole reason the Vatican claims women"*: "Mother Angelica Sounds Off."

241   *Sister Mary Ann Walsh*: ibid.

241   *"I'm going to blast them."*: A.I. with Mother Angelica, 2001; and A.I. with Bill Steltemeier, 2003.

241   *"Yesterday I made a mistake" and subsequent quotes from "The Hidden Agenda"*: *Mother's Corner*, EWTN, August 14, 1993.

243   *A cheer erupted*: OLAM History, August 14, 1993; A.I. with Sister Antoinette and a former nun, 2001.

243   *Reaction of bishops conference*: "Mother Angelica Sounds Off"; A.I. with Mother Angelica.

243   *"senseless and heartless condemning"*: "Milwaukee Archbishop Criticizes Mother Angelica's Telecast," *Arlington Catholic Herald*, September 23, 1993.

244   *"darkness and fear"*: Jim Sheehan, "Mother Angelica," *National Catholic Reporter*, October 29, 1993.

244   *"At that moment, she threw down the gauntlet"*: A.I. with Bishop Robert Lynch, 2003.

244   *In a joint statement, a group of prominent Catholics*: Zimmerman, "Group Outraged That Woman Depicted Christ at World Youth Day."

244   *EWTN picked up more than two hundred cable affiliates*: EWTN's Marketing Department; A.I. with Chris Wegemer.

245   *the group of nuns began a private novena*: A.I. with Sister Antoinette, 2001.

246 *"This is a risk we take"*: OLAM History, December 23, 1993.

247 *Background on Garabandal*: Dr. Courtenay Bartholemew, *Her Majesty Mary Queen of Peace* (Goleta, Calif.: Queenship Publishing, 2002).

247 *"[The] warning. It will be an act of God's mercy"*: Mother Angelica Live, EWTN, February 8, 1994.

247 *"satanic cruelty" and "This flood"*: Mother Angelica Live, EWTN, July 27, 1993.

248 *"War is long overdue."*: Mother Angelica Live, EWTN, August 31, 1993.

248 *"I have to stick up for my friend" and "I've got to"*: Mother Angelica Live, EWTN, September 1, 1993.

248 *"prelude" and subsequent quotes*: Mother Angelica Live, EWTN, November 23, 1993.

249 *"The Vatican has approved altar girls"*: Mother Angelica Live, EWTN, April 12, 1994.

249 *"I think when this program's over"*: Mother Angelica Live, EWTN, November 2, 1993.

250 *"Something needs to be done"*: Rod Dreher, "TV Abbess Scourge of Catholic Liberals," *Washington Times*, April 25, 1994.

250 *Bishop Emil Wcela*: Michael S. Rose, "Mother Angelica: Healed and Reviled," *St. Katherine Review*, March–April 1998.

CHAPTER 16: HAMMER OF THE HERETICS

251 *"foundation of pain" and "Why?"*: Mother Angelica Live, EWTN, January 10, 1995.

251 *". . . my head was wet with perspiration"*: letter from Mother Angelica to EWTN employees, March 3, 1995, OLAMA.

252 *Sister Mary Raphael's cancer diagnosis and treatment*: OLAM History, June 2, 1995, and June 9, 1995.

252 *"Conditions around the world"*: EWTN press release, June 7, 1995.

252 *Details of search for monastery land*: OLAM History, August 16, 1995, August 17, 1995, and October 12, 1995.

253 *Details of Hanceville purchase*: A.I. with Sister Antoinette, 2004.

253 *Details of Mother Angelica meeting with the Pope*: A.I. with Mother Angelica, 2001; A.I. with Sister Margaret Mary and Chris Wegemer, 2003.

255 *Background on shrine of Divino Niño*: Father Eliecer Salesman, *Novena: Nine Sundays in Honor of the Divine Infant Jesus* (Bogotá, Colombia: Apostolado Biblico Catolico, 2003).

255 *"Well, there is a good John Rizzo!"*: OLAM History, June 20, 1996.

257 *"like a second founding"*: A.I. with Michael Warsaw, 2003.

257   *"[God] was very fussy about the Temple"*: Greg Garrison, "Mother Angelica's Dream," *Birmingham News,* August 15, 1997.

257   *the monastery would cost $3 million:* ibid.

257   *Donations ranging upwards of $48.6 million:* Father Gregory T. Bittner, "Tensions in Subsidiarity," *CLSA Proceedings* (Canon Law Society of America, Washington, D.C.) 65 (2003).

258   *Foley requested a "visitation":* OLAM History, April 17, 1997.

258   *Mother refused his visitation request:* OLAM History, April 18, 1997; A.I. with Bishop David Foley, 2003.

258   *voted on May 20, 1997:* OLAM History, May 20, 1997.

259   *Cardinal Mahony among those writing on behalf of EWTN:* Art Babych, "EWTN: Canadians Divided on Merits of a Catholic Network," Catholic News Service, April 16, 1997.

259   *"there's no need for confession" and subsequent quotes: Mother Angelica Live,* EWTN, November 12, 1997.

261   *"For you to state publicly on television":* John Allen, "Mahony Sees Nun's Critique as Heresy Charge," *National Catholic Reporter,* December 5, 1997.

261   *"For you to call into question":* Tod Tamberg, "EWTN Head Apologizes for Questioning Cardinal's Faith," Catholic News Service, November 26, 1997.

261   *"I think she took offense":* A.I. with Michael Warsaw, 2003.

261   *"I must insist you issue a formal retraction" and Mother Angelica's comments: Mother Angelica Live,* EWTN, November 18, 1997; Monica Seeley, "Thou Must Retract," *LA Lay Catholic Mission* 4 (1998): p. 1.

263   *"strikingly truncated theology of the Eucharist":* John Allen, "Liturgy Watchdog Group Blasts Mahony," *National Catholic Reporter,* December 26, 1997.

263   *"pastoral leadership" and "ecclesiastical taboos":* Tom Fox, "Mahony Offers Welcome Sign of Hope," *National Catholic Reporter,* May 5, 2000.

263   *Mahony-Bernardin connection:* Tom Fox, "Mahony's Pastoral Concern Shows in Liturgy Letter," *National Catholic Reporter,* February 23, 1998.

263   *Advocates of female ordination, critics of:* Stephanie Block, "Facing De Facto Schism: LA's Call To Unholy Action," www.rcf.org, April 4, 1998; Paul Likoudis, "A Parody of Faith," *The Wanderer,* June 2001.

263   *"profound commitment":* ibid.

263   *"the latest example of the absolute contempt":* "Thou Must Retract."

264   *"Mother Angelica has the guts to tell him what we do not":* OLAM History, January 22, 1998.

264   *"I must respectfully state that your November 18th program":* "Mahony Takes Case Against Mother Angelica to Rome," *The Wanderer,* January 15, 1998.

265   *"I gave him his apology and clarification":* OLAM History, December 3, 1997.

265 *"I have dedicated my life to the Eucharist"*: ibid.

265 *Bishop Foley and Father Deitz worked on a retraction*: A.I. with Bishop David Foley, 2003.

266 *Letter written at the insistence of Cardinal Mahony*: letter from Virgil Dechant to Mother Angelica, December 10, 1997, OLAMA.

266 *On the same day, the auxiliary bishops of Los Angeles wrote*: letter from the auxiliary bishops of Los Angeles to Congregation for the Institutes of Consecrated Life and Societies of Apostolic Life (hereafter CICLSAL), December 10, 1997, OLAMA.

266 *Mention of complaint by Bishops Lynch and Trautman*: letter from CICLSAL to Mother Angelica, December 12, 1997, OLAMA.

266 *"No, I'm seventy-four years old"*: A.I. with Bishop David Foley, 2003; OLAM History, December 15, 1997.

266 *"So I phoned Mahony"*: A.I. with Bishop David Foley, 2003.

267 *"amount to a denial of" her "belief"*: letter from Mother Angelica to Cardinal Roger Mahony, December 23, 1997, OLAMA.

267 *"The cardinal wants the Holy See to do something"*: John Allen, "Mahony Appeals to Rome About Angelica," *National Catholic Reporter,* January 30, 1998.

267 *"reoriented"*: ibid.

268 *"just penalties"*: ibid.

268 *Definition of interdiction*: Catholic Encyclopedia (www.Newadvent.org).

268 *"Is Mahony looking for Rome to slap an interdict"*: John Allen, "Mahony Appeals To Rome about Angelica."

CHAPTER 17: MIRACLES AND CHASTISEMENTS

269 *reignited the quarrel*: letter from Cardinal Roger Mahony to Mother Angelica, January 2, 1998, OLAMA.

270 *Mother notified her direct superior*: letter from Mother Angelica to CICLSAL, January 7, 1998, OLAMA.

270 *"My grace is sufficient for thee"*: The Holy Bible (London: Catholic Truth Society, 1957), 2 Corinthians 9.

271 *Background on Paola Albertini*: Maureen Flynn, "An Interview with Paola Albertini," *Signs and Wonders* 9, no. 4 (Spring 1998).

271 *"special message from Our Lady"*: ibid.

271 *"bright glow"*: Gerald Renner, "Nun Hangs Tough in Tiff with Cardinal," Religious News Service, February 13, 1998.

271 *"What joy you give"*: OLAM History, January 28, 1998.

272 *"Lord, all these years You've used me"*: A.I. with Mother Angelica, 2001.

272 *Details of Paola Albertini's interaction with Mother Angelica:* Maureen Flynn, "An Interview with Paola Albertini"; A.I. with Sister Agnes and Sister Mary Claire, 2002.

272 *Details of reaction to healing:* OLAM History, January 28, 1998.

272 *Paola Albertini and Mother prayed:* ibid., January 29, 1998.

274 *"from people suggesting that Mother":* John Allen, "Pain Healed, EWTN Approved, Angelica Says," *National Catholic Reporter,* February 13, 1998.

274 *Cardinal Mahony lamented her non-response:* letter from Cardinal Roger Mahony to Mother Angelica, February 5, 1998, OLAMA.

275 *"Nothing further can be gained":* fax from Mother Angelica to Cardinal Roger Mahony, February 26, 1998, OLAMA.

275 *Mahony relayed details:* letter from Cardinal Roger Mahony to Mother Angelica, February 28, 1998, OLAMA.

275 *Mother urged to accept the invitation:* letter from Archbishop Oscar Libscomb to Mother Angelica, March 4, 1998; letter from Cardinal Martinez Somalo to Mother Angelica, March 5, 1998, OLAMA.

275 *"it would be highly inappropriate":* fax from Mother Angelica to Cardinal Martinez Somalo, March 6, 1998, OLAMA.

276 *"cast out the confusion":* letter from Mother Angelica to Cardinal Joseph Ratzinger, March 11, 1998, OLAMA.

276 *"I don't believe this":* OLAM History, March 21, 1998.

276 *Details of meeting with Cardinal O'Connor:* transcript of March 21, 1998, meeting, OLAMA; A.I. with Mother Angelica, 2001; and A.I. with Bill Steltemeier, 2003.

277 *"I couldn't walk into that chapel" and ensuing conversation:* A.I. with Mother Angelica, 2001.

277 *"I love you":* OLAM History, March 21, 1998.

277 *"I find it extremely beneath the dignity":* fax from Mother Angelica to Cardinal John O'Connor, April 7, 1998, OLAMA.

277 *Cardinal O'Connor requested an edited transcript:* faxes from Cardinal John O'Connor to Mother Angelica, April 8, 1998, and April 15, 1998, OLAMA.

277 *Hospital stay for asthma:* OLAM History, April 23, 1998.

278 *CICLSAL elected to do nothing:* letter from CICLSAL to Mother Angelica, June 27, 1998, OLAMA.

278 *"Eternal Word Television Network is neither owned":* letter from Mother Angelica to Cardinal Martinez Somalo, July 17, 1998, OLAMA.

278 *"The real issue raised by your letter":* letter from Bill Steltemeier to Cardinal Martinez Somalo, July 22, 1998, OLAMA.

278 *"programming attacking bishops"*: John Thavis, "Cardinal Mahony at Vatican," Catholic News Service, October 2, 1998.

279 *"theological and ecumenical developments"*: NCCB doctrine committee's text modifications, "Popular Devotional Practices: Basic Questions and Answers," November 9, 2003.

279 *"average person in the hubbub" and subsequent remarks: Mother Angelica Live,* EWTN, September 2, 1998.

279 *Details of Shrine chapel:* A.I. with Mother Angelica, 1999; *Come and See* (Hanceville, Ala.: OLAM, 2002).

280 *"The new monastery will enhance"*: OLAM History, November 7, 1998.

281 *"Who owns EWTN?"*: minutes of board meeting on October 17, 1998, OLAM History, October 17, 1998.

281 *"had an obsession"*: OLAM History, October 17, 1998.

281 *$49 million in assets:* Greg Garrison, "Building for Eternity," *Birmingham News,* August 10, 1998.

CHAPTER 18: THE LAST THINGS

282 *"This is David Foley,"*: A.I. with Bishop David Foley, 2003.

282 *Mother confided in Foley:* A.I. with Mother Angelica, 2000.

283 *Meeting with Bill Steltemeier and Bishop Foley:* OLAM History, May 26, 1999.

283 *clear definition of the relationship among four entities:* letter from Bishop David Foley to Bill Steltemeier, June 3, 1999, OLAMA.

283 *Blessing of monastery:* OLAM History, August 6, 1999.

283 *One open house drew:* OLAM History, August 29, 1999.

283 *Sister Raphael's diagnosis:* ibid., August 12, 1999, and August 13, 1999.

284 *The chief liturgist for the Birmingham diocese:* A.I. with Bishop David Foley and Father Joseph Wolfe, 2003.

284 *on August 24, the same day:* OLAM History, August 24, 1999.

284 *Medication became difficult to swallow:* OLAM History, August 24, September 3, September 14, 1999.

285 *Y2K preparations:* ibid., December 21, 1998; A.I. with sisters and staff, 2002.

285 *pious manuals:* See Kimberly Hawn et al., *Millennium Insurance: A Christian's Guide to Y2K and How to Prepare Wisely for It* (San Diego: Basilica Press, 1999).

285 *she begged the construction team:* OLAM History, September 17, 1999.

285 *"I appreciate and honor your authority"*: letter from Mother Angelica to Bishop David Foley, September 13, 1999, OLAMA.

285 *consultation with the liturgy office:* Father Gregory T. Bittner, "Tensions in

Subsidiarity," *CLSA Proceedings* (Canon Law Society of America, Washington, D.C.), 65 (2003).

286 *flatly forbade the use:* letter from Bishop David Foley to Mother Angelica, September 29, 1999, OLAMA.

286 *"misinformed by his consulting canonists":* letter from Mother Angelica to Bishop David Foley, October 10, 1999, OLAMA.

286 *"obedience issue":* A.I. with Bishop David Foley, 2003.

286 *"beyond Birmingham":* Father Gregory T. Bittner, "Tensions in Subsidiarity."

286 *Mother Angelica's asthma attack:* OLAM History, October 6, 1999.

287 *"political statement" and subsequent quotes:* "Letter To Priests Concerning Decree," *One Voice,* November 26, 1999.

288 *hypocrisy of the Pharisees:* OLAM History, October 19, 1999.

288 *"No custom presumed or otherwise":* Bittner, "Tensions in Subsidiarity."

289 *"As abbess of a Monastery within [Foley's] diocese":* ibid.

289 *recruited Archbishop Oscar Libscomb:* A.I. with Bishop David Foley, 2003.

289 *Foley and his liturgist:* Bittner, "Tensions in Subsidiarity."

289 *"I explained the matter to the president":* A.I. with Bishop David Foley, 2003.

289 *"Many meetings and discussions ensued . . .":* Bittner, "Tensions in Subsidiarity."

290 *"suitable decree could be promulgated":* ibid.

290 *"In my farming way,":* A.I. with Bishop David Foley, 2003.

290 *"since the faxes he sent":* ibid.

290 *"The threat of suspension was to get the attention of Rome":* ibid.

291 *Foley petitioned Rome:* A.I. with Bishop David Foley and source close to apostolic visitator, 2003.

291 *Cardinal Somalo wrote to inform the abbess:* letter from Cardinal Martinez Somalo to Mother Angelica, December 4, 1999, OLAMA.

292 *"Reverend Mother" and "I'm not going out there":* A.I. with Sister Antoinette and Mother Angelica, 2001; OLAM History, December 19, 1999.

293 *Sister Raphael's gastric system spasmed:* ibid., December 22, 1999.

293 *"everywhere":* ibid.

293 *"I know I am dying":* ibid.

294 *"Don't say just because January 1st":* ibid., January 4, 2000.

294 *"Mother Vicar's death will be very hard on me":* ibid., January 1, 2000.

294 *"Don't leave me":* ibid., January 6, 2000.

295 *"O yes my love, oh yes" and subsequent quotes:* ibid., January 9, 2000.

296 *"packs of nasty letters" and subsequent remarks:* Mother Angelica Live, EWTN, January 18, 2000.

296   *Details of the meeting in Rome*: A.I. with Bishop David Foley, 2003; Bittner, "Tensions in Subsidiarity."

297   *"in appreciation for the work being done"*: OLAM History, February 14, 2000.

297   *"I know the Holy Father gives gifts"*: *Mother Angelica Live*, EWTN, February 15, 2000.

297   a *"sign of the Pope's solidarity with Mother Angelica"*: A.I. with Vatican official, 2003.

298   *"the two options carry with them no theological"*: Jerry Filteau "Vatican Rejects Some Claims of Best Way to Offer Mass," *One Voice*, February 25, 2000.

298   *"technical issues"*: EWTN memo, March 12, 2000.

298   *"central" and "it seems necessary"*: Bittner, "Tensions in Subsidiarity."

299   *questions to be explored*: ibid.

299   *Kenedy Foundation, Bishop Gracida, and Archbishop Gonzalez*: Evan Moore, "Church Pitted Against State," *Houston Chronicle*, June 23, 1996; Stephen Michaud and Hugh Aynesworth, "Showdown in Texas," *Philanthropy Roundtable*, March 2003; "The Dioscese of Corpus Christi Is Slashed," *San Antonio Express*, May 18, 1996.

299   *"You're going to fix this"*: OLAM History, February 28, 2000.

300   *A major concern for the visitator*: ibid., February 29, 2000.

301   *"We want you to remain doing what you're doing"*: ibid., March 2, 2000.

301   *"Are you saying" and subsequent quotes*: A.I. with Mother Angelica, 2001.

302   *Before leaving, Archbishop Gonzalez*: OLAM History, March 2, 2000.

302   *Archbishop Gonzalez told them*: ibid., March 3, 2000.

303   *"They don't want to control you"*: ibid., March 4, 2000; transcript of EWTN board meeting on March 17, 2000.

303   *Bishop Foley drove . . . to the guest house*: A.I. with Bill Steltemeier, 2003.

304   *Mother Angelica signed a letter of resignation*: OLAM History, March 6, 2000.

304   *"that the only apostolate"*: Letter of resignation from Mother Angelica to Bill Steltemeier, March 6, 2000, OLAMA.

305   *"Take this network"*: A.I. with Chris Wegemer, 2003.

305   *It was actually pneumonia*: Mother Angelica's medical history and report of physical, March 14, 2000, Cullman Regional Medical Center, Cullman, Alabama.

305   *the archbishop penned a note to Mother Angelica*: note from Archbishop Gonzalez to Mother Angelica, March 17, 2000, OLAMA.

306   *Details of board meeting on March 17, 2000*: EWTN transcript of meeting; A.I. with Bill Steltemeier, Bishop David Foley, Helen Hull Hitchcock, Sister Antoinette, Bishop Thomas Daily, 2003; and A.I. with Mother Angelica, 2001.

308   *"the Holy See . . . could have authorized"*: Bittner, "Tensions in Subsidiarity."

309 *Cardinal Somalo sanated the donation*: letter from Cardinal Martinez Somalo to Mother Angelica, June 26, 2001, OLAMA.

309 *"beyond our competency"*: Bittner, "Tensions in Subsidiarity."

311 *"In my heart I really feel I died"*: OLAM History, July 7, 2000.

CHAPTER 19: PURIFICATION

314 *claims to have seen the child Jesus*: OLAM History, August 26, 2001.

314 *"Why? I don't feel anything . . ."*: A.I. with Sister Margaret Mary, 2003.

316 *"as good as this one"*: OLAM History, November 17, 2001.

317 *Details of fall at Books-A-Million*: A.I. with Sister Margaret Mary, Sister Michael, and Sister Antoinette, 2003; and A.I. with Mother Angelica, 2001; OLAM History, December 11, 2001.

317 *"her face like a basketball"*: A.I. with Sister Margaret Mary, 2003.

318 *Details of Mother Angelica in the ICU*: A.I. with Sister Margaret Mary and Dr. Richard May, 2003.

319 *"We must suffer . . ."*: OLAM History, December 16, 2001.

319 *"points to ponder" and subsequent quotes*: ibid., December 20, 2001.

320 *Details of Mother Angelica's brain surgery*: A.I. with Dr. J. Finley McRae, 2003.

321 *"Mother Angelica has been a star"*: Bishop David Foley, "As I See It," *One Voice*, January 4, 2002.

322 *Mother Angelica could read aloud*: EWTN press release, February 22, 2002.

322 *"I want to get rid of those creeping characters"*: Author's personal notes, June 2002.

323 *"That's not necessary"*: OLAM History, March 15, 2002.

323 *"Why don't we go out for dinner?"*: Greg Garrison, "Mother Angelica Experiences a Rebirth of Her Original Ambition," *Birmingham News,* April 20, 2003.

324 *"[God] has a definite plan in mind"*: Mother Angelica, *The Healing Power of Suffering* (Birmingham, Ala.: EWTN Catholic Publishers, 1976), p. 33.

330 *"the New Faithful"*: Colleen Carroll, *The New Faithful* (Chicago: Loyola Press, 2000).

331 *"I'm glad you're going to Lourdes"*: *Mother Angelica Live*, EWTN, July 27, 1993.

333 *Mother Angelica on February 2, 2004*: A.I. with Sister Mary Gabriel and Sister Antoinette, 2004.

ACKNOWLEDGMENTS

IF THERE IS GOOD to be found in these pages, it is principally due to the many people who graciously offered their time, resources, and memories to this project.

Firstly, I must thank my subject, Mother Mary Angelica, PCPA, for her candor, bravery, and incredible faith. Once the interviews began for this biography, she unflinchingly unveiled hard truths she could have easily kept to herself. At times wheezing and crushed by infirmity, she kept our interview appointments and supported the project when others might have been tempted to turn away. Writing her story has left a deep impression, one I will carry with me the rest of my life.

This book would have suffered mightily were it not for the contribution of Sister Mary Antoinette, the community historian of Our Lady of the Angels Monastery. She assembled letters, gathered photographs and hundreds of pages of community history, and corralled the appropriate sisters whenever this biographer hit a snag. Her skills as an archivist are rivaled only by her exquisite mastery of the violin. A thank you must also go to the late Sister Mary Raphael. Her record of Mother's comings and goings for more than forty years, her observations, and her interviews with Sister Mary David (Mother Angelica's mother) provided me with rich source material, much of it never seen before.

I am in the debt of the following people, who shared their memories and endured all manner of interrogation over the last five years.

In Canton, Ohio:

Joanne Simia, Mother's first cousin, and June Peterson Francis, Mother's aunt, could not have been more gracious. They gave me precious insight into the Gianfrancesco clan and an honest appraisal of life in southeast Canton.

For their remembrances of young Rita Rizzo, I must thank Elsie Machuga Johnston; Margaret Glazer, who was the bridge to a good number of Rita's high school peers; Blodwyn Nist; Ilene Keller Hall; Rylis Guist; Steven Zaleski; Sabatino Pentello; Gordon Schulte; Dr. Norma Marcere; Margaret Santilli; Elizabeth Morgese; Mary Murphy; and many others. Karen Sigler's study of Rhoda Wise and assorted materials from the Wise house proved exceedingly helpful. Mother Marian Zeltmann, the abbess of Sancta Clara Monastery, indulged me as I rooted through the archives there. I am grateful for her kindness and for her permission to reproduce excerpts from Sancta Clara's day calendars and protocols. I thank, too, Mother Mary James, PCPA, at the St. Paul's Shrine in Cleveland for willingly chasing down material in that monastery's archive, despite a flu epidemic in the cloister. Harold Zeigler must also be thanked for chauffeuring me around Canton during my first visit.

For a picture of Sister Angelica's activities in the Sancta Clara Monastery, Joan Frank's memory proved indispensable. Equally important were the memories of Sister Mary Joseph, PCPA; Sister Mary Michael, PCPA; Sister Mary Anthony, PCPA; Sister Mary Assumpta, PCPA; Sister Mary Bernadette, PCPA; and those sisters who requested anonymity.

The intimate portrait of Mother Angelica presented in these pages owes much to Sister Mary Catherine, PCPA; Sister Mary Agnes, PCPA; Sister Margaret Mary, PCPA; Sister Mary Gabriel, PCPA; Sister Mary Regina, PCPA; Sister Mary Faustina, PCPA; Sister Mary Clare, PCPA; Sister Ester Marie, PCPA; former nuns who asked not to be mentioned; and all the Poor Clares of Perpetual Adoration at Our Lady of the Angels Monastery. Their prayers and sacrifices did much to bring this work to completion.

In Birmingham:

My appreciation goes out to Jean Morris for many delightful hours; Matt Scalici, Jr.; Phyllis Scalici; Tom Kennedy; Chris Harrington, whose affection for Mother Angelica and knowledge of her broadcast output is astounding; Marynell Ford; Tim Brown; Walter Anderton; Father Mitch Pacwa, S.J.; Dr. Richard May; Dr. David Patton; Dr. L. James Hoover; Dr. Stanley Faulkner; Dr. Rex Harris; Dr. J. Finley McRae; Bishop David Foley; Bill Steltemeier; Michael Warsaw; Doug Keck; and countless others, whose names are too numerous to mention here.

For sharing their memories of the public and private Mother Angelica, I am indebted to Dick DeGraff; Robert Corazzini; Father Bob Bonnot; Father John Geaney; Father Francis Mary Stone, MFVA; Father Joseph Wolfe, MFVA; Father Richard Motaconis; Father Benedict Groeschel; Monsignor Michael Wrenn; Father Nevin Hammon; Father Robert DeGrandis; Cardinal Bernard Law; Cardinal Edmund Szoka; Cardinal J. Francis Stafford; Cardinal Francis Arinze; Archbishop Charles Chaput; Bishop Dermott Malloy; Archbishop Phillip Hannan; Bishop Robert Lynch; Bishop Anthony Bosco; Bishop Raymond Boland; Bishop Rene Gracida; Bishop Macram Gassis; Bishop Thomas Daily; Bill Bomberger; Helen Hull Hitchcock; Tom Rogeberg; and Virgil Dechant.

Bill Steltemeier and Michael Warsaw of EWTN must be singled out for permitting me to reproduce excerpts from *Mother Angelica Live; Mother Angelica's Answers Not Promises;* and Sister Mary Raphael's book, *My Life with Mother Angelica.* Our Lady of the Angels Monastery granted permission to quote extensively from the following unpublished materials: the history of Our Lady of the Angels Monastery; the letters of Mother Angelica; and Sister Mary Raphael's manuscripts, "Mother Angelica and Her Mother" and "Behind the Wall and Over the Hill." Mr. James Finefrock very kindly allowed me to quote from a letter written in 1945 by his uncle, Dr. Wiley Scott, addressing Rita Rizzo's medical condition, for which I am most grateful.

To my many sources at the Vatican and in the United States: You know who you are, and we'd better keep it that way. As Mother Angelica would say, "You're awesome."

The crucial work done by a handful of resourceful and dedicated souls added immeasurably to the final product. The research of Sharon Shriver, my fairy godmother in Canton, Ohio, lent the early chapters of the book a texture and color they would have lacked otherwise. For her zeal and commitment to the project, I am eternally thankful. In New Orleans, Peter Finney III did yeoman's work transcribing hours of the *Mother Angelica Live* programs. Some of the quotes sprinkled throughout the book are the result of his sharp eye. Mary Ann Charles at EWTN Creative Services helped locate and refurbish some of the priceless images in the book, including the author photo. My mother, Lynda Arroyo, went arthritic transcribing the interviews I conducted with Mother Angelica and her sisters. For this and so much more, she has my love and appreciation. And for the corner table they allowed me to occupy for the better part of a year, I thank Mr. Joe Paternostro and the staff of Caffe Caffe for their boundless hospitality.

Without some good friends and supporters, I could not have written this book. They include Umberto Fedeli; Joseph Canizaro; Danny Abramowicz; John Marra; Peter Spitalieri; George Schwartz; Paul and Barbara Henkels; Charlene and John "Packy" Hyland; Bowie Kuhn; George Weigel; Chris Sadowski; Jim and Kerri Caviezel; Beverlee Dean; Saint Anthony; Michael Paternostro; Kathryn Lopez; Robert Royal, president of the Faith and Reason Institute in Washington, D.C., who named me a research fellow; Doug Keck, who has been so patient and supportive over the years; and Christopher Edwards, my faithful producer, who sustained *The World Over Live* each week and offered me moral support just when I needed it.

Then there are the brave individuals who agreed to read the manuscript, offering advice and wisdom. They include Ron Hansen, a literary inspiration and a great soul; Father Richard John Neuhaus, a friend and towering intellectual presence in the Church; William Burleigh, whose keen editorial eye is overshadowed only by his big heart; Kate O'Beirne, who gifted me with her incredible insights and a hell of a subtitle; and Nicholas Sparks, who offered this rookie feedback and support. I am indebted to you all.

Loretta Barrett, my feisty agent, and her cohorts Nick Mullendore, Gabriel Davis, and Emily Saladino did everything to get this book into the right hands. Loretta was the first person with whom I shared the idea for this project, and from the start she saw its merit and importance. We both believed Doubleday the perfect home for Mother Angelica's story, and so it was. Thank you, dear Loretta.

I wish every first-time author an editor like Michelle Rapkin at Doubleday. She snatched this project up instantly and has never let go. Her patience, attentiveness, and belief in this story have been a great comfort to me throughout the arduous publishing process. Frances O'Connor and Jen Kim, Michelle's assistants, helped in so many ways. I thank them for each and every one.

To my television family, thank you for your long-standing support and love. I would not be here but for you. I look forward to many shared years together in print and broadcast, exploring all that is seen and unseen.

Personally, I am grateful to my parents, Lynda and Raymond, and to my brother, Scott, for their encouragement.

Finally, my wife, Rebecca (the Angelica widow), sacrificed much for this work. For years, she endured weekends and most nights without me, and when I did appear, she dutifully listened to every draft as if it were the first time. She is a splendid woman and a cherished wife. Anything I have ever done, including this work, pales next to the great gifts she has given me: our sons, Alexander and Lorenzo. I love you all very much.

INDEX

McFadden, Bishop James, 52, 56,
57, 58, 60
McInerny, Ralph, 244
McLane, Gene, 312
McNulty, Father Frank, 205
McRae, J. Finley, 319–20
Mellett, Don, 12
Michael, Saint, 226, 318
Michael, Sister. *See* Mary Michael,
Sister
Miller, Fredrick, 150
Mooney, Mike and Martha, 149
Moore, Albert, 129
Morris, Jean
and charismatic movement, 135
and Mother Angelica's talks, 122,
312
and television, 138–42, 144–45,
155, 157, 163
as travel companion, 126, 186
Mother Angelica Live (TV), xix,
181–83, 192–94, 248, 315,
330
Mother Angelica Presents (TV), 163
*Mother Angelica's Answers Not
Promises* (book project),
198
Mother's Corner (TV), 239, 241
Myers, Kathleen, 61

National Conference of Catholic
Bishops (NCCB)
and changes in the Mass, 230,
249–50
and CTNA, 168–70, 176, 209–15
and Foley issue, 285–86, 289–90,
296, 297
and Mahony affair, 263–67, 275,
276, 278–79
and papal visits, 203, 205–8
rivalry with, 167, 168, 178, 250
working relationship with, 177,
223–24
and World Youth Day, 240–44

National Religious Broadcasters
Association, 194
Neuhaus, Father Richard John, 329
Nist, Blodwyn, 20

Oblates of Mary Immaculate, 249
O'Connor, Cardinal John, 259,
276–77, 278, 299
Oddi, Cardinal Silvio, 160–61, 178,
195
Oddo, Tony, 94, 97, 100, 102
O'Dea, John and Ida, 52, 54
O'Donnell, Bishop Cletus, 214
O'Donnell, Bishop Edward, 224
OLAM. *See* Our Lady of the Angels
Monastery
Olson, Elizabeth, 61
Order of the Eternal Word, 201–2,
221, 228–29, 327, 328
Our Hermitage (TV), 139–42
Our Lady of the Angels Monastery,
Birmingham
books published by, 125–30,
132–33, 256, 322
building projects in, 143, 145–47,
222, 252–53
charismatic gifts in, 123, 202
Church probe of, 291, 298–303
construction of, 97–100, 301
contemplative traditions of, 200,
202, 229–30, 245–46, 280,
298, 306
design of, 106–7
donations for, 77, 85, 94, 98, 102,
115, 129
financial concerns of, 101–2, 107,
109, 116, 127, 129, 146,
301–2
and Hanceville facility, 252–53,
280
history of, 191, 226, 269, 314
hostility aimed at, 103, 104–5
idea for, 67, 74–75, 77–81, 301
land search for, 94, 95, 96–97

The *New York Times* bestseller

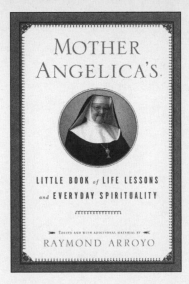